W9-AZT-226

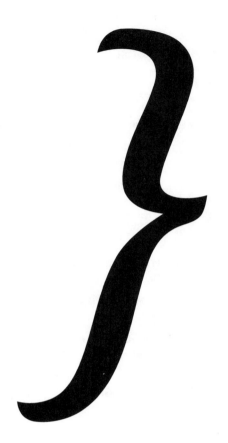

Python Power!

THE COMPREHENSIVE GUIDE

Matt Telles

THOMSON

COURSE TECHNOLOGY

Professional ■ Technical ■ Reference

ISBN-10: 1-59863-158-6
ISBN-13: 978-1-59863-158-6

Library of Congress Catalog Card Number: 2006923270

Printed in the United States of America

08 09 10 11 12 TW 10 9 8 7 6 5 4 3 2 1

THOMSON

COURSE TECHNOLOGY

Professional ■ Technical ■ Reference

Thomson Course Technology PTR, a division of Thomson Learning Inc.
25 Thomson Place
Boston, MA 02210
http://www.courseptr.com

Publisher and General Manager, Thomson Course Technology PTR:
Stacy L. Hiquet

Associate Director of Marketing:
Sarah O'Donnell

Manager of Editorial Services:
Heather Talbot

Marketing Manager:
Mark Hughes

Acquisitions Editor:
Mitzi Koontz

Marketing Assistant:
Adena Flitt

Project and Copy Editor:
Marta Justak

Technical Reviewer:
Michael Dawson

PTR Editorial Services Coordinator:
Erin Johnson

Interior Layout Tech:
Value Chain International, Ltd.

Cover Designer:
Mike Tanamachi

Indexer:
Sharon Hilgenberg

Proofreader:
Steve Honeywell

This book is dedicated to the ladies in my life: Teresa, Jenny, Rachel and Sarah.

} Acknowledgments

The author would like to acknowledge the aid of the Python community and Usenet newsgroups in finding answers to all of the questions that eluded me.

A special thanks to Mike Dawson, who went well above and beyond the call of duty to help a poor programmer out with this book. Thanks, Mike, you did a great job!

Also, a small note of thanks to Marta, without whom this book would never have gotten off the ground. Thank you, dear. Now get back to work.

} About the Author

Matt Telles is a 22-year veteran of the computer wars. Having moved from the mainframe world, with his beloved DEC 1091, he is now ensconced in the PC world of Windows and Linux. A long-time C++ programmer, he has since moved on to more modern languages like C#, Python, and PHP. The high point of his career is in writing his own biography for books.

✹ ✹ ✹

TABLE OF ∮ Contents

❋ ❋ ❋

} Introduction

What You'll Find in This Book

Welcome to the world of Python! Within this book, you will find a complete introduction to the language, including insider tips and tricks, and basic knowledge that you will need to get started. If you are a beginning Python programmer, you will find enough here to get you going. If you are an experienced Python programmer, you will likely find a trick or two worth the price of admission. Within these covers, you'll learn how to:

* Write basic Python code.
* Work with databases.
* Work with Web pages and Web servers.
* Create reusable Python code.
* Work with files.
* Create your own Python types.

Who This Book Is For

This book is intended for a programmer with some experience in the world of development. Although no prior expertise in Python is assumed, you will do just fine if you have worked with the language in the past. Beginning developers will learn enough to get started with the language and become proficient quickly. Experienced developers will quickly get up to speed with the language, and previous Python programmers will learn new things about the language they are accustomed to.

How This Book Is Organized

The book consists of 16 chapters, each of which addresses a specific area of Python programming. The chapters are set up individually so that you need not read them in any specific order. Simply leaf through to the section you are most interested in and refer to the content in that chapter.

Chapter 1 introduces the Python language, explains where it came from, what it is used for, and explains how to download the interpreter and related applications.

Chapter 2 consists of an overview of the elements of the language, including types, conventions, and structure of code.

Chapter 3 discusses the individual tools that are a part of the Python distribution, including the Command Line compiler, the editor, and the integrated development environment.

Chapter 4 discusses the basic data types in Python, showing you how to create them, use them, and convert between them.

Chapter 5 introduces control flow and allows the reader to learn how to change the behavior of a Python application through looping and conditional structures.

Chapter 6 introduces input and output functionality in Python, discussing how to write to the console window, files, and work with directories and drives.

Chapter 7 introduces the concept of functions and modules, allowing the developer to encapsulate code for later reuse and integration into other applications.

Chapter 8 discusses the topic of exception handling, discussing how to create, handle, and work with the exception functions in Python.

Chapter 9 gives the developer a brief overview of object-oriented development, introducing the concepts and terminology used throughout the remainder of the book.

Chapter 10 extends the concept of object-oriented development as it applies in Python, introducing the developer to classes, methods, and attributes.

Chapter 11 discusses modules, both those that are built into the language and developed by external developers.

Chapter 12 works with the default GUI library for Python, TkInter, discussing how to create and work with graphical user interfaces. The various components of TkInter are used to create forms for inputting and displaying user information.

Chapter 13 covers working with the Apache Web server, receiving information from HTML forms, generating HTML on the fly, and working with cookies.

Chapter 14 deals with the MySQL relational database and how it is used from Python. The concepts involved in relational database are covered, as is the syntax of adding, deleting, and modifying records in a database table.

Chapter 15 creates a full-blown Web application utilizing HTML pages, Python scripting code, database technology, and the Apache Web server.

Chapter 16 covers graphics in Python using the PIL library. The developer will learn how to draw graphics, display existing images, and work with graphical concepts.

All of the code for the book can be found at http://www.courseptr.com/ptr_downloads.cfm.

Simply enter the ISBN, Title, or author name to be able to access it.

❄ **Code Numbering**

Note that all of the code in the book will be on the Web site, whether or not the file name is listed in the text. Each code sample will be in numerical order, which can lead to some "missing" numbers in the text. This is by design and not an error.

1} About Python

What Is Python?

"What does the word *Python* make you think of?" If someone on the street asked you that question, you might come up with a variety of possible answers. Perhaps you would say that it reminded you of a large snake that squished people and ate them. Alternatively, you might think of the wonderful old British comedy show, Monty Python's Flying Circus. The odds are, however, that you would not think about a programming language. Reading this book should change that attitude, hopefully, and make you think of the programming language first, or at least just after Monty.

So what is this programming language called *Python?* Put simply, Python is an interpreted object-oriented language that is available on multiple platforms (hardware systems) and multiple operating systems (software systems). You can take the same Python script file and run it on Microsoft Windows™, Apple Macintosh™, Unix™, or a dozen other potential platforms that the language has been implemented for. The language itself is a standard, so any valid Python script will run, unmodified, on any platform that supports the interpreter.

Python is an extensible language, meaning that you can add to it with your own source code, modules, and components that can then be reused in other applications. Python is a small language, meaning that it has a tiny memory "footprint," and, in fact, is used in many handheld devices for programming. The Python interpreter is distributed under an approved open-source license that means that it is now, and always shall be in the future, a free language. Nobody can charge you for the interpreter, nor can they suddenly charge you to make your script files work.

Python is one of the foundations of LAMP (or WAMP) application development. LAMP stands for the four pillars of the open source community, Linux, Apache, MySQL, and Python (or PHP). In addition, three of the same pillars can be used in the Windows community to provide free development for Microsoft Windows developers as well. Python can be used to create

I

❋ ❋ ❋

stand-alone scripted applications for use on a single machine, or as a scripting language for Web-based applications that can run all over the known computer universe.

Python gives you the capability to interface to databases, to create CGI scripts that can be run from a Web browser, to create applications that can be run in a Windows environment, and to create extensible scripts that function in the business or scientific world. Python has been used in everything from business Web sites to online games, from simple conversion scripts to complex Internet update routines for banks and other financial institutions.

To give you just a brief idea of what sorts of people use Python, the language has been used successfully in such large-scale operations as Industrial Light and Magic (the film people) to such small-scale operations as running the semi-conductor line at Phillips. If people of this magnitude think the language is ready for prime time, it is hardly a surprise that the average programmer is interested in it.

A Brief History of Python

Now that you have a vague idea of what Python is, it might be useful to know exactly where it came from. After all, knowing our history is what separates men from animals, or something like that. If you are all fired up to learn the language itself and not worry about where it came from, or what drove the original development of the language, feel free to skip this section of the book. However, you should know that by understanding the underpinnings of the language, you would get a pretty good idea of what the original developer intended. Understanding the history and purpose of a language helps to understand some of the design choices and approaches made by the language developers, and Python is certainly no exception.

In the late 1980s, in the Netherlands, a programmer named Guido van Rossum, then working at CWI (the National Research Institute for Mathematics and Computer Science in the Netherlands) was working with a language called *ABC* on a platform called the *Amoeba operating system*. Amoeba was an experimental, microkernel-based distributed operating system developed by Andrew S. Tanenbaum and others at the Vrije Universiteit. The aim of the Amoeba project was to build a timesharing system that made an entire network of computers appear to the user as a single machine. Mr. Van Rossum liked the language a lot, but recognized that it had a number of shortcomings.

The basis for the Python language was ABC, which was very similar to BASIC or Pascal. It was an excellent teaching language, did not require variable declarations, and used indentation for nesting of statements. These bits of functionality, you will find, are core to the Python implementation as well. While ABC was more of a monolithic language that tended to produce large, hard-to-debug applications, Python was designed more to be object-oriented and modular.

Similar to modern programming languages, ABC consisted of a complete environment including interpreter, editor, multiple workspaces, and a syntax sensitive command system. This made it popular for beginning students, who liked the idea of an all-in-one environment that helped them as they went along.

By this point in the computer world, the advantages of an interpreted language had already been recognized. BASIC was a standard, popular with people who needed to write quick, easy-to-implement and easy-to-modify scripts that would accomplish simple tasks. It was just becoming clear, however, that the concepts inherent in interpreted languages could be used to accomplish much more complex tasks than they had been used for before.

Python itself came from frustrations van Rossum encountered when trying to work with ABC. For one thing, the language had no really well structured error handling. For another, ABC had such a monolithic structure that it could not easily be extended or modified. Realizing that these disadvantages would make it impossible for the language to grow and be used externally, van Rossum took the best features from ABC and then built a new language around them calling it Python.

Python was designed to be a highly readable language. It aims toward an uncluttered visual layout, uses English keywords frequently where other languages use punctuation, and has notably fewer syntactic constructions than many structured languages such as C, Perl, or Pascal. Because it is a simple language, Python is very easy to learn and master, and therefore lends itself well to a first language for most developers. At the same time, because the language is so well crafted, it is amazingly powerful and can accomplish incredible tasks with a minimum amount of coding.

The really exciting changes to Python came after van Rossum's work at CWI was complete. He and his team of programmers had moved from CWI to the BeOpen labs. This open-structured programming laboratory led the team to explore new directions for the language. In the great tradition of all programming tasks, the team "borrowed" from other languages to extend their own. Much in the same was that the C language borrowed constructs from previous languages such as Pascal or FORTRAN, Python 2.0 borrowed from a language called *Haskell* and acquired its most important feature: list comprehensions.

List comprehension gives a language the capability to work in terms of sets and lists. The language itself understands a list and can construct one from a collection of individual units, from a collection of other lists, or from selected "slices" of existing lists. For example, you might have a list that consisted of four items:

List 1:

Apple

Pear

Pomegranate

Grape

You might then have a second list, which consisted of vegetables:

List 2:

Potato

Celery

Tomato

Carrot

Yes, I know, a tomato is not a vegetable; it is a fruit. Let's not get bogged down in minutiae here. In any case, the two lists contain four separate items. Suppose that you wanted to create a new list that contained all of the items in both lists. In a typical non list-based language, you would have to allocate a block of memory big enough to hold all eight items and then copy the items one by one into the new list. In a language such as Haskell or Python, however, you can create a new list by simply defining a variable to be the concatenation of lists one and two. More importantly, you can then "slice" this list any way you want, returning individual components or sublists quickly and easily. It may not be evident at this point why this is useful, but I assure you that by the end of your reading of this book, you will see just how useful this can be.

We digress, however, since the original topic of discussion was the history of Python. At this point, Python had been released (or escaped) into the international community, and many people were interested in it. The simplicity and power of the language, not to mention the built-in exception handling capability, made the language a natural replacement for programming environments like BASIC, which, to this point, had been the most popularly used interpreted language. Python was on its way to stardom.

With the release of Python version 2.0, however, Python really became noticed by the main-stream development world. The addition of garbage collection, which allowed the programmer to focus on development and stop worrying about things like memory leaks and the like, made it desirable. The ability to extend the language through the use of internal and external classes made it possible to use Python in production environments. Up to this point, however, Python had been somewhat schizophrenic. The language had its own types (string, integer, floating point, and so forth) that were implemented in the underlying implementation language (Python was originally written in C, and the mainstream implementation still is, so that's what the underlying types were implemented in), while new classes that were implemented in the Python language were treated differently. With the release of Python 2.2, however, this all changed. The language treated all types the same way, paving the way for true object-oriented development, a basic goal from the initial releases of the software. It should be noted that in addition to the C implementation, there are several other editions of Python available today, including Jython (Java), IronPython, and many others.

The biggest change for Python came in the release that was centered around the second major version. Python had become a standard language, with a group responsible for its development and for approving all enhancements to the language standard. The Python Software Foundation was created. This board used a standard method, called the *Python Enhancement Proposal* (PEP), to offer up to the programming community suggestions for new language enhancements. These enhancements have been gathered and streamlined and will become Python 3.0 when it becomes available. The biggest change for the third major release will be the first break with backward compatibility to fix perceived errors in the language. Whether or not this will actually happen is still in debate. In any case, the future of Python is quite rosy, and the spirited debate on its functionality and future ensure that it will be around for a long time to come.

That's where Python came from. Where is it going? While nobody really knows for sure, we do know that Python is here to stay, and learning the language will help you in your future endeavours in the software development world. So let's take a look at why you should learn Python and what it will mean to you.

Interpreters Versus Compilers

The first thing that is important to understand about Python is that it is an *interpreted* language. There are two sorts of programming languages: interpreted ones and compiled ones. A compiled language is what you are probably used to if you have done any programming in the past. The process for a compiled language is as follows:

Create source file using text edit → Use compiler to syntax check and convert source file into binary → Use linker to turn binary files into executable format → Run the resulting executable format file in the operating system.

Let's take a look at the steps here, so you can get a better idea of what is going on beneath the covers.

1. **Create source file using text editor.**
   Source files are human-readable text files that represent the actual programming language in which you are working. For example, in C, you might have a file that looks something like this:

   ```
   #include <stdio.h>
   int main(int argc, char **argv)
   {
       printf("Hello world");
   }
   ```

   This little program just prints out the string Hello world to the user's console. You will notice that the program doesn't run. It is the input to a compiler. You can type out the file using system tools, or print it, or save it to a source code repository, but it will never be anything more than text. There is a complete disconnect between the source code file and the final running application in the compiler version of a language.

2. **Use the compiler to check syntax and convert source into binary format.**
The purpose of a compiler is to do two things. First, it runs through the tokens in your source code, comparing them to the rules that the language requires. Again, as an example, consider a Pascal assignment statement. The language requires that the statement look something like this:

```
a := 3;
```

In this statement, there are four pieces:

* a—This is the name of a variable in the program, or a memory address if you prefer.
* := —In Pascal, the := statement means *assign a value to*. It takes the variable on the left-hand side of the equation and puts the value on the right-hand side of the equation into that location in memory.
* 3—This is a value; in this case, a constant value. We are going to place the value 3 in the memory address represented by the variable a.
* (;) —The semicolon is the last piece of the equation. In Pascal, this character represents the end of the statement. Now, looking at the whole statement, realize that the code is there only for the benefit of the programmer. To the compiler, the instruction breaks down into "move the constant value 3 into the memory address that was allocated for the variable a."

In C, the same statement looks like this:

```
a = 3;
```

In BASIC, it would be `a = 3`

No matter what language you choose, the output of the compiling process will be the same: a binary instruction that moves the value 3 into a memory address. Once the compiling process is complete, you have a bunch of binary files that represent the "source code" as it is viewed by the computer.

3. **Use linker to turn binary files into executable format.**
The purpose of the "linking" phase of the compiling process is to assemble all the various pieces of the final executable together. The linker takes the individual pieces, whether they are C functions, C++ classes, or Pascal modules and finds all of the pieces that need each other. When you call a function, for example, the linker is responsible for finding

that function in the group of source files that you have given it and creating the proper binary instructions to the computer to "jump to" the right place in memory to being executed.

An example might be useful here, since this is about as clear as mud.

Imagine that you have a bit of code in your program. This bit of code is going to output some data to the user. For this example, we will use C and assume that the data you are outputting is a simple string that says "Hello world."

In the source code file, you have a statement that says:

```
printf("Hello world");
```

The compiler takes this statement, assembles it into two separate instructions to the computer:

Take the string `"Hello world"` and place it in a memory address.

Call the function `printf` and point it at that memory address.

The first part of the process is easy enough. There is an instruction to store the string in a memory address, and this is independent of any other pieces of the program. The second part of the process, however, is more complicated.

The call to the function `printf` requires the system to find the function and load its address into memory. The compiler can't do this job, because it has no idea what `printf` does or where it is. This is the job of the linker. It finds the `printf` function in all of the compiled source code and matches it up to the function call.

The result of this finding and matching up and generating is the executable file.

4. **Run the resulting executable format file in the operating system.**

   After the linking process is complete, the compiler and linker are no longer necessary for the program to run. It has become a permanent part of the operating system, and can run anytime you want it to with no external requirements.

The interpretative process, on the other hand, is quite different. The interpretative process looks more like this: Create source file using editor → Load the source file into the interpreter → Run the interpreted code.

1. **Create the source file**.

   Creating the source file using the text editor is exactly the same as it was in the compiled step of the same name. You use a text editor and generate some text in the format of the interpreted language that you want to use.

2. **Load the source file into the Interpreter**.

   The interpreter for given languages usually has a load, or run, option. This option is used to take the human-readable code and load it into the interpreter. Python uses a bytecode interpreter, so the input source code is loaded, parsed, and turned into byte codes for later execution. Unlike a compiler, the interpreter does not process the input file at this point. (There are some exceptions here, but the general rule applies.) The important thing to realize is that interpreted code is not processed until the user requests it to be run.

3. **Run the interpreted code.**

Once the user requests that the interpreted code be run, the process begins. The interpreter reads each statement of code and validates it. If an error occurs, the process stops, and the user is presented with an error message. This is quite different from the compiled stage, in that the end user can be presented with syntax errors, whereas the compiled version will only allow the developer to see syntax errors.

As each statement is validated, the interpreter is either directly executed, or, in the case of languages like Python, is converted into a bytecode version that can then be loaded into a processing environment. In any case, the results are immediately displayed for the end user to view.

The biggest difference between interpreted code and compiled code is that an interpreted application need not be "complete." You can test it in bits and pieces until you are satisfied with the results and put them all together later for the end user to use.

When to Use (or Not Use) an Interpreted Language

As with any approach to a problem, there are advantages and disadvantages to using an interpreted language. Let's take a look at some of these, so you can get a sense of the balance you need to use in determining when a language such as Python makes sense, and when it does not.

Disadvantages

1. **You need to do more things to the end user.**

Obviously, since the interpreter loads and runs the individual source code files at runtime, you need to distribute all of the files that are needed by the interpreter. This means sending out a potentially large number of source files. Contrast this with the compiled approach, where all you generally have to distribute is the single executable file that contains the application you want to give to the user.

2. **The source files can be modified by the end user.**

Source code files are simple text files, especially in Python. This means that they are in human-readable, and thus human-modifiable, form. Since the end user can read the files, it is not unreasonable to assume that the person can modify the files. This can lead to confusing problems, especially if the user happens to delete a file that is needed by the system. Python does provide the ability to distribute bytecode versions (called `*.pyc` files) of the source code to alleviate this concern to some degree.

The flip side to this is that you can easily detect what files have changed by using simple tools available in nearly any operating system environment.

3. **Errors aren't found until runtime.**

   Since an interpreted file is processed line by line, any problems that exist in a given module will not be found until that module, and the line containing that module, are loaded and processed. This can lead to unexpected problems with end users and applications. It also requires that testing be much more complete than it would need to be in a compiled application.

   While a logical error can occur in any sort of code, whether it be interpreted or compiled, a syntactical error can only occur in interpreted code for the end user. It looks particularly unprofessional to see an error such as "Syntax error in line nn in file xxxx.py" show up on your user's screen. The use of interpreted code, therefore, requires a higher degree of path testing than the equivalent use of compiled code.

Advantages

1. **Easier to debug and maintain the code.**

   Obviously, when you can load a small section of code and try it out without having to worry about compiling and linking the entire application, the process is going to go a lot faster. In addition, since you can try things out without having to have them work completely, you can step through a process, see if the individual pieces work, and then stop the process before it completes.

2. **Easier to update the application code quickly.**

   Since the edit, compile, link, and deploy process is now reduced to edit the file and replace the existing file with the updated version, the process for updating an application is streamlined. More importantly, since there are no longer any issues about whether or not the program is running, whether or not the executable file is in use, and whether or not the user has the rights to change the file, everything becomes much easier to modify. Obviously, doing a file comparison between two text files is vastly easier than trying to figure out what changed in a binary executable file. As a result, it is easier to determine what changed between two versions on the user's machine. This makes management of applications and users easier as well.

3. **Errors can be fixed quickly without the need for complete redistribution.**

   For most stand-alone applications, the executable file is only a small part of what needs to be sent to the user. There are subsidiary files that must be kept in sync, settings that need to be made on the user's machine, and so forth. The ability to simply drop a text file into a directory and have the application behave in a new, or improved, manner is a huge benefit not only to the developer, but also to the support personnel and the maintainers of the user's system.

In addition, since "patch" files can be issued that modify small parts of text within a file, this makes it trivial to change a running application to behave in a different fashion.

4. **Can be embedded in other languages.**

   One of the more interesting things about Python as an interpretive language is that the interpreter itself is rather small. The interpreter itself is a binary component that can be included in other applications without including the entire GUI system that supports the interpreter. This permits third-party applications to embed this binary component in their own applications and to run scripts in Python from within their own GUIs.

   When you think about it, most applications these days need some sort of scripting capability. The ability to run commands automatically, or to extend the functionality of an application through scripting, is so powerful that it has become a standard part of most complex applications. Python provides the best of both worlds here. It allows you to maintain the security and speed of a compiled application, while permitting the ability to customize that application via scripting.

So, as you can see, there are a mere three reasons not to use an interpreted language, whereas there are four reasons to use one. Now, it is vaguely possible that this balance might be biased because of the subject of this book, but it still indicates that Python is a very valid alternative to compiled languages.

Understanding Bytecodes

As mentioned previously, Python uses "bytecodes" to actually do the work of processing the source code. The bytecode idea is not new, as there are quite a number of languages that use something similar. The idea is that a statement is broken down into a "code," indicating what it is going to do, and then a series of arguments to that code. For example, you might have something like this:

```
print value1
```

The "code" for print might be 0x01 (it doesn't really matter what the value is). The argument to the print statement is a value. So, in the byte code version of the source code, you might see something like this:

```
<0x01><value><end-of-statement>
```

When the interpreter loads the bytecode version of the file, it reads a code and recognizes it as a print statement. The interpreter then knows to read in arguments until the end of statement marker is encountered. This is quite different from the compiled version of the program, where the statement is literally turned into a series of machine statements that the native operating system can process.

Why Use Python?

We've looked at the differences between compiled languages and interpreted ones. We've also looked at the advantages and disadvantages of using interpreted languages in general. The real question, then, is why would you choose Python over some of the other interpreted languages out there? Let's look at the reasons you *should* use Python. Of course, since you are reading this book, the odds are good you've already made this decision for yourself, but hey, what's wrong with a little shameless promotion?

Object-Oriented

Python is an object-oriented language. Most existing interpreted and scripting languages are simple line-oriented, sequential languages, which indicates that reuse is virtually impossible and debugging and maintaining the code is difficult. Python is a structured language constructed around classes and reusable components called *modules.* This allows you to easily move your Python code from project to project, saving you enormous amounts of time.

Cross Platform

Some languages, particularly ones like Java claim to be "write once, run anywhere" as the tagline goes. Unfortunately, the reality is far from that simple. Most scripting languages require major changes to run on different platforms, because the core components are written in machine-specific languages. Python code is written in Python itself, so any platform that will run the interpreter will run them. This allows you to move forward knowing that no matter what changes the company you work for decides to make with respect to hardware and software, your Python code is going to work like a champ. This particular attribute is one of the main reasons that so much Internet code is written in Python, because it makes it easy to port it from server to server.

Broad User Base

When you are writing code in a particular language, it is good to know that there are others out there who are writing code in that same language. Not only does this give you someone to commiserate with when things don't go the way you want them to, but it also gives you someone to ask for help. The Python community is quite large, as you will see in just a bit. There are entire Web sites devoted to Python programming, Usenet newsgroups that specialize in helping new and expert users, and lots and lots of code out there that you can steal (I mean, borrow) and use in your own applications.

There is really nothing more frustrating than having to reinvent the wheel each time you do something, simply because you can't find any examples of how to do it. Because Python has such a broad user base, the chances are good that someone has done what you are trying to do. Combine that fact with the aforementioned object-oriented approach, and you can likely find existing code that just drops into your application and does what you need it to do. This can be important when the boss calls you at 4:30 on a Friday wanting some new feature added to his Web site.

Well Supported in Third-Party Tools

When you are trying to implement a new application, it is good to know if the existing third-party tools out there will help you out. Python is well supported in such third-party tools as MySQL, an open-source database package, and Apache, an open-source Web server. These are two of the most popular packages for using scripting tools with, and as such, using a well-supported scripting tool is a definite bonus.

In addition to being used by third-party tools, Python can be embedded in other applications. There are a number of examples of this, which makes it easier to convince other people to use Python rather than a less supported engine.

Good Selection of Tools Available

It is one thing to start writing code with a Command Line compiler and a language specification. It is quite another to have the ability to use a fully compliant Integrated Development Environment (IDE), debugger, and Help system. The former allows you to write code. The latter allows you to write code that you can actually trust in a reasonable period of time.

Python comes with an excellent set of pre-built tools, for which source code is available. This makes it easier to develop high-quality code, which in turn makes it easier to worry about your application features and not about whether or not your system is going to crash the first time someone uses it.

Good Selection of Pre-built Libraries

As mentioned previously, Python lends itself well to developing reusable code because of its object-oriented approach to development. This means that there is a lot of already developed code out there that you can reuse. Many of these classes are of general-purpose functionality that you will probably need in your own applications. Email, complex math, and collections are but a few of the libraries that you can easily import into your own applications.

Remember, the less time you spend developing code that the user never sees, the more time you can spend creating functionality that the user really wants. When all is said and done, that is what it is all about, from the perspective of management anyway.

Where Is Python Used?

So where do people use Python? The areas that the language finds itself used would surprise you. Here is just a small group of areas in which Python has found itself utilized to make the world a better place:

❉ Cinematography
❉ Sports
❉ Clothing
❉ Aviation
❉ Business information
❉ Document management
❉ Pharmaceuticals.
❉ Education
❉ Government
❉ Public safety
❉ Biology
❉ Chemistry
❉ Weather
❉ GIS
❉ Marine
❉ Engineering.
❉ Web pages
❉ Application development tools

Bear in mind that this is only a small fraction of the places in which you will find Python code, so it's likely that your application space has already been used in the past and that code exists to do the more common things you might need.

How Is Python Licensed?

Python is distributed in open source, and is licensed under a public access license. If you go to the Python Foundation Web site (`www.python.org`), you will find a complete description of the license for the language and all of its components. Essentially, however, you can consider the language to be free of all encumbrances and licensing fees.

You need never worry about paying for Python, or any of its source code.

Where Do I Get Python?

Although Python can be obtained from lots of places on the Web, the "official" release of the software is always available at www.python.org/download. To download the software, go to the Web site and find the version that corresponds to your operating system. For example, for this book, I have chosen to do my work on Windows XP. All of the Windows versions are supported with a single installer, the Windows installer.

From that point, you must decide whether you want only the development system, or whether you want the source code for the system, or both. The source is available as a tarball, which can be unzipped using the GNU gzip application, available at the GNU Web site, www.gnu.org. As of the writing of this book, the gzip application was available on the main download page for GNU software, which is http://directory.fsf.org/GNU.

If you do not want the source code for the system and simply want the binaries, you can download them directly. For Windows, the download is a standard Microsoft installer file (msi). For UNIX, the download is a tarball that contains all of the applications and installer files. You may also want to download the documentation, which is available in various flavors, from HTML to compiled help (CHM) files.

In any case, once you have downloaded the software, it is time to install it.

Installing Python

For the purposes of this book, we will look at only the Microsoft Windows version of Python. There are a variety of reasons for this, not the least of which is that Windows is the most prevalent operating system out there. However, the language and tools we'll discuss will work with any operating system and any installation of the current version of Python. Note that differences between versions may arise due to changes in the core language. Installing Python on Microsoft Windows is a fairly straightforward affair. After you have downloaded the installer file from the python.org Web site, and placed the file somewhere you can find it on your local computer, simply double-click the installer executable file to get started.

At the time of this writing, the current version of the Python system is 2.5. The installer for the 2.5 Python install is called python-2.5.msi, and is a standard Microsoft Installer file. Running the installer will display a security warning in Windows first, since the publisher cannot be determined from the application file. This warning screen looks like the one shown in Figure 1.1.

Saying yes to this screen is pretty straightforward; just click the run button and move onward. Doing so will bring up a second window, which prompts you to decide whether you want to install this application for just yourself or all users. Your answer to this one determines whether or not the application will show up on the Start menu for just the user you are logged in as, or for all users that use this machine. The default here is for all users. This is probably what you

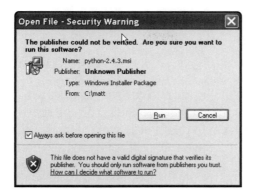

Figure 1.1
Security warning for
Python 2.5 installer.

should use, unless you have a compelling reason not to install the system for other users. The screen looks like the one shown in Figure 1.2. Whether you select all users or just yourself, click the Next button to move on to the next screen.

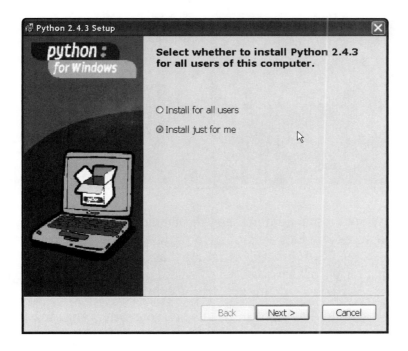

Figure 1.2
Determining user installation to install Python 2.5.

Following the user determination, you will be prompted for a directory to use for installing the system. You can select whatever directory on whatever drive you want for this prompt, but write down the directory that you are using since you will need it in just a moment.

The next dialog prompts you to select the tools you want to install. By default, Python will install all of the tools that you will look at in the next chapter. If you have particular disk space problems, or know in advance that you will never need certain components, feel free to remove whatever pieces you don't want.

After you have made your location and detail install choices, the installer will go off and start copying files into the right places on your hard drive. Depending on the speed of your system and the hard drive you are copying to, this could take a little while. Finally, the installer will grind to a halt, and a Finish screen will be displayed. Once this happens, Python is installed on your system. You can verify this by looking at the Start button menus. You should see an entry that reads Python 2.5 in the main menu, along with entries in that menu entitled IDLE, Module Docs, Python Command Line, Python manuals, and Uninstall Python. To verify that all is working properly, click the Python Command Line selection. You should see a window pop up that looks like Figure 1.3.

Figure 1.3
The Python Command
Line window.

If the window pops up properly, your install went fine, and you should be all set. If you get an error message, check to be sure that everything went properly in the install directory and that no errors are displayed on the screen. The most likely errors are that you had insufficient disk space to install the system or that you did not have sufficient privileges to install the application. In either of these cases, contact your system administrator for resolution of the problems.

Congratulations! You now have a full-blown Python installation on your system and can begin to write programs.

Getting Information on Python

You might wonder where to find really good information about Python, besides this book. The Internet, of course, is a great source of information, but you always have to know where to look.

Here are just a few of the Web sites that you might take a look at for source code, answers to questions, and general tips about the language and the tools.

The most obvious source of information is `www.python.org`, the main site for Python. This is the place you will find the documentation, latest applications and patches, and other official information about the language. Anyone starting out with Python should at least browse the site to see what is available here for download or reading.

The `www.planetpython.org` site is a good source of information about Python, as well as downloads, commentary and discussions.

If you are working on the Apache Web server and want information related to Python, how to use it, where to get the modpython (we'll discuss this later) modules and how to configure things, the `www.modpython.org` Web site is the place to be. There's some general Python discussion here as well.

For those of you who are into the whole .Net environment from Microsoft, `www.codeplex.com/IronPython` is the place to be for sure. This Web site contains the download of Iron Python, allowing you to integrate Python code with .Net libraries to develop specifically for .Net compatible platforms, primarily Microsoft Windows. They have a nice mailing list to keep you updated on changes to the system and discussion areas to talk about the language and the implementation.

There is an excellent mailing list for learning Python and discussing it with people that are experts in the field at `http://mail.python.org/mailman/listinfo/tutor`. It is a very friendly place for people new to the language to ask questions without being made to feel stupid.

Finally, for those of you who want to use Python as an embedded interpreter within the C++ language, the world gives you boost.Python. Go to this site, located at `www.boost.org/libs/python/doc`, and you will learn more than you ever wanted to know about how Python can be used inside a C++ application using the open source boost libraries.

Python Communities

The Web sites listed previously often have discussion areas where you can talk about Python, post your problems, or just read what other people are doing with the language. Another excellent source of information about Python is the Usenet newsgroup community. If you have a newsgroup reader, or can point your Web browser to `groups.google.com`, you can read these newsgroups and post your own comments or questions. Some of the newsgroups you might want to read include the following:

* `comp.lang.python`—The official newsgroup for Python development. You will find the majority of expertise here, along with people who are more than happy to help a newcomer feel at ease with the language.

* `comp.lang.python.announce`—An official release newsgroup where you can read about the latest and greatest Python developments and where to download them.

Finally, there are operating system specific newsgroups. For example the `linux.debian.maint.python` newsgroup contains information about Python on the Debian installation of Linux.

Other Software

As we begin to discuss other segments of the programming world with respect to Python, you will need to obtain and download other software for use with the language. Specifically, you will probably want to download and install the MySQL database system and the Apache Web server system. These two packages are available on the Internet free of charge.

MySQL is a relational database system that is used by a large percentage of the development world because of its stability and lack of cost. It compares well to commercial database systems, such as Oracle™ or SQL Server™, but does not require the same level of administration or the upfront cost to purchase. You can find the most current version of MySQL at `www.mysql.org` in the Downloads section. Be sure to download the Python interface libraries, which can be found at `www.mysql.org/downloads/python.html`.

The Apache Web server has become the standard open source Web server for creating and maintaining Web sites. Since Python has become so closely associated with creating CGI scripts and Web pages, it only makes sense for us to discuss the building of various components for the Web. You can find Apache at `www.apache.org`. The actual Web server (http server) is found at `http://projects.apache.org/projects/http_server.html`. In this book, we will be using Version 2.2.3, which is available for download. You will also need to download the `mod_python` module for use with the server. You can download this at `www.modpython.org`.

And Now for Something Completely Different...

Aw, come on, you didn't really think we could go this whole chapter without a gratuitous Monty Python® reference, now did you? Remember, Python has a lot in common with Monty Python. They are both a bit offbeat, both well loved, and both often blow up rabbits. No, actually, Python doesn't blow up rabbits—I made that part up. Anyway, it is time to move on to the actual meat of the language, looking at syntax and writing code. So, let's get on with it!

2 } Python Language Overview

In order to really understand a language, you need to know the components that make up that language. In the case of a programming language, the elements that make up the language are its syntax, its keywords, and the style with which the language expresses itself. To begin with, let's take a simple look at some Python code. Since Python is an interpreted language, there is really no need for the usual start and end blocks; you can simply select the pieces that you want to run and type them into the interpreter. In a compiled language, for example, you would need an entry point, and some sort of termination point. We will be using the IDLE interpreter for this example. We'll get into a fuller discussion of IDLE and the other tools in the next chapter, but for now just follow the directions, and you'll do just fine.

To start up IDLE, just select it from the Start menu in windows (Start Menu | All Programs | Python 2.5 | IDLE (Python GUI)), or run `pythonw.exe` from the directory in which you installed Python. When you bring up the IDLE editor, it will look like the image shown in Figure 2.1. IDLE, of course, comes from the name of one of the Monty Python actors, Eric Idle.

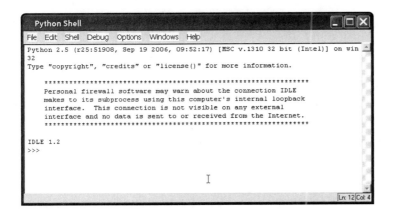

Figure 2.1
The IDLE editor.

Python Syntax

You've seen some simple examples of the ways in which Python statements are entered and executed by the interpreter. Let's take a closer look at what the actual syntax of Python looks like and what the rules are for using that syntax.

Comments

When you are writing code, it is often useful to place a comment in place to indicate what you are doing. This is particularly useful if you want someone else to be able to ever read your code. The Python language supports comments, using the hash (#) character. The hash character indicates that everything from that point on to the end of the line is a comment. For example, you can use it as a line unto itself:

```
# This is a comment.
```

Alternatively, you can use the comment character at the end of a line of code:

```
x = 1 # Initialize x to be the first element.
```

In either case, the text following the comment character is ignored by the interpreter when it is reading and processing the code.

Indentation

If you are accustomed to programming in another language, such as Pascal, C++, or Java, you may be used to the idea of statement termination. For example, in C++, if you want to assign the value 12 to a variable named a, you would write a statement that looks something like this:

```
a = 12;
```

The variable name is a, the action you are taking is "assignment" (using the = operator), and the value you are assigning to the variable is 12. The compiler knows that the statement is finished when it encounters the end-of-statement token, which in C++ is the semi-colon (;). Likewise, in Pascal, you might write something like this:

```
a := 12;
```

Once again, the statement has a variable, an operator (in this case := which is the Pascal version of the C++ operator=), and a value. The statement is terminated by a semi-colon. Older languages, such as FORTRAN, use a different scheme to indicate the end of a statement. In order to terminate a statement, you use the carriage return to indicate that the statement is finished. Python, which aims for simplicity in all things it does, uses a combination of indentation and end-of-line characters (carriage returns) to indicate statements. So an assignment in Python looks like this:

```
a = 12
```

That certainly seems simple enough, but what do you do when your line is too long for a single line of code? For example, suppose that you want to assign a really long string to a given variable. You might do something like this:

```
s = "This is a really, really long string that should not be this long, but it
is. How long do you think it will get before it does something bad?"
```

As you can tell, the above line is too long to appear on a single line in the interpreter. Wrapping text is a bad idea in any language, since the editor often inserts some sort of carriage return character to mark a line wrap. That character inserted indicates to the interpreter that the statement ends. So the Python interpreter would read the above statement as:

```
s = "This is a really, really long string that should not be this long, but it
is. How long do you think it will
```

and then follow that with the statement:

```
get before it does something bad?"
```

The first statement is an error because it does not terminate the literal string with a closing double quote. The second statement is an error because, well, it isn't a statement at all! So, how do you get around this little problem? Fortunately, Python provides a solution, the line continuation character. You can write the above as:

```
s = "This is a really, really long string that should not be this long, but it
is. How long do you think" \
" it will get before it does something bad?"
```

Now, there are a few rules here that you will need to become aware of later. First of all, this rigmarole is not necessary if the line in question is actually a list of items. For example:

```
month_names = ['January', 'February', 'March',     # These are the
               'April',   'May',      'June',       # names
               'July',    'August',   'September',   # for the months
               'October', 'November', 'December'] # of the year
```

The interpreter knows that there is more coming, because each line ends with a comma and the "statement" cannot end until the closing bracket (']') is found.

Secondly, you can't have a comment on a line that contains a continuation character. Thus, something like this:

```
str  = "This is a test" \ #
        " more of the test"
```

will not be parsed properly and will end up with an error from the interpreter.

So what is important about indentation? In the world of Python, indentation is everything. For example, consider the following example in a language such as C++:

```
if (x == 2 )
{
        printf("X is 2\n");
}
```

This example compares the variable x to the constant value 2, and if they compare to the same value, it then prints out some debugging information. In a language such as Pascal, this same statement would look like this:

```
if ( x = 2 ) then
begin
        WriteLine("x is 2");
end;
```

As you can see, in either case, there is a delimiter for a block. In the case of C++, the delimiter is a set of braces { and }. In the case of Pascal, the block is delimited by the begin and end statements. The compilers recognize that these delimiters mean that everything within the block will only be executed if the conditional is wrapped around the block (in this case, whether or not x is equal to 2) is true.

We will spend a fair amount of time looking at conditionals and loops and all the rest of the block-oriented statements in Python. For now, however, it is only important to know that Python has no real delimiters. It does not use "begin" and "end" statements or sets of braces to indicate that anything is supposed to be a part of something else. Python, instead, uses the simplicity of indentation to indicate whether or not something is a part of a block.

For Python, the above block would look like this:

```
if  x == 2:
        print "x = 2"
```

If you want to try this out, bring up the IDLE editor that you just installed in the previous action. Now, enter the following lines into the IDLE editor. First, let's assign the variable a value:

```
x = 2
```

Enter the line just as it appears above and press the Enter key. The IDLE editor will create a local variable in the editor called x and assign it the value 2. Now, we are going to try to compare it to something:

```
if x == 2:
    print "This is a test"
```

There are a couple of things worth noticing here. First, as you type, Python will highlight (change the font color) the text of words it recognizes within the lines you enter. In this case, the words *if* and *print* will be highlighted, because they are keywords within the Python environment. Next, notice that the colon : at the end of the `if` statement automatically causes the editor to indent the next line, because the editor knows that the colon at the end of an `if` statement means that you are trying to create a block of statements to follow if the conditional statement within it is true. When you type the print statement and press the Enter key, the editor will automatically indent the next line, indicating that it feels you are trying to create a new line in the block. You can add another line, and it will only be executed if the block is entered, or you can press Enter without entering any text. If you do the latter, the editor assumes you are done with the block and terminates it. In "immediate" mode, which is what we are doing right now, the interpreter executes statements as you enter them. Don't worry about the differences between immediate mode and program mode, as we will discuss that in the next chapter. In any case, once you press the Enter key on the blank line, the interpreter interprets the line, realizes that the variable x is, in fact, equal to the value 2, and prints "This is a test" on the output console. The whole thing looks like this:

```
>>> x = 2
>>> if x == 2:
        print "This is a test"


This is a test
>>>
```

As you can see, it works the way that you'd expect. Indentation is a very important part of Python, and this is one of the main reasons that it is built directly into the editor. However, you might wonder whether the indentation level is important. The answer is, well, kind of. You can change the level of indentation when you are typing, simply by hitting the backspace key. This will automatically wipe out all indentation, since the editor uses a single tab to auto-indent. Once you have done this, you can then indent your own level, such as two spaces, for example. Try it.

First, enter the line:

```
if x == 2:
```

Notice that the editor auto-indents the next line in about eight characters. (It varies, depending on your settings, but that is the default.) Then press the backspace key. Notice that the cursor moves back to the left hand side of the screen. Type some number of spaces, say two, and enter:

```
    print "This is a test"
```

Press the Enter key again, and you will see that the editor indents two spaces as well. The indentation level doesn't matter, except that it should be consistent. Now, why did I say it "kind of" matters as to the level of indentation? Well, let's take a look at our example. We've got:

```
x = 2
if x == 2:
    print "This is a test"
```

This is what is presently in the editor buffer. Now, if you press the Enter key again and then press backspace, you can change the indent level, right? No, in fact, you can't. Suppose, for example, that you try to indent in one space (indenting more than the current level would be okay, as we'll see later).

```
>>> if x == 2:
    print "x = 2"
   print "x = 1"
IndentationError: unindent does not match any outer indentation level
(<pyshell#7>, line 3)
```

The editor "knows" that the indentation level doesn't match, so it complains about it to you. The levels have to match, or it is an error. So while you might play around a bit until you discover a level of indentation that appeals to you, you need to be consistent about it. Indentation is extremely important in Python, so be sure that you understand how to read and interpret the indentation levels in code. Now that we've covered the keywords and indentation, it is time to start slowly getting into the meat of the language. Let's next take a look at the naming and usage of variables in Python.

Python Reserved Words

One of the nice features of the IDLE environment is that you can actually ask Python to list all of the keywords that it supports. A *keyword* is one that means something to the language. In other words, you can't use a reserved word as the name of a variable, a function, a class, or a module. You can only use keywords the way in which they were meant to be used. To list the keywords in IDLE, just enter the following lines into the interpreter, pressing Return after each one:

```
import keyword
print keyword.kwlist
```

Obviously, you will be spending a fair amount of time with IDLE and with the various syntax components of Python, so just accept that this is a capability of the environment that you can use to remember the keywords.

When you run the above commands in the interpreter, you will see a list of words, enclosed in single quotes, and separated by commas. This is the way in which IDLE displays a list. We'll talk about lists a bit more in Chapter 3, "Tools." The list you see should look like this:

```
['and', 'as', 'assert', 'break', 'class', 'continue', 'def', 'del', 'elif',
'else', 'except', 'exec', 'finally', 'for', 'from', 'global', 'if', 'import',
'in', 'is', 'lambda', 'not', 'or', 'pass', 'print', 'raise', 'return', 'try',
'while', 'with', 'yield']
```

Let's take a look at the keywords, along with a brief description of what they mean, and a very simple example of how you might use them. This will be your quick and dirty introduction to the syntax of Python.

Decision Making and Iteration Keywords

Python contains multiple keywords used for looping, decision-making, and controlling of execution statement order. Here's a list of those keywords, along with a simple example of each one. You will learn more about decision-making and iteration control keywords in Chapter 4.

✳ **break**: The break statement stops execution of a loop in Python. For example, you might want to stop a given loop when a condition is met. The following example will break out of a loop when the index value is odd.

```
index = 0
while index < 100:
    if index % 2 == 1:
        break
    print index
    index = index + 1
```

This block of code will print out only the number 0, because as soon as the value of 1 is reached, it will break out of the loop as per the break statement.

✳ **continue**: The continue statement allows a loop to pick up again at the top of the iteration, rather than executing any statements following the continue statement in the loop. For example, you might want to skip certain values in a loop. The following example will skip all odd values in a loop.

```
index = 0
while index < 10:
    index = index + 1
    if index % 2 == 1:
```

```
        continue
    print index
```

This block of code will print out every even number between 1 and 10. The `continue` statement skips all of the odd numbers.

❄ **elif**: The `elif` statement is Python shorthand for "else if." An `elif` statement should follow an `if` statement, and the code within the `elif` block will only be executed if the condition is True. This does not mean that every `if` statement must have a corresponding `elif`. Note that an `elif` statement must be at the same level as the `if` statement it follows. Finally, once any condition is evaluated to True, the entire block of `if`'s and `elif`'s is exited. The following example shows how you might test for three different conditions.

```
x = input("Enter a value: ")
if x == 1:
    print "You entered one"
elif x == 2:
    print "You entered two"
elif x == 3:
    print "You entered three"
```

When the user enters a value, the series of statements is interpreted. If the user entered, for example, a 2 at the prompt, the first `elif` would be evaluated to True, and the block would exit.

❄ **else**: The `else` statement corresponds to an `if` statement somewhere in an application. If the preceding if statement (or `elif` statement) is not true, the `else` statement code will be executed. The following example shows testing a single value and printing out some information, depending on whether the value is odd or even. The `else` statement can also be used with a `while` or `try` statement, as you will see later.

```
x = input("Enter a value: ")
if x % 2 == 0:
    print "Even"
else:
    print "Odd"
```

❄ **for**: The `for` statement allows you to iterate over a sequence of values. The following example prints out the elements of a set.

```
myList = [1,"Hello world", 2.5]
for i in myList:
    print i
```

❊ **if**: The if statement allows you to evaluate an expression and take action, depending on whether the statement is True or False. The following example simply prints out a string if a variable is the proper value.

```
x = 1
if x == 1:
        print "Yes!", x
```

❊ **while**: The while statement implements a looping mechanism that will continue to execute until a given condition is no longer true. The following example shows a loop that counts up to (but not including) 10.

```
index=0
while index < 10:
        print index
        index = index + 1
```

Debugging Keywords

Python provides built-in methods for debugging and observing your application's actions while it is running. Let's take a quick look at the keywords involved here.

❊ **assert**: The assert statement is used to ensure that a given condition is true. If the condition is violated, the program will throw an exception (see the "Exception Handling Keywords" section) and most likely terminate. For example, this code snippet would ensure that the user never entered a value outside the range from 1 to 10.

```
x = input("Enter a value from 1 to 10: ")
assert x >= 1 and x <= 10
print "Thank you"
```

❊ **print:** The print statement is a multi-use statement that allows you to output the value of variables along with text and formatting instructions in Python. For example, you might output a value in octal format as the following snippet shows.

```
print "%o" % 12
```

Package and Module Handling Keywords

As you will see later, Python provides ways to organize your code. The methods include pack-aging your code or writing your own modules. To utilize these organizational techniques, you use the package and module handling keywords. We will learn more about these keywords and their usage in Chapter 6, "Input and Output."

* **global**: The global statement makes a variable that would otherwise be defined locally to be available outside the scope of the function you are using it in. For example, if you have a global variable called BAD, and you want to assign a value to that variable within a function, you must declare it to be global within the function. Otherwise, a local variable of that name will be created. An example would be useful here:

```
BAD=1

def foo():
    print "Foo Called"
    global BAD
    BAD = 2

def foo1():
    print "Foo1 Called"
    BAD = 12

foo() #1
foo1() #2
print BAD
```

Notice that when this code snippet is run, the value of BAD following the execution of the lines marked #1 and #2 is 2, rather than 12. In the function Foo1, we assign to a local variable called BAD, because it is not marked as global.

* **import**: The import statement, similar to the C or Java include statement, allows you to bring external code into the currently running application. For example, to use one of the libraries that ships with Python, such as the math library, you import it into the interpreter.
* **import math from:** The from statement is used in conjunction with the import statement to import only selected entries, such as modules, classes, functions, or constants from external code. For example, you might want to import only the value of Pi from the math library.

```
from math import pi
print "Pi = ", pi
```

❋ **class**: The Python language allows you to encapsulate your logic in your own code blocks called *classes.* These classes can contain data and methods that you can expose to the outside world. In this simple example, you create a class with one method and then use that class in the actual application.

```
class MyClass:
    "A simple example class"
    i = 12345
    def f(self):
        return 'hello world'


# Program begins here.
print "Start of program"
x = MyClass()
s = x.f()
print s
```

❋ **def** : The def keyword allows you to define your own functions in Python. A function is simply a group of statements that is executed only when it is called from a piece of application code. Here's a simple example of a function that simply doubles the value that is input.

```
def doubleit(x):
    return x * 2


# Execution begins here.

x = 1
print "Doubled: ", doubleit(x)
x = doubleit(x)
print "Doubled: ", doubleit(x)
```

❋ **return**: The return statement allows you to return values from a function. If you return a value from a function, you must assign a value to the return value in order to use it. See the def keyword above for an example of how to use the return statement.

Exception Handling Keywords

Exception handling is a way of creating, dealing with, and notifying the user of errors in the application. An exception is considered to be an extraordinary (or, if you prefer, exceptional) event that has occurred within the application, which cannot be dealt with in the normal course of running. We will look more at exception handling in Chapter 8. "Exception Handling."

❋ **finally**: The finally statement is used in an exception handling block for things that must be done before any exception in a try block is thrown. You can save the exception information, close files, or whatever you might want to do when a serious error occurs. You cannot handle an exception in a finally statement, as illustrated in this example.

```
x = input("Enter a number: ")
y = 0
try :
    y = 10 / x
    print "Y = ", y
finally :
    print "In Finally Y = ", y
```

❋ **raise**: The raise keyword allows you to raise your own exceptions in your own Python application code. An exception should be raised whenever an exceptional event (one well outside the scope of expected errors) occurs. For example, consider the case of a user entering a value that is outside the valid range of values for a given input.

```
try:
    x = input("Enter a non-zero value: ")
    if x == 0:
        raise Exception
    print "You entered a legitimate value!"
except:
    print "Exception caught!"
```

❋ **try**: The try statement executes a block of code that might throw an exception. See the previous raise statement for an example of how this works in Python. Anything within the indented block will attempt to run. If an exception is thrown, it will skip all remaining statements in the block.

❋ **except** : The except statement is used to catch exceptions. In the example used in the raise statement code, the except block (indented code following the except: statement) will be executed only if there is an exception. Otherwise, this block will be skipped during normal execution.

General Language Keywords

The Python language has a number of keywords that can be used in virtually any kind of a statement, from a decision to a print statement. Here are a few of them that should be reasonably obvious to any programmer.

❈ **and**: The `and` keyword is used to combine two values for boolean True or False equivalence. If `a` is True, as well as `b` being True, then a and b are True together. This is a normal programming convention.

❈ **in**: The `in` keyword is used to see if something is a member of any sequence or collection. For example, you can test for a value in a list or set by using the `in` keyword. You can see an example of this in the following interpreter exchange:

```
>>> x = [1,2,3]
>>> if 1 in x:
        print "Yes"

Yes
>>> if 4 in x:
        print "yes"
```

Note that the second query `4 in x` returns False and thus does not print out the `yes` statement.

❈ **is**: The `is` keyword is used to test for object equality. Any two objects that reference the same object will be alike for the `is` comparison. For example:

```
>>> s = 1
>>> ref = s
>>> if s is ref:
        print "s is copy"
else:
        print "s is NOT a copy"


s is copy
>>> if x is copy:
        print "x is copy"


>>> t = 1
```

```
>>> if s is t:
        print "s is t"

s is t
```

* **not**: The not keyword simply negates a comparison. It is not really useful by itself, but you can use it to ask if something is not equal in object equality:

```
if s is not t:
```

This statement will do an object equality test of the variables s and t and if they are not the same ,will execute the code following the if statement.

* **or**: Similar to the and keyword, the or keyword returns True if either of the two values are True. So, if the variable a is True and the variable b is False, then a or b returns True because one of them is True. If both a and b are False, then a or b returns False.

Other Keywords

This section contains keywords that do not fit in anywhere else.

* **pass:** The pass keyword is what used to be called a noop. That is, the statement does nothing. It can be used anywhere that a valid statement is expected. For example, you could do something like this:

```
>>> t = 1
>>> s = 2
>>> if t == 1:
        pass
else:
        print "Something is very bad"
```

If t retained its assigned value, the pass statement would be executed, and the program would simply move on to the next line following the if block.

* **lambda**: At the risk of starting a linguistic war, the lambda statement is by far one of the most useless things in the Python language. Essentially, lambda allows you to create a "nameless" function with some inline code in it. An example is probably easier than trying to explain this keyword, or why you might want to use it.

```
>>> g = lambda x: x*x
>>> g(8)
64
```

Why would you want to create an inline, unnamed, function? I have no idea.

❋ **yield**: The `yield` statement is used only in generator functions in Python. A generator is a function that can stop what it is doing at any given point in the function body, return a value back to the caller, and, later on, resume from the point it had paused. This appears quite confusing, but can be very useful under certain circumstances. Let's look at a simple example now to see the syntax and then talk about it later in the book.

```
>>> def genfunc():
        print 'first call'
        yield 1
        print 'second'
        yield 2

>>> a = genfunc() # note that nothing happens here
>>> a.next() # call the function the first time
first call
1
>>> a.next()
second
2
>>>
```

Notice that the `yield` statement allowed us to pick back up where we started after we called the "next" iterator of the generator function object.

❋ **del**: The `del` statement simply removes a variable from the interpreter memory. Once a variable has been deleted, it can no longer be referred to:

```
>>> x = 1
>>> print x
1
>>> del x
>>> print x

Traceback (most recent call last):
```

```
  File "<pyshell#55>", line 1, in -toplevel-
    print x
NameError: name 'x' is not defined
>>>
```

❋ **exec** : The exec statement simply executes a string. The string can be any valid command within Python. It can be either a literal string or a string variable.

```
>>> x = 2
>>> exec "print x"
2
>>> s = "print"
>>> s += " x "
>>> exec s
2
>>>
```

Variable Usage

Python, like most languages, has a set of rules for variables. A variable is a memory address that can change. This is different from a memory address that can't change, which we normally refer to as a "constant." Variables are the holding cells of the computer world, the place in which you place data that you are going to need later. (I'm sure you know this, but it never hurts to actually take a moment to understand what it is we are talking about.) Note that in Python, all variables are references, which is different than many languages, which do not use the reference concept.

Python is not a "strongly typed language." By this, we mean that variables do not have specific types, which they can only be assigned to. In fact, you don't have to predefine variables in Python at all. A variable comes into existence as soon as you refer to it by its name. Which brings us to the first variable topic: naming and conventions.

Python allows you to define a variable using a combination of letters, numbers, and the underscore (_) character. There are a few rules: a variable must begin with a letter or an underscore, and the variable name is case sensitive. That is, you cannot have the following variable names:

```
1x = 2
?x = 3
x% = 4
```

However, all of the following are legal Python variable names:

```
x = 1
_x = 2
__x = 3
x_y = 5
```

On the other hand, while these variable names are all valid, they are also all different:

```
aXb
AxB
Axb
```

For example, if you bring up the IDLE editor and enter the following lines:

```
>>> aXb = 1
>>> AxB = 2
>>> Axb = 3
>>> print aXb
1
>>> print AxB
2
>>> print Axb
3
>>> print AXB

Traceback (most recent call last):
  File "<pyshell#12>", line 1, in <module>
    print AXB
NameError: name 'AXB' is not defined
```

Notice that all of the variable names contain the same letters, "a," "b," and "x" but in different combinations of cases. Yet each one has a different value assigned to it. It is important to keep track of the actual combination of letters you use to define a variable name, since it can lead to some rather strange problems in the code if you do not. In short, Python uses case-sensitive variable names.

Once you have the actual rules out of the way, there are the conventions. As the movie *Pirates of the Caribbean: The Curse of the Black Pearl* taught us, these aren't really rules; they are more guidelines. In Python, it is customary to begin a variable with a letter, not an underscore. There are no hard and fast rules for this, but under certain circumstances that we will discuss later, underscores can mean different things in different places, so it is best to avoid them as starting characters. Consistency is more important than style in a Python application, so if you use a lowercase letter as the starting letter of your variables, do so consistently throughout the application. Numbers are allowable in variable names, and they often are used to differentiate between different types of values. For example, you might have t0, which represents a starting time, and t1, which might indicate an ending time. Numbers are best at the end of variable names, but this is not a hard and fast rule.

The next thing that is often hard to understand about Python is that you do not need to define your variable. That is, if you are used to doing things like this:

```
int x;
int y;
double z;
x = 1;
y = 2;
z = (double)(x+y);
```

in your applications, you might as well get over it for Python. Python is quite happy with the following lines instead:

```
x = 1
y = 2
z = x+1
```

In fact, if you try to define a simple variable ahead of time, you will get an error, since there is no way to "define" a variable in Python.

The Continuation Variable

Now, remember that I said that using the underscore to begin a variable name is a bad idea? There's a reason for this. The IDLE editor (and, in fact, the interpreter in general) supports the notion of a continuation variable. This is probably one of the oddest things in the Python environment, but it does have its uses. It is a lot easier to just show you this one, rather than try to explain it up front:

```
>>> 5+6
11
>>> _+22     # Continuation!!
33
```

Notice the second statement, the one marked with the comment "Continuation!!" The continuation character, "_", forces the interpreter to take the last value that was stored and to apply whatever additional work you want done on it. Why would you do something like this? Because all Python expressions in immediate mode have a side effect, which is that they store the current value in the interpreter. You can think of this value as the "immediate variable." You can work with this variable to do shortcuts in your work. This does not work with variables, however. Consider this example:

```
>>> x = 1 + 2
>>> _+ 33


Traceback (most recent call last):
  File "<pyshell#18>", line 1, in <module>
    _+ 33
NameError: name '_' is not defined
```

[Note: The above session assumes you just started the IDLE Editor. If you have been typing along with the chapter, you would not see an error.]

As you can see, the continuation variable is only valid when you are working in immediate mode in the editor, and only when you are creating values as you go. This is particularly useful when you are using the Python environment to do mathematical calculations for you and want to see the intermediate values as you go along. If you didn't use this method, you would have to things like this:

```
>>> x = 5+6
>>> y = x + 22
>>> print y
33
```

Python is all about making life as easy as possible for the programmer to get his or her job done as quickly and easily as possible, and the continuation character is an expression of that.

Watching Out for Spelling Mistakes!

Here's an important caveat for working with Python: spelling matters! This is particularly true if you use rather odd names. For example, consider the following example:

```
>>> x_y_z = 1
>>> y_z_a = 2
>>> a_b_c = x_y_z + y_z_a
>>> x_y_a = 3
>>> b_c_d = x_y_z + y_z_a
>>> print b_c_d
3
```

Now, this code works just as it was written, but there is a major problem here. Instead of adding the first and second values and referencing the result in the variable b_c_d, I really meant to add the second value (y_z_a) and the last value (x_y_a). Because I misspelled a variable name, however, I got the wrong result, with no indication of the error. If I had actually used a variable name that didn't exist, I would have gotten an error. Unfortunately, there is no such check for what you meant to have happen. This is a danger in any language, but it is particularly prevalent in interpreted languages that do not have strong type checking, which describes Python. So remember what your third grade teacher told you and mind your spelling!

Predicates

The term *predicate* is used in a lot of languages, and has a variety of meanings. In Python, you will see the term bandied about quite a bit in the literature, so it is worth mentioning here. There is no "predicate" keyword in Python. It is a term that describes functionality in the language, much the same way that "variable" does. A predicate is a function that tests a condition and returns a Boolean value. That is, the function returns a value that is either true or false, depending on the condition evaluated. We haven't gotten into a discussion of functions yet, and won't for some time, so why bring this up now? The answer is, there are lots of functions that you use every day that you don't even think about. For example, consider the following bit of Python code:

```
x = 1
y = 2
if x+y < 4:
    print "Yes!"
```

If you enter this code into the interpreter, you will see the following display in IDLE:

```
>>> x = 1
>>> y = 2
>>> if x +y < 4:
        print "Yes!"


Yes!
```

What does this mean? Obviously, when you add one and two, you get a value less than four, so the print statement is executed. The conditional expression here is "x+y < 4". The expression that you are invoking is the if statement in Python. So, the entire expression "if x + y < 4" is the predicate in this expression. This might not seem important now, but it will certainly become important later on as you develop your own functions and use them in your code.

Identifier Scope

Scope is another issue that comes up constantly in programming languages. Put simply, scope is the lifetime of an object and where it may be accessed. The scope of a variable in Python is determined by two things: first, the place at which it is first used, and second, whether or not it is global. As you may recall, the keyword *global* was mentioned a bit earlier in this chapter. At the time, we merely glossed over what it meant, but now it's time to actually understand why this keyword exists at all.

There are two times in which the scope of a variable becomes important. One, in functions, we will discuss a bit later in the book. The second, within blocks, we can talk about now.

Let's consider the following example:

```
x = 1
if x == 2:
    y = 2
print "y = ", y
```

Entering the code into the IDLE editor, you get the following output:

```
>>> x = 1
>>> if x == 2:
        y = 1



>>> print y

Traceback (most recent call last):
  File "<pyshell#70>", line 1, in <module>
    print y
NameError: name 'y' is not defined
>>>
```

Why is this? The answer is *scope*. The variable y in this example is only defined within the block that is defined from the start of the if statement until the end of the if block two lines below. You can't refer to the value outside of that block, because it was never defined as the code never entered the block. We could fix this easily enough:

```
>>> x = 1
>>> y = 1
>>> if x == 2:
```

```
        y = 2


>>> print y
1
```

As you can see, by moving the initial definition of y outside of the if block, you fix the problem. However, you may not want to do that under all circumstances. Instead, you can extend the scope of the variable y by using the global statement:

```
>>> x= 1
>>> if x == 1:
        global y
        y = 2


>>> print y
2
>>>
```

As you can see, the variable y is now defined both inside and outside the block. We have changed the scope of the y variable to be global, that is, available anywhere from that point on in the application. When we talk about functions and modules, this will become more important, so it is fairly imperative that you understand what scope means at this stage.

By the way, this brings up an important aside. You may have noticed that once a variable is defined in the IDLE editor, it hangs around forever. There are two ways that you can fix this, if you happen to want to get rid of a variable. First, you can use the del statement:

```
>>> y = 2
>>> print y
2
>>> del y
>>> print y

Traceback (most recent call last):
  File "<pyshell#87>", line 1, in <module>
    print y
NameError: name 'y' is not defined
>>>
```

The `del` statement removes a variable from the memory of the interpreter. This is useful if you just want to get rid of a single variable. If, on the other hand, you want to get rid of all of the work you have done, there is a better way. The IDLE editor has an option, tucked under the Shell menu called *Restart Shell.* If you run this function, it will remove all of the variables you have in memory, as well as any code you may have loaded in the form of modules or functions. This can be useful when you have no idea what is set and what is not and just want to start with a clean slate.

Figure 2.2 shows a typical run of the IDLE editor, showing some of the things you have done in this session, along with a shell restart and the repercussions of that restart.

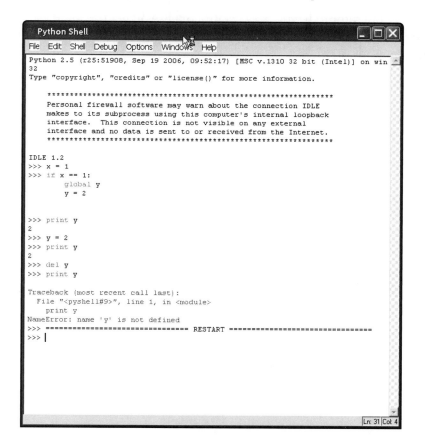

Figure 2.2
Restarting the IDLE editor.

That about covers the concept of scope, leaving us only one more topic to talk about in this chapter before we get into some real coding. So, let's move on to that final topic: the notion of operators.

Operators

There are two different kinds of operators in Python, as in most languages. First, there are unary operators. Unary operators are those that operate on a single value. The unary operators are:

~ : The bitwise NOT operator

- : The negative operator

+: The positive operator.

The latter two are fairly self-explanatory. If you have a value and apply the negative operator to it, you get a negative result, assuming that the value is a numeric type. Likewise, if you have a value and assign the positive operator to it, you get ... well, actually, you get the same value. The positive operator is really just used for circumstances where you want to emphasize the fact that something is positive. That is:

```
>>> x = 1
>>> y = +x
>>> print y
1
>>> x = -1
>>> y = +x
>>> print y
-1
>>>
```

The "~" operator, on the other hand, is a little more complicated if you have never worked with it before. The idea here is that the ~ operator reverses all of the bits in a value. That can be useful for certain mathematical expressions, but it is generally used to reverse the values 0 and -1, to be used as numeric values for true and false. So, if we do the following:

```
>>>   x = 0
>>> print x
0
>>> x = ~x
>>> print x
-1
>>> x = ~x
>>> print x
0
>>>
```

As you can see, the ~ operator is simply flipping the bits of the value of x. By definition ~(~x) will always be the value x, no matter what x started out as:

```
>> x = 123
>>> x = ~(~x)
>>> print x
123
```

That about covers unary operators, which brings us up to the second type of operator in Python, binary operators. In this case, binary doesn't mean the mathematical base that consists of only zeroes and ones, it means the idea of operators that have two arguments. This sounds strange, but I assure you, you have been using them most of your life without even thinking of them as binary. For example, x + y uses the binary operator "+." It applies to two variables, x and y.

Python supports the basic binary operators that you would expect:

+ The addition operator

- The subtraction operator

* The multiplication operator

/ The division operator.

For numeric values, these operators work the way you would expect. There are a few catches and caveats work mentioning, however. Python will assume data type, depending upon the information supplied. Consider the following example.

```
X = 10/3
```

Python has no way of knowing what you intended the data types to be in the above statement. It will therefore assume that both operands are integers, as there is nothing to suggest otherwise, and as you know, you do not declare variable types in Python. The result of the above statement will also be an integer. So, instead of getting a result of 3.333, you will get the result 3. How do you fix this? That's also quite simple; just change one of the arguments to a floating point value:

```
>>> x = 10/3
>>> print x
3
>>> x = 10.0/3
>>> print x
3.33333333333
>>>
```

There are also shorthand versions of the above operators that work on a single variable. For example, suppose that you want to increment the value of x by 1. You could write:

```
x = x+1
```

However, Python provides a better way, the += operator:

```
>>> x = 1
>>> x = x + 1
>>> print x
2
>>> x = 1
>>> x += 1
>>> print x
2
>>>
```

Likewise, there are versions for all of the other standard operators, as show in Table 2-1.

Table 2-1   The Python Standard Operators

Operator	Meaning
+	Add two values
+=	Add a value to a variable (shorthand)
-	Subtract two values
-=	Subtract a value from a variable (shorthand)
*	Multiply two values
*=	Multiply a variable by a value (shorthand)
/	Divide two values
/=	Divide a variable by a value (shorthand)

Note that all of the above only work on numeric types, which means that integers or floating point numbers can be added, subtracted, multiplied, and divided. This does not apply to string types.

Modulo Operator

One of the less common operators, at least outside of the computer world, is the modulo operator. This operator, is represented by the percent sign '%'. This operator does a division between two values and returns the remainder of the division. For example, if you divide 10 by 3, you get the result of 3, with one left over. The modulo operator returns the 1, in this case, as you can see in the following example:

```
>>> x = 10 /3
>>> print x
3
>>> x = 10 % 3
>>> print x
1
>>>
```

You might wonder what the use is for the modulo operator. Actually, there are quite a number of really good uses for it. The first, and most heavily overused example is that of determining whether or not a given year is a leap year. If you are unaware of the rules, a leap year is a year that follows these constraints:

❊ It is divisible by 4.

❊ It is *not* divisible by 100, unless it is divisible by 400.

Thus, 2004 is a leap year, 2000 is a leap year, but 1900 is not a leap year, nor is 1901. Note the "is divisible by." You can think of "is divisible by" as the same as "divisible with no remainder." In other words, a given year is a leap year if:

```
>>> year = 2004
>>> isLeapYear = (year % 400 == 0) or ( year % 100 != 0 and year % 4 == 0 )
>>> year= 2000
>>> print isLeapYear
True
>>> year = 2004
>>> isLeapYear = (year % 400 == 0) or ( year % 100 != 0 and year % 4 == 0 )
>>> print isLeapYear
True
>>>
>>> year = 1900
>>> isLeapYear = (year % 400 == 0) or ( year % 100 != 0 and year % 4 == 0 )
>>> print isLeapYear
False
```

Another use of the modulo function is in calculating change, which is probably more useful and less widely used. For example, imagine that you want to know how many quarters to return to someone based on the value of the bill that they hand you. By dividing by the value of the coin you want to use, you find out how much of that coin will be returned as change. Then, by using the modulo operator, you can determine how much change is left to figure out the next coin value for. This is actually a very common operation in point of sales systems.

Naturally, there is a shorthand version of the modulo operator, %=, which takes a value, applies the modulo of a value to it, and then stores the result back in the original variable.

Exponential Operator

How many times have you thought to yourself: "How much is 2 multiplied by itself 4 times?" Why, I find myself doing this half a dozen times a day, at least. You mean you don't? Gee, what is wrong with you, anyway? Seriously, though, the idea of multiplying a number by itself is called "raising that number to a power" or exponentiation. This particular function is very useful for working with bit values, for doing mathematical calculations, and for various other uses in the software world. In Python, the exponentiation operator is represented by the symbol "**", or a double asterisk.

For example, suppose that you are told to find the value of 2 raised to the 5th power. In math terms, this is represented as 2^5, and in Python, it would be expressed as 2**5. Entering this into the IDLE editor, you can see that the result is:

```
>>> 2**5
32
```

Can you apply the exponentiation operator to a variable itself using shorthand? Yes, just as you would expect:

```
>>> x = 2
>>> x **= 5
>>> print x
32
```

Logical Operators

The next batch of operators we are going to discuss is the set known as *logical operators*. These operators are called this because they are used by the logic statement in Python. The set of operators is shown in Table 2-2.

Table 2-2   Python Logical Operators

Operator Name	Purpose
or	Logical or statement
and	Logical and statement
not	Logical not statement

The logical operators are generally used in conditional statements, such as the 'if' statement. For example, consider the following scenario: You want a number that is between 1 and 10, inclusive. That is, the values 1, 2, 3, 4, 5, 6, 7, 8, 9 and 10 are legitimate, all other values should be rejected. You could write something like this:

```
if x < 1:
    print "Error!"
if x > 10:
    print "Error"
# Otherwise, legitimate value.
This, of course, works fine as you would expect:
>>> x = 1
>>> if x < 1:
        print "Error"


>>> if x > 10:
        print "Error"


>>> x = -1
>>> if x < 1:
        print "Error"


Error
>>>
```

Wouldn't it be nice, however, to combine those two conditions into a single if statement? That way, you would know exactly what it was you were testing for. This is a perfect case for the logical or operator:

```
>>> x= -1
>>> if (x < 1) or (x > 10):
        print "Error"


Error
>>>
```

If you happened to major in English and not in "programmerese" as a language, the logical or is not quite what you expect. When you write x or y, you get results according to Table 2-3:

Table 2-3   Logic OR Truth Table

X	y	Result of x OR y
True	True	True
True	False	True
False	False	False
False	True	True

In other words, the result of two expressions or'd together is True if either of those expressions is True.

The and operator works exactly the opposite way. The expression "x and y" is True only if both x and y are True:

```
>>> x = 1
>>> if x != 2 and x != 3 and x != 4:
        print "X is ok"


X is ok
>>>
```

Using our truth table (Table 2-3) above for and, we get the following table results:

Table 2-4   Logic AND Truth Table

X	y	Result of x AND y
True	True	True
True	False	False
False	False	False
False	True	False

Finally, you have the not logical operator. The not operator does the opposite of whatever you apply it to. So, if you say not x == 2, then it is the same as x != 2. Here's a simple example to show you what is meant:

```
>>> x = 2
>>> if not x == 2:
```

```
      print "x is not 2"



>>> if not x == 1:
      print "x is not 1"



x is not 1
>>>
```

Likewise, you can use the `not` operator with the `and`, or `or` operators. For example:

```
>>> x = 1
>>> if not ( x == 1 and x != 2 ):
      print "Help!"
```

In this case, you take the expression (x == 1 and x != 2) and evaluate it. Since the variable x is equal to 1, the first half of the expression is True. Since x is not equal to 2, the second half of the expression is True. Using the truth tables above, you can see that since True and True is True, the value of the expression within the parentheses is, in fact, True. Now, you apply the `not` operator to that. This says that you take True, and make it not True, or False. So the result of the expression is False, and should result in the print statement not being executed. Running the above code in the IDLE environment verifies this.

Comparative Operators

Like all programming languages, Python provides a way in which to compare values for equality and inequality. In addition, for numeric and string values, there are operators for checking for magnitude differences, less than, greater than, and so forth. Table 2-5 shows the list of valid comparative operators in Python.

Table 2-5 The Python Comparative Operators

Operator	Meaning
<	Less than operator
<=	Less than or equal to operator
>	Greater than operator
>=	Greater than or equal to operator
<>	Not equal operator (deprecated)
==	Equal operator
!=	Not equal operator

Yes, you read that correctly, there are two `not` equal operators. Why? I really don't know, to be honest, except that different languages, such as Pascal and C++ use different operators, and it was easier to support both when the language was being created. Note that the <> version has been deprecated and shouldn't be used in new code. It is shown here just in case you run into it in some old code.

Here are a few simple examples of the comparative operators in use, just to give you an idea of how they work in practice.

```
>>> x = 1
>>> y = 2
>>> print x <> y
True
>>> print x != y
True
>>> print x == y
False
>>> if x < y:
        print "x is less than y"
else:
        if x > y:
                print "x is greater than y"
        else:
                print "x = y"


x is less than y
```

As you can see, not only can you compare two values, but you can also print out the result of that comparison as a value itself. Finally, Python does proper comparisons for both integer values and floating point values:

```
>>> x = 10.0
>>> y = 9.99
>>> print x > y
True
>>> print x < y
False
```

There you go, a whirlwind tour of the reasonably straightforward comparison operators in Python.

Bitwise Operators

A few pages back, you learned about the logical and, or, and not operators. These operators worked on the state of logical values, True and False. The computer world, however, often deals in much smaller increments than True and False. Computer programmers are taught early on to think in terms of bits. A bit is a single 0 or 1 value. In many cases, especially in older applications, a lot of data was stored as individual bits within a numeric value. For example, you might have a single 16-bit value that meant the following:

```
Bit 0:  Whether or not option 1 is enabled.
Bit 1:  Whether or not option 2 is enabled.
...
```

And so forth until:

```
Bit 15: Whether or not option 16 is enabled.
```

To accomplish this, Python offers three operators: the "&" bitwise and operator, the "|" bitwise or operator, and the "~" bitwise not operator.

The bitwise or operator works by combining bit values. It is probably easier to show you how this works and then explain it than to try to explain it alone. Take a look at the following simple Python code:

```
>>> a = 1
>>> b = 2
>>> c = a | b
>>> print c
3
```

Okay, now to understand what is going, first you have to understand how binary values are represented. A number like 1 is really represented as a 16 bit value:

```
0000000000000001
```

The value 2 is represented as:

```
0000000000000010
```

The value 4 would be:

```
0000000000000100
```

And so on. When you "or" two values together, you use the same rules you used for the logical `or` condition, but on a bit basis. Let's look at the numbers you select, 1 and 2:

```
1:   0000000000000001
2:   0000000000000010
```

You first look at bit 0 (the rightmost bit). If either bit is set in the two values, the "output" bit is set to 1. Since there is a 1 in the value 1, and no 1 in the value 2 for the rightmost bit, the "output" bit is set to 1. So, at this point, you have:

```
0000000000000001
```

Now, you repeat the process for the next bit. The value 2 has bit 2 set, whereas the value 1 does not. So the output bit is set and the result is now:

```
0000000000000011
```

The remainder of the bits is not set for either the first or second values, so all of the output bits are set to 0. This means that the result has only two bits set. To figure out what the number is, you just multiply each position by the power of 2 that it represents:

```
1 * 2^0 = 1
1 * 2^1 = 2
```

And so forth. Since none of the rest of the bits are set, you just add the 1 and the 2 and get 3 for the output value. Thus, 1 | 2 is 3. Wow, talk about a complex explanation of a really simple concept. Computers know how to do this instantly.

Now that you understand all that, the rest of it goes pretty fast. The bitwise `and` operator, &, works by determining which bits are set in common between two values. So, 1 & 2 is 0 since there are no bits in common. 3 & 2 is 2 because only a single bit is set in common, the second bit from the right.

Finally, the bitwise `not` operator: ~. This operator flips the bits of a given value; however, it doesn't really result in what you expect to have happen, so it is probably worth a bit of explanation.

Imagine you have the value 0. The value 0 is represented by sixteen zero bits:

```
0000000000000000
```

If you flip those bits, you get:

```
1111111111111111
```

Now, you might imagine that would be a really big number, but you are wrong. In fact, that's a really small number. The reason is that the computer uses the high bit (the leftmost bit) to represent the sign of the value. So, if the leftmost bit is set to 1, the value is negative. In this case, the remainder of the bits adds up to be -2.

Take my word that this works for now. If you really want to understand the representation of negative numbers as a binary value, feel free to look it up on the Internet. Suffice it to say that the bitwise `not` operator accomplishes this by flipping bits.

Membership Operators and String Operators

We will talk a great deal more about membership and string operators in later chapters when we talk about sets of data and strings. For completeness, Table 2-6 shows the various operators and a short description of what they do.

Table 2-6   Membership Operators in Python

Operator	Meaning
in	Indicates whether a given collection contains a value.
not in	Indicates whether a given collection does not contain a given value
X[index]	Returns the element at a given location in a sequence.
X[startindex:endindex]	Returns a slice of a given sequence.

Identity Operators

Finally, Python contains two identity operators. The `is` and `not is` operators check to see if a given variable refers to the same object as another variable. We will discuss the identity operators when we talk about classes and instances later in the book.

In Conclusion

That sums up our quick introduction to the Python syntax. At this point, you have just enough information to be slightly dangerous in the language. Next up on our tour will be an examination of the tools that are provided with the Python environment, examining how to use things like the editor, the Command Line compiler, and the documentation. We'll look at creating Python files, and how to run them in the interpreter. We'll also take a little look at the structure of Python, including modules and packages and files.

3 } Tools

A carpenter cannot create works of art without his hammer, saw, and drill. An electrician is helpless without a circuit tester. A politician is hopeless without his script writer. What do all of these things have in common? Simple—they are all tools that are used for professionals to accomplish their jobs. The job of a Python programmer is to create, maintain, enhance, and debug Python applications. Like any other sort of profession, the Python programmer needs tools to accomplish his or her task. In this chapter, we are going to look at some of the tools that are already built into the Python distribution that will be used in your unrelenting pursuit of Python perfection.

Also, we are going to explore the tools that actually come with the standard Python distribution. There are plenty of third-party libraries, packages, and tools that can be used with Python, but they are a subject for external sources, such as Web site reviews, because they have a tendency to change so quickly and move around so much. Refer back to the Web sites listed in Chapter 1 for a good list of places to look for other Python tools and libraries.

IDLE

Of all of the tools you are likely to use in the Python development process, IDLE is by far the most common. The IDLE integrated development environment provides syntax highlighting, loading, and running of Python scripts, debugging facilities, integrated help, and many other features that will aid you in producing high-quality Python code. The IDLE environment, which was created specifically for Python, is a vast improvement over various other possibilities for editing and running code, and it should be your first choice among tools to use.

Actually, you don't really need to use IDLE, unless you are so inclined. Python is all about flexibility, so you can use other tools if they are more familiar to you. There are Python language templates for the popular UNIX editor Emacs, and for many other common editors out there. By using your favorite editor along with the Command Line interpreter/compiler, you can easily edit and run Python scripts to your heart's content without ever having to learn IDLE. If this is your choice, feel free to skip this section and read about some of the other features of the language tools or simply move on to the next chapter and read about the language itself.

To begin the discussion, let's look at the IDLE environment. Figure 3.1 shows the IDLE editor as it looks when you first load it from the main menu [Start -> All Programs -> Python 2.5 -> IDLE (Python GUI)]. The IDLE application, by the way, on the Windows side is called pythonw.exe, not to be confused with python.exe, which is the Command Line compiler.

Figure 3.1

The IDLE editor.

Before we talk about the functionality of the IDLE editor menus, it is important to note that IDLE recognizes two "modes." First, there is "immediate" mode. In this case, the interpreter immediately executes a statement as soon as it is entered into the editor and the Enter key pressed. For example:

```
x = 1
```

followed by the Enter key will immediately create a variable called x in the interpreter memory and assign that variable the value 1. Likewise, entering the statement `print x` and pressing the Enter key will immediately display the value of x (in this case, 1) to the immediate window.

The other "mode" that IDLE recognizes is editing mode. In this case, you are using the IDLE editor as a text editor, creating a set of commands that you want to run as a single application script. Only when you are done and select Run from the Editor window will the interpreter be invoked and the individual statements within the script executed. Immediate mode statements disappear when you close down the editor; edit mode statements are normally saved to a file at some point during the development and debugging process. Now let's take a look at the functionality that is built into the IDLE editor.

Let's briefly look through the menu structure of the IDLE editor, so you can get a good handle on where everything is, and know where to change things when you need to change them during the editing and running of a Python script.

File Menu

The File menu consists of the following options.

New Window

The New Window option pops up a new editing window that you can use to create a new Python script window. The IDLE editor allows you to open as many windows as memory permits on your system. You can keep each module or file in a separate window, if that happens to be your preference. We'll look at this option a bit later when we talk about creating Python files. Opening a new window does not invoke a new copy of the interpreter, nor can you actually run a given script module in one of these separate windows. They are solely for loading and editing text. Think of them as small editors, and you will do fine.

Open

The Open command loads a module that you have written in the past, or one that someone else has written, for editing or running. After a module has been loaded into the interpreter, all of the functions, statements, and definitions within the modules are available to the interpreter (although not available to you in Immediate mode, as you shall see later). This allows you to load a given Python module and run some functions within it to do testing, or just to experiment with how things work, without making any changes in the "production" version of the code. This is a powerful capability and one that is not really available in the compiled world. Sometimes, interpreters are really better than compilers overall.

Recent Files

The recent files entry is really just a placeholder for a pop-up menu that contains a list of the most recently used files that you have loaded into the editor or saved from the editor. You can quickly and easily move between files that you have loaded by selecting them from the Recent

Files menu. Note that the first time you bring up IDLE, this menu will be empty, since you will not have worked on any files yet.

Files that are loaded from the Recent Files menu will be loaded into a new window, as per the new window command. In fact, selecting something from the Recent Files list is the equivalent of selecting a new window, followed by using the File menu on that new window to load an existing file. Files loaded by the recent files menu are not automatically interpreted, so you will have to issue the Run command on them to load the functions and data in them into memory for use in the interpreter.

Open Module

We will look at modules a bit later in this chapter, but for now, just consider a module to be a collection of functions and classes in Python. You can use the Open Module command to load a module the same way that you use the Open command under the File menu to load a given Python script file. The difference is that the Open file command allows you to browse for a given file in a given place on your computer system. The Open Module command, on the other hand, takes the name of a module and finds it somewhere within the search path defined in the IDLE editor. The difference, really, is between browsing for something when you know where it is, and searching for something when you know its name. The Open Module command launches a single dialog, shown in Figure 3.2, which prompts you for the name of a module to load.

Figure 3.2
The Open Module
dialog box.

You might be wondering what the "sys.path" is to which the dialog refers. We will examine that in just a moment when we look at the path browser in the IDLE IDE.

Let's take a quick look at how a module load works in IDLE. In the dialog box, type in the name **pdb.py**. This is the Python debugger module, which you'll learn about later in the chapter. Here, you'll get your first look at a real Python file. Enter the name and press the **OK** button in the dialog. You should then see a window showing the pdb.py module (see Figure 3.3).

The module loads and is ready for you to edit, run, or do whatever you want to do with it. Note also that the window used to display a loaded file is different from the IDLE Immediate mode window, and contains other commands, which you'll learn about in just a bit.

Class Browser

The Class Browser allows you to view the makeup of a given class within the Python environment. In general, using the class browser from the main IDLE window is pointless, since the

Figure 3.3
The Python debugger
module loaded into IDLE.

modules are generally loaded into separate windows. The same command, however, exists on open file windows. Looking at the Python debugger module that was loaded in the last example, you can look at the File | Class Browser result in that window. Move over to the pdb.py window and select File | Class Browser. You should see a pop-up window appear that looks just like the one displayed in Figure 3.4.

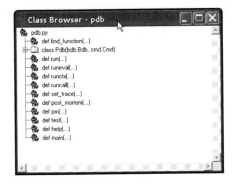

Figure 3.4
The Class Browser
displayed for the Python
debugger module.

As you can see, the Class Browser lists all sorts of interesting things about the module. Any classes that are encountered when loading the module are displayed. In this case, there is only a single class, the Pdb class. You will notice that there is a little expansion box to the left of the class name. Clicking that box will expand the class definition and show you all of the methods within the class. In addition, outside of the class definition will be a list of functions that were found at a global scope within the module. At the top of the Class Browser window, for example, you will see a definition for a function called `find_function`. Don't worry about understanding how functions work in Python quite yet, as we will get into a much more complete discussion of creating and using functions in Chapter 7.

One last note on the Class Browser: One of the nicest features of the Class Browser is its ability to go directly to the source line in the actual module file from the definition of the function. In the Class Browser, simply double-click the function name that you want to inspect. Figure 3.5 shows a good example of this. In this case, I've selected the "reset" function in the Class Browser and double-clicked it. This brought up the pdb.py file in a window (I had closed it to illustrate the point) and moved the cursor directly to the line that defines the function reset within that file. This can be a very handy way to navigate the source code in a module, or to pick up where you left off in your last editing session.

Figure 3.5

The Class Browser used for navigation.

Oh, one last note that isn't important right now but may be to you in the future. The Class Browser, like the rest of Python, works by interpreting the source. That means that it does its very best to parse a given source module and extract all of the functions and classes within that module. The really nice side-effect of all of this is that a class need not be complete, nor compile properly, to load it into the Class Browser. So you can easily use the Class Browser on your work in progress. This is a nice feature that I think you will learn to appreciate as you go along.

Path Browser

Ah yes, the joys of paths. The Python system uses the `sys.path` value to determine the roots from which to load all modules and search for things. For example, in the Open Module menu selection, the `sys.path` path is used to define the directories on the local system and any network paths to use to find things. Now, you might wonder where this information comes from. There is no setting in the IDLE application to define the system path, but the Path Browser is something else entirely. So before we get to the Path Browser, let's take a quick look at the `sys.path` variable and determine where it is set and how.

In the Windows environment, and specifically for Python 2.5 installations, there is a registry key that is used to determine the path that will be used for the installation. You will find this key in the registry at the following location: `HKEY_LOCAL_MACHINE\SOFTWARE\Python\PythonCore\2.5\PythonPath`

In addition, you will find the installation path there, as well as the documentation paths and the modules loaded into the system at startup. It is not generally a good idea to modify these values, because most of them can be modified outside of the registry as well.

For the specific example of the `sys.path` variable, you can set an environment variable in your system to modify the path that the IDLE editor (and Python interpreter) uses to search for modules. The environment variable is called `PYTHON_PATH` and is expected to contain a list of directory paths, separated by a semi-colon. You can place this environment variable in either the system environment or your local user environment, and the IDLE environment will find it properly. Note that changing this variable requires you to restart the IDLE environment in order to reload it.

Finally, you may change the path through a `.pth` file placed in the Python directory. A `.pth` file contains a list of subdirectories from the directory it is stored in that are to be used to search for modules. For example, imagine that you have your Python directory at `c:\Python25` for Python 2.5. Within that directory, you have a directory called `MySource` in which you want to add the files that you create to the general search path. Let's look at how you would go about doing that right now.

First, create the directory `MySource` in the `c:\Python25` (or wherever you installed Python on your system) directory. Next, bring up the Path Browser. You should see something like the display shown in Figure 3.6. Note that the `MySource` directory is not displayed in the list.

❋ ❋ ❋

Figure 3.6
The initial Path Browser
display.

Now, we are going to create a new file in the main directory (c:\Python25, or the directory in which you installed the system). Using your favorite text editor, or even IDLE itself, create a new file and call it MySource.pth (for path file). Place the following lines into the file:

```
# Add MySource to the main path
MySource
```

Save the file and close it. Make sure that you close down the IDLE environment; then restart it. Re-enter the Path Browser dialog, and you will see that the MySource directory has now been added to the list of searchable paths. You can repeat this for any number of paths you want, by simply adding the lines to the .pth file, or by creating a new .pth file in the main directory.

❋ **Warning About Invalid Paths!**

```
If you add a name that does not exist, or is not a directory, IDLE will not
add it to the search path, nor will it tell you about it. Always verify that
your search path has been updated when you make a change to the main search
path or you will get unexpected results.
```

The Path Browser Dialog

Now that you understand what path is being browsed, it is worth mentioning that the Path Browser dialog itself is used to show you all of the files that are located along the various branches of the search path. You can select any given directory in the search path and view the Python (.py) files that are located along that directory path.

Save

The Save saves a file that has been previously opened or created within the environment. Selecting the Save menu selection on a newly created script file will prompt the user for a name for the file, as well as a directory in which it should be stored. If the file has already been saved and has been loaded into the IDLE environment, selecting the Save option will save it back to the same file name, overwriting the existing file.

Note that there are three file types that are supported by the IDLE environment:

* ❋ **TXT files** (`.txt`) are simple text files. Anything can be saved as a text file and will be assumed to be plain text. IDLE will attempt to look for Python code stored within a TXT file just as it does with any other sort of file.
* ❋ **PY files** (`.py`) are considered to be Python source code files. The `.py` extension is the default extension for Python and is the extension you will normally see on the Internet.
* ❋ **PYW files** (`.pyw`) are Python Microsoft Windows files. Normally, there is no difference between a `.py` file and `.pyw` file. However, if you are using functionality for which Windows extensions are somehow needed, you should use the `.pyw` extension rather than the `.py` extension to indicate to other people that this file will only work on a given operating systems. Needless to say, it is considered rude and poor form to create a Python script that only runs on a given operating system.

> ❋ **File Naming Tip**
>
> If you do not name your files correctly, the IDLE editor will not do syntax highlighting for that file.

Save As

The Save As functionality is the same as the Save functionality, except that it will change the name of the output file. The original file that was loaded into the environment will not be affected by a Save As, whether the file name or the file extension has been modified, unless you save it to the same name. It is okay to save a file as the same name as another file that already exists; however, you will be prompted that the file already exists.

Save Copy As

The Save Copy As functionality is exactly the same as the Save As functionality with one noticeable difference. When you use the Save As functionality, not only is the file saved by the new name, but also the copy that is maintained in memory is renamed to that new name. That is, when you do a Save As to the name `test1.py`, work on the file for a bit, and click Save, then the `test1.py` file will be updated on disk. With the Save Copy As functionality, when you save the `test.py` file as `test1.py` and then modify the file, the next time you click Save, it will be saved to disk as `test.py` rather than `test1.py`. This is rarely worth mentioning, but can lead to confusing results for you if you selected the wrong one and then went back later to work on it.

Print Window

The Print Window functionality seems simple, doesn't it? You click the main window, click Print Window, and the results of the window are printed. Sigh. Unfortunately, it isn't that simple. Python lacks the capability to actually print to a Windows printer. As a result, the system launches the standard text editing program, Notepad for Windows, loads the text into it, and then invokes the Print command from Notepad to print it. You might think that there is no difference here, but there is. For one thing, Notepad assumes that there is a default printer installed. If your system does not have such a default printer, or if the default printer is not enabled or running, your print job will not show up on the printer. Worse, you will get a very odd message about the RPC server not running instead of a printer error. Should you happen to see this message, you will now know what is going on.

If a default printer is installed, or you are running on a non-Windows platform, the contents of the current window will be sent to the printer as plain text, in the default font and color displayed.

Close

The Close button will close the window for which it is used. If the Close button is used on the main window, the behavior is the same as selecting Exit.

Exit

The Exit button will close all open Python IDLE windows and exit the application. IDLE does not prompt you to save your work, so if you do not want to lose anything that is in the current edit buffer, you will need to save it before selecting exit or close.

Edit Menu

The Edit menu on IDLE consists of the following options:

Undo and Redo

Undo and Redo are fairly well understood terms in the computer world. If you make a mistake, you can click the Undo button to revert the current document to its previous state. In IDLE, Undo and Redo only work within the context of the current statement. That is, once you complete a Python statement, the Undo functionality is lost. So, if you are typing on a line and enter **print x** and click the Undo menu selection, it will remove the last thing you typed, which is "x." Clicking it again will remove the space. Clicking it a third time will remove the word "print." Undo isn't necessarily as intuitive as you might imagine.

Likewise, Redo does exactly what Undo does, but in the opposite order. If you type **print x** without pressing Return, and then click Undo three times, you will end up with a blank line. If you click Redo three times, you will end up with "print x" back on the line again. Anywhere in between, of course, will result in some partial amount of the "print x" line.

Unfortunately, IDLE does not gray out menu options when they do not apply, so even if you have a blank line and have done nothing with it, you will still see the Undo and Redo menu options available.

Cut, Copy, and Paste

The cut, copy, and paste actions work on the current line in the editor. For cut and copy, the currently selected item or items will be copied or removed from the edit buffer into the paste buffer. For the paste command, whatever is in the current paste buffer will be placed into the edit buffer at the current cursor location. Note that IDLE does not really pay much attention to whether or not pasting a given block at the current location makes any sense, so if you copy out of another document and paste into the IDLE environment you may get what you want and you may get total garbage followed by error messages. It is best to use these as simply and in as straightforward a manner as possible.

One difference between the "standard" Windows copy and cut functionality and that implemented in IDLE is the case where nothing is selected. In this case, most Windows applications assume that if you have selected nothing, then you want to copy (or cut) the entire line. However, IDLE assumes that you want to copy (or cut) nothing. If you select a block of text and copy (or cut) it, then select another block of text and select paste, the copied text will overwrite the highlighted text.

IDLE considers text that is cut, copied, or pasted to be part of the current line buffer, and unless that text contains an embedded carriage return character, it will not immediately interpret the line when in "immediate" mode. In editing mode, the text will always be pasted in and treated simply as text.

Select All

The Select All menu item simply selects, and therefore highlights, all of the text that is displayed in the window, whether or not it is currently visible to the user. That is, the entire edit buffer is selected. This can be useful for copying text to another window, or for saving it into a file that exists in another editor, or for clearing the entire window by selecting it all and deleting it. There are no real surprises in the Select All command.

Find, Find Next, Find Selection, Find in Files, Replace

The various find and replace options in IDLE work pretty much the way you would expect them to. In Immediate mode, the Find, Find Next, and Find Selection commands work on the entire edit buffer, allowing you to search not only the text of your script, but the system display and error messages. In Edit mode, the Find functions work in the file that is displayed and allow you to search and find any piece of text from the current location either upward or downward in the current file. The Find functionality uses the (ill-named) dialog shown in Figure 3.7.

As you can see from the Find dialog, you have various options within the function. The Regular Expression check box allows you to use regular expressions within the string in order to match

Figure 3.7
The Search dialog.

wildcards, single words, various permutations of strings, and so on. The options available when using regular expressions are, not surprisingly, the same as those exposed by the Regular Expression package for Python, which we will be discussing in Chapter 11. The Match Case check box allows you to force the search to be exactly the same as the string you type in. That is, if you enter the string `"hello"` and you do not check this box, then the search will match the following strings:

```
"Hello"
"hEllo"
"HELLO"
"hello"
```

Naturally, all other variants will match as well, with any of the characters being in upper- or lowercase. On the other hand, if you check this option, the string `"hello"` will only match that exact string in the text, so all other variants will be ignored.

The whole word option indicates whether the string that is checked can be a part of a bigger string or not. So, if the check box is not selected, then `hello` will match `hellothere`, as well as `shellop`. If the check box is selected, then the string must exist as a separate delimited string. A delimited string may be delimited by the start of the line, the end of the line, or by a non-letter character, such as a space or a period.

The Wrap option indicates whether the search should wrap around to the beginning of the file or buffer if the string is not found from the current location. If your cursor is in the middle of the file, for example, and you tell it not to wrap, then the search will progress from the character position of the cursor to the bottom of the file and stop. If the Wrap option is selected, and the string is not found by the bottom of the file, then the search will pick up at the top of the file and progress to the cursor location.

The Up or Down radio buttons indicate whether the search should progress from the cursor location to the bottom of the file (down) or from the cursor location to the top of the file (up).

Finally, since the Find dialog can be displayed and used at any time, the Close button is included to make it go away. The Find dialog is modal, meaning that while it is displayed, you can't do anything else. The Find Next command can be used to repeat the search using the same arguments as the previous search, but moving the starting location to the current cursor location.

Find Selection works just like Find, but it uses the currently highlighted text as the target of the search. Basically, you can select a block of text (or double-click a word to select it) and then select Find Selection to find the next occurrence of the text in the buffer.

The Find in Files function can be amazingly useful when you are trying to figure out where a given string, or function, exists somewhere in your source tree. By using the dialog shown in Figure 3.8, you can search an entire raft of files for a given string, rather than the current edit buffer.

Figure 3.8
The Find in Files dialog.

The options for this dialog are exactly the same as the Find dialog, with three noticeable differences. First, the Wrap option is gone, since it makes no sense to consider your current cursor position when searching other files. Secondly, the File Mask is now added to the dialog, allowing you to specify what file names you want to search for. Wildcards are supported in the File Mask, so you can ask to search all Python (`*.py`) source files. The default mask is `*.py`. In addition, you can specify whether to search the current directory, or the current directory and all directories below that.

❄ **Changing Your Current Directory**

The "current directory" for IDLE is always the installed directory for the pythonw.exe application. If you want to search other directories, just enter the directory as part of the file name in the File Mask box, such as c:\MyFiles*.py.

Finally, the Replace command looks just like the Find dialog, but allows you to specify a string to replace the found text with. In addition, you can find the string, replace the string, or replace all occurrences of the string using the Replace command.

Go to Line

As the command suggests, the Go to Line menu option allows you to move to a specific line number within the Editor window. When you select this menu option a small dialog pops up asking what line number you want to move the cursor to. Enter a numeric value and press the OK button, and the Editor will scroll itself up or down, if necessary, to move to the line number that you have entered.

Being a programmer, you are going to try something dumb here, such as entering a non-numeric value or a negative value into the dialog box. Don't bother, because the writers of IDLE were smarter than that. If the value entered is out of range, it will just beep at you and ignore you. If you try a non-numeric value, you will see an error message telling you to enter only numeric values. Sorry.

Show Call Tips

This rather odd sounding function gives you some very useful functionality in the IDLE editor. If you are working with a function that IDLE is aware of, such as one that has been loaded into the editor from an outside source, or one that you defined in the current module you are working on, you can enable Call Tips for the module. A call tip is a little pop-up window that shows you information without getting in the way. For example, take a look at Figure 3.9.

Figure 3.9

A Call Tip window display in IDLE.

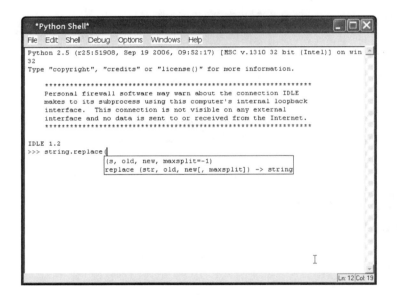

As you can see from the display in Figure 3.9, a small window opens up indicating what information the system expects to see for the `string.replace` function in Python. This can be really useful when you can't quite remember the number or order of arguments that are supposed to be used for a given function. Unlike some of the newer IDE systems, IDLE does not allow you to enter things by default for functions using the Call Tip window. That doesn't really make the functionality any less useful, however.

Show Completions

One of the new features for the IDLE Python 2.5 editor is the addition of completion showing in the editor. When you enable completion showing (it is off by default), the editor will pop up a little list box that allows you to view the possible endings for the string you have started typing in. Not only does this work with functions that are built into classes, but it also works on ordinary typing within the editor itself. For example, let's look at Figure 3.10, which shows a good example of how this works.

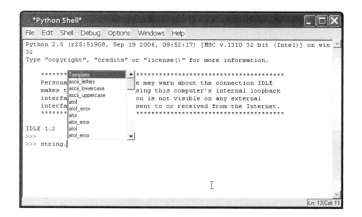

Figure 3.10
Edit completion in Python.

If you are accustomed to working in some of the more popular commercial development systems, you've probably seen this functionality before. It allows you, the programmer, to think less about how things are spelled and what exact wording was used for a given feature or keyword, and more about writing your code to accomplish whatever task you have at hand. This feature alone would make IDLE worth buying, if anyone were actually charging for the editor. That you get the feature and the editor for free just indicates what an incredible bargain Python is to developers.

To use the function to insert keywords or function names into your source code, simply use the up and down arrow keys to select the word you want and press the Enter key. The pop-up list will disappear, and the word will be inserted at the current cursor position in the editor.

Show Surrounding Parens

This is also a new feature in IDLE 2.5, and a very nice one. The Show Surrounding Parens function will allow you to type in an expression such as x = 1 + ((2*3)+4) and see which sets of parentheses match up on the line. When you enable this feature, the editor will automatically highlight both of the parentheses when you type a closing parenthesis. When you are working with a complex expression with a lot of parentheses, this can be a real lifesaver. You no longer have to sit there and count the number of closing parentheses to see whether or not you have the right number of them for an expression. By watching which of the opening parentheses the closing one matches up with, you know how many you need to still add. For those of us who once worked in languages such as Lisp, this feature alone makes everything else worth the experience.

As a simple example of the matching parenthesis function, try the following. First, type in an expression like this:

```
x = 1 + ( 2*(3+4) + (4*5) + 6 * ( (1+2) *(1+2) )
```

Now press the Enter key. You will notice that the editor continues to indent the statement, rather than executing it in Immediate mode. Why is that? Because we do not have the right number of matching opening and closing parentheses.

Now, try it again, but leave the setting for Show Surrounding Parens on. When you type the last parenthesis in the above expression, you will see it matched up with the second one on the line. This tells you that you need to enter one more parenthesis to make it all work. Enter that one, and you will see it match up with the first one on the expression line. Now, you can press the Enter key and see that the value of x has been set in the interpreter.

I think that once you play with this one a bit, you will agree that it is an amazingly useful function.

Expand Word

The Expand Word function is a form of auto-completion that a lot of Command Line shells have these days. For example, you might want to copy one file named "fred.txt" to another one called "fred.new." The Command Line shell can auto-complete the name of the first file, since it exists, saving you some typing time and some backspacing, at least if you type like I do.

To see the Expand Word function at work, try this: go into the IDLE environment and type **str**. Now enter the auto-complete command, **ALT-/**. You will see the environment automatically fills in the string to read "string," since that is the best match it can find for the letters you typed.

What if there is more than one possible match for what you typed? Pressing the Alt-/ keyboard combination multiple times will slowly go through the entire list of possible matches for that string selection. When you find the one you want, just keep typing and the match will be placed into the edit buffer.

Shell Menu

The Shell menu consists of only two options, but both are rather useful.

View Last Restart

This command will scroll the Shell window to the position of the last user restart. If there has been no restart of the Shell, the cursor position will not change. This can be useful for when you want to know exactly what variables you have set, and what conditions have been created within a given session. Each time the Shell is restarted, a message is displayed in the window indicating that a user restart has occurred. Note that the first time you start up the Shell, this is a non-user restart and does not count in the display.

Restart Shell

Restarting the Shell deletes all variables, clears out all function definitions, and unloads all modules that are not automatically loaded at runtime. In addition, all memory is cleared, all breakpoints are reset, and all data in the Edit window is erased. Restarting the Shell can be very useful for a number of reasons, including not being sure what variables have been set or what functions have been modified. Restarting the Shell is much akin to shutting down the Python IDLE editor and then starting it again, without having to go through the pain of having to stop and start the process. In slow environments, or those with limited memory, this can be a slow and painful process, and a restart is much easier.

For the programmer, another important consideration when you are debugging a system is to restart the system to be sure that the interpreter is in a "clean" state before running your program. This can help you identify problems that are being caused because you have been mucking about in the interpreter in Immediate mode and then running a program that relies on certain interpreter settings. If you run the program a second time and don't see the same behavior, it is likely that you simply left some stray garbage running around in memory and needed to clear it out. It could also be an indication that your application is relying on things you were unaware of set in the interpreter. Either is a matter for some concern and should cause you to at least scan the offending code.

Debug Menu

The next menu on the IDLE 2.5 system Interpreter window is the Debug menu. This menu consists of commands related to the running, debugging, and maintaining of existing code. The available commands on the menu are the following.

Go to File/Line

This option would appear to be the same as the Edit menu version of Go to Line. It is quite different however, as you will see. First, with the IDLE editor open in Immediate mode, and no modules listed, select the menu item. You will see an error message displayed that says:

```
The line you point at doesn't appear to be a valid file name followed
by a line number.
```

Well, that was clear as mud, wasn't it? Actually, what the error is telling you is absolutely true. You may remember a while back we looked at the Find in Files command. This command, among others, generates a list of files and line numbers upon which a given statement or string is found. Another good place to find such things is in the error statement from the interpreter when an invalid token is encountered during the parsing of the interpreted lines of a function or class.

Let's go back and re-run the Find in Files command and search for the string "copyright" in all Python (`*.py`) files in the current directory and all subdirectories below it.

After you run the command, a window will appear that looks a lot like the one shown in Figure 3.11. Notice that it is a list of files, along with the line number in the file, and then the string that the search indicated contained the word *copyright*. Oddly enough, you will also notice that the Find in Files window does not contain any Debug command, nor is there a Go to File/Line command under any of the windows in that window. Seems rather silly, doesn't it? The format shown here, with the file name followed by the line number, is the same format that is expected by the Go to File/Line command. All is not lost, however, since you can simply copy the lines you are interested in, in the Output window, and paste them into the IDLE editor window; then use the command on the line to view the file that the search found.

Figure 3.11
The Find in Files output.

See? Python isn't perfect, but it certainly provides ways around problems when you encounter them. This is the hallmark of a great system.

Debugger
Virtually all good development environments contain a debugger of some sort that will aid the developer in tracking down problems in his or her source code when it is running. Often, problems occur only while the program is running, and in a way that can't be found by simply printing

things out as you go along. We will spend more time discussing the debugger in just a bit, but for now, you can see what sort of tools you have available to you in the debugger. Figure 3.12 shows you the Debug Control window and shows you the various options available in it.

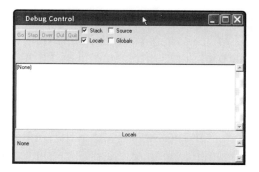

Figure 3.12
The Debug Control window.

The debugger offers the usual assortment of commands that all good debuggers offer: the ability to set breakpoints, the ability to single step through code, the ability to step into and out of functions, and the ability to restart the application by quitting the debugger. In addition, you can look at variable values and view global values within your application.

For those of you who have used, or at least tried, Python in the past, the debugger has always been available and was called the `pdb module`. The current release, Python 2.5, now integrates the debugger into the IDLE environment where it belongs.

Stack Viewer

Without a doubt, the most annoying thing there is for a programmer is when the program just dies without any real indication of why. In Python, exception handling is a built-in part of the language, so it is natural for programmers to throw exceptions when error conditions occur. Unfortunately, if the programmer before you didn't catch the exception properly, the program has an annoying tendency to simply abort and drop you back into the IDLE editor. This isn't exactly a useful thing. Yes, the editor will tell you what the exception was, and possibly where it occurred, but that information is usually not terribly useful without knowing how you got to the point of the exception.

The Stack Viewer option will display a stack trace indicating how you got to the point of the last exception. This can be more useful than I can really explain to you if you've never tried to backtrack through an application. We will certainly make use of this viewer later in the book as we explore exceptions and exception handling.

Auto-Open Stack Viewer

The Auto-open Stack Viewer menu option is a toggle indicating whether or not to automatically open the Stack Viewer when an exception occurs. You would think this would be the sort of thing that you could set once and forget about, but unfortunately, it isn't. Every time you shut down IDLE, the editor will "forget" the setting you used for this option. So, each time you bring up IDLE, remember to turn this on—it really should have defaulted itself to on. This one is too good a piece of functionality not to use it, and remembering afterward forces you to go through a lot more work than you need to in order to figure out where something went wrong.

Like most editors, the IDLE editor permits you to configure virtually anything for the way in which you add, modify, or display code. The configurable items are all found under the Options menu item.

Configure IDLE

The IDLE environment is extremely configurable. It provides ways to change virtually all of the key bindings, colors, and behaviors of the system. This is done within the configuration dialog. When you select the Configure IDLE option in the menu, you will be presented with the following dialog and the following tab on that dialog, as shown in Figure 3.13.

Figure 3.13
IDLE configuration—
Fonts/Tabs tab.

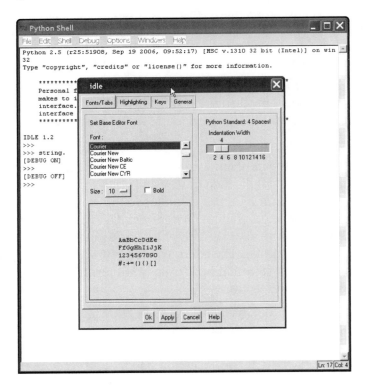

The font part of the tab is fairly straightforward: you can select the font that you want the text displayed in for the code in the editor. In general, fixed fonts work the best, since you can easily line up code in columns, but your preferences may vary from mine.

The Tab setting is probably one of the most religious items on the screen. This setting, set by a slider control that we will discuss when we work on the Tk GUI elements of Python, allows you to set the number of spaces used for a tab character. This is important, because the tab character is the way in which you normally indent code in Python. As discussed in Chapter 2, indentation is a major part of the Python language, and you should be comfortable with the way in which the code is displayed. If you set the Tab setting too high, you will have lines that wrap around to the next line, which are very hard to read. If you set the tab setting set too low, it is very difficult to tell when code is indented, especially with a proportional font. The Default setting for the tab value in IDLE is 4, and it seems to work well under most circumstances. If you don't like it, you can change it, and if the changes don't work out, you can always change it back, so feel free to experiment with the settings until you find something that works well for you. For this book, we will be using the Default setting of four spaces to a tab.

The second tab on the configuration screen is the Highlighting tab. This tab, shown in Figure 3.14, allows you to specify the colors that are used for displaying various kinds of high-lighted text in the editor. IDLE uses the concept of "themes" so that you can save a set of preferences, and then use them depending on what you feel like or what your environment looks like. I prefer different settings at home and at work, because of the lighting available in the different locations.

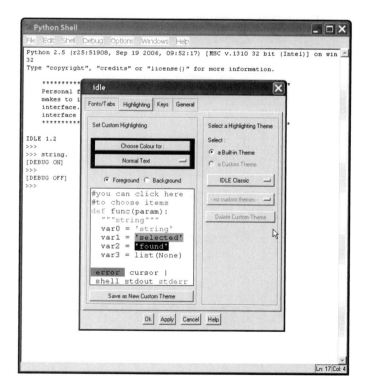

Figure 3.14
IDLE configuration
Highlighting tab

You will notice, if you play with the drop-down box on the screen, that you can set the colors for a wide variety of elements in the system. For example, if you want to show keywords in the system in a bold red color, it is quite easy to do. Simply select the "Python keywords" from the first drop-down box (the one that says "Choose Color for:"), or you can simply click on the section you want to change within the display box. The drop-down box will automatically change to reflect your selection. To actually change the color, just click the Choose Color for: button, and a color dialog will display. Pick the color you want and apply it and the keywords will then be displayed in that color in the editor.

Once you have set the various colors to be the way you want them, the next thing you get to play with is the keyboard bindings for the editor. Keyboard bindings match up a set of key combinations to a command in the editor. The editor is quite flexible, so if you want to model it after a favorite editor of yours, it is usually possible.

You can see the tab in Figure 3.15. The left-hand side is a list of possible key bindings, or commands, that you can modify along with their current keyboard combinations.

Figure 3.15
IDLE configuration—Keys
tab

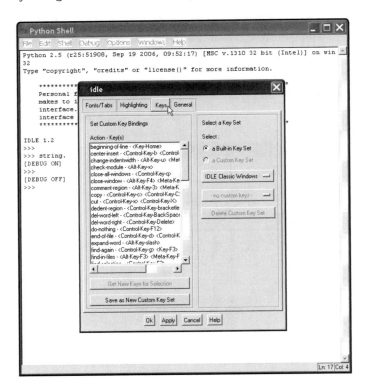

To modify a keyboard setting, you simply select the one you want and then click the Get New Keys for Selection button. A dialog will appear allowing you to set the key that you want. You can select any combination of the Control, Shift, and Alt keys to use with your keyboard entry. For example, suppose that you want the "move to start of line" key to be Control-Shift-H. I'm not entirely sure why you would want this, but let's say that you did.

First, select the keyboard binding you want. In this case, it is "Beginning-of-line" and is bound by default to the Home key on your keyboard. Now, click the "Get New Keys for Selection" button. In the displayed dialog, click the Control and Shift check boxes. Now, find the "h" key in the listbox on the right-hand side of the dialog. Select it and press OK in the dialog. That's all there is to it! From now on, when you use this keyboard map, pressing Ctrl-Shift-H will move you to the beginning of the line.

You might notice that the dialog displayed has an "advanced" button. If you have no great desire to search through the list of things and have been using Python for some time, you may find it easier to simply select this and type in your keyboard combination in Python-key syntax. It's a bit tricky at first, but once you see a few in the Basic view, you will get used to it.

Finally, we have the General tab of the options menu. This option shows you the general options available in Python. The tab is shown in Figure 3.16.

Figure 3.16
IDLE configuration—
General tab

Most of the options of the General options tab are straightforward and need little commentary. The first option simply tells you what window to bring up when you start IDLE, the second asks whether or not you want the system to save your work before you run a script. If you do not automatically save your work, IDLE will prompt you before running a script. The reason for this is obvious: if you do something horrible and crash the interpreter, your work would be lost forever. If you save it before you run, this is not an issue.

The window size is a default. You can probably leave it as it is, unless you have particularly special environments in which you are running. The size selected tends to be about half the screen. The page reformat width is simply the number of characters wide the page is before it wraps around to the next line. The default source encoding is an interesting one. The encoding scheme used for Python is the character set that you use to store your scripts. Normally, you would use plain text, since that is the most portable between different operating systems. If, however, you are going to be displaying characters in your script that are in a different character set, such as a different language, you will want to select either the current locale, which is a Windows system setting, or you will want to select UTF-8, which is the standard for wide character sets across all operating systems. Note that Python code itself is in plain text at all times.

The additional Help source list needs a bit of explanation. If you are using third-party libraries or tools within your Python IDLE environment, you may want to include the Help files that come with these tools. To do so, simply click the Add button to the right of the additional Help files list box. Python will then load these Help sources whenever it starts up.

The Windows menu in Python is a variable one. The first entry changes the height of the main window to be the same as the height of the screen. After that, a list of windows is maintained, corresponding to all of the individual windows that are available within the IDLE editor. For example, if you do a search within files, an Output window will be displayed by the IDLE editor environment. That window will then be added to the bottom of the Windows menu on the main screen.

The final menu on the IDLE main menu is the Help menu. This menu consists of three or more Help entries. The first, About IDLE, simply gives you version information about the system. An example of the IDLE About box is shown in Figure 3.17.

The most interesting information in the About box are the versions of Python and of Tk that are being used to implement and run with the IDLE environment. In this case, the Python version, as expected, is 2.5 since that is the version we installed and ran. The Tk version, which is the version of the GUI components that Python uses to create windowing applications, is 8.4. Why the discrepancy? Well, for one thing, Tk has been around longer than Python and is better established. For another, there are more changes on a more frequent basis in Tk than in Python.

Oh, one last note on this screen. You will note that the actual name of IDLE is displayed. There is a lot of controversy over where the name came from, and the IDLE folks finally decided to

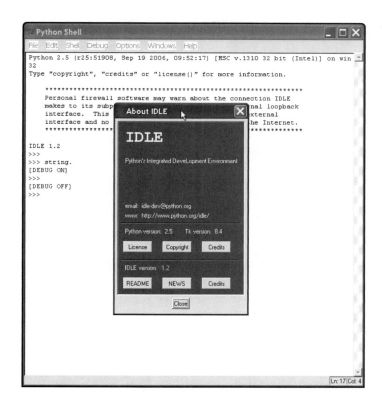

Figure 3.17
IDLE About box

actually reveal the secret. IDLE stands for Integrated DeveLopment Environment. If you do not think it is a stretch to make that particular acronym work for this, you really haven't been paying attention.

The Edit Window

There are quite a few other windows within the IDLE environment, and we will discuss most of them as we get to them. The most important one to consider, for now at least, is the Editing window. To get to the Editing window, select File | New Window from the main menu in IDLE. You should see a window that looks remarkably like the one shown in Figure 3.18.

The majority of the menus and functionality of the Editing window are very similar to, if not the same as, the main IDLE Interpreter window. The differences are primarily around the functionality needed to actually write and run code in the system. The Editing window is designed to help you write code, edit code, and maintain code. The Interpreter window, on the other hand, is generally designed to interpret Python statements and display the results of those statements. The Interpreter window certainly can be used to write code, but that is not what it is best at. When you are writing actual Python scripts to be deployed external to the system, it is best to use the Code Editor window.

Figure 3.18
IDLE Editing window.

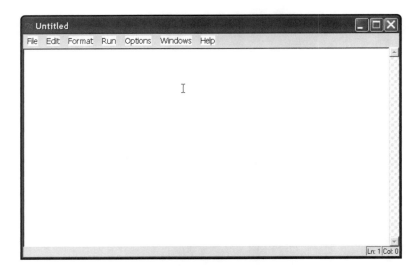

The biggest differences between the Code Editing window and the Interpreter windows are in the two menus labeled Format and Run. There are other differences, as we will see shortly, but these two are where we will focus the majority of our energies in this chapter.

Format Menu

The Format menu, as should be obvious from its name, is used for formatting Python code according to your own desires. The options in the Format menu are the following.

Indent Region

As we have mentioned repeatedly, Python is all about indentation. As a result, you will want to be able to control what is indented and what is not indented. The Indent Region command simply indents the selected area by one tab stop. You might do this if you were taking a block of code and placing it within a conditional statement such as an `if` statement, or maybe within a looping construct, as you will see in the next chapter. You may indent a region as many times as you want, because indenting it will not unselect the area, nor will it change the behavior of the application.

The indent behavior is dependent on the indent setting, which is set in the Options panel of either the main window or this one. If you want a faster way to change this setting, look at the New Indent Width menu option on this very menu.

Dedent Region

If there were any need to prove that Python was a programmer's tool, and not something written for anyone with the slightest grasp of the English language, instead of the Python language, this menu option would dissuade them from any other belief. Really, who would call something *dedent*? The proper term would be *unindent*, or perhaps *outdent*. Then again, *outdent* sounds no better than *dedent*, so let's just let it go, shall we?

Needless to say, the Dedent function does the opposite of the Indent function. A block of selected code will be indented less by using this function when the editor applies the menu option. If the code block selected is already at the leftmost margin, there will be no effect from this command, except for a warning noise from the editor.

Unlike the indent command, however, dedenting (can this really be used as a verb?) a block can cause problems. Remember, the indentation level determines what a block of code "belongs to" and how it is executed. Moving a block of code out of an indented block causes that block to be executed after the block it was in finishes, and, more importantly, whether or not the conditional or loop enclosing the old block is executed at all.

For example, let's imagine that we have a loop that does something. It might look something like this:

```
for i in range(1,10):
        if i & 1 == 1:
                print "The number is odd"
        print "This number is ", i
```

Don't worry about how the code works. We'll certainly discuss this, and many other features of loops, in the next few chapters. The point is, the code that is indented within the `for` loop is all executed when the `for` loop runs. Now, if we modify this block by dedenting the final line, as follows:

```
for i in range(1,10):
        if i & 1 == 1:
                print "The number is odd"
print "This number is ", i
```

We get a completely different result from this block than we would from the original block of code. The original block, when run in the IDLE interpreter, prints out the following output:

```
The number is odd
The number is odd
The number is odd
The number is odd
The number is odd
This number is  9
The number is odd
This number is  1
```

```
This number is  2
The number is odd
This number is  3
This number is  4
The number is odd
This number is  5
This number is  6
The number is odd
This number is  7
This number is  8
The number is odd
This number is  9
```

As you can see, the block of code simply prints out the numbers from one to 10, indicating which ones are odd and which ones are not. It does its job, and is nothing flashy. However, when we unindent that last line of code, we get the following output from the scriptlet:

```
The number is odd
The number is odd
The number is odd
The number is odd
The number is odd
This number is  9
```

As you can see, the indentation makes a huge difference. Oh, one final note here. You can't actually type in the second block of code into the interpreter. If you try, you will get an error saying that the indentation levels don't match. That is because the interpreter works by processing one line at a time. If you want to run this little scriptlet, you will need to enter it into the Code Editor window and save it; then run it in the interpreter.

Comment Out Region

One of the hallmark methods of debugging an application is to remove code until you find the offending statement. Python is no exception to that rule. You often find that you want to see where a problem is occurring, and the easiest way to do that is simply to get rid of all of the code until the problem goes away. Alternatively, you may have a block of code that does something you don't want it to, or aren't ready for. In any of these cases, you often find it necessary to comment out an entire block of code at once. The Comment Out Region command was designed for you! Imagine, for example, that you have the following set of Python code in your little application:

```
x = 1
y = 2
z = 3
print "x = ", x
print "y = ", y
print "z = ", z
a = x + y * z
print "a = ", a
```

When you run this chunk of code in the interpreter, you get the following output shown in the console window:

```
x =   1
y =   2
z =   3
a =   7
```

Obviously, we are displaying a lot of information here. The first three print statements, for example, are there just to show what the input to our little equation to calculate "a" might be. We might want to see that information when we are initially writing the application, and perhaps when we are debugging it, but not during the real "run" of the system. So, rather than deleting the lines, we might want to comment them out for now. To do this, select the three print statements above the assignment to the variable a and then click the Comment Region menu option. You should see the following code in your Code Editor afterward:

```
x = 1
y = 2
z = 3
##print "x = ", x
##print "y = ", y
##print "z = ", z
a = x + y * z
print "a = ", a
```

As you can see, the editor has commented out the lines, and thus suppressed the unneeded debug statements. They aren't gone, but they won't be executed, as you can see when you run the scriptlet in the interpreter.

Uncomment Region

As you might have guessed from the trend here, the IDLE creators were very fond of completeness when they were implementing features. If there is a way to do something, there is a way to undo it. For the Comment Region function, the mirror function is to, of course, uncomment the region. Using the example from our previous block of code in the Comment Region function, applying the Uncomment Region command to it results in:

```
x = 1
y = 2
z = 3
print "x = ", x
print "y = ", y
print "z = ", z
a = x + y * z
print "a = ", a
```

Somehow, I really doubt this came as a huge surprise. When you are putting back in a large chunk of code that you have commented out in the previous step, using the Uncomment Region is a quick and easy way to accomplish your task.

One thing you might wonder about, does the Uncomment Region work on code that you have commented out on your own? The answer is yes. If I comment out a line of code by doing something like this:

```
# x = 1
```

Then if I select that line and press the Uncomment Region menu option, the line will be turned into the proper code again:

```
x = 1
```

One warning here: If you have a line that is commented out with some space in front of it, like this:

```
#    x = 1
```

And if you "uncomment" it, you will keep the spaces in front, which will result in a possible indentation issue. Just something to be aware of.

Tabify Region
The Tabify command reformats a block of code using a tab setting specified by the user at the time the reformatting is done. Essentially, the Tabify function allows you to override on a local basis what the editor does for you automatically. For example, suppose that you typed the following block of code into the editor:

```
x = 1
y = 2
```

```
for i in range(1,10):
    print "i = ", i
    if i & 1:
        print "I is odd"
    else:
        print "I is even"
```

Assuming that you used spaces in the above code, the Tabify region command will convert the spaces into tabs at the rate you specify in the dialog box that pops up when you select Tabify. If you select, say, four spaces to a tab, then each four spaces that lead each of the lines in the above block will be replaced by a single tab character. Tabs are better than spaces, at least in the Python world, because they make it easier to line things up, and much easier for people to reformat code to look the way they want it to. If you use spaces, the user will have to go through and either replace each set of spaces with a tab character, or actually physically modify the code to look the way they like.

Untabify Region

As you might have guessed from the rest of the formatting options, the Untabify command undoes the results of the Tabify command. That is, Untabify (which isn't a word either) converts tabs back into spaces. To use the command, select a block of code and then click the Untabify Region menu command.

When you select the Untabify Region, the editor will display a small dialog prompting you for the number of columns to use for each tab it encounters in the lines marked. As with the comments above on the unindent section, you have to be careful with this command. If you did not use tabs in all of the code, which would be a bad idea, you might accidentally change the indent levels of the code and produce a different result. Because indentation is such a huge part of the Python language and editor, it is generally a good idea to settle on a single way of doing the indentation levels and stick to that way throughout your code.

If you work in a corporate environment, it is important that you establish standards for coding including the use of tabs and spaces, as well as the indentation levels. Without such standards, you will find that combining different people's code into a single application becomes a nightmare.

Toggle Tabs

In the editor, by default, when you move to a given column, the editor will use a combination of tabs and spaces to reach the given result. For example, if you have eight character tab settings, and you are in column 10, the editor will use a single tab (eight spaces) and two spaces to reach the tenth column. If you turn off tabs, using the Toggle Tabs command, only spaces will be used to reach the column number. Once again, this can have an impact when you are using other people's code (OPC), so you should select this option with some care.

Oddly enough, there is no Untoggle Tabs command. Go figure. You would have thought, for completeness, that there would be a Use tabs and Unuse tabs command. There isn't. The toggle is a single menu command that is either on or off. Unfortunately, there is no indication that you are in one mode or the other. If you want to change this setting, you may have to click the menu item twice to get the results you want. The editor does warn you when you select it as to which one you are trying to accomplish.

New Indent Width

The New Indent Width command sets the indentation level. Instead of having to go into the Options panel and setting the indent level, you can do it here directly. One annoying feature of the IDLE editor, or a good feature I suppose, depending on how you look at it, is that the setting here only applies to the current Edit window, and only as long as the Edit window is open. As soon as you close this window, this setting disappears. If you open a different Edit window, the default value from the Options panel will be used instead of this one. Even if you reopen this file with another Edit window, a different value will be set. This is not the same as changing the indent level in the Options panel, which is a system wide preference and persistent across different editing sessions.

Format Paragraph

The format paragraph is exactly the same functionality as the Emacs editor command fill region, and is useful for working with blocks of comments. The format paragraph command should not be used on code, as it will hopelessly mess up your code style and indentation level and will render the resulting code uncompilable (if that is a word at all).

The purpose of the format paragraph command is to allow you to reformat a comment block so that it appears in a single paragraph. For example, suppose that you had the following comments in your text:

```
# This is a comment.
# This is another comment, except this one is longer and will probably wrap
around to another line in a wrapped environment.
```

As you can see from the above, the comments are on two lines, and one of them is too long to actually fit on a single line in the Editor window without extending off to the right and requiring scrolling. If you then apply the Format Paragraph command to the two lines, you get the following:

```
# This is a comment. # This is another comment, except this one is
longer and will probably wrap around to another line in a wrapped
environment.
```

Unfortunately, the above will not compile. You only want to use the Format Paragraph command in actual documentation you are writing, not in code. Yes, Python developers are expected to write documentation.

In addition to the Format menu, the Edit window also contains one other completely new main menu item, the Run menu. This menu consists of commands related to compiling and running source code.

Python Shell

Depending on how you start up the IDLE system (see the Options panel discussion earlier in this chapter), you may or may not have a Shell window visible when you are in the Edit window. If you do, this command will simply bring that window to the front. If you do not have a Shell window visible, this command will create one and bring it to the front. The Shell window is the same as the Interpreter window, and is used for running scripts and displaying Immediate mode values.

Note that there is simply no way, in the current version of Python, to run a program or scriptlet without invoking the Interpreter window. This might change in future versions of the IDLE editor, but for now, you might as well get used to the Shell window. It isn't going anywhere. Of course, even this statement isn't entirely true. If you name a file with the extension .pyw, you can launch it and suppress the display of the console window by double-clicking it in the Explorer window. This is a nice feature, especially when you want to provide users with quick and dirty utilities.

Check Module

In any interpretive language, just as in any compiled language, there are really two steps to running a program. First, you have to verify that the code is correct. Then you actually run the program. Python is no exception to this rule. You have to first check over your script to verify that it is all proper for the language rules. The purpose of the Check Module command is to do exactly this. Without actually running the code, this command will see if all of the code is valid Python code.

For example, consider the following script file:

```
x = 1
y = 2
for i in range(1,10):
    print "i = ", i
    if i & 1:
        print "I is odd"
    else:
        print "I is even"

This is an error
```

If you will notice, there is a line of text at the bottom of the script that is quite obviously an error. It even tells you that it is an error, so how can you (or the interpreter) miss it? Okay, sarcasm aside, the point is, there can be code in the script that is invalid. Now, there are two kinds of errors in Python. First, you can have syntax errors. These are lines of code that are invalid according to the standard. These can be statically checked by the interpreter without having to actually run the code. This is the purpose of the Check Module command. If a piece of code contains a syntax error, the error will be flagged by the interpreter, and the editor will return you to the exact line that contains the error, indicating what the problem is, if possible. At no time will the code be run or any output generated.

The second form of error in the Python environment is a runtime error. These are errors that occur because you pass bad data to a function, or because you try to open a file that doesn't exist, or something of that ilk. It is not possible for the interpreter to determine whether or not something will generate a runtime error, so this sort of error can only be found by running the program.

Run Module

Once you have written a chunk of Python code, and checked it for syntax errors using the Check Module command, the next logical thing to do would be to run it and see if it does what you want and expect. The Run Module command is designed to accomplish exactly that. When you run a module, the interpreter first checks it for syntax errors, then loads the script into the interpreter and executes it one line at a time. If an error occurs, such as an unhandled exception being thrown, the process halts and an error is displayed on the output window console. If the process completes normally, the output from the application is displayed and the interpreter returns to a waiting state.

We will look at a complete example of creating a simple Python application a bit further into this chapter.

Rather than look at the individual menus on the Edit window from this point on, we will only look at the menu items that are different from the main interpreter (Shell) window.

Under the Options menu on the Editor window is the Code Context option. This is a toggle that can be turned on or off. Turning it on will reveal a blank area at the top of the window that displays nothing initially. This might not seem like the most useful option, but the reality is that it does quite a bit.

Code Context means where you are in the source code. When the entire source code listing fits into the Editor window, as it has for all of the examples we have looked at so far, it obviously accomplishes nothing. Let's look at a good example of how the code context can be useful. To accomplish this, we are going to load in some existing code that ships with the Python system.

Under the File menu, select the Path Browser option. You will see the Path Browser window that you have seen in the past. Now, navigate to the `<drive><base>\lib` directory. The

<drive> will be whatever drive you installed the system on, and the <base> will be the base directory into which the Python 2.5 install was made. For most users, the entire path will be c:\Python25\lib. Select the idlelib package entry in the list. You should see a display that looks like Figure 3.19.

Figure 3.19
Path Browser showing the IDLElib package.

Now, select the AutoCompleteWindow.py file and double-click it in the window. In a moment, an Edit window will display showing the contents of this file. You will notice that the entire file does not fit into the Edit window at all. Go to the Code Context menu option and toggle it on. For reasons unknown, this particular toggle option does indicate that it is active by placing a check mark next to the menu option when it is selected and removing the check mark when it is cleared. Notice that nothing appears in the little context area. Now, page down by clicking on the scrollbar on the right-hand side of the Editor window.

You should see a display similar to the one shown in Figure 3.20. As you can see, the lines above the lines displayed at the top of the Editor window are now visible in the Code Context window. This is the purpose of the window, to put the code you are looking at into "context" in terms of what class and method you are currently viewing in the editor window.

It can often be difficult to tell exactly what function you are working on when you are in the middle of a file. The IDLE developers realized this and provided a way in which to control this display.

That wraps up our whirlwind tour of the IDLE editor. Next, we will look at the underlying Command Line compiler/interpreter that is actually the core of the Python language.

Figure 3.20
Path Browser showing the
IDLElib package with
context.

```
CodeContext.py - C:\Python25\lib\idlelib\CodeContext.py
File  Edit  Format  Run  Options  Windows  Help

class CodeContext:
    def __init__(self, editwin):
        # self.info is a list of (line number, indent level, line text, block
        # keyword) tuples providing the block structure associated with
        # self.topvisible (the linenumber of the line displayed at the top of
        # the edit window). self.info[0] is initialized as a 'dummy' line which
        # starts the toplevel 'block' of the module.
        self.info = [(0, -1, "", False)]
        self.topvisible = 1
        visible = idleConf.GetOption("extensions", "CodeContext",
                                     "visible", type="bool", default=False)
        if visible:
            self.toggle_code_context_event()
            self.editwin.setvar('<<toggle-code-context>>', True)
        # Start two update cycles, one for context lines, one for font changes.
        self.text.after(UPDATEINTERVAL, self.timer_event)
        self.text.after(FONTUPDATEINTERVAL, self.font_timer_event)

    def toggle_code_context_event(self, event=None):
        if not self.label:
            self.pad_frame = Tkinter.Frame(self.editwin.top,
                                           bg=self.bgcolor, border=2,
                                           relief="sunken")
            self.label = Tkinter.Label(self.pad_frame,
                                       text="\n" * (self.context_depth - 1),
                                       anchor="w", justify="left",
                                       font=self.textfont,
                                       bg=self.bgcolor, fg=self.fgcolor,
                                       border=0,
                                       width=1, # Don't request more than we get
                                       )
            self.label.pack(side="top", fill="x", expand=True,
                            padx=4, pady=0)
            self.pad_frame.pack(side="top", fill="x", expand=False,
                                padx=0, pady=0,
                                after=self.editwin.status_bar)
        else:
            self.label.destroy()
            self.pad_frame.destroy()
            self.label = None
        idleConf.SetOption("extensions", "CodeContext", "visible",
                           str(self.label is not None))
Ln: 14 Col: 9
```

Command Line Compiler

The Command Line compiler, or interpreter, is the core of the Python interpretive system. Rather than being a complete integrated development environment (IDE), the Command Line executable is just a little program you can run in your Command Shell. To launch the Command Line version of Python, simply open a Command Shell in Windows (located under Start | All Programs | Accessories | Command Prompt). On some versions of Windows it will be called the *Command Shell*, on others the *Power Shell*. Whatever you call it, it is basically the MS-DOS shell that older programs know and hate.

The first thing you will need to do in the command prompt, if you have not already done so, is to set your path variable to point to the location of the Python executables. For a normal install, the Python executables will be located in c:\Python25. The actual executable for the interpreter is called, surprisingly, `python.exe`. To run the Command Line version of the interpreter, simply type **python** and press Enter. You should see a display similar to Figure 3.21.

The interpreter looks exactly the same in the command prompt as it does in the IDLE editor. There is really no surprise here—that is the Command Line interpreter you are looking at in IDLE, just displayed differently.

Within the Command Line environment you can do all of the things you did in IDLE with some notable differences. Obviously, you can't change the font or color display, and you will not be using a GUI interface to load files. However, there are lots of bits of functionality available to you. To find out what is there, type **help()** and press Enter at the prompt. You will be informed of the high level Help topics available. There are three main levels of Help available:

- ❊ **Keywords**—This entry will list all of the available Python keywords. We have looked at these in Chapter 2.

- ❊ **Modules**—This entry will list all of the available modules that you can look at help for in the system. A module is a package of classes, functions, and definitions in the Python system. Once you are in the modules Help subsystem, entering the name of one of the modules will give you more information about it.

- ❊ **Topics**—This entry will provide you with a list of Help topics that are available within the Python environment. Note that to view the documentation for a given Help topic, you will need to set an additional environment variable, called PYTHONDOCS. In addition, you will need to install the Python HTML files that contain the documentation.

Otherwise, the Command Line interpreter works the same way that IDLE does. You can type an expression at the interpreter prompt (>>>), and it will be immediately processed and, if necessary, output displayed. For example, enter the following commands and look at the output within the environment:

```
>>> x = 1
>>> print x
1
```

As you can see, the interpreter works exactly the same way at the command line as it does in IDLE. However, there is one important feature that the Command Line interpreter supports that IDLE does not, which is the ability to immediately "run" a script from the command line. Let's look at a very simple script and then run it in the environment. You don't need to worry about what the script does at this point, just type it in as requested.

1. Create a new file in your favorite text editor (Notepad works fine) and enter the following text into the file:

```
fp = open("test.xml", "w")
fp.write("<XML>\n");

sName=input("Enter a name: ")
sColor=input("Enter a color: ")
sNumber=input("Enter a number: ")

fp.write("<object name=\"" + sName + "\">")
fp.write("   <color>"+sColor+"</color>")
fp.write("   <number>"+sNumber+"</number>")
fp.write("</object>")
fp.write("</xml>")

fp.close()
```

2. Save the file and call it `runme.py`. Make a note of the directory in which you saved the file.

3. Open the command prompt and navigate to the directory that you saved the file in. For example, if you saved the file in `c:\MyFiles`, type the following commands into the command prompt:

```
C:
Cd\Myfiles
```

4. Run the script by entering the following command into the command prompt:

```
python runme.py
```

5. You will notice that the Python header information, telling you how the system works and so forth, does not come up. Instead, the prompt displays the following:

```
C:\MyFiles>python ch7_1.py
Enter a name:
```

As you can see, the program is actually running and prompting you for input. This is the big difference between the Command Line executable and IDLE. In IDLE you would see the usual interpreter display; you would need to load your file into the Editor window and select Run to make the thing run. When you need to test command line-style programs, this is the best way to go about it.

So now you know how to use the IDLE editor and how to use the Command Line compiler. Let's take a very brief tour of creating a new file in IDLE and running it. That will take you through the entire process, the rest is just details.

Creating Python Files

So you want to create a Python script and run it. How do you go about it? Well, we've seen a lot of the pieces so far, but we haven't done an end-to-end discussion of the process. Let's do that now, so that we don't have to go over it again and again through the book.

1. **Determine what the program is going to do.**
   It should be obvious that the first step you are ever going to take in developing application software is to determine what you want the software to do, but too many people skip this step. We aren't going to go into a complete discussion of the art of designing a software application, because there are many fine books out there, including books in this series that will help you to do software design. From a Python perspective, however, you need to decide what the application is going to do, and what modules you will need to implement that application.

2. **Create a new file in the Editor window.**
   The first step to creating a new application is to create a new file in which to store the source code. Using IDLE, select File | New Window from the main menu. A new Editor window will be displayed that contains no code. Notice that the title of the window is "Untitled."

3. **Create the application code in the Editor window.**
   For the purposes of this simple example, you are going to create a very simple application that prompts you for your first name, last name, and middle initial, and then greets you by name. You don't need to understand how it works, at least not yet, just follow along to get a feel for the process involved.

In the Edit window, add the following code, one line at a time. Notice that as you type Python keywords, they are highlighted in the window. If a word does not highlight immediately, go back and check it for misspellings.

```
fName = input("Please input your first name    : ")
lName = input("Please input your last name     : ")
mInit = input("Please input your middle initial: ")
sFullName = fName + " " + mInit + " " + lName
print "Hello ",sFullName
```

4. **Save the file.**
   There are several ways to save a file in IDLE, and the easiest is to press Control-S. This will bring up the Save File dialog. Save the file as `ch3_1.py` (for the first program we have worked on for Chapter 3) and save it to a place that you want to use for Python script storage. Click OK, and the file will be saved.

5. **Run the file.**
   From the Run menu, in the Code Editor window, select Run Module (or press F5). The Python Shell window will come to the front of the window stack and will display:
   Please input your first name :
   Enter the following string: 'Matt'.
   You have to enter it with the quotes included, but it doesn't matter if they are single quotes or double quotes. The reason for this is that if you simply enter the value Matt into the editor, it will be processed as a variable and will be undefined and generate an error.
   Once you press Enter, the Shell window will then display:
   Please input your last name :
   Enter "Telles" in quotes (or, if you are really bold and daring, go ahead and enter your own last name). Press Enter.
   The Shell window will now display:
   Please input your middle initial:
   Enter 'A' in quotes, or your own middle initial, and press Enter.
   The Shell window will display:
   Hello Matt A Telles
   And will then return itself to a waiting state.

6. **That's it.** You have just written and executed your first Python application. You can now reload this application any time you want, by selecting File | Open from the main menu and selecting the `ch3_1.py` file from your disk operating system.

Documentation

The final topic of discussion for this chapter is documentation. There are three forms of documentation available in the Python system. First, only in the Windows operating system version, we have the compiled Help file (.CHM) that is available from the IDLE editor under the Help menu. The actual Help file is stored under the menu option "Python Docs" in IDLE.

The second form of documentation exists within the interpreter itself. This is the built-in Help system that is accessible by typing **`help()`** into either the Command Line interpreter or the Python Shell window in IDLE. Within this Help system, you can type topics, as we have seen earlier, to get a list of help topics. Typing one of these topic names into the Help system, however, will result in the following error being reported:

```
help> DELETION
Sorry, topic and keyword documentation is not available because the Python
HTML documentation files could not be found.  If you have installed them,
please set the environment variable PYTHONDOCS to indicate their location.
```

Now, really, why would anyone give you the ability to display a Help topic and then give you an error message when you try to follow his directions? The IDLE editor creators, of course. Well, really, it isn't their fault. The Help HTML files, you see, are really a part of the Python system as a whole. On the Microsoft Windows system, however, the download does not include them by default. The Python official Web site, www.python.org has them at http://docs.python.org/download as HTML files for download. You can go there now, download them, and install them on your system. Fair warning: The entire Help file system download is over four megabytes, and on some systems that might take quite some time to download. Once you have the file downloaded, decompress it into the doc directory of your Python installation tree. You will then need to set the PYTHONDOCS environment variable to allow the IDLE editor to find the location of these files. Set the PYTHONDOCS environment variable to be the root of the directory in which you installed the documents. For example, if you installed the files in c:\Python25\doc\Python2-5-docs\ with all of the directories below that (ref, api, doc, etc), then use that directory rather than the actual location of the reference files.

After you have done all this and everything is working properly, you can use the Help topics from within either IDLE or the Command Line Python interpreter.

The final way in which you can utilize Help within the Python system is to use the index.html that is stored in the PYTHONDOCS root directory. Bring this file up in your favorite Web browser, and you will have access to all of the Help files within Python.

In Conclusion

Hopefully, you've enjoyed this tour of the various Python tools. I realize that it is frustrating to be three chapters into a book and not have the opportunity to write code, but at the same time, I hope you realize just how big of an area we have covered so far. The Python system is quite large, and has a lot of really useful and important features. In the next chapter, we start coding real Python, so you will get that itch scratched. Hang in there, just one more page.

4 } Data Types

Like most programming languages, Python is made up of building blocks called *types*. These types define the kinds of data that you can reference in the system and how you can manipulate that data. As with most languages, there are restrictions in Python on what sorts of information you can refer to various data types. Rather than data storage spaces, which is what variables are in most languages, Python uses data references for variables. This means that a variable "refers to" a given piece of data in memory. Unlike many languages, however, Python is not a strongly typed language. By strongly typed, we mean that a particular variable can only refer to a particular data type. For example, in the C programming language, if you were to do something like this:

```
int x;
x = "Hello world";
```

This would be flagged as an error by the compiler. I have defined the variable x to be of type "int" (or integer). By doing so, I have instructed the compiler that the variable x can only be used to store numeric values within a certain range. (The actual range is defined by the operating system on which the compiler is running.)

Python, on the other hand, does not require you to define the type that you are going to store in a variable. In fact, Python does not allow you to define the data type for a given variable. The data referred to in the variable defines its type implicitly, and in so doing, defines what operations can be performed on the variable.

In the Python language, there are two sorts of data types. First, we have the "built-in" data type. These are types that have simple assignments and functionality. Built-in types tend to directly model real-world types. For example, one of the built-in types is a number. We run into numbers all the time, from the negative ones in my checkbook to the massively large ones in the Federal budget. It is easy to understand how the built-in types work, because we are accustomed to working with most of them in our everyday noncomputer lives.

The second type of data in Python is what we refer to as "advanced" data types. Advanced data types are classes and instances of those classes, as well as the types that are made up of basic types. As an example of the second sort, consider the complex math type. This type, made up of an "imaginary" half and a "real" half, is useful for all sorts of mathematical and engineering calculations. It has a representation (usually shown in the form of "4 + 2i," for example) and a set of rules that goes along with it. The capability to extend a language with your own user-defined types is the difference between classic languages, such as FORTRAN and COBOL, and more advanced languages, such as C++ or Eiffel. Python falls somewhere on the advanced side of that equation, with the ability to extend itself, as we will see, through classes and functions.

When we discuss data types, we will consider a number of things. First, the ways in which you can use the data types, such as ranges and conversions must be thought about. Ranges are the allowable values over which the value is defined. For example, a numeric type range consists of all of the numbers, but not characters, strings, or images. After the range, we will consider the notion of usage. Some types, for example, allow you to convert their value directly to strings quickly and easily. Some allow you to manipulate pieces of their values, such as the complex data type mentioned previously. Yet others allow you to define your own manipulations for working with them, such as classes. We will discuss classes more completely when we get into writing functions and class definitions in Chapter 10, but for now let's look at the capabilities of those classes in Python.

Numeric Types

The first type is the numeric type. Python supports two basic numeric types: integers and floating point numbers.

Integers

Integers are whole numbers having a range that depends upon the hardware upon which Python is running. You can have negative integers, positive integers, and zero, which is neither negative or positive. Integers support the full range of arithmetic operations: adding, multiplying, dividing, and subtracting.

The first question is: How big of a number can I store in an integer? The answer is that it depends on the machine on which you are running. Since determining what kind of processor that you are using can be annoying, Python defines a few constants that you can use for manipulating very large or very small numbers. The most important variable that you care about with respect to integers is the `maxint` constant. This constant is defined in the "sys" modules in Python. To see the value of `maxint`, try the following lines in the IDLE editor:

```
>>> import sys
>>> print sys.maxint
2147483647
```

Understanding the `sys.maxint` value can be a little confusing. Where does that number come from? Actually, it is really simple. The number of bits on the machine determines the size of the largest integer value that you can store. To determine the maximum value, look at the following list:

❋ For a 32-bit machine, this is (2 ** 31) -1

❋ For a 64-bit machine, this is (2 ** 63) -1

❋ For a 128-bit machine, this is (2 ** 127) -1

To display the `maxint` value, you simply import the sys (or system) module into the IDLE editor. The sys module contains lots of definitions of operating system specific data and functions. You might think that the maximum negative integer, therefore, would be - 2147483647. Surprisingly, it is not. In fact, it is -2147483646. Because of the way in which binary numbers are stored, the highest value is going to have to use the highest bit to indicate that it is negative, which "eats up" one bit value and thus makes the negative value smaller. So, for the 32-bit operating system that makes up Windows XP, the range of normal integers is -2147483646 to 2147483647, inclusive. You can assign any such value to a numeric variable and not have any problems.

Demonstrating Long Integers

Python also has what it calls *long integers*. A long integer is limited in size only by the storage available on the machine upon which it is running. A long integer is signified in Python by adding a suffix, L, like this: 5000000000L. Long integers use multiple words to store their values, so they can hold very long numbers. The advantage to a long integer is that you can store a very large number without losing precision. So why wouldn't you use long integers at all times? Well, for one thing, it takes time to process all those digits when you are doing math upon them. So, unless you have a compelling reason to use a long integer, you should probably stick with normal ones.

Older versions of Python used to display an error if a variable was set with an integer value (by not using the L suffix) if the variable was subsequently set to a value greater than `maxint`. Now Python simply changes the variable to a long integer. This is a nice convenience, and works well with the IDLE environment. To illustrate this, consider the following example.

Repeating the exercise of displaying `maxint`, but adding one (+1) to the value demonstrates this:

```
>>> x = sys.maxint
>>> x = x + 1
>>> print x
2147483648
>>>
```

Even though the editor does not bother to print out the trailing "L," indicating that this is a long value, it is obviously bigger than a `maxint` and yet is not having any problems. If you were writing, say, an accounting package in which all dollar values were stored as pennies, and happened to be working with a chief executive's salary that was in the millions of dollars, you would definitely appreciate the ability of Python to store such large numbers! The real advantage is that you can do math on big numbers, or small numbers, in the same way.

Look at the following code, entered into the IDLE environment in Immediate mode:

```
>>> x = 10000000
>>> type(x)
<type 'int'>
>>> x *= 12
>>> print x
120000000
>>> x *= 22
>>> print x
2640000000
>>> type(x)

<type 'long'>
```

As you can see, no matter what size the integer value represents, and what type of data variable is used to refer to it, the same math operations can be applied to it. Note also that you can verify that the type has changed by using the `type()` method built into Python. When you first initialize the value, it references an integer value. After doing math to force it to contain a long integer, it now references a long integer value.

Octal and Hexadecimal

Python also understands other number bases, such as hexadecimal and octal. To tell Python you are using a value in octal (base 8), simply add a preceding zero. For example, suppose that you wanted to write the number 9 as an octal number. In base eight, the number nine is represented as one eight and one one. So it would be 11, in octal. However, if you tell Python that the number is 11, it is going to think that you mean the decimal (base 10) value 11. So, instead of writing:

```
x = 11
```

when you want something in octal, write:

```
x = 011
```

then, print out the value:

```
>>> print x
9
```

So the interpreter recognized that you wanted the value to be in base eight and not in base ten. Similarly, you can work in programmers' other favorite base, sixteen or hexadecimal. To accomplish hexadecimal constants, you add the string "0x" in front of the value.

```
>>> x = 0x11
>>> print x
17
```

Once again, note that the `print` statement displays the value in decimal integer format. Now, you might wonder, how do you output numbers in other bases? To print out in hexadecimal format, you use the `hex()` function. For example, using our previous conversion:

```
>>> print hex(x)
0x11
```

Likewise, there is a built-in function called `oct()` that will return a value in octal format (with the preceding zero indicating it is an octal value):

```
>>> print oct(x)
021
```

Python supports binary values too, but in a slightly more complex manner. We will discuss the binary support when we get to built-in functions and libraries.

Floating Point Numbers

What would the world be like without floating point numbers? You certainly couldn't have a half of something, nor could you deal in quarters, eighths, or sixteenths. None of these are whole numbers, so they can't be represented by integers. As a result, to handle little things like this, Python contains a complete floating point library for working with rational, or floating point, numbers.

To assign a floating point number, you use a floating point literal:

```
>>> f = 1.2
>>> print f
1.
```

Other than the fact that the floating point number system in Python allows you to enter more than integers, there isn't all that much exciting about floating point numbers. You can use floating point literals, as above. You can add, subtract, multiply and divide floating point numbers. You can also mix integers and floating point numbers. For example:

```
>>> x = 1.23
>>> y = 2
>>> z = x / y
>>> print z
0.615
```

You can convert an integer into a floating point value in a variety of ways. For one thing, you can simply assign one to the other:

```
>>> a = 1
>>> b = 2.0
>>> b = a
>>> print a
1
```

You can create a floating point number from either an integer or a string by using the built-in `float()` function:

```
>>> c = float("2.3")
>>> print c
2.3
```

There are also quite a few built-in functions that you can use on floating point numbers. For example, there are the `floor()` and `ceil()` functions. These functions return the lowest and highest integers that are represented by a given floating point number, respectively. An example is likely to help here:

```
>>> import math
>>> x = 4.5
>>> print math.floor(x)
4.0
>>> print math.ceil(x)
5.0
```

The `floor` function, which is part of the math library, returns the integer portion of the value of the number you give it. The ceil function returns the next highest integer representing the floating point value. Any value over the integer value will result in a ceil value of the value plus one. Note that to use the math functions, you must first import the math library in the IDLE environment:

```
>>> import math
```

After you have done this, you can use the functions in the library, as long as you fully qualify them by placing math in front of them, followed by a period. This is the Python way of qualifying a function within a module.

Strings

Although Python is used for a variety of mathematical and engineering functions that require heavy use of numeric types, by far the most common use of the language is in areas that require heavy string processing. Searching functions, e-commerce applications, pattern matching, and mailing list processing are but a few of the areas where you care a lot more about text processing than number crunching. Python provides a rich array of functionality dedicated toward working with strings.

String Variables

The most obvious use of a string is in the storage, printing, and inputting of strings. Python variables can be used to store strings. You can assign string literals to string variables, copy string values into other values, and manipulate string values using a variety of string functions that are either built into the language or in the string module. This is probably the most common module you will use when writing Python code, so it behooves you to understand it as well as you possibly can.

To create a string variable, you normally assign a variable a string literal. A string literal is a series of characters, normally enclosed in quotation marks. There are actually a few ways in which you can define a string literal. Let's look at the three most common:

Enclosed in Quotes

The most obvious way you would work with a string is to place something in quotation marks. For example:

```
name = "My name is Matt Telles"
```

This creates a variable called `name`, which refers to the string literal "`My name is Matt Telles`." You can use either single or double quotation marks to create a string in Python:

```
>>> name_single = 'My name is Matt Telles'
>>> name_double = "My name is Matt Telles"
>>> print name_single
My name is Matt Telles
>>> print name_double
My name is Matt Telles
```

As you see, it doesn't matter to the interpreter which form you use. There are exceptions to this, such as when you want to enclose a single quote within a literal string:

```
>>> name_quote = "This is Matt's string"
>>> print name_quote
This is Matt's string
```

The reverse works just as well:

```
>>> quote = 'And I said, "Hello there" to him'
```

If you don't like this method, you can use another way to place a double quote within a string:

```
>>> quote = "And I said, \"Hello there\" to him"
>>> print quote
And I said, "Hello there" to him
```

This works just as well the other way around, too. You can escape (that's what placing a backslash in front of the character means) a single quote within either a single or double quote-delimited string.

Spanning Multiple Lines

It is quite often useful to have a single string that spans multiple lines. Whether you are outputting some help text, or just have a quotation that turns out to be too long for a single line of text, Python provides methods for entering multiple lines of text into a single variable. The easiest way to do this is simply to continue a line to the next line by using the line continuation character:

```
>>> aQuote = "This is a really really really long line that"\
        "needs to be continued to the next line"
>>> print aQuote
```

```
This is a really really, really long line that needs to be continued to the next line.
```

As you can see, the line is continued, and does not contain any line breaks. If, for some reason, you actually want to continue the line and embed a line break in it, simply use the carriage return escape sequence (\n):

```
>>> aQuote = "This is a really really really long line that\n"\
        "needs to be continued to the next line"
>>> print aQuote
This is a really really, really long line that
needs to be continued to the next line.
```

The other direct way to continue a line is to use the "raw" delimiter, the character "r," in front of the string. If you do this, Python considers everything in the string to be copied literally until it finds the closing quotation mark:

```
>>> aRawQuote = r'This is a raw string that will be interpreted\
to contains whatever the heck I type into it'
>>> print aRawQuote
This is a raw string that will be interpreted\
to contains whatever the heck I type into it
```

One problem with the raw syntax is that, in the interpreter, it will force you to use the backslash to continue the line while typing; however, the interpreter itself will count the backslash as part of the line. You can't have everything. Oh, and finally, the line continuation character isn't restricted to strings; it can be used for any sort of input line.

Triple Quotes

The third method for continuing lines in Python was designed for use in printing out things like Help texts or copyright statements. Certainly, you have seen blocks like this:

```
Help - use this command for getting help.
Our interpreter understands the following commands:
    Print
    Quit
    Store
```

This syntax is so popular, in fact, that Python provides a special way to enter it, the triple quote. The triple quote, which is literally three quotation marks in a row, treats everything within the block defined by the quotes as literal text to be rendered just as it appears:

```
>>> print """
Help - use this command for getting help.
Our interpreter understands the following commands:
    Print
    Quit
    Store
"""

Help - use this command for getting help.
Our interpreter understands the following commands:
    Print
    Quit
    Store
```

The triple quote syntax, which is very familiar to HTML programmers as the `<pre>` tag format, is quite useful when you are displaying things like help, usage, or other block-oriented data. It does make the code a little harder to read, so if you are going to use it, be sure to keep the sections of your scripts that print in triple quotes on their own and with plenty of white space around them to make it clear to the reader that what they are seeing is really literal text and not potentially code.

Concatenating Strings

After storing and printing, the most utilized function of strings is concatenating, or combining, them into longer strings. For example, I might have an output line that was going to print something based on certain criteria. The beginning of the output might always be the same, say, "The answer is: "where the end of the string would vary, depending on exactly what that answer was. Python provides the string concatentation operation, '+'", for working with strings. Much as the plus operator adds two numbers, the string plus operator adds two strings:

```
output = "The answer is: "
# Decide what the answer should be...
output += "green"
print output
```

In the above little piece of code, the final result printed would be:

```
The answer is: green
```

Concatenation can be used with variables, as shown above, to concatenate to a single variable. It can be used with two variables:

```
quest = "The question is: "
q1 = " why me? "
qtotal = quest + q1
```

This creates a variable called `qtotal` that combines the two strings found in quest and q1. Note that there are no automatically appended spaces, punctuation marks, or quotation marks. If you combine "a" and "b" by writing "a"+"b," you get "ab."

Finally, please note that simple concatenating a string to another string does not modify either string, unless the result is assigned to one of them. In this case, the result becomes the new reference of the string variable. So:

```
s1 += "this"
```

does modify the string s1, since it is assigned back to the original string. However if you look at this example:

```
>>> s2='b'
>>> print s2+'c'
bc
>>> print s2
b
```

You can see that the string s2 was not modified, even though it was used in the print statement to output a concatenated string.

As a side note, you might wonder if Python contains the reverse operator, a "-" or deconcatenation operator, that would do something like this:

```
s1 = 'abc'
s2 = s1 - 'a'
```

The answer is no, nor is there a "-=" operator that will remove a given character or string from a string reference. I guess completeness only goes so far with language developers. As you will see shortly, however, implementing the functionality of a minus operator is not hard with the functionality given to us by the string functions in Python.

Repeating Strings

Python does contain a unique operator in all of the programming languages. The times operator "*," when applied to strings, allows you to repeat a string some number of times. For example:

```
>>> a = "Hello"
>>> a += 5*"there"
>>> print a
Hellotheretheretheretherethere
```

The times operator (or repeat operator) "multiplies" a string and produces a result that is the string concatenated with itself the number of times you want. The repeat operator can be used on either side of a string:

```
>>> a += "there"*3
>>> print a
Hellotheretheretheretheretheretheretherethere
```

While it might appear that this is one of those times that an operator is included simply to create a cool feature, if you've ever had to generate filled strings for a database, you will realize just how useful this function is. The reason for this is that you can use a variable in place of the literal value shown previously. That allows you to do things like filling a string with a variable number of spaces, based on some criteria. A simple example shows this:

```
>>> a = "Test"
>>> i = 10
>>> a += i*" "
>>> a += "done"
>>> print a
Test           done
```

As you can see in the preceding example, we chose the value 10 to be the number of spaces to "pad" the variable "a" with, before appending the string "done" to it. However, suppose that you wanted to do something more exciting, like padding the string to be 25 characters at all times. As you will see in just a moment, there is a way to determine the length of the string. That function, combined with the repeat operator, allows you to pad a string to an arbitrary size:

```
a = 'word'
# Pad the string out to 25 characters
l = 25-len(a)
a += l*" "
```

Substrings

A common problem, when you are working with strings, is to be able to extract a piece of a string. This is particularly important when working with fixed length files, for example, where each character in a string might mean something else. Another good example of this need is in telephone numbers, where you might want to input the number as 212-555-5555, but then store it as the area code (212) and the rest of the number in separate fields in a database or other storage mechanism. Python provides some excellent manipulation capabilities for strings, especially when you are working with pieces of them.

The first way in which you can manipulate a string is by indexing. An index provides a single character in the string, or can be used to provide a complete substring within an existing string. The general form of the index operator in Python is:

```
String[start[:end] ]
```

Where:

* Start is the starting index of the character you want to work from
* End is the ending index of the character you want to process to.

You do not have to specify anything more than the start or end index. For example, suppose that you wanted the third character in the string `Hello world` referenced to by the variable `str`. This character, which would be an `l` would be retrieved using the following bit of Python code:

```
Str[2]
```

The index value 2 is chosen, rather than 3, because Python is a 0-based indexing language. That is, numbers start at zero and progress to the number of characters minus one. So, in the string `Hello world`, which has eleven characters, the indices run from 0 to 10.

One important point about Python strings and indexes. Unlike other languages you may have worked with, such as C, Pascal, or Visual Basic, you cannot change a string via the index mechanism. That is, you cannot write something like this.

```
Str[2] = 'b'
```

There are a variety of reasons for this, but the upshot is that you can't. There are lots of ways to accomplish the same thing without having to directly modify memory, so this isn't a particularly big problem. Just remember that strings accessed via index are read-only and cannot be modified. Strings are immutable, meaning "unchangeable." In Python, variables are either mutable (able to be changed) or immutable (unable to be changed). You'll see this come up over and over in the next few chapters.

Oh, by the way, if you don't happen to know how long a given string is, or don't feel like doing the math, Python provides a rather interesting method for accessing strings backward. You can use negative numbers to access the string from the right-hand side. Thus, with the string variable `str` equal to the string `Hello world`, if you use the value -1 for the string index (i.e., `str[-1]`) you will get the `d` at the end of the string. Likewise, the string index -2 gives you a `l` and so forth, until you get to the beginning of the string. Python strings will not allow you to access values outside the range of 0 to the length of the string minus 1, using positive indices; anything outside that range will give you an error. Likewise, you can't use a value in the negative range outside of -1 to the length of the string, because it will give you an error. To illustrate this point:

```
>>> s = "Hello world"
>>> s[12]

Traceback (most recent call last):
  File "<pyshell#23>", line 1, in <module>
    s[12]
IndexError: string index out of range
>>> s[-11]
```

```
'H'
>>> s[-12]


Traceback (most recent call last):
  File "<pyshell#25>", line 1, in <module>
    s[-12]
IndexError: string index out of range
```

Slicing

A variant of the single index access is multiple index accessing of strings, or slicing of strings. This is done by providing a range of characters that you want. For example, you might want the characters from position three through position eight in the string `Hello world`. In Python, this is done by using the slicing syntax [3 : 8]. In fact, if you look at the result of this operation:

```
>>> s[3:8]
'lo wor'
```

You can see that you get exactly what you'd expect. In a range operation, unlike a single character operation, giving numbers outside the bounds of the string is okay. So, you can look at, for example, characters four through 100:

```
>>> s[4:100]
'o world'
```

Python will automatically check the string bounds and will only allow you to work with the ones that are valid. Likewise, if you work with negative numbers and "go off the end" to the left, you will get the beginning of the string.

There are some rather handy shortcuts that can be used with string slicing. First, you do not have to supply either the beginning or ending values. Python will use the remainder of the string in that direction. For example, you can use the following syntax to obtain the characters in a string from position 3 to the end:

```
>>> s[3:]
'lo world'
```

Naturally, you can also retrieve the first batch of characters in a string. For example, suppose that you wanted everything up to the third character in a string. In this case, you would use syntax like this:

```
>>> s[:3]
'Hel'
```

Now, let's go back to the problem we talked about a bit earlier—setting a given character in a string. As mentioned, you can't simply say `s[2] = 'a'` and have the string now read `Healo world`. However, using the combination of the two pieces above, you could write:

```
>>> s1 = str[0:2] + 'a' + str[3:]
>>> print s1
Healo world
```

Obviously, you can change a single character, but you just have to use a little bit more code to do it. However, you can also insert a set of characters at a given position using the same syntax. For example, instead of the `a` in the concatenation of strings, you could have put an entire line of text. This is something you can't do in languages that support changing a single character index. So, really, Python can do everything they can do and more.

String Functions

Python supports two sorts of string functions. First, there are the built-in operators that support indexing and assignment. There is also the string module, which contains quite a number of different sort of functions. However, before we get there, let's discuss the one other built-in function that applies to strings, and any other sort of sequence type: the `len()` function. The `len()` function will return the length, in characters, of a given string that is passed to it.

A string that contains no characters, for example, a character string represented by "", is defined to have a length of zero. A string that contains any other characters, such as `Hello world`, contains a length of the number of characters in the string, in this case 11. String objects that are not assigned a value, such as those assigned the special value type "None" have no length, and trying to determine the length of such an object will generate an error. The remainder of the string methods are actually part of the string module, which is the class that represents strings in Python. Let's look at those functions now.

String manipulation in the string module consists of a variety of types of functions and definitions. They are the following:

- ❄ string constants
- ❄ Conversion functions
- ❄ Search functions
- ❄ Formatting functions
- ❄ Escape sequences

Let's look at each of these groups and see how they apply to strings in Python.

String Constants

The Python string module defines quite a few constants that can be used in your own applications. The major ones that you are likely to run into are listed in Table 4-1. Take a look at them and then we will look at an example or two of how to use them:

Table 4-1   String Constants In Python

Function Name	Purpose
ascii_lowercase	The set of ASCII characters in lowercase. This is the letters a-z, but not the punctuation or space characters.
ascii_uppercase	The set of ASCII characters uppercase. This is the letters A-Z but not the punctuation, space, or other characters.
ascii_letters	This is the combination of the two groups above uppercase and lowercase ASCII characters.
digits	These are the digits 0–9
hexdigits	These are the hexadecimal digits 0–F
punctuation	These are the punctuation marks, period, comma, semi-colon, and so forth. This includes all of the Shifted-number keys on the keyboard.
printable	This is the complete set of characters made up of the groups above: letters, numbers, and punctuation.

How do you use these constants? There are a variety of ways, but let's consider the most obvious case. The user inputs a string, and you want to check to make sure that it only is made up of certain characters.

First, you need a way in which the user can input some data into the application. We'll discuss various input and output functions in Chapter 6, but for now, let's just use a function and assume that you can figure it out enough to write the code. The function is called input and just takes a single argument, the string you want to use as the input prompt. You use the function like this:

```
s = input("Please input a string: ")
```

The return value from the input function is the evaluation of an expression. So long as you enclose your input in quotation marks, you will get back a string. We will see in Chapter 6 that there is another function, called raw_input, which will return you only the string. You may use raw_input instead if you want. You can convert the string, or you can use it directly as a string as you are going to do right now. So the process is as follows:

1. Input a string from the user.

2. Check all of the characters to see if they are valid for our application.

3. If an invalid character is found, tell the user and stop.

4. If no invalid characters are found, print the string back to the user.

In this case, we will consider all valid characters to be those that are in either lowercase ASCII or uppercase ASCII. Anything else is an invalid character. So, given what we have learned in Python so far, and a little bit of code that we have not learned yet, let's try it:

1. Create a new file in the editor of your choice. Call it Ch4_1.py.

2. Enter the following code into the Ch4_1.py file:

```
# Import the string module for the constants we need.
import string


# Input the string from the user and assume that it is okay.
s = input("Please input a string using only lower and upper case letters: ")
valid = True


# Loop through all of the characters, checking to see if they are all
# in the valid groups we allow
for c in s:
    if ( c in string.uppercase ):
        continue
    if ( c in string.lowercase ):
        continue
    print "You have entered an invalid character: [" + c + "]"
    valid = False
    break


# If the whole string was valid, echo it back to the user.
if valid == True:
    print "You entered a valid string: "+s
```

3. Save the file in the editor and then load it into the Python IDLE shell by using the File | Open command.

4. Run the program in the shell by using the Run Module (or F5 in Windows) command.

5. You should see some sort of interaction similar to the following in the Shell window. Note that we have run the program several times here with different sets of input, as denoted by the Restart messages:

```
>>> ================================ RESTART ================================
>>>
Please input a string using only lower and upper case letters: 'hello'
You entered a valid string: hello
>>> ================================ RESTART ================================
>>>
Please input a string using only lower and upper case letters: 'hello world'
You have entered an invalid character: [ ]
>>> ================================ RESTART ================================
>>>
Please input a string using only lower and upper case letters: 'hi.'
You have entered an invalid character: [.]
```

As you can see, the program works as specified. We'll get into what the various pieces are as we discuss the components of Python later in the book. Let's just look at a few little things here:

The statement for c in s: simply loops through the contents of the string s, allowing the variable c to get each character. The for loop iterates over the character array (which is what a string really is) and returns each character in turn. Then once you have the character, you can check to see if it is a member of the various string values uppercase and lowercase using the in operator again.

You may also note the user of the True and False values. They do have to be capitalized in Python, but otherwise can be treated as any other sort of value. As you can see, working with the string values, and strings, in general, is quite simple and straightforward in Python.

Conversion Functions

The next group of functions we will consider in the string module are the conversion functions. These are functions that manipulate and return a given string in some way. Some of them change the string type into other types, while others simply manipulate the contents of the string in a useful fashion. Table 4-2 shows the functions we are going to be considering in this group:

Table 4-2   Python String Functions

Function	Purpose
atof	A deprecated function that converts a string into a floating point number. For future work, use the float() function instead.
atol	A deprecated function that converts a string into a long value. For future work, use the long() function instead.

Function	Purpose
atoi	A deprecated function that converts a string into an integer value. For future work, use the int() function instead.
capitalize	A function to capitalize the first letter of a string and make all other letters in the string into lowercase. Used primarily for displaying names.
lower	Converts an entire string into lowercase.
upper	Converts an entire string into uppercase.
join	Concatenates two strings, using a separator character supplied by the programmer.
lstrip	Strips leading spaces (or optionally other characters) from a string
rstring	Strips trailing spaces (or optionally other characters) from a string.
strip	Strips leading and trailing spaces (or optionally other characters) from a string.
replace	Replaces one or more characters in a string with a replacement set of characters.

The first three functions are marked as *deprecated*. In programming lingo, *deprecated* means that these functions have been replaced by newer functions and may not work in the future. You can use a deprecated function, especially if you are never planning on upgrading your version of Python, but it is generally a good idea not to do so. You never know when someone else might decide that they want some new whizbang feature in a newer edition of the libraries and upgrade the system, breaking your Python scripts. When something is marked deprecated and replaced, you should not use it in new code, and find all occurrences of it in old code and replace those occurrences with the newer function.

In this case, we are talking about converting strings to various types of numbers. The old way of doing this was:

```
s = "123.35"
f = string.atof(s)
```

The variable f will now reference the floating point number 123.35.

In modern versions of Python, starting with version 2.0, the proper way to do this same function is to use float:

```
f = float(s)
```

The variable f will, once again, reference the floating point value 123.35. The variable s will not be modified in either case.

The two functions atoi and atol convert a string into an integer value, allowing you to specify an optional mathematical base to use in the conversion: The base is the numeric system (usually decimal, but can be octal, hexadecimal, or any other valid numeric base) to use in the conversion. To see how this works, consider the following simple example:

```
>>> s = "100"
>>> i = string.atoi(s)
>>> print i
100
>>> i = string.atoi(s,8)
>>> print i
64
```

As you can see, if you do not specify a base, the default decimal system (base 10) is used for conversion. If, on the other hand, you specify a base, which in this example was octal, the conversion function uses that numbering system to convert the number. Obviously, the output is in decimal in either case.

The new functions, int() and long(), both accept the same arguments, so you can pass in a base there as well:

```
>>> i = long(s,8)
>>> print i
64
```

The capitalize, upper, and lower methods work on the case, upper, or lower of a given string. The upper and lower methods simply return the string mapped into the upper- or lowercase characters, whereas the capitalize method changes the case of the first character in the string to be uppercase and all other characters to be lowercase. Here's a simple example to give you an idea of how they work:

```
>>> s = input("Enter your first name: ")
Enter your first name: 'matt'
>>> print string.lower(s)
matt
>>> print string.upper(s)
MATT
>>> print string.capitalize(s)
Matt
```

As you can see, these functions can be very useful for output. The lower and upper functions are extremely useful when you are trying to match strings, without worrying about the case of the input, such as when you ask the user to input a command. Imagine, for example, that you want to have a "menu" of commands, such as copy, delete, and exit. You wouldn't want to check for every variation of input of the commands, depending on how the user felt like typing them that day. Instead, you might compare the input converted always to lowercase to make things easier for you.

You might wonder what happens if a non-alphabetical character is used in the string and then passed to the upper or lower functions. The answer is, nothing. Conversions on non-alphabetical functions are not performed; the characters are left alone:

```
>>> print string.lower('#$%^&*()')
#$%^&*()
>>> print string.upper('#$%^&*()')
#$%^&*()
```

The "join" function is an interesting one. Suppose, for example, that you had a database that contained the user first name, last name, and middle initial. Now, suppose that you needed to print out their name, in proper format, for use in a mailing label. You could simply print out the first name, a space, the middle initial, a space, and the last name. That certainly works, but there is an easier way using the functions that we have learned so far:

```
>>> first = 'matt'
>>> last = 'telles'
>>> middle = 'a'
>>> print string.join([string.capitalize(first),string.capitalize(middle),
string.capitalize(last)], ' ')
Matt A Telles
```

The only thing that looks funky here is the bracket syntax ([ ]) to create a list. Don't worry about it for now, as we'll be talking about it later in this chapter.

The strip functions (lstrip, rstrip, and strip) remove leading and trailing spaces (or other characters) from an input string. Going back to our example of inputting menu commands, you might worry that the user would input a string with a leading or trailing space in it. The lstrip function removes leading spaces, the rstrip function trailing spaces, and the strip function both leading and trailing spaces. The reason that the description above says "or other characters" is that the functions work on spaces by default. If you want to remove leading underscores, you can use them for that as well, by simply adding a second argument, which is the character to remove. Looking at an example of using the strip functions:

```
>>> s = "     hello world     "
>>> print "[" + string.lstrip(s) + "]"
[hello world     ]
>>> print "[" + string.rstrip(s) + "]"
[     hello world]
>>> print "[" + string.strip(s) + "]"
[hello world]
```

As you can see, the functions will remove the leading spaces by default. If you wanted to use, say, lstrip to remove leading underscores from a string, you would use string.lstrip(s, "_") as your function call.

The final function we will consider in the conversion set for strings is the replace function. The replace function replaces characters that you do not want to appear in a string, with characters you would prefer to find. A good example of this is using a string with spaces in a file system that does not support spaces in file names. The conventional thing to do in this case is to replace all of the spaces with underscores. So, we might have something like this as an example:

```
>>> f = input("Enter file name: ")
Enter file name: 'this is a file name with spaces'
>>> print string.replace(f, ' ', '_')
this_is_a_file_name_with_spaces
```

That's about all there is to it to the conversion functions. Now, let's look at the search functions.

Search Functions

When you are working with strings, in Python or any other language, it is normal to need to be able to search through the string for various things. Perhaps you want to know if the string contains any invalid characters, or perhaps you are looking for a wildcard character that indicates the need to do further processing. You might care how many times a given character or string appears within an input string, or want to break an input string down into component words. Whatever your need, the Python string functions will likely provide a method for accomplishing the task.

Table 4-3 shows the search functions that are supported by the Python string module, along with a brief description of what they do. Take a look at them and then we will take some time to look at how they are used with some examples.

Table 4-3   String Search Methods

Method	Purpose
find	Locates a given character or string in a given string if it exists, searching from the beginning of the string to the end.
rfind	Locates a given character or string in a given string if it exists, searching from the end of the string to the beginning.
index	Locates a given character or string within a string, starting from a given position and moving forward within the string.
rindex	Locates a given character or string within a string, starting from a given position and moving backward within the string.
split	Allows you to split a string into component words, using user-defined delimiters.
zfill	Pads a given string with zeroes until a given length is reached.

The searching functions seem reasonably straightforward. In fact, if you understand the `find` functions, forward and backward, you really understand the `index` functions, since they are the same thing. The main difference is that in case of an error, `find` returns a -1 for the index of the next position, whereas `index` raises an exception in your code. We'll be looking at exceptions and exception handling a bit later in the book, so let's just examine the find function for now. The syntax is the same for both.

To search forward through a string for a given substring, you use the `find` function. To search from the rear of the string backward, you use the `rfind` function. To see how this works, consider the following example:

```
>>> s = "my name is my passport, verify me"
>>> print s.find("my")
0
>>> print s.rfind("my")
11
```

If you examine the output of both functions, you will find that they refer to different instances of the string "my" within the original string. The first string is at the very beginning of the string and is found by the `find()` function. The second string is in the middle of the string, and is found by counting backward eleven positions from the end of the string by the `rfind()` function.

The split() function breaks a string down into substrings, using a delimiter specified by the user. In the previous example, we have a string with seven substrings in it. Using the `split` function we get the following:

```
>>> s.split(' ')
['my', 'name', 'is', 'my', 'passport,', 'verify', 'me']
```

Notice that the `split` function returned the word `passport` along with the comma that followed it. The `split` function doesn't understand that you wanted words; it understands that you wanted everything that was delimited by the character(s) that you gave it. You can't specify more than one delimiter, because the function assumes that a multi-character separator is really a string that separates the words. So, if we try:

```
>>> s.split(', ')
['my name is my passport', 'verify me']
```

As you can see, we don't get what we expect. The string is split into two words, separated by a comma and space, rather than all words that are separated by either a comma or a space. Note that you can omit the separator entirely, and get back a list that is separated by any form of white space.

```
>>> s.split()
['my', 'name', 'is', 'my', 'passport,', 'verify', 'me']
```

This is, of course, the same as the case where we specified the delimiter.

The zfill() function is one of those things you just scratch your head at and wonder why people included it. In fact, if you have ever worked with an accounting system, you would understand. In some applications, such as accounting, numbers are supposed to be a fixed width. This requires leading zeroes, so as to not change the value of the number, to be printed. This is the purpose of the zfill() function:

```
>>> s = "123"
>>> print s.zfill(10)
0000000123
```

Formatting Functions

It isn't unusual for programmers to use Python to write applications that have to produce reports for the user. One of the most common needs when writing a report is the ability to justify text within a column or region of the report. Python provides three string methods in the string module for justification, whether you need things right or left justified, or centered within a block. The three methods are shown in Table 4-4.

Table 4-4   Formatting Methods

Method	Purpose
ljust	Left justify a string within a given width
rjust	Right justify a string within a given width
center	Center a string within a given width.

The functions should be somewhat self-explanatory, but let's give a simple example of how to use them anyway, just in case you might have some questions about them.

```
>>> s = "1234"
>>> print s.ljust(10)
1234
>>> print s.rjust(10)
      1234
>>> print s.center(10)
   1234
```

As you can see, the justification functions work about the way you would expect. You can combine various string functions, since most of them return a string. The exception is the split function, which returns a list of strings. In Python, if a function returns a given object, you can invoke other methods of that object. For example:

```
>>> s.zfill(5).center(10)
'  01234   '
```

The ability to apply multiple methods to what appears to be a single object is quite powerful, especially when those methods do not change the object(s) to which they are initially applied. Let's imagine, for example, that Python provided no way to strip both the leading and trailing spaces for a string. You might have to do something like this to create the same functionality as strip().

```
>>> s = "    hello world    "
>>> s1 = s.lstrip()
>>> s2 = s1.rstrip()
>>> print s2
hello world
```

Alternatively, however, you could just do this:

```
>>> print s.lstrip().rstrip()
hello world
```

As you can see, the application of multiple methods does just what we want and in a much more convenient and compact format.

Escape Sequences

One thing that you might run into when working with Python code is the notion of "escape sequences" in the strings. An escape sequence is a character that cannot normally be used in a string literal, but can be if you convert it into something that the interpreter understands and can process. Good examples of escape sequences that you would need to understand would be carriage returns, line feeds, tabs, and quotation marks.

There are two sorts of escape sequences. First, we have escaped characters. For example, if you want a string that reads Matt's Farm, you need to escape the quotation mark within the string, because otherwise, Python thinks you are stopping the literal string and then creating a variable called s Farm, which isn't legal. To do this, we place a backslash in front of the escaped character: Matt\'s Farm. Then the interpreter understands that you want to embed a single quotation mark within the literal string and everything is good.

The other sort of escaping is to use a special sequence of characters to replace a character that cannot be used in a normal literal string (or, for that matter, in an HTML page or certain kinds of documents).

Table 4-5 lists the more commonly used Python escape sequences along with their meanings:

Table 4-5   Python Escape Sequences

Escape Sequence	Meaning
\r	ASCII carriage return
\n	ASCII line feed
\b	ASCII backspace
\t	ASCII horizontal tab
\f	ASCII form feed
\v	ASCII vertical tab
\\	The backslash character
\'	Single quote character
\"	Double quote character
\unnnn	The 16-bit unicode character represented by the hexadecimal value nnnn
\Unnnn	The 32-bit unicode character represented by the hexadecimal value nnnn.
\onn	The octal value nn
\xnn	The hexadecimal value nn

There really isn't a lot to using an escape sequence in Python. You simply choose the ones you want, and then place them in a string:

```
>>> print "This is a tab \t followed by a return \n and then a funky character \xE4"
This is a tab    followed by a return
 and then a funky character ä
```

I'm sure you get the general idea here. That about covers the string module in Python. You will have noticed that while we were discussing strings, we came across some interesting things that looked like arrays. These are called *sequences*, and they will be the next topic we are going to cover.

Sequences

Sequences in Python are collections of data, shown in various forms. The three specific forms that make up all of the other types in Python are lists, tuples, and dictionaries. They are roughly equivalent to various types of arrays in other languages, but in Python they have special meanings. Let's look at each one of them so that you can understand how they work, what they look like, and how you can use them in your own Python programs.

Lists

In Python, a list is simply a collection of ordered objects, although the objects need not be of the same type. Lists are formed by enclosing a collection of objects in a set of square brackets, separated by commas. Well, at least that's what the official Python definition says. What does a list look like? A list looks like, well, a list of items:

```
x = [ 1, 2.45, "This is a string", 0 ]
```

The Python interpreter will take the previous statement and allocate a block of memory to store it. Once it has done so, you will have a list. The question is—what can you do with a list once you have one?

First, you can determine how many elements a list has, using the `len()` function:

```
>>> print len(x)
4
```

As the above code illustrates, the list referenced by the variable x contains 4 elements. We can look at a given element of a list using the index function (`[]`) to index into the list. As with all other Python data structures, lists are zero based, and thus this list has the elements 0, 1, 2 and 3.

```
>>> print x[0]
1
>>> print x[1]
2.45
>>> print x[2]
This is a string
>>> print x[3]
0
```

You can iterate through a list, using the `for..in` syntax we've looked at briefly before:

```
>>> for e in x:
        print e


1
2.45
This is a string
0
```

So far, at least, lists appear to be the same as arrays in any other language. Lists in Python, as with most other languages, are mutable, meaning that you can change the elements in the list in place:

```
>>> x[2] = "This is a different string"
>>> for e in x:
        print e


1
2.45
This is a different string
0
```

On the other hand, lists can also be modified and extended at the same time. This is done using "slicing," which we've looked at before as well. For example, I can refer to the first and second elements of the list by saying x[0:1]. You can do that with strings, but you can't change them. Even more impressive, you can insert data into a slice of a list:

```
>>> x[0:1] = [1,2,3,4,5]
>>> print x
[1, 2, 3, 4, 5, 2.4500000000000002, 'This is a different string', 0]
>>>
```

As you can see, lists support the concept of mutability and also the idea of insertion. If you insert a list of objects at a given slice, you get a new list that contains all of the old elements (aside from those in the slice) and all of the new elements, as a single list. If, however, you insert a new list at a given position in a list:

```
>>> print x
[1, [2, 3, 4, 5], 3, 4, 5, 2.4500000000000002, 'This is a different string', 0]
```

In this case, you get something very different. As you can see, the second element in the list (or position 1) contains both a single element, and a list of elements. This brings up an interesting attribute of lists: Lists may contain other lists. And since any list can contain any other list, a list may be made up of lists of lists, or matrices. If you have a mathematical background, I'm sure you can see how useful this kind of thing can be. How do you access the embedded lists? The way you would expect:

```
>>> print x[1][2]
4
```

You can think of the above syntax as "the second element of x, then take the third element of the list stored at that position." The result of an embedded list element that is extracted via a slice or index is always a list itself, and thus you can do operations on it. For example, suppose that you wanted to know how many elements were in that embedded list:

```
>>> print len(x[1])
4
```

Pretty fancy stuff, isn't it?

Adding, Removing and Inserting with Lists

If you have a list, and it is mutable, it makes sense that you can add, remove, and insert things into that list. We've covered one form of adding things into a list, using the slicing mechanism to replace a range of items with a potentially longer list of items. Adding items to the end of the list is accomplished via the `append()` method (there are other methods for adding items to a list in other places):

```
>>> x.append(3)
>>> print x
[1, [2, 3, 4, 5], 3, 4, 5, 2.4500000000000002, 'This is a different string', 0, 3]
```

The `append` method can add a single element, a range of elements from another list, or even an entire other list to the list. If you append a new list to the end of the list, you get a new element in x that contains an embedded list:

```
>>> x.append([1,2,3])
>>> print x
[1, [2, 3, 4, 5], 3, 4, 5, 2.4500000000000002, 'This is a different string',
0, 3, [1, 2, 3]]
```

If you want to insert a new item in the middle of a list, you use the insert method. This is pretty straightforward, as methods go:

```
>>> x.insert(0,"front")
>>> print x
['front', 1, [2, 3, 4, 5], 3, 4, 5, 2.4500000000000002, 'This is a different
string', 0, 3, [1, 2, 3]]
```

Once again, this is pretty straightforward. There is a catch, of course. Consider the following line of code:

```
>>> x[0:0] = "fronter!"
```

You would think that this would create a single new element at the beginning of the array, since the slice 0:0 is really just the first element of the array, and it would replace the current element with the string "fronter." It does not do that. Instead, you get the following:

```
>> x[0:0] = "fronter!"
>>> print x
['f', 'r', 'o', 'n', 't', 'e', 'r', '!', 'front', 1, [2, 3, 4, 5], 3, 4, 5,
2.4500000000000002, 'This is a different string', 0, 3, [1, 2, 3]]
```

This happens because a string really is a sequence in Python. As a result, when you inserted the string as a single element, you got the list of characters inserted into the array at that position, just as if you had inserted a list of elements at a range of positions. This is, admittedly, a bit strange, but you get used to it after a while. If you wanted to insert the string as a single element, you would use the considerably less intuitive format:

```
>>> x[0:0] = ["fronter!"]
>>> print x
['fronter!', 'front', 1, [2, 3, 4, 5], 3, 4, 5, 2.4500000000000002,
'This is a different string', 0, 3, [1, 2, 3]]
```

Items can be removed from a list using the remove method. You can remove a single element if you know the value of it using remove, or you can use the del function to delete items by their index:

```
>>> x.remove(0)
>>> print x
['f', 'r', 'o', 'n', 't', 'e', 'r', '!', 'front', 1, [2, 3, 4, 5], 3, 4, 5,
2.4500000000000002, 'This is a different string', 3, [1, 2, 3]]
>>> del x[0:5]
>>> print x
['e', 'r', '!', 'front', 1, [2, 3, 4, 5], 3, 4, 5, 2.4500000000000002,
'This is a different string', 3, [1, 2, 3]]
```

Notice the difference here. The remove() method searched for, found, and removed the value 0 in the list. The del operation (which is not a part of the list class) removed the elements from 0 to 5 of the list. The difference is quite dramatic and easy to overlook.

There are three other operations that are worth mentioning about lists. First, there is the index method. Given a list x, the x.index(value) method will return the position of the first index of a list element equal to "value" in the list.

```
>>> print x
['fronter!', 'front', 1, [2, 3, 4, 5], 3, 4, 5, 2.4500000000000002,
'This is a different string', 0, 3, [1, 2, 3]]
>>> print x.index(1)
2
```

Next, we have the `reverse` method. Given a list, this method will reverse in place the elements of the list:

```
>>> l = [1,2,3]
>>> l.reverse()
>>> print l
[3, 2, 1]
```

Finally, there is the `sort` method. The `sort()` method, which can be quite powerful, allows you to sort the elements of a list in place. Given the above definition of a list, we can then say:

```
>>> l.sort()
>>> print l
[1, 2, 3]
```

You might wonder what the `index()` and `sort()` methods do with embedded lists. It's a valid question and one we should examine:

```
>>> print x
['fronter!', 'front', 1, [2, 3, 4, 5], 3, 4, 5, 2.4500000000000002,
'This is a different string', 0, 3, [1, 2, 3]]
>>> print x.index(2)

Traceback (most recent call last):
  File "<pyshell#44>", line 1, in <module>
    print x.index(2)
ValueError: list.index(x): x not in list
```

Why do you think you would get an error trying to find the value 2 in the list? Looking at the list, it is quite obvious that there is, in fact, a value of 2 stored in the list, which is stored in position 3. So, why didn't Python find it there? The answer is that the index function finds the exact match of an element in the list. The element at position 3 in the x list is actually a list itself with the value [2,3,4,5]. Thus, it does not match the single element 2.

What happens when you sort the above list?

```
>>> x.sort()
>>> print x
[0, 1, 2.4500000000000002, 3, 3, 4, 5, [1, 2, 3], [2, 3, 4, 5],
'This is a different string', 'front', 'fronter!']
```

If you allow Python to use its default comparing technique, the sorting algorithm first looks at numeric values, then at strings, because the ASCII values of numbers will be lower than the string values. As a result, the items are sorted in numeric order and then string order, which looks a bit strange, but is absolutely accurate.

There will be more to learn about lists as we go along through the book. Hopefully, at this point, you know enough to understand the odd syntax elements that we will be learning.

Shared References

One last point worth mentioning, since we are discussing references and values of variables. In Python, everything is a reference. That is, a given variable "refers" to a given value. Multiple variables can refer to the same location in memory. This is especially a problem in lists. Consider the following example:

```
>>> x = [1, 2, 3]
>>> y = x          # not copied, shared reference
>>> y[0] = "a"
>>> x
['a', 2, 3]
>>> y
['a', 2, 3]
```

Note that in this case, although we modified one variable, we also modified another reference to the same memory location, within a list. This can be a problem for programmers who are accustomed to variables being actual containers.

Tuples

Once you understand lists, understanding tuples is easy. A tuple is just like a list, except that it is immutable. In short, you can create a tuple, and iterate over it, but you can't modify the contents of the tuple after it has been created. A tuple is created using a similar syntax as a list:

```
aTuple = (1, 2.15, "This is a test")
```

You can print them out:

```
>>> print aTuple
(1, 2.1499999999999999, 'This is a test')
```

Note that the floating point value, being stored as a "true" float, will be displayed as an approximation, so it does not look like 2.15.

Naturally, just like a list, you can slice them and print out or access pieces of them:

```
>>> print aTuple[1]
2.15


>>> x = aTuple[2]
>>> print x
This is a test
```

The biggest difference is that you simply cannot modify the individual pieces of a tuple the way that you do a list. For example, if you try to update one of the components of the tuple:

```
>>> aTuple[1] = 3.14


Traceback (most recent call last):
  File "<pyshell#5>", line 1, in <module>
    aTuple[1] = 3.14
TypeError: 'tuple' object does not support item assignment
```

Unlike lists, the tuple is considerably less picky about syntax. For example, you don't really need to include the parentheses to make a tuple in the interpreter:

```
>>> anotherTuple = 1, 2, 3, 4, 5, "end"
>>> print anotherTuple
(1, 2, 3, 4, 5, 'end')
```

Once again, just like a list, a tuple is sliceable, meaning that you can get at chunks of it at once. For example, in the previous example, suppose that you wanted to get the second through fifth elements of the variable `anotherTuple` and print them out. You could write something like this:

```
>>> print anotherTuple[1:4]
(2, 3, 4, 5)
```

As with lists and other data structures in Python, the tuple type is zero based for access, meaning that elements one through four correspond to the second through fifth data elements in the tuple.

Tuples can be nested within each other, forming a two or three or more dimensional data structure. If you have two tuples and then want to form a third tuple created from the first two, you can do so easily:

```
>>> t1 = 1,2,3,4
>>> t2 = 2,3,4,5
```

```
>>> t3 = t1,t2
>>> print t3
((1, 2, 3, 4), (2, 3, 4, 5))
```

Note in the above example, the variable t3 consists of two elements, not eight. The two elements are each tuples and contain four elements each. If you look at the length of the tuple, you will see this:

```
>>> print len(t3)
2
>>> print len(t3[0])
4
>>> print len(t3[1])
4
```

There are two other important aspects of tuples that we need to cover before we move on to the next data structure. First, you can create a tuple that contains no elements at all. This is called an "empty tuple." You may never want to create one directly, but if you are returning a tuple that contains data from some user query, it is important to know that the returned value could be empty:

```
>>> t = ()
>>> print len(t)
0
```

As you can see, the empty tuple has a length of zero, which really should be no surprise at all. You can create empty versions of any type of sequence, such as a list ([]) or a string (""). Now, what about the other strange case of tuples, the case of a single element? There is nothing surprising about the fact that a tuple can contain only a single element, but the syntax is a bit strange:

```
>>> t1 = 4,
>>> print t1
(4,)
```

Notice the extra comma at the end of the line assigning the value 4 to the newly created tuple t1. This is necessary because it is the only way in which to tell the interpreter that you want to create a tuple of length one and not simply assign a variable the value 4. Notice that this syntax works for more than one element, as it would have to in order to make the language complete:

```
>>> t2 = 4,5,6,
>>> print t2
(4, 5, 6)
```

You never have to include the comma at the end of a tuple definition if there is more than one element in the tuple, but it won't hurt things either.

Tuples, by the way, support the usual functionality of data structures in Python. You can print them out, and you can concatenate them:

```
>>> t3 = t1 + t2
>>> print t3
(4, 4, 5, 6)
```

When you concatenate two or more tuples, you are creating one long tuple; you are not embedding one tuple in another, as you might have thought from our discussion about lists. Finally, you can unpack a tuple. This is definitely one of the stranger elements of Python, so take a careful look at it to understand what is going on here:

```
>>> x1,x2,x3,x4=t3
>>> print x1
4
>>> print x2
4
>>> print x3
5
>>> print x4
6
```

The comma syntax on the left-hand side of the equation tells Python to "unpack" the tuple elements, one at a time, into the variables defined on the left side, from the tuple on the right side. Note that the number of elements on the left side must exactly match the number of elements in the tuple:

```
>>> x1,x2,x3=t3

Traceback (most recent call last):
  File "<pyshell#34>", line 1, in <module>
    x1,x2,x3=t3
ValueError: too many values to unpack
```

So, what have we learned so far? If you use the square bracket notation, you get a list. Lists are mutable. If you use the regular parentheses notation, or just assign a variable a list of comma separated items, you get a tuple. Tuples are immutable. Now, you can forget all that and work on the next item, dictionaries.

Dictionaries

A dictionary is a mapping of key value pairs. The idea comes from our own word *dictionary*, which consists of words and their meanings. Likewise, a data structures dictionary consists of keys and values that are associated with those keys (like definitions, but less so). For example, suppose that I had a list of names, and wanted to associate a list of addresses with those names. I could use two lists to do so, having the first list contain the names and the second list hold the addresses. Of course, by doing so, I set myself up for failure. What if I delete something from the first list? I have to remember to do so in the second list. What if I want to sort the first list based on some criteria? I have to remember to sort the second list in the same order as the first list so that everything stays in sync. In short, it is a bad idea to implement two dependent data structures in independent format. For this reason, the designers of Python created the dictionary, which is a single data structure with two dependent data fields in it.

There is one important aspect to a dictionary that you need to understand. The key to a dictionary can be any valid object type. The key, however, must be an immutable value type. That is, you can't use lists as keys in a Python dictionary. There are a variety of reasons for this, but the major one is that dictionaries are allocated in a fixed way, so that allowing change would overly complicate the underlying code. However, this requirement does explain the need for tuples in Python. The entire purpose of a tuple is to provide an immutable construct. Needless to say, you can use tuples as value types in dictionaries.

Creating a Dictionary

The first step toward working with any new data structure is creating one, and dictionaries are certainly no exception to that rule. As we have seen, Python is all about creating things using strange syntax. The dictionary uses yet another odd character set to define it, in this case the braces ({}) characters:

```
>>> dict = {}
```

This line creates an empty dictionary. There is no particular reason why a new dictionary has to be empty. We could easily create one that had an initial element:

```
>>> dict2 = { "fred":"1010 Elm Street" }
>>> print dict2
{'fred': '1010 Elm Street'}
```

Multiple entries into a dictionary are made by separating them by a comma in the construction phase:

```
>>> dict3 = { "fred":"1010 Elm Street", "ralph":"2020 Maple Lane" }
>>> print dict3
{'ralph': '2020 Maple Lane', 'fred': '1010 Elm Street'}
```

The above code creates a dictionary with two keys in it, 'ralph' and 'fred'. Note that the order of things in a dictionary is not guaranteed in any way. We created the dictionary with 'fred' first and 'ralph' second, but when we printed them they were in the opposite order.

❋ Dictionaries and Keys

Never assume anything about the order of a dictionary and its keys. Dictionary keys may be stored in any order, and should never be assumed to be sorted.

Adding to a Dictionary

After you have defined a dictionary, the next logical step is to add new items to it. The syntax for adding items to a dictionary is actually amazingly simple, especially compared to some of the other methods used in Python:

```
>>> dict3['irving'] = '2662 Fremont Blvd'
>>> print dict3
{'ralph': '2020 Maple Lane', 'irving': '2662 Fremont Blvd', 'fred': '1010
Elm Street'}
```

To add a new key value, you simply use the indexing method to define it as a key for the dictionary. Likewise, if you want to change the value for a given entry in a dictionary, you use the same syntax:

```
>>> dict3['fred'] = '1020 Elm Street'
>>> print dict3
{'ralph': '2020 Maple Lane', 'irving': '2662 Fremont Blvd', 'fred': '1020
Elm Street'}
```

You can add or update key values using the same method. This is rather handy, especially if you aren't sure if a given key exists in the dictionary. If you want to know if a dictionary has a given value, you can use the has_key method:

```
>>> if dict3.has_key('fred'): print 'yes!'


yes!
```

Retrieving Values for Keys

When you have added keys and associated values to a dictionary, the real question is how do you get them back? There are a couple of ways to get data back from a key. The first uses the same syntax as setting the data:

```
>>> print dict3['ralph']
2020 Maple Lane
```

There is also a method called `get()`, which will return either the value of a key, or a default value, depending on whether or not the key was found in the dictionary. The thought process goes like this. If there is a key in the dictionary for the requested key value, return it. If there is no key value, you probably want to do something with it anyway, so allow the programmer to define a default value to return that can be set in the dictionary. You use the `get()` method this way:

```
>>> dict3.get('ralph', 99)
99
```

If the key "ralph" is found in the dictionary, the actual value of the key will be returned. If the key "ralph" was not found, then the value 99 will be returned. As you can see in our example, the key was not found. It is generally a good idea to return a signal value that tells you that the value was not found; otherwise, it is difficult to know if this is a new entry or an update of an existing key.

Iterating Over Keys

Let's imagine that you have a dictionary that represents a list of names and their identification numbers within a company. Such a dictionary might look something like this:

```
>>> dict = {'adam':1, 'bert':2, 'charlie':3, 'devon':4 }
>>> print dict
{'bert': 2, 'devon': 4, 'adam': 1, 'charlie': 3}
```

By the way, this also shows that you can create a dictionary with keys and values that are of different types, but I digress. Suppose that you wanted to list all of the keys available in the dictionary. The dictionary class defines a method called `keys()` that provides access to the key components of the dictionary object:

```
>>> for k in dict.keys() :
        print k


bert
devon
adam
charlie
```

There is a similar entry for the value entries for a given dictionary:

```
>>> for v in dict.values() :
        print v



2
4
1
3
```

Once again, please notice that the order of the keys and values within your dictionary bear no relationship to the order in which you put them into the dictionary. In fact, they are completely mixed up in relation to the original definition of the dictionary. You can never rely on the order of a dictionary.

Now, if you want to retrieve a value for a given key, you could simply iterate over both lists, looking for a given key and then finding the corresponding value in the other collection. That, however, would be silly. Remember, given a key, you can directly get back the value for it in the dictionary. You could, for example, dump a dictionary and get back both the key and value assigned to it using the following code:

```
>>> for k in dict.keys() :
        print "key: ["+k+"] = value: ["+str(dict[k])+"]"



key: [bert] = value: [2]
key: [devon] = value: [4]
key: [adam] = value: [1]
key: [charlie] = value: [3]
```

Note that you have to convert the value into a string in order to be able to print it. If you didn't do this, because the type is an integer, Python thinks that you are trying to add a string and an integer, which is an invalid operation.

Removing Keys from a Dictionary
The last topic to cover with respect to dictionaries is the removal of keys and values from the data structure. As with lists, the removal of entries in the dictionary is accomplished via the del() function, which is a part of the basic Python functionality. Assuming that you are using the dictionary from our last example, let's get rid of poor *bert*, who is no longer with the company:

```
>>> del dict['bert']
>>> print dict
{'devon': 4, 'adam': 1, 'charlie': 3}
```

That's all there is to it. Once you've deleted an item from a dictionary, it is gone forever, never to rear its head again. With that, we complete our discussion of dictionaries, and wrap up our discussion of the basic types in Python.

Advanced Type

In addition to the basic types in Python, there are quite a few advanced types. Some of them, we will discuss later on in the book, but a few are worth mentioning here. Whether or not you ever use some of these advanced types, it is always good to know that they are available, so that if you do need them you will know what to look for.

Classes and Objects

Python is an object-oriented scripting language. We will look at the complete issue of object-oriented programming and what it lends itself to in Chapters 9 and 10 of this book. For now, however, just know that Python allows you to define your own classes, which are encapsulations of data and functionality. The class keyword allows you to define a class, as in the following example. We'll be looking at what all this means later in the book, in the aforementioned chapters.

```
class MyClass :
    def __init__(self) :
        print "Initializing MyClass"
        self.x = 0

    def print_x(self) :
        print "MyClass::x = ", self.x
```

You don't really need to understand this example, but it is nice to see some real code for a change. Note that the "class" keyword is used to define a class, and that the "def" keyword is used to define methods within the class. Programmers used to object-oriented languages such as C++ or Java will have little trouble recognizing the constructs shown here. Also, please notice that indentation plays a major part in the definition of classes.

If you are accustomed to object-oriented programming, you are probably accustomed to the notion of constructors. A constructor is used to initialize an object when it is created. In Python, the notion of a constructor is handled by the __init__ method. If you are used to C++, you probably know all about the "this" pointer, which is a reference to the actual object you are working on. In Python, this is handled by the self object We will talk about the remainder of the class code in Chapter 10.

As a last example, before we leave classes, let's just look quickly at how you create an object and invoke a method upon it:

```
>>> x = MyClass()
Initializing MyClass
>>> x.print_x()
MyClass::x =   0
```

As you can see, it really isn't all that difficult. Classes are a very powerful part of the language, and well worth the two chapters we will devote to them.

Complex Type

If you are of a mathematical bent, you have almost certainly worked with complex numbers before. A complex number is part "real" and part "imaginary." Normally, you write a complex number as:

```
x + nj
```

where:

x is some real number that represents the magnitude of the real portion of the number.

j indicates the imaginary portion

n is some real number that represents the magnitude of the imaginary portion of the number.

This book is really not long enough to explain what imaginary numbers are, or how they work. Suffice it to say that the definition of an imaginary number is the square root of minus one. Yes, I know, they told you in school that you can't take the square root of a negative number. You can, so get over it.

You can add complex numbers, multiply them by either real numbers or other complex numbers, subtract them, and take their square roots and divide them by either real numbers or other complex numbers.

For example, consider the following simple example of multiplying two complex numbers:

```
>>> (4+3j)+(2+6j)
(6+9j)
```

Other than that, if you want a background in imaginary and complex numbers, please consult a general college math book. I'm not entirely sure why Python chose to implement complex numbers, but having used them in a project, I can say that it does an excellent job with them.

Generator Type

Python provides a generator type function. A generator function is one that can come up with a return value and then yield control back to the calling function. Now, of course, any function can do that. The difference is, when you call a generator function again, it picks up where it left off, and continues until it is next interrupted. The generator type function makes use of the reserved word `yield` in the Python lexicon, and can be invoked with the `next()` function. Let's look at a simple example, just to illustrate what it is we are talking about here:

```
def foo():
      # 1
      print 'call 1'
      yield 0
      # 2
      print 'call 2'
      yield 1
      # 3
      print 'call 3'
      yield 2
      # 4
```

The `foo()` function is a generator function. When it is invoked, it will print out information indicating what stage in its existence it is at. To invoke it, you use a variable that is "created" by `foo`:

```
>>> a=foo()
```

Notice that there is no output from this function. That's because it hasn't actually done anything yet. To make the generator work, you call the `next()` function:

```
>>> a.next()
call 1
0
```

As you can see, the function is invoked the first time, and proceeds until it encounters a yield statement. The yield value, the number following the yield statement in the function, is the result of the function call. At this point, the function has run from the line marked with the comment #1 to the line marked with the comment #2. If you invoke the generator object again, you get a different result:

```
>>> a.next()
call 2
1
```

Naturally, the second time you invoke the generator, it picks up where it left off and executes until another yield statement is encountered. You can run the function a third time:

```
>>> a.next()
call 3
2
```

At this point, the generator is sitting at the point marked # 4 in the code listing. The function is essentially complete. If you run the function another time:

```
>>> a.next()

Traceback (most recent call last):
  File "<pyshell#19>", line 1, in <module>
    a.next()
StopIteration
```

The interpreter recognizes that the function has finished, and that generates a StopIteration exception, which can be caught by the calling program. There is no defined way to restart a generator function; you need to recreate it and call next() on it once more to make it start over.

There are a variety of good reasons to use generator objects. Perhaps you want to process some database records in the background. Perhaps you want to calculate the value of pi to the thousandth digit. Whatever your process, you can call the generator function when you want to, and let it continue until it has processed a single iteration of its functionality. When it returns, you can continue with whatever you were doing. An excellent use of the generator pattern is to do background spell checking in an editor. Your mileage may vary, of course.

None Type

Python considers the type of an object to be a type unto itself. Integers, for example, are of type int. Strings are of type string (or something str). User defined classes are of the type defined by the class. You can do things based on the type of an object. Python provides a function and a keyword to work with types. The type() function will return you the actual type of an object:

```
>>> x = 'this is a test'
>>> print type(x)
<type 'str'>
```

You can test the type of one object against another type using the is keyword:

```
>>> x = 'this is a test'
>>> print type(x)
```

```
<type 'str'>
>>> y = 'this is another test'
>>> if type(x) is type(y) :
        print "They are the same!"
```

```
They are the same!
```

As you can see, the types match, and thus the objects are of the same type. You can return a value of a given type from a function, in exactly the same way. What happens, however, if you don't know what type of value to return for a given variable? The answer is, you use the None type. The None type means exactly what it says, that the object has no valid (or discernable) type. It is much the same as using null as a value in C++ or Java.

Please do not confuse the None type with an undefined variable type. For example, if you have a program that hasn't ever used the variable z, then you can't write something like this.

```
>>> if type(z) == None :
        print "z has no type"
```

Not only does the statement not work, it generates an error.

```
Traceback (most recent call last):
  File "<pyshell#56>", line 1, in <module>
    if type(z) == None :
NameError: name 'z' is not defined
```

Unicode Type

The Unicode type is used for supporting systems that support Unicode strings. A Unicode string (sometimes incorrectly called a *wide string*) is one that uses multi-byte characters to allow support for foreign language character sets. You create a Unicode string by adding the string "u" to the front of a string:

```
>>> x= u"This is a Unicode string!"
>>> print x
This is a Unicode string!
```

Depending on your computer setting, Unicode strings may or may not compare exactly to non-Unicode strings. For Windows, for example, they are the same:

```
>>> y = "This is a Unicode string!"
>>> if x == y :
        print "They are the same"
```

```
They are the same
```

For some flavors of UNIX, this will not be true.

In Conclusion

That concludes our tour of the basic and advanced data types in Python. From this point on, I'm going to assume that you understand the data types, so I won't take the time to explain them or how they work. Feel free, of course, to refer back to this chapter any time you feel you need to refresh your memory.

In the next chapter, we'll begin to explore the structure of Python statements by looking at condition and looping syntax. Once you understand the basics of the language, you can do pretty much anything in Python.

5 } Control Flow

In the beginning of computer programming, languages really only allowed you to do things in sequential order. You wrote your programs by inputting instructions to the machine to do a given task, following a set of commands that were always executed in the same order and the same direction. Eventually, programmers realized that not all conditions were the same. You had to have some control over whether or not certain instructions were executed and when the machine would execute them. This led to the rise of "conditional" programming. Conditional programming was considered to be an "if .. then" style of programming.

Consider, for example, a very simple script that does the following pseudo tasks:

1. Asks the user for a file name.

2. If the file name exists, copies it to a backup directory.

3. If the file name does not exist, creates the file from a template.

4. Asks the user if he wants to do it again.

5. If the user says yes, returns to step 1.

6. If the user does not say yes, exits the script.

There is nothing particularly complicated or surprising in the above task list. This is the sort of thing that we do every day in the computer world. However, notice the two bits of logic in the list. First, you need to be able to compare two things (whether or not a file exists, and whether or not the user says "yes" to a question) and take actions based on that result. Second, you need to be able to go back to another point in the script and start running from there.

The ability to change the behavior of a piece of code based on certain information in the environment (variables, conditions, input) is known as *conditional code flow*. The ability to change the order of a program so that it moves back and reruns a block of code is known as *looping code flow*. This chapter is dedicated to working with these two concepts.

Conditionals

The conditional logic in Python is primarily based on the "if … else" structure. The keywords we are generally concerned with in Python are the ones shown here in Table 5-1.

Table 5-1   Conditional Keywords in Python

Keyword	Meaning
if	Checks a condition. If the condition results in a "True" case, the code following the if statement is executed.
elif	Shorthand for "else if." Must follow an if statement, and if the condition compared is True, the code following the elif statement is executed
else	Must follow an if statement. If the code for the if (or elif) statement is False, the code following the else statement is executed. May also be used in a loop structure

As you can see from the list above, there are really only three keywords that we care about in the Python language. The if statement is the only one of the three that can be used on its own; the other two are dependent on other statements in the code.

The if Statement

The if statement is used to test a condition and to check whether or not the comparison results in a True value or False value. The simplest form of an if statement is as follows:

```
if condition :
    statement
```

Note that the if statement always consists of three elements. First, there is the if keyword. This tells the interpreter that you want to do a comparison. Next, there is the condition section. A condition can be any valid Python comparison, the result of a function or method call, or, in the case of a Boolean variable, a simple variable name. Finally, there is the colon (:) that indicates the end of the if statement and the beginning of the statement block to execute in case the condition is True.

Let's look at a couple of examples of the if statement in action to get an idea of how it works. First, consider the simplest case, a variable that is assigned either the value True or False.

```
>>> v = True
>>> if v :
        print "v is True!"


v is True!
```

As you can see from the above listing, first you create a simple Python Boolean variable and set it to True. Then you write an `if` statement that seems to do no comparison; it merely has a single variable name on the `if` line. The reason this works is that Python implicitly compares the variable to the True value. The `if` statement could have been written this way:

```
if v == True :
```

but this way saves us a couple of bytes and is understood by the interpreter. In general, I happen to frown on this sort of code in my own applications. I find it more difficult to read on first scan and thus more error prone. But your mileage may vary, and you should work in the way in which you are most comfortable.

As you can see, the `if` statement does work, the variable is True, and the `print` statement is executed. What if the variable were False? You can easily test this by entering the code in a slightly different way:

```
>>> if not v :
        print "v is False"
```

As noted in this example, nothing is printed out. The `not` operator modifies the tested condition, so that if the variable is True, the condition is not True, which is `False`. If the variable had been False, the condition would have been not False or True.

That is the simplest form of the `if` statement. A slightly more complex version would be a comparison:

```
>>> x = 1
>>> y = 2
>>> if x < y :
        print "x is less than y"
        print "please change x to be greater than y"
        x = y + 1


x is less than y
please change x to be greater than y
>>> print x
3
```

Looking at this example, you can see that comparisons can be slightly more complex than we have examined previously. In addition, you can see that we can have multiple statements within an `if` block. Once again, Python indentation comes to the rescue. By indenting the block, you indicate to Python that you are going to execute all of the statements in the block when the if statement is True. If the if statement is False, none of the statements in the block are executed. It is an all or nothing proposition.

Before we move on to the next part of the "if logic, let's take a look at one more thing you ought to be aware of, which is the idea of nested if statements.

```
>>> x = 1
>>> y = 2
>>> z = 3
>>> if x < y :
        if z > x :
            print "Z is bigger than X"
        if z < x :
            print "Z is smaller than X"


Z is bigger than X
```

There are a couple of interesting things in this code snippet. First, you will notice that an if block can contain other if blocks. This is important for cases such as sorting or comparing multiple values. Notice that the indentation of the blocks indicates which lines go with which blocks. Because the print statements are indented from the if statements within the main if block, they are only executed if the if statements they belong to are True. Otherwise, the flow of the application continues with the next statement outside of that block.

Next, note the two if statements within the main block. If x and z are the same value, of course, neither of these statements is going to be executed. Fortunately, we have taken care of that by assigning z a larger value than x. If they are not the same, then obviously, one of the two if statements is going to be True, and the print statement within it will be processed and executed.

Oh, one last thing about if statements. You don't have to have separate lines or blocks for statements. You can have everything on one line, but the if statement still has to have the colon separating the condition from the executing statements:

```
>>> if x + y == z : print "The equation is TRUE!"


The equation is TRUE!
```

When you are tying the above statement in the IDLE environment, you will notice that you have to press the Enter key twice at the end of the statement for it to execute. This is because even though the first line is not indented, subsequent lines can be, so the editor waits until it is sure you are done typing in lines for the `if` block before executing them.

Let's take a look at the second of the three pieces of the conditional block, the `elif` statement.

The `elif` Statement

The `elif` statement is a combination of the `else` clause and the `if` statement. Essentially, you are saying, "if this one thing is not True and if this other thing is True, then do this." As a result of this, the syntax of the `elif` statement is exactly the same as the `if` statement, but with the following caveat. An `elif` statement must appear in an `if` block. It cannot appear on its own. That is, you can't write:

```
elif x == 1:
   print "x = 1"
```

This isn't valid, because there was nothing for the `else` part of the `elif` statement to apply to. Instead, you would have written:

```
if x == 0 :
   print "x = 0"
elif x == 1 :
   print "x = 1"
```

The important thing to remember about `elif` is that it is the same as an `if` statement in terms of syntax and usage.

That is, it must be followed by a conditional statement and then a colon before you can place any statements to be executed.

Any valid statement block that can be placed in an `if` statement block can be placed in an `elif` statement block:

```
>>> x = 3
>>> if x == 0 :
      print "X is zero"
elif x & 1 == 1 :
      print "X is ODD"
elif x & 1 == 0 :
      print "X is EVEN"


X is ODD
```

In the above code, the value of x is compared to three different things. First, you check to see if the value is zero, since zero is neither odd nor even. If the value is not zero, the first `elif` statement is invoked and the lowest bit is tested to see if it is on or not. If it is on, the value is, by definition, odd. If the bit is not set, the code will then drop down to the next `elif` statement, which tests to see if the bit is not set, which would indicate that the value was even.

In this instance, we give the value three to x, which makes it not zero and odd. Note that the only block of code that is executed is the one for the odd case, and none of the others. This indicates that the program has done what we expected it to do. In addition to seeing that the `elif` statement works properly, this example also indicates that you can nest `elif` statements the same way in which you nest `if` statements. The difference, however, is that an `elif` can only be nested within an `if` statement and not within another `elif`. Each `elif` is paired with the closest `if` statement. Thus, you can't write something like this:

```
if x == 0:
    print "x = 0"
elif x == 1:
    print 'x = 1'
    elif x & 1 :
        print "x is odd"
```

For one thing, this would make no sense at all. What exactly are you trying to accomplish? You can nest `if .. elif` blocks, however:

```
>>> x = 3
>>> if x == 0 :
        print "Zero"
elif x & 1 :
        print "ODD"
        if x > 3 :
                print "Unlikely"
        elif x < 3 :
                print "Even more unlikely"
        elif x == 3 :
                print "There you go!"
elif x & 1 == 0 :
        print "Even"


ODD
There you go!
```

In the above example, there are two separate conditions that you are testing for. At the outside level, you want to know whether x is zero, even, or odd. At the inside level, if x is odd, you want to know if it is less than, greater than, or equal to three. If x is odd, you would expect to see two print statements executed, and you do, indicating that the structure and its indentation are correct.

The else Statement

The final piece of our conditional logic puzzle is the else statement. The else statement, as you might imagine, is what happens when no other conditions in an if block are found to be True. There can be only a single else statement that is a part of the if structure, although nested if statements can each have their own else block. Unlike the elif, the else statement must appear at the end of the list of conditional alternatives, following the if and any elifs that exist subsequently. You do not need to have an elif statement to have an else, but you must have an if statement.

Here is a very simple example of an if statement with an else clause:

```
>>> x = 0
>>> if x & 1 :
        print "X is odd"
else :
        print "X is even"


X is even
```

If you look at the logic here, it goes like this. The conditional (x&1) is evaluated. Since zero doesn't have the lowest bit (bit 1) set, the condition is False. As a result, the if statement condition doesn't evaluate to True, and the block of code following it is not executed. The interpreter then looks for the next token within the block at the same level as the if statement. If you consider a block of if, elif, and else statements, the levels go like this:

```
if  #1
elif #2
    if #3
    elif #4
    else #5
elif #6
else #7
```

Looking at the blocks, you have an outer block and an inner block. The outer block is made up of statements 1, 2, 6, and 7. Notice that there is only a single `if` and a single `else` in that grouping. That is the most of each that you can have at any level. The inner block consists of statements 3, 4, and 5. Once again, there is one `if` and one `else` statement in the block. In the outer block, you have two `elif` statements: 2 and 6. You can have as many of these as you want.

Wrapping Up the Conditionals: A Cool Example

That really wraps up all of the functionality available in the conditionals in Python. We will look at some other uses for at least one of the statements here, the `else` statement, when we talk about looping, since it is used there as well. However, before we leave the subject, let's look at a really cool example, using some of the functionality that you've learned in this chapter and the last chapter.

Imagine, for a moment, that you are writing some sort of a command driven system. The user enters a command, and you then invoke a given function based on that command. Let's say, for argument's sake, that you have three commands possible. You have `print`, `copy`, and `exit`. Certainly, you could add new commands to the system, but for now we'll stick to those three. Let's just assume that there is a way to input the command into the system. We are merely concerned with writing a chunk of code that processes the command. We'll further assume that there are three functions already written by someone else that do the actual work. We'll call those three functions `print_function()`, `copy_function()` and `exit_function()`. Very original, isn't it?

Given the code that you've already seen in the sections above in this chapter, you could write something like this:

```
if command == 'print' :
    print_function()
elif command == 'copy' :
    copy_function()
elif command == 'exit' :
    exit_function()
else :
    print "Invalid command"
```

Now, this code will certainly work. If you enter a valid command, it will call the proper command. However, it suffers from a very annoying flaw, in my opinion. Each time you want to add a new command, you have to add a new block to the `if` statements. The `if` block can very quickly become long and unwieldy, and is going to leave you prone to mistakes. What if you could replace all of the comparison and processing logic to four lines, and could extend that logic infinitely without having to modify those four lines? Would you be interested in something like that? Of course, you would. But wait, there's more! Hmmm. Why do I suddenly feel like a late-night TV salesperson? Oh well. We are going to use a bit of functionality that we learned in the last chapter, by using the dictionary data structure to implement all this. Now what would you pay for all of this? Oh, wait, sorry. Anyway, take a look at this code:

```
def copy_function() :
    print "copy function"

def print_function() :
    print "print function"

def exit_function() :
    print "exit function"

# Definition piece.
func_dict = {}
func_dict["copy"] = copy_function
func_dict["print"] = print_function
func_dict["exit"] = exit_function

# Processing piece
command = input("Enter command: ")
if func_dict.has_key(command) :
    func_dict[command]()
else :
    print "invalid command: "+command
```

As you can see, the processing code for this entire script is, as promised, only four lines long. The definition piece, which can be expanded as much as you need it to be, sets up a dictionary and then adds commands to it. The value part of the dictionary is the function to invoke. How can this work? Well, as you might recall, in the previous chapter we said that the key could be any valid immutable Python data type. That certainly is the case here, with the key being a string value. The value part of a dictionary entry does not have to be an immutable entity within Python. A function is most certainly an immutable thing; you can't change it without modifying the code and reloading it. As a result, Python is more than happy to allow you to store functions in dictionary values. Of course, you aren't really storing the function there; instead, you are storing a reference to the function. When you retrieve the function reference by getting the key value, you then apply the function call syntax [function()] to it, and Python does the rest. The only reason this works is because Python is an interpretive language. Any other language would, at the very least, require a bunch of casts and conversions before it would let you try something like this.

Let's try the thing out and see if it works as advertised:

1. Create a new file in Python using the IDLE editor's File | New Window command.

2. Enter the code above into the new window and select File | Save. Save the file as `ch5_2.py` in the directory of your choice.

3. Press the F5 key or select Run Module from the Run menu of the Editor window.

4. Enter a command when prompted.

5. Repeat steps 3 and 4 until you are satisfied that the script works the way it was promised to.

6. You should see something like the following dialog displayed in the console window of IDLE:

```
Enter command: 'print'
print function
>>> ============================ RESTART ===============================
>>>
Enter command: 'print'
print function
>>> ============================ RESTART ===============================
>>>
Enter command: 'copy'
copy function
>>> ============================ RESTART ===============================
>>>
Enter command: 'exit'
exit function
>>> ============================ RESTART ===============================
>>>
Enter command: 'fred'
invalid command: fred
>>>
```

As you can see, it works! Now there is something you aren't going to find in the average introduction to Python Web page.

Loops

Modern programming languages all contain some sort of looping mechanism. Some contain quite a few different varieties, from `for` loops, to `do` loops, to `while` loops, to `repeat until` loops. Python contains two varieties of looping constructs. First, there is the `for` loop, which is the main workhorse for looping. The `for` loop in Python can do pretty much anything any other sort of loop can do, and then some. If that were not enough, Python contains the `while` loop, which is more of a conditional looping structure than anything else. In this section, we will take a look at the two kinds of loops and how they work in Python.

The `for` Loop

The for loop is the basic looping structure in Python. The `for` loop is used for a lot of things, but primarily it is a "foreach" style loop, always working its way through a set of data values. If you are accustomed to working in another language, such as C or C++, you may be used to a `for` loop structure looking something like this:

```
for ( int i=1; i<10; ++i )
    // do something.
```

The basic structure of a `for` loop (or `do` loop, in some languages) in most languages is three-phase. First, there is an initialization step. Next, there is a termination clause. Finally, there is an incremental stage. The initialization step sets the starting condition for the loop. For example, in our C++ example above, the index variable `i` is initialized to one to start the loop. The termination clause is the middle conditional section of the loop, and is checked each time the loop is entered from above or by looping back. While the condition is True, the loop will continue. In our example, the loop continues until the value of `i` exceeds nine. Once it hits 10, the loop will exit. Finally, we have the incremental phase, where the index value (and any other values) is modified each time through the loop. You can think of the C++ `for` loop as looking like this:

```
index = initial_value;
target: do_something
        increment index
      if index < final_value go to target
```

This is the style of most looping constructs in programming languages. Python, however, takes a slightly different approach to the loop mechanism. In Python, the for loop looks something like this:

```
for value in setofvalues :
    do_something
```

As with all other Python block-oriented statements, the `for` loop executes all of the statements that are indented within it while it is running. Naturally, you can have all sorts of other statements in that block, including conditionals and other looping constructs. Here is the simplest example of a Python `for` loop:

```
>>> for i in 1,2,3,4,5 :
        print i
```

```
1
2
3
4
5
```

The above loop will execute, as you can see, five times. There are five values in the set of values to work with, so it goes through each of them once. There is no notion of incrementing the loop, nor of a terminating clause to speak of. You can drop out of a loop, but you cannot change the processing order of it. By the way, I lied. The absolutely simplest form of a loop would be the following:

```
>>> for i in 1,2,3,4,5 :
        pass
```

The `pass` statement in Python does just about what you would expect it to. It means "pass this line without doing anything." The `pass` statement is a placeholder when you must have a valid statement in place, but don't want the code to do anything. If you are accustomed to other languages, it is the equivalent of a line containing nothing but a semi-colon in C, C++, or Pascal.

So, if all you can do with a `for` loop is loop through a bunch of values, what good is it? Actually, it is quite useful. You don't have to list every value in the set of values over which to execute; instead, you can use a variety of other alternatives. Let's look at a few of these.

The `range()` function will allow you to define a set of values over which the `for` loop can execute, as long as your value list is in sequential order. For example, let's imagine that you want to add the numbers from one to a given value. The range() function accepts two values, a starting and ending value, and generates a set of numbers between those two numbers, inclusively. So, if you wanted to add the numbers from one to 10, you would create a `for` loop like this:

```
>>> total = 0
>>> for i in range(1,10) :
        total = total + i


>>> print total
45
```

If you sit down with a calculator and add the numbers from one to 10, you will find that the result is incorrect. The actual value for adding all of the numbers from one to 10 is 55, not 45. So what happened? The answer isn't that complicated. The actual syntax of the range function is as follows:

```
range( start, stop [,step])
```

You don't have to specify a step value; one will be assumed if you don't tell it otherwise. However, the start value is where the range begins, and the stop value is the number at which to stop before adding another to the range. If you really want to generate the full range of numbers from one to 10, you have to add one more to it. Remember, Python is zero based. So what you really want is this:

```
>>> total = 0
>>> for i in range(1,11) :
        total = total + i


>>> print total
55
```

As you can see, the range is now correct, and the value generated is what was expected.

You don't have to use the `range` statement. The `for` loop also works on lists. In this case, it is really a `foreach` loop, working its way through all of the values in the list. For example, suppose that you wanted to multiply three numbers together. You could do this:

```
mtotal = n1 * n2 * n3
```

However, if you want to add new numbers to the list to multiply, this could get ugly in a hurry. Let's use a looping construct to do it instead:

```
>>> nums = [1,2,3,4]
>>> mtotal = 1
>>> for i in nums :
```

```
        mtotal *= i
```

```
>>> print mtotal
24
```

Now, if you want to add new numbers to multiply by, you simply add them to the end of the list. Let's take a quick look at the `for` loop usage here, to understand what is really going on. Note that we use the "in" operator. Each time through the loop, the loop variable `i` is assigned the next element in the list. The first time through the loop, the `i` variable is 1, the next time it is 2, and so forth until it reaches the end of the list. Unlike the `range()` function, looping through an list will process each and every element in the array.

It might appear that you can only use this construct on numeric lists, but nothing could be further from the truth. In fact, Python allows you to process any type of list in a `for` loop. For example, suppose that you wanted to print out the letters of a string individually. Remember that a string is really just a sequence of characters, so:

```
>>> s = "this is a test"
>>> for i in s:
        print i
```

```
t
h
i
s

i
s

a

t
e
s
t
```

Before continuing, there is one more aspect of the `for` loop that is worth mentioning. As you may remember, I said originally that you could loop through a list of values on the `for` loop line:

```
for i in 1,2,3,4,5 :
    do something
```

There is no requirement whatsoever that the numbers be in order, nor do they have to be consecutive:

```
>>> for i in 1,3,2,5,4,400 :
        print i


1
3
2
5
4
400
```

Naturally, you can nest loops. Imagine, for a moment, that you wanted to determine all of the prime numbers between one and 10. A prime number, you may recall from school, is a number that is divisible only by one and itself. It turns out that you can determine if a number is prime by trying to divide it by all the numbers between one and itself divided by two. You can determine all of the prime numbers between one and a given number by two loops:

```
for n in range(2, 10):
    prime = True
    for x in range(2, n):
        if n % x == 0:
            prime = False
    if prime == True :
        print n, " is a prime number"
```

If you run the above little script in the interpreter, you will see the following output:

```
2   is a prime number
3   is a prime number
5   is a prime number
7   is a prime number
```

As you can see, the nested looping structure works quite well, and is an important part of the Python programming language. This example, however, is quite inefficient. Even after it determines that a given number is not prime, it continues to find factors that divide into it. This seems rather silly, because it should probably stop processing the inner loop as soon as it finds that a number is not prime. Not surprisingly, Python provides a way in which to accomplish this, the `break` statement:

```
for n in range(2, 10):
    prime = True
    for x in range(2, n):
        if n % x == 0:
            prime = False
            break
        print "Inner loop: ", x
    if prime == True :
        print n, " is a prime number"
```

The `break` statement stops the processing of a loop and "breaks out" of it when the statement is encountered. I've added a `print` statement to the inner loop so you can see what is going on while the loop executes. If you look at the output from this script now, you'll see what I mean:

```
2   is a prime number
Inner loop:   2
3   is a prime number
Inner loop:   2
Inner loop:   3
Inner loop:   4
5   is a prime number
Inner loop:   2
Inner loop:   3
Inner loop:   4
Inner loop:   5
Inner loop:   6
7   is a prime number
Inner loop:   2
```

As soon as a factor that the number divides by evenly is found, then the loop stops. That is the purpose of the `break` statement. On the other hand, you might want to run through a loop and only process certain numbers. Let's say that you want to process only the odd numbers in a given range. You might write something like this:

```
for i in range(1,11) :
    if i & 1 :
        print "Processing ", i
```

```
        print "Doing something here"
    else :
        print "NOT processing ", i
```

Now, if your code is just doing this, there is no particular reason not to write the code this way. If you execute this code, you will see the following output from the interpreter in IDLE:

```
Processing  1
Doing something here
NOT processing  2
Processing  3
Doing something here
NOT processing  4
Processing  5
Doing something here
NOT processing  6
Processing  7
Doing something here
NOT processing  8
Processing  9
Doing something here
NOT processing  10
```

It isn't always that ideal to have to do things this way, however. If you want to simply skip to the next value in a `for` loop, Python provides a simpler way. The `continue` statement allows you to skip to the next iteration of the loop:

```
for i in range(1,11) :
    if i & 1 == 0:
        continue
    print "Processing ", i
    print "Doing something here"
```

This code is considerably easier to read, and doesn't require that you remember to indent each line within the `if` statement properly. The output from this, with the exception of not printing out the "not processing" entries, is exactly the same as the previous example, but the code is shorter and more efficient. The `continue` statement drops to the bottom of the loop and continues with the next entry in the range that is being processed. This example also shows how the `if` statement can be used within a Python `for` loop to do individual processing on range elements.

The final keyword that is important to the `for` loop structure is, oddly enough, the `else` statement. As you have seen, there are two ways for a `for` loop to terminate. First, it can run through all of the values assigned to it to process. The `for` loop can also exit because you inserted a `break` statement, which was processed during the running of the code. If you want to know whether or not the `break` statement was processed, you can either insert some sort of signal variable, as we did in the prime number case, or you can use the `else` statement. Let's take another look at the prime number loop, this time using the `else` statement:

```
for num in range(2, 10):
    for x in range(2, num):
        if num % x == 0:
            break #1
    else: #2
        print num, 'is prime'
```

For each iteration of the inside loop, one of two things can happen. The first thing that can happen is that a number will be evenly divisible by one of the numbers that leads up to it. In this case, the `break` statement will be executed. The second thing that can happen is that none of the numbers leading up to the number in question will be evenly divisible. In this case, the loop will terminate normally. However, when the loop finishes, the interpreter will execute the `else` statement, because nothing interrupted the flow of the loop. This might seem a tad counterintuitive. Normally, the `else` command is executed when something doesn't happen the way you expect, and a loop flowing through all of its values is the normal behavior. Hey, nobody said everything had to make perfect sense. The `else` clause will only be executed when the normal behavior of the loop is followed. In our case, if the loop finishes normally, we didn't find a factor of the number, so it must be a prime number. In this case, we print out the fact to the user:

```
>>>
2 is prime
3 is prime
5 is prime
7 is prime
```

You'll find that the `for` loop is an amazingly versatile and powerful tool in your Python arsenal. You should get quite used to using it, since we will be relying on the power of this construct quite a bit through the rest of the book.

Oh, one last note on the `for` loop. The behavior of the loop is set at the time you define it, and it is not safe to modify the contents of the range you are processing over. That is, if you do something like this:

```
arr = [1,2,3,4,5]
idx = 0
for i in arr :
    if i & 1 :
        del arr[idx]
    idx = idx + 1
```

...then you are just asking for trouble. The odds are good that it will work, most of the time. The problem is that if it doesn't work, you are stuck with a program that crashes intermittently with no real indication of what the problem might be. If you have to do something like this, make a copy of the array by using the slicing operator:

```
arr = [1,2,3,4,5]
idx = 0
for i in arr[:] :
    if i & 1 :
        del arr[idx]
    else:
        idx = idx + 1
```

Notice that you now only increment the index if the value was not deleted. That's because the array was modified when the index was deleted, and the index will not be pointing at the proper place. This is the problem with in place modification of an array in a loop. Oh, and finally, the break and continue statements can be used outside of simple loops, in if statements, and other places such as the while loop, which we will talk about now.

The while Loop

The final construct we are going to look at in Python is the while loop. Nearly all languages have something equivalent to the while loop. Put simply, the while loop is a looping construct that continues to execute while a given condition is True. In its simplest form, the while loop looks like this:

```
while (something) :
    do something
```

For example, let's imagine that you want to count upward from a given number until you run across a number that is evenly divisible by 3. Since you do not know how many values might be involved, the for loop is not a good choice. Instead, you use the while loop to process numbers until the condition is satisfied:

```
>>> start = 5
>>> while start % 3 != 0 :
```

```
        print start
        start = start + 1
```

```
5
```

In this case, because the very next number in order happens to be divisible by three, the loop terminates very quickly. However, if you started at 10 instead:

```
>>> start = 10
>>> while start % 3 != 0 :
        print start
        start = start + 1
```

```
10
11
```

In this example, there are two numbers between the starting value and the terminating value. This kind of thing is harder to do with a `for` loop, because the ending point is not well known. The `for` loop doesn't really have a condition for an open-ended terminator, whereas the `while` loop doesn't have a condition for a particular ending. When you think about a loop, the best way to approach the decision of which looping structure to use is to decide whether or not you know exactly when it will end. If you know the ending value, use a `for` loop; if you do not know the ending value, use a `while` loop instead.

There is one very serious warning about the `while` loop construct in Python. Unlike the `for` loop, there is no way for the interpreter to determine when, or whether, a `while` loop will exit. There is no valid way to create an infinite loop using the `for` loop construct. With a `while` loop, unless you are very careful, you will easily create loops that cannot possible exit. Consider the following, very simple, example of an infinite loop using the `while` construct:

```
>>> i = 5
>>> while i < 10 :
        print i
```

```
5
5
5 <this line repeats forever until you hit control-c in the editor>
```

Why does this happen? You told the interpreter to continue printing inside the loop until the value of i equaled 10 or more. The problem is that you never changed the value of the variable inside the loop. The `while` loop contains no automatic incrementing facility, so the value of the variable stays the same forever.

The other potential problem in Python `while` loops is the loop that never actually executes. Consider the following, simple example of such a loop:

```
>>> while False :
        print "In Loop!"
```

This loop never prints out "In Loop!" or anything else when you enter it into the interpreter window. The condition for which it executes is never True, so the loop itself is ignored. This might seem like a strange thing to allow, but it can happen in less obvious ways. If you write a loop that has a variable condition such as this, you can see what I'm talking about:

```
while !done :
    do something
```

This loop might execute once, it might execute a number of times, or it might execute forever. It is impossible to say, without knowing what the value of `done` is before the loop is entered, and what happens to the value of `done` within the loop.

The Python `while` loop is an extremely powerful construct, but one that needs to be used with considerable care. Always study the terminating condition of your loop and make sure that you know what will cause it to end, and whether or not that condition can ever be met. The most dangerous of all possibilities is a logic error that leads to an infinite loop in your code. As a bonus, here's a loop that looks perfectly safe, but will never end under a certain circumstance. See if you can figure out what the circumstance is before you look at the answer:

```
while value != 0 :
    if value & 1 :
        print "Value ", value, " is odd "
    else :
        print "Value ", value, " is even "
    value = value - 1
```

Can you figure out what value of "`value`" will cause the problem? Give yourself a gold star if you said a negative number. If the `value` variable is initially set to, say, -1, the loop will continue more or less endlessly. I say more or less, because eventually it will loop around to a number that is too big to be negative (yes, this actually makes sense) and will become positive. At that point, the decrement will eventually take it down to 0, and the loop will terminate.

However, this is a condition you really don't want to wait for—it could take years. Be careful with your loops!

In Conclusion

The difference between a simple first-generation programming language and a more advanced second-generation or later programming language is the ability to interrupt the flow of a program, to change the flow, and to repeat instructions. In Python, the two methods we looked at for interrupting the flow of behavior were conditional statements and looping statements. We looked at the `if` statement, the `for` loop, and the `while` loop, as ways to change the behavior of a program at runtime.

The ability to perform statements conditionally in a scripting language makes that language immensely powerful. You can customize code based on user preferences, or security concerns, or anything else that your little heart desires. Likewise, the ability to perform looping within a program means that you can repeat a process until you are happy with the result, or until the end user tells you that he is satisfied with the outcome. In either case, it is a lot nicer to be able to do something "n" times until the user says "stop" than it is to make the user start and stop a process "n" times.

That about covers all of the basics of Python. We've done a little bit of real programming, written some scripts that perform real tasks, and learned about the components of the language. In our next chapter, we will cover that most wondrous of all topics: the input and output of data in a Python program.

6 } Input and Output

From the programmer's viewpoint, a programming language is all about the code: how easy it is to read, how easy it is to accomplish the task at hand, and how good are the tools that come along with the language. From the user's perspective, however, it doesn't matter what the language is. What matters is how they get information into an application, and how the information they get back is presented. As a result, the input and output features of a language are key in the user's eyes, even if they aren't quite as important to the developer. In this chapter, we will explore some of the basic input and output functions of Python. This chapter does not discuss graphical user interfaces, which will be discussed later in the book. Instead, we will focus on the programmer's interface to user input and output. You will learn about displaying simple data, getting information from the user, formatting the data so that it looks nice, and then working with files. We'll discover how to open and close files, how to read and write using files, and how to work with the operating system to discover what files and directories exist on the user's machine.

User Input

Without user input, the computer world would surely be extremely boring to the end user. It is all very nice to watch data endlessly scroll across the screen, as it always seems to be doing in bad technology movies, but unless you have some control over what information is doing the scrolling, it really doesn't help you a lot. In order to have any sort of control over what comes out of the system, you have to have some control over what goes into the system. That system input is usually in the form of the user being prompted for information and entering the requested information into the system in the easiest and most straightforward method possible.

The two most basic functions provided with the Python environment are `input()` and `raw_input()`. These two functions will do most of the work you need to do, at least when working in a Command Line environment. Remember, however, that Python is not a strongly-typed language. You can reference any sort of data from a variable, and the language will not do anything to stop you. This same approach tends to apply to the more simplistic input and output functions. You can input pretty much anything from the command line, because the language really does not care. The two functions we will be discussing now simply output a prompt and wait for the user to enter a string. They do no range, bounds, or syntax checking, nor do they worry about how long the string is going to be or what sort of variable you are going to utilize for storage of the string. All of the details of the input are left to the programmer. This can be a good, or bad, thing depending on how you look at it. For now, let's not worry about the details of the implementation, but let's just focus on getting some information into a Python program, so that you can work with it in your scripts.

The `input` Function

The `input()` function is the first of the ways in which you can get data from the user in Python Command Line programs. The syntax of the input function is really quite simple. It looks like this:

```
<return> = input( "<prompt>")
```

Where:

`prompt` is a string that will be displayed for the user to view, which should give some sort of indication of the usage and type of data you are expecting.

`return` is the returned value from the function. This will be the evaluated version of whatever is input. Normally, you assign the return value to a variable, although you may not always do this.

In its simplest form, without worrying about the returned data from the user, the `input()` function can be used to indicate that the user should do something. For example, consider the following small Python script, which outputs a series of data points and then waits for the user to read them before going on:

```
for i in range(0,50) :
    if i % 10 == 0 and i != 0 :
        x = input("Press return to continue")
    print i
```

If you run this little scriptlet, you will see that it runs in the IDLE interpreter and generates output that looks like this:

```
0
1
2
3
```

```
4
5
6
7
8
9
Press return to continue' '
10
11
12
13
14
15
16
17
18
19
Press return to continue
```

You will notice that in order to handle the Return key input from the user, you are forced to
have the user enter a single space in quotes. The reason for this is that the `input()` function
expects the user to input either a string or a variable. For example, consider the following
interactive session:

```
>>> c = 'hello world'
>>> x = input('enter a value: ')
enter a value: c
>>> print x
hello world
```

That seems rather odd, doesn't it? We typed in the letter "c" into the input field, and yet the
variable `x` that was assigned the return from the `input()` function got the value `hello`
`world`. That can't be right, can it? The answer is, yes, it can. The `input()` function allows you
to enter variable names, and it inserts the variable value into the input string. Why does it do
this? The answer is somewhat convoluted. The actual definition of the `input()` function is
that it is the same as `eval(raw_input(prompt))`, at least according to the Python documentation. The input value from `input()` is really expected to be any valid Python expression.
That means it can be a variable, an expression, or a string. Let's look at an example to illustrate
exactly what we are talking about here.

```
>>> x = input('enter a value: ')
enter a value: 1+2+3
>>> print x
6
```

As you can see, the input is not the string "1+2+3", but rather the evaluation of the expression "1+2+3", which happens to be the integer value 6. As you might have guessed, the `input()` function was written for Python programmers by Python programmers. It really isn't intended for getting simple input from the end user. When you want to get input from the end user, you should probably choose the `raw_input` function, which we will look at next. Remember, Python is primarily a scripting language. It was not intended for general-purpose user input and work. Instead, it was meant to make it easier to develop scripts that could quickly and easily work to accomplish simple tasks. As the popularity of the language has grown, so have its capabilities, adding a GUI interface, working with databases, and all of the other topics that you will learn about later in the book. At the core, however, Python is still that simple scripting language.

The `raw_input` Function

The `raw_input()` function is a better choice for getting simple information from the user. Imagine, for example, that you want to have the user simply press the Return key to continue. You might be scrolling information across the screen and want to pause it so that the user can see what is going by. Or you might be displaying an error message before going back to processing, or perhaps to exiting, the application. Whatever the reason, what you want is the ability to output a string, have the user press the Return key, and then continue. This is one of the best uses for the `raw_input()` function:

```
>>> raw_input("Press return to continue")
Press return to continue
' '
```

You can also prompt the user for some sort of input and retrieve it with the `raw_input` function. In fact, even when you don't enter anything, the system does retrieve the value. As you can see, just below the prompt line above, the interpreter has printed out what you typed in, since you didn't assign it to a variable. In IDLE, the interpreter always prints out the return value of a function when it is finished executing, unless that return value is assigned to a variable. So, if we do this:

```
>>> raw_input("Enter your name: ")
Enter your name: matt telles
'matt telles'
```

You can see that the interpreter received the value of my name and then printed that value out to the console because it wasn't used. Now, on the other hand, if we do this:

```
>>> name = raw_input("Enter your name: ")
Enter your name: matt telles
```

You will notice that in this case, nothing was printed out, because it was assigned to the name variable in the application. We can print out the value of the variable in the IDLE interpreter:

```
>>> print name
matt telles
```

As you see, the name was stored referenced by the variable. How do you deal with numbers? The answer is that raw_input() does not deal with numbers, at least not directly. Look at this example:

```
>>> x = raw_input("Enter your age: ")
Enter your age: 45
>>> print x
45
>>> print x + 2


Traceback (most recent call last):
  File "<pyshell#11>", line 1, in <module>
    print x + 2
TypeError: cannot concatenate 'str' and 'int' objects
```

In the above code, the "age" is input, but it is stored as a string. When you try to manipulate that variable as if it were a numeric entry by adding the value two to it, you get an error, because you can't add a number to a string. So, how do you make the age value into a string? The answer is by conversion. For an integer value, for example, you use the int() function:

```
>>> x = int ( raw_input("Enter your age: ") )
Enter your age: 45
>>> print x
45
>>> print x + 2
47
```

Likewise, you can convert floating point numbers using the `float()` function:

```
>>> x = float( raw_input("Enter a floating point number: ") )
Enter a floating point number: 55.2
>>> print x
55.2
```

You might wonder what would happen if I entered a value that was not in the proper format for the conversion type I selected. Imagine that I wanted the user to input a number in integer format, and he entered the string representation of the integer, like this:

```
>>> x = int( raw_input("Enter a number from one to five: ") )
Enter a number from one to five: one

Traceback (most recent call last):
  File "<pyshell#17>", line 1, in <module>
    x = int( raw_input("Enter a number from one to five: ") )
ValueError: invalid literal for int() with base 10: 'one'
```

As you will see when we talk about exceptions and exception handling in Chapter 8, there are ways to handle this sort of problem. For now, just be careful when you enter a value to make sure that it is in the right format for the variable type you are expecting in the Python script.

From the perspective of simple input, the `input()` and `raw_input()` functions are what are available to you in Python, and for the majority of simple cases, they are enough. When you need something more advanced than this, there are a couple of other choices. One is file-handling input, which we will discuss in this chapter. Another is GUI input, which we will talk about in Chapter 12.

User Output

It only makes sense that if you can input data from the user, you will want to output data to the user. Python supplies a number of ways in which to output data. The most basic one is the `print` statement, which we have been looking at throughout the book. The general form of the `print` statement is:

```
print expression[,]
```

where expression can be any valid Python expression, from a variable name to an evaluated formula, to a simple string. The `print` statement normally outputs a carriage return at the end of its processing, unless the last character on the print line is a comma.

For example, you might write some Python code that looked like this:

```
print "This is one line"
print "This is on a line",
print "But so is this"
```

The first line contains no trailing comma, so it will be output and then followed with a carriage return. The second line contains a trailing comma, so it will be output and no carriage return will follow. The third line will be output on the same line as the second, and will terminate with a carriage return. In fact, if you enter the code above into an Editor window in IDLE and then run it in the interpreter, you will see the following output from your script:

```
>>>
This is one line
This is on a line But so is this
```

Isn't it nice when things work the way they are expected to? The trailing comma, by the way, is intended for use in applications in which you want to build up an output string, such as in reports, or error processing, where you want to output some text, then do some work, but have it all look like a single line to the end user.

You can print the value of a variable using the `print` statement, and the value of the variable will be displayed for the user:

```
>>> x = 42.7
>>> print x
42.7
```

You can combine string literal with variables to display information for the user, such as showing them the name of the variable along with the value of that variable, as follows:

```
>>> print 'x = ', x
x =  19
```

An important rule to remember is that the print statement takes a single expression. This expression must be a valid Python statement, and it cannot break any of the rules in the interpreter. Thus, you can append strings together in the expression using the "+" operator, but you cannot append an integer to a string. Instead, you must use the comma operator "," to display different data types together, as you see in the example above. If the variable x contained a string, that would be a different matter. Strings can be concatenated with the "+" operator:

```
>>> x = 'hello world'
>>> print 'x = '+x
x = hello world
```

If you want to use special characters in your output, you need to escape them with the backslash character. Special characters for an output string would include quotation marks, for example:

```
>>> print 'x = \"'+x+'\"'
x = "hello world"
```

Note the use of the backslashes in the string to indicate to the interpreter that you want the quote marks to appear in the output, and not be used for delimiting strings. The `print` statement isn't very complicated, nor is it very smart. The only thing that remains to discuss with respect to the `print` statement is the issue of formatting.

Formatting

The `print` statement in Python supports a limited form of formatting. You will probably not see a lot of good examples of its formatting capabilities, simply because it is really quite confusing to use. Here is an example of formatting a string:

```
>>> print "There are %(#)03d entries" % { '#' : 3 }
There are 003 entries
```

Yes, it really looks like that. Here's the scoop on formatting. In order to use formatting in a `print` statement, you first have to use a name for the item you are going to format. In the example above, the "name" is the "#" character in the left-hand string portion of the `print` statement, for example, the part that reads "There are %(#)03d entries." The `03d` means that you are printing out an integer value, that it should be displayed as three digits, and that it should be zero filled for any portion of the three digits that would otherwise be blank. In other words, if you have fewer than three digits, you get zeroes on the left-hand side. Table 6-1 shows the various permutations of the value and the output string:

Table 6-1   Output Options for `print` Statement

Value Range	Output
0-9	00n
10-99	0nn
100-999	nnn

As you can see from the table, if you have a number from zero to nine, you get two zeroes plus the number. A number from 10 to 99 has one zero plus the number, and anything over 99 displays the number itself. What if you have a number bigger than the three digits you allowed?

```
>>> print "There are %(#)03d entries" % { '#' : 1103 }
There are 1103 entries
```

The answer is that the `print` statement considers the formatting width to be more of a guideline than a rule. If your number is too big to fit in the formatting specification, it will be output normally, since it is assumed that you cared a lot more about the value of the number than the width of the space it is going to print in.

You can specify names of variables in the list, as well as the special character "#." For example, suppose that you want to output the last name, first name, and middle initial in a `print` statement, all formatted to a specific width:

```
>>> print '%(first)20s %(last)30s %(middle)2s' % {'first':"matt", 'last':
"telles", 'middle':"a"}
             matt                         telles  a
```

As you can see, the various components of the name were carefully aligned to the widths you specified in the print formatting statement. The key to the formatting, by the way, is the "%" sign following the initial formatting string. This tells the interpreter that the remainder is to be formatted using the dictionary that follows. You might wonder, since the second half of the formatting string is a dictionary, whether or not you can use a variable there instead of a hardcoded list of values. You may absolutely do so, as you can see in this example:

```
>>> names = { "first":"matt", "last":"telles", "middle":"a" }
>>> print '%(first)20s %(last)30s %(middle)2s' % names
             matt                         telles  a
```

Once you understand that you can do things like this, the formatting options in the `print` statement make a bit more sense. The next thing you might wonder is what sort of formatting options exist. Table 6-2 shows the formatting string options and what they mean to the `print` statement.

Table 6-2   The Formatting Options in Python

Conversion Character	Meaning
d	Signed integer decimal
i	Signed integer decimal (same as "d")
o	Signed octal decimal
u	Unsigned decimal
x	Unsigned hexadecimal (displayed as 0x)
X	Unsigned hexadecimal (displayed as 0X)
e	Floating point exponential (displayed as e^power)
E	Floating point exponential (displayed as E^power)
f	Floating point decimal
F	Floating point decimal (uppercase)

Conversion Character	Meaning
g	Floating point format. Uses exponential if power is greater than -4 or less than precision, decimal format otherwise.
G	Floating point format. Same as "g" but uses uppercase
c	A single character (integer or character string)
r	String (converts any object using the `repr()` function).
s	String (converts any object using the `str()` function)
%	No argument, results in a % sign in the output string.

To get an idea of how these work, consider the following simple example:

```
>>> print '%(v1)x %(v2)f %(v3)e' % { 'v1':12, 'v2': 25.4, 'v3': 45678.434 }
c 25.400000 4.567843e+004
```

You can output numbers in various formats. The first entry is the lower-case hexadecimal version of the value "12," whereas the last entry is the value "45678.434" in scientific notation, using the lowercase version of the "e." The remainder of the entries, hopefully, is obvious.

That's really all there is to say about formatting. When you are writing reports, or other fixed size output, the formatting functions in Python can be useful, but they really are nothing to write home about. You can accomplish the same thing with most of the string formatting functions discussed in Chapter 3.

Just as a last note on the matter, the formatting characteristics we have discussed are not actually a part of the `print` statement. In fact, you can use them by themselves. Consider the following statements in the IDLE interpreter:

```
>>> k = 'value'
>>> v = 'a string'
>>> x = "%s=%s" % (k, v)
>>> print x
value=a string
```

It might not seem obvious, but you do not need the names in the list. The formatting functions will accept an array, but they have to be in the same order as the usage in the format string. What the formatting statement is looking for is a tuple of values. A dictionary allows you to order the tuple by name, and refer to it that way in the format statement, but it isn't a requirement.

File Input

Not all input into an application is from the user on the command line. Quite often, it is necessary to read data from an existing data source, such as a file. Other forms of file input are databases, but we will talk about those later in the book. For now, let's look at the basic file functionality provided with Python and its libraries.

The first thing you need to understand is that a file object is a part of the basic Python library. There are no imports necessary to work with files or their functions. Next, you need to know how to create a file object to work with it. The file object is created in response to an attempt to open or create a new file in the operating system. For our purposes, we are going to assume that there is a file in the system that already exists. The following is the contents of my example file; you can use whatever data you want for your own application.

```
This is a test
This is another test

This is a third line of the test that is fairly long and contains odd
characters &*^(^(^
```

The purpose of this example is just to show that file input and output work properly in Python and to illustrate some of the potential issues that might be expected to come up. This is far from a comprehensive file full of strange characters and really long lines and blank lines and such. The file contains some text, some non-alphabetical characters, and a single blank line, just to illustrate how Python handles those cases.

So, how do you work with files? The first step is to open the file. This is accomplished through the open() function. The open() function accepts two arguments. The first is the name and path of the file to open for access. The second is the mode of access. Modes include reading, writing, reading and writing, and whether or not the file is of text format or binary format. Our open() statement looks like this:

```
infile = open("c:\\temp.dat","r")
```

Note that the infile variable doesn't need to be defined anywhere, because it will come into existence as soon as the statement is executed successfully. The infile variable is a "file" object, and you can use the file methods with it. The open statement is a function call that invokes a built-in function in the Python library. The first argument to the function is just the complete path of the file you want to open. In my case, the file is stored on the root directory of my primary hard-drive. The file name is "temp.dat," for simplicity for me. You can call yours whatever you want, and place it wherever you want. The final option, "r," means that you are opening the file for read access. There is actually one more option available, which is the buffer size to use when loading the file, but in general you do not have to worry about that one.

The available modes for the `open()` function are as follows:

* r—Opens the file in read access. Writing to the file will not be permitted. The file must exist.

* w—Opens the file in write access. If the file does not exist, it will be created. If the file does exist, it will be truncated to a zero length.

* a—Opens the file in append access. Both reads and writes will be permitted to the file. If the file does not exist, it will be created. If the file does exist, it will be opened, and the current position moved to the end of the file for writing.

* b—The b attribute is added to one of the above attributes, so you actually have rb, wb, and ab. The b attribute indicates that the file is binary, for operating systems that treat binary and text files differently.

If the `open` function fails, an exception is thrown, and the process stops. If, on the other hand, the `open` function succeeds, the file is opened in the mode you specified and can be accessed using the other functions in the file class. Let's look at a simple example that shows how to work with the file object to read in the contents of a file.

1. Create a new file, using either the IDLE editor or the editor of your choice. Give the file the name ch6_1.py.

2. Enter the following text into the ch6_1.py file:

```
infile = open("c:\\temp.dat","r") #1
while infile:
    line = infile.readline()
    if line == "" :
        break
    print line,
infile.close()
```

❋ A Note on File Naming Conventions

```
If you have chosen another name, or location, for the file, substitute the
file name of your choice in the line marked with the comment #1.
```

3. Save the file to a location of your choice by using the File | Save command.

4. Run the file in the interpreter by either selecting Run | Run Module in the Editor window or by pressing the F5 key on Windows.

5. Observe the output from your new program. It should look something like this:

```
>>>
This is a test
This is another test
This is a third line of the test that is fairly long and contains odd
characters &*^(^(^
```

That's all there is to creating a file reader in Python. However, there is a considerable amount more that you can do with the file object for a file, once you have it open. Table 6-3 shows a list of the file methods and what they do.

Table 6-3   File Methods in Python

Method	Description
flush	Flushes out the contents of the file to the operating system; useful for files opened in write mode.
fileno	Returns the file descriptor number for this file. Really not useful for anything but external functions that require it.
next	Uses the file object as an iterator and returns the next line in the buffer. Rather than returning a blank line on end of file, it raises an exception.
read(size)	Reads at least size bytes from the file if there are at least that many left to read.
readline	Reads one complete line from the file. A line is defined to be the characters until a newline character is encountered. The newline is included.
readlines	Reads lines in one at a time until the end of file is encountered; then returns them as a list.
seek	Moves to a given position in the file, starting at either the beginning, the end, or the current position.
tell	Returns the current position in the file. The opposite of seek.
truncate	Truncates the file to a given size
write	Writes a batch of data from the application to the file.
writelines	Writes out a list of lines to the file all at once.

File Output

We've already looked at the methods for reading lines from a file. The next thing to examine is how to write data to a file. For this exercise, it makes sense to work with a real-world example. Let's imagine that we need to be able to log information to a file while our program is running.

Now, later on in the book, we would probably use a function that could be used anywhere. However, for now, we will just use interactive statements to accomplish the task.

The process of writing to a file is three-fold. First, you need to open the file, specifying write access to it in order to be able to output data into the file, instead of reading data from the file. Next, you need to do the actual writes to the file, outputting whatever kinds of information you want to output. Finally, you need to close the file, which flushes the data back to the operating system disk files and frees up the memory associated with the file object in the Python interpreter. It sounds like a lot to remember and do, but the reality is that it is very simple and straightforward in Python.

1. Create a new file in the IDLE editor, or use the editor of your choice. Name the file `ch6_2.py`.

2. Place the following code into the ch6_2.py file and save it.

```python
log_file = open("c:\\debuglog.log", "w")
log_file.write("Starting program")

# Prompt the user for data, reverse the string
# and write it out to the console and log file
done = False
while not done:
    s = raw_input("Enter a string to reverse (exit to quit): ")
    if s == 'exit':
        break;
    log_file.write("The user entered: "+s)
    # Reverse the string
    sr = ""
    for c in s :
        sr = c + sr
    log_file.write("The reversed string is: "+sr+"\n")
    print "The reversed string is: " + sr

log_file.write("Ending program");
log_file.close()
```

3. Run the script in the IDLE interpreter, using either the Run | Run Module command or pressing F5 in the Editor window.

4. You should see an output session that looks something like this:

```
Enter a string to reverse (exit to quit): fred
The reversed string is: derf
Enter a string to reverse (exit to quit): george
The reversed string is: egroeg
Enter a string to reverse (exit to quit): ralph
The reversed string is: hplar
Enter a string to reverse (exit to quit): exit
```

5. Now, examine the debug log file (`c:\debuglog.log`). It should look like this:

```
C:\>type debuglog.log
Starting programThe user entered: fred
The reversed string is: derfThe user entered: george
The reversed string is: egroegThe user entered: ralph
The reversed string is: hplarEnding program
```

Notice that since we did not place a carriage return (`\n`) character at the end of the first `write` statement, the debug log does not contain a carriage return between the first and second `write` statements.

As you can see, writing to a Python file really isn't very difficult. You can write out any type of data you want to, simply by converting it into a string using either the `repr()` function or the `str()` function, depending on your preferences. The `repr()` function returns a representation, which the interpreter can handle, while the `str()` function returns a human-readable string representation. For example, if you had a value of 123.456 in a floating point variable, you could convert it with:

```
>>> x = 123.456
>>> print str(x)
123.456
>>> print repr(x)
123.456
```

Closing Files

With earlier versions of Python, it was very important to close the file when you were done writing to it. Closing a file when you are reading from it is a less important issue, since no data can be lost if the file doesn't change. However, with the version 2.5 release of Python and the file library functions, it is less important to force the file to close. If you do not specifically call the `close` function on the file object, then it will be automatically closed when the object is reclaimed by the Python interpreter. This will happen when either the object goes out of scope, or when the program ends, whichever happens first.

Closing a file, however, is a good habit to get into. If you always rely on the interpreter to clean up after you, and you continue to run the program forever, you may end up with serious memory leaks that are not at all easy to detect. With files, failing to close a file will result in data potentially being lost, especially if the program ends unexpectedly.

As a result of these reasons, and just to be safe, always call the `close()` method on the file object when you are done with it. To do this, just call the method with no arguments:

```
fileObject.close()
```

Once you have closed a file, it is no longer available for either reading or writing, depending on the mode in which it was opened. Using that file object after the `close` method has been called is an error.

Positioning in Files

Once upon a time, files were stored on sequential media, like paper tape and magnetic tape. It was possible to write to files, then rewind the tape and read from them. However, writing to the file, then moving back and reading it while the program was running was, at best difficult, and at worst impossible. Quite often you had to request that a tape be remounted for writing by a human operator. Fortunately, those bad old days are long behind us now.

Python, like most programming languages, supports the ability to move around randomly within a file. You can jump to a given position, read some data, then jump to a new position and either read or write more data. The operating system deals with extending the file, moving blocks around, and making sure that everything stays in sync. This has led to the use of files as "conduits" of data in applications, especially when the data is being written on one end, and read on another. In addition, it has made it possible to skip around a file to read pieces of it only when you need to.

The Python functions for moving around a file are taken from the "C" programming language libraries. The two functions you should care about are `seek()` and `tell()`. The `seek` function positions the file "cursor" at a given place, at which point all reading and writing will commence. The `seek` function has the following usage:

```
seek( offset[, whence )]
```

The offset parameter is a long integer representing the number of bytes into the file to move the cursor. The actual position is a combination of the offset and the whence parameter.

The whence parameter specifies where the offset should begin from. By default, this parameter is set to 0, which indicates the beginning of the file. You can also use the values 1, which means from the current position in the file, or 2, which means the end of the file moving backwards.

For example, if you opened a file and wanted to move to the one-thousandth byte before reading, you would do the following:

```
fileObj = open(fileName, "r")
fileObj.seek( 1000 )
```

Since the whence parameter defaults to the beginning of the file, this statement will always move to the position one thousand in the file. Note that if the position does not exist, such as being before the beginning of the file or after the end, the position will be set to the closest legal place, such as the start or end of the file.

The `tell` function, on the other hand, returns the current position in a file. The offset returned will always be usable by the `seek` function to return to a given position. This brings us to an excellent example program to use for seeking around files. We will write a little script that prompts the user for a file name and a keyword to search for, and then returns all of the lines in the file that contain that keyword. The user can then go to the individual lines by entering the number, and viewing the text at that line position.

1. Create a new file, using either the IDLE editor or the editor of your choice. Give the file the name `ch6_2b.py`.

2. Enter the following text into the `ch6_2b.py` file:

```
# Read in the lines, looking for that keyword. If we
# find it, add the line number and position to the list
lineNo = 0
linesFound = []
done = False

while not done :
    pos = inFile.tell()
    sLine = inFile.readline()
    if sLine == "" : # end of file
        done = True
        break

    if sLine.find( sKeyword ) != -1 :
        # Print out the line number
        print "Found at line: "+str(lineNo)
        # Build a tuple to store the info
        tTuple = lineNo, pos
```

```
        linesFound.append( tTuple )
    lineNo = lineNo + 1


# Now, see what they want to do.
done = False
while not done :
    command = int( raw_input("Enter the line you want to view: ") )

    if command == -1 :
        done = True
        break

    # see if we can find it in the list
    for tT in linesFound :
        if command == tT[0] :
            # Go to that line
            inFile.seek( tT[1] )
            # Read in the line again
            lLine = inFile.readline()
            print "The line at position " + str(tT[1]) + "is: " + lLine
```

3. Save the file to a location of your choice by using the File | Save command.

4. Run the file in the interpreter by either selecting Run | Run Module in the Editor window or by pressing the F5 key on Windows.

5. Observe the output from your new program. It should look something like this:

```
Enter the file name to search: d:\PythonBook\ch6_3.py
Enter the keyword to find: done
Found at line: 11
Found at line: 18
Found at line: 22
Found at line: 34
Found at line: 35
Found at line: 39
Enter the line you want to view: 18
The line at position 438is: while not done :

Enter the line you want to view: 34
```

```
The line at position 878is: done = False

Enter the line you want to view: 39
The line at position 1005is:          done = True
Enter the line you want to view: -1
```

The functionality to move around files works quite well. You should also note the use of tuples, lists, and string functions in this example. The next important thing to know is how to work with the operating system to retrieve directories and file names.

Directories and Files

One of the most common problems that faced by programmers is to work with files and directories. The user often wants to load an existing file, save a file to a specific directory, or validate that a given file exists and is of the correct format. It is no surprise, therefore, that the Python libraries provide functionality that will aid you in supporting these user needs. The majority of the functionality we will be discussing in this section comes from the `os` module. To use this package in your own Python scripts and in the interpreter, you will need to import it into the system with the following statement:

```
import os
```

In addition, we will be working with the `os.path` module. Here is how to import all of the submodules into your program (or into the interpreter).:

```
import os.path
```

The most commonly used functions that we are going to discuss in this section are the `listdir`, `access`, `chdir`, `getcwd`, `isdir`, and `stat`. There are lots of other functions in the `os` package. Table 6-4 lists the `os` package methods and what they do.

Table 6-4 The `os` Methods for Files and Directories

Method	Description
access	Provides access to the file information, such as whether or not a file exists, whether you have permission to read it, or write it, or execute it.
chdir	Changes the current directory to the one passed into the function.
fchdir	The same as chdir, but uses a file descriptor to an open directory, rather than a directory name.
getcwd	Returns the current working directory name.
chmod	Changes the mode of a file to allow permissions to read, write, or execute the file.
listdir	Returns a list of all entities within a given directory. An entity is a file, link, or subdirectory. Does not return "." or "..".

Method	Description
major	Returns the major version number for a given device.
minor	Returns the minor version number for a device.
mkdir	Creates a new directory within a given file system.
makedirs	Creates a list of nested subdirectories recursively from a given point downward
remove	Removes (unlinks) a given file.
removedirs	Recursively loops through and removes directories down to a given level.
rename	Renames a given file or directory in the file system.
rmdir	Removes a given directory from the file system. One level only.
stat	Returns file statistics
tempnam	Returns a temporary file name that is guaranteed to be unique.
tmpnam	Returns a temporary file path that is guaranteed to be unique. Used for temporary files that will be deleted after a program terminates.
unlink	Removes a file from the file system.
utime	Sets user times (access time, creation time, and so forth) for a given file.
walk	Does a recursive walk through a directory structure returning all elements of the structure.

But it is one thing to sit there and look at the functions, and it is quite another to put them together into a cohesive module. Let's create a simple Python script that will go through and show us a directory list for a given path. Now, this isn't quite as simple as it seems. When you are looking at the contents of a directory, it is not completely obvious how you go about determining whether or not the entities you are processing are files, directories, or other things.

To accomplish our task, we will prompt the user for a path name and then enumerate all of the entities we find under that path. Each entity will be checked to see whether or not it is a file. If it is not, then it must be a directory.

1. Create a new file, using either the IDLE editor or the editor of your choice. Give the file the name ch6_4.py.

2. Enter the following text into the ch6_4.py file:

```
# Import the packages we need
import os
import os.path

# Prompt the user for the path
sPath = raw_input("Enter the path: ")
if sPath[len(sPath)-1] != '\\' :
```

```
    sPath += '\\'

# Get a list of ALL of the entities for the path
eList = os.listdir(sPath)

# Now, determine which of these is a directory
for e in eList :
    if os.path.isdir(sPath + e) :
        print "Directory: " + e
```

3. Save the file to a location of your choice by using the File | Save command.

4. Run the file in the interpreter by either selecting Run | Run Module in the Editor window or by pressing the F5 key on Windows.

5. Observe the output from your new program. It should look something like this:

```
Enter the path: c:\windows
Directory: addins
Directory: AppPatch
Directory: assembly
Directory: Config
Directory: Connection Wizard
Directory: CSC
Directory: Cursors
Directory: Debug
Directory: dell
Directory: Downloaded Installations
Directory: Downloaded Program Files
Directory: Driver Cache
Directory: ehome
Directory: Fonts
Directory: Help
Directory: ie7beta3
Directory: ime
Directory: inf
Directory: Installer
Directory: java
Directory: LastGood
Directory: Media
```

```
Directory: Microsoft.NET
Directory: Minidump
Directory: msagent
Directory: msapps
Directory: mui
Directory: network diagnostic
Directory: nview
<remainder deleted to save space>
```

Now, the real question is, how does this all work? The user is first prompted for a path name. In Windows, a path consists of a drive letter, a path, and a trailing backslash. Since users cannot always be relied upon to enter things completely, we check to see if the path they gave us contains the trailing backslash or not. If it is not already there, we will append it to the string before processing it, since the methods we are using require it.

After the path name is specified, the next step is to get back a list of all of the entities within that directory name. This is accomplished by using the `os.listdir()` function. This function returns a Python list, which you can then process using a `for` loop. For each element you process, check to see if it is a directory, using the `isdir` method of the `os.path` package. Once you know that something is a directory, you print it out for the user. Notice that the above is the listing of the directories in the standard Windows directory for Windows XP. I've removed a number of the directories in the list simply because they would scroll for page after page and accomplish nothing. We certainly have more to talk about than looking at the subdirectories on a computer!

The `stat` Module: File Statistics

When you are working on a computer, you often want to know things about the files on your file system. For example, it is nice to know what files have been modified in a given directory, so that you can back them up to some sort of an archive system. When I am writing a book, for example, I often ask the file system for a list of files that have been modified most recently, in order to make sure that my backup copies are up-to-date. Have you ever wondered just how the file system knows what files have changed and when those changes took place? The answer lies in file statistics. In Python, the file statistics commands are all handled by the `stat()` method of the `os` package.

The `stat` method accepts a single argument, the full path of the file or directory name for which you want the statistics. It returns an array of values, which need to be interpreted properly to use. Let's take a look at the use of the `stat` function, and the information you can retrieve for a given file or a directory.

1. Create a new file, using your favorite editor or the IDLE editor that ships with Python. Call the new file `ch6_5.py`.

2. Enter the following code into the ch6_5.py file:

```python
import os, sys
from stat import *


sName = raw_input("Enter the file name: ")

# First, see if the file exists
if os.access( sName, os.F_OK ) == False :
    print "That file name doesn't exist!"
    exit()


# The file exists. Get some information about it
sStat = os.stat( sName )

# The first thing we need is the 'mode' of the file
mMode= sStat[ST_MODE]
if S_ISDIR(mMode) :
    print "The path is a directory"
elif S_ISREG(mMode) :
    print "The path is a file"
else :
    print "I have no idea what the path is"


# Now, let's get some information about the file.
userID = sStat[ST_UID]
print "The user id that owns this file is: " + str(userID)


fSize = sStat[ST_SIZE]
print "The size of the file, in bytes, is: " + str(fSize)


accessTime = sStat[ST_ATIME]
print "The last access time is: " + str(accessTime)
```

```
modTime = sStat[ST_MTIME]
print "The last modification time is: " + str(modTime)
```

3. Save the file to a location of your choice by using the File | Save command.

4. Run the file in the interpreter by either selecting Run | Run Module in the Editor window or by pressing the F5 key on Windows.

5. Observe the output from your new program. It should look something like this:

```
Enter the file name: c:\Python25\README.txt
The path is a file
The user id that owns this file is: 0
The size of the file, in bytes, is: 56691
The last access time is: 1171030703
The last modification time is: 1158684398
```

If you take a look at Figure 6.1, you will see the actual Windows directory listing (using a command prompt) of the directory in question. As you can see, the file size that is listed in the directory listing is the same value we came up with in our Python program.

Figure 6.1

Directory listing of

c:\Python25 directory.

The time values that are used by Python are something called *epoch-seconds*. This happens to be the same value that is used by the operating system to store times. The value itself is the number of seconds since some base date. In the case of Windows, the base is normally 1970. That particular number, however, isn't terribly useful to those of us who work in the realm of months, days, and years. Fortunately, there is a `datetime` module in Python that will allow you to convert these strange numbers into more human readable forms.

6. Modify the Python script, ch6_5.py as follows. Note that the lines to modify are shown in bold print:

```
import os, sys
from stat import *
import datetime

sName = raw_input("Enter the file name: ")

# First, see if the file exists
if os.access( sName, os.F_OK ) == False :
    print "That file name doesn't exist!"
    exit()

# The file exists. Get some information about it
sStat = os.stat( sName )

# The first thing we need is the 'mode' of the file
mMode= sStat[ST_MODE]
if S_ISDIR(mMode) :
    print "The path is a directory"
elif S_ISREG(mMode) :
    print "The path is a file"
else :
    print "I have no idea what the path is"

# Now, let's get some information about the file.
userID = sStat[ST_UID]
print "The user id that owns this file is: " + str(userID)

fSize = sStat[ST_SIZE]
print "The size of the file, in bytes, is: " + str(fSize)

accessTime = sStat[ST_ATIME]
print "The last access time is: " + str(accessTime)
print "As a date, this is: " + str(datetime.datetime.fromtimestamp(accessTime))
```

```
modTime = sStat[ST_MTIME]
print "The last modification time is: " + str(modTime)
print "As a date, this is: " + str(datetime.datetime.fromtimestamp(modTime))
```

7. Once again, run the program. You should see the following output from the file:

```
Enter the file name: c:\Python25\README.txt
The path is a file
The user id that owns this file is: 0
The size of the file, in bytes, is: 56691
The last access time is: 1171030703
As a date, this is: 2007-02-09 07:18:23
The last modification time is: 1158684398
As a date, this is: 2006-09-19 10:46:38
```

As you can see, the date that the file was modified does correspond to what we saw in the directory listing in the command prompt. It is also displayed in a human readable format that is a lot easier to read than a timestamp.

As with all of the other methods in the directory processing system, you should spend some time browsing through the online documentation to see what is available to you. There is simply not enough space in this book to go over each and every method that is in the library, and you never know when you might need one that we haven't covered.

Command Line Arguments

When you are working in the IDLE editor, it is normal to simply prompt the user for whatever information you want, or to simply set a variable equal to whatever you might want to use in your program in the interpreter. However, in the real world, it is quite common to use Python scripts from the command line to accomplish things. We do this sort of thing all the time, and rarely think about it. For example, we might want to use the command prompt to rename a file. To accomplish this, you open a command prompt (in Windows, in UNIX, you would simply type at a shell prompt) and enter the following command:

```
ren myFile.old myFile.new
```

where the name `myFile` is the existing name of the file, and `myFile.new` is what we want to call it. The command here is `ren`, indicating you want to rename a file. The two entries `myFile.old` and `myFile.new` are called *command line arguments* to the application (`ren`). Python supports the use of command line arguments. The `sys.argv` variable will hold the current Command Line arguments to your application. To see how this works, let's create a very simple example script to print out whatever arguments you pass to the thing.

1. Create a new file, using your favorite editor or the IDLE editor that ships with Python. Call the new file `ch6_6.py`.

2. Enter the following code into the `ch6_6.py` file:

```
import sys

if len(sys.argv) == 0 :
    print "There were no arguments passed to the program"
else :
    print "There were " + str ( len(sys.argv) ) + " arguments passed to the program"
    for arg in sys.argv :
        print "Argument: " + arg
```

3. Save the file to a location of your choice by using the File | Save command.

4. Run the file in the interpreter by either selecting Run | Run Module in the Editor window or by pressing the F5 key on Windows.

5. You should see the following output in the Python interpreter:

```
There were 1 arguments passed to the program
Argument: E:/Python/ch6_6.py
```

Now, that doesn't seem very useful, does it? We knew the name of our program, since we wrote it and executed it. How do we get user arguments to the program from outside the program?

Unfortunately, it is simply not possible to pass arguments to a program within the IDLE environment. This makes sense since you aren't likely to want to pass information to something within an interpreted environment. To pass the arguments to the program as it is run, you need to run the program from a command prompt. To do this, just launch a command prompt (in Windows, or just run the command from the shell in UNIX) and enter the following command at the command line:

```
E:\Python>c:\python25\python ch6_6.py 1 2 3 4 5
```

Note that you may need to modify the path of the python.exe program file, if you have not already set your path variable to point to that directory. If you've done everything right, you should see the following output from at the command prompt window:

```
There were 6 arguments passed to the program
Argument: ch6_6.py
Argument: 1
Argument: 2
Argument: 3
```

```
Argument: 4
Argument: 5
```

There are two important things to note about this particular example. First, you obviously can get the arguments passed on the command line. The first argument (`index 0`) is always going to be the name of your program script. The remaining entries are the values passed on the command line. Secondly, and more importantly, you will notice that when you run the interpreter from the command line directly, the interpreter runs the script you pass and then terminates it. No prompt to enter values, and no waiting in immediate mode for you to enter values. This can be very important when you want to run a simple script in Python to accomplish something and then move on to some other task.

Command Line arguments aren't something new, and they certainly aren't rocket science. Note, however, that not all environments will set the initial argument to be the name of the program, so you should always check to see if the `argv` variable in the system module actually contains data before processing it.

Pickle

The pickle module is the standard way in which Python objects are written to a file. You may have noticed that the read and write functions of the file object work only with strings. That is, if you have a string `s` and want to write it to a file `f`, you just do this:

```
f.write(s)
```

However, if you have a numeric value, say a floating point value, and want to write it to a file, you can't simply write:

```
f.write(f)
```

You will get an error from the interpreter, because the file object write method is not written to accept a floating point number. Instead, you have to write:

```
f.write( str(f) )
```

or

```
f.write( repr(f) )
```

This can be rather annoying, especially when you are working with more complex types, such as complex variables, or user-defined class types. The designers of Python recognized that this was likely to become a problem, so they wrote the pickle module just for this purpose. The pickle module is a generalized serialization process for Python. If you have a type `t` and a file `f` that you want to write that a variable of that type's values into, you just use the pickle module to accomplish it:

```
import pickle
```

```
pickle.dump(t, f)
```

Then, if you want to read a type back in from a file, you use the `load()` function:

```
import pickle
t = pickle.load(f)
```

You can read about the pickle module more completely in the Python documentation, but here is a very simple example of using the module to save and restore data from a file:

1. Create a new file, using your favorite editor or the IDLE editor that ships with Python. Call the new file ch6_7.py.

2. Enter the following code into the ch6_7.py file:

```
import pickle

# Create the file for storing data in
dFile = open("storage.dat", "wb")

# Store some values
x = 123.467
pickle.dump( x,dFile )
y = 10
pickle.dump( y,dFile )
z = { 1 : "Hello", 2 : "Goodbye" }
pickle.dump( z, dFile )

# Close the file so that the data values are written to disk
dFile.close()

print "Done with save. Restoring"

iFile = open("storage.dat", "rb" )

# Read in values
d1 = pickle.load(iFile)
print d1
d2 = pickle.load(iFile)
print d2
```

```
d3 = pickle.load(iFile)
print d3

iFile.close()
print "Done"
```

3. Save the file to a location of your choice by using the File | Save command.

4. Run the file in the interpreter by either selecting Run | Run Module in the Editor window or by pressing the F5 key on Windows.

5. You should see the following output in the Python interpreter:

```
Done with save. Restoring
123.467
10
{1: 'Hello', 2: 'Goodbye'}
Done
```

Pretty much any data type can be "pickled," although if you write your own classes, you may need some effort to make them serialize properly. We will discuss this again when we talk about creating new classes in Python. For now, you can simply use the pickle module to save and restore data anytime you want. Note, however, that pickle does throw some exceptions, particularly if you try to read something that isn't available in the file (such as storing three values, and trying to read back four). How do you know if you have more data to *unpickle*? Actually, the pickle module simply moves through the file, reading each element. As a result, you can use the following code to determine whether or not the process is complete:

```
# Are we at the end of the file?
curPos = iFile.tell()
iFile.seek(0, 2)
endPos = iFile.tell()
iFile.seek(curPos)
print iFile.tell(), endPos
```

If the two values printed at the end are the same, you have reached the end. So you could rewrite your unpickling (loading) process to be:

```
# Re-read, using a more generic system.
iFile = open("storage.dat", "rb" )

# Determine how big the file is:
curPos = iFile.tell()
```

```
iFile.seek(0, 2)
endPos = iFile.tell()
iFile.seek(curPos)


# Read in values
while iFile.tell() < endPos :
    d = pickle.load(iFile)
    print d
```

If you add this code to the bottom of your script and re-run it, you will see the following output in the interpreter:

```
Done with save. Restoring
123.467
10
{1: 'Hello', 2: 'Goodbye'}
Done
123.467
10
{1: 'Hello', 2: 'Goodbye'}
```

As you can see, you get the same result, with a more generic approach to the loading process. This can be useful if you don't know what is stored in the file.

In Conclusion

This chapter has been a fairly quick-paced coverage of the input and output functionality in Python. You've learned about printing to the console, reading from the console, working with files, and working with the serializing subsystem in Python. Take some time to play with the functions you've learned, so that you can get a good idea of how they will apply in your own applications. When you are done, come on back, and we'll move to the next topic in our Python exploration, in which we'll talk about these mysterious classes and functions that we've been using so blithely up to this point.

7 } Functions and Modules

The single biggest difference between early, first generation programming languages and later programming languages is the addition of functions. Functions made it possible to stop copying blocks of code from one place to another and to begin the process of reusing code entities. Not only did that make applications smaller, but it also made it easier to debug, maintain, and extend them. Python supports functions, as we will see in this chapter, and gives you a number of features that so-called "more advanced" languages do not.

What Is a Function?

According to the dictionary, "In mathematics, a function is a relation, such that each element of a set (the domain) is associated with a unique element of another (possibly the same) set (the codomain, not to be confused with the range). The concept of a function is fundamental to virtually every branch of mathematics and every quantitative science." Fortunately, we don't have to deal with definitions like that. A function, in the computer science sense, is a set of code that performs a given action. It may have parameters, or arguments, which modify the behavior for a specific set of values. It may choose to return data to the caller of the function. For our purposes, however, a function is simply a block of code that can be reused easily across one or more applications.

Defining Functions in Python

The keyword for defining functions in Python is `def`. You use the `def` keyword (which has nothing to do with rap music or other musical things) in the following manner:

```
def func() :
    # statements
```

When the Python interpreter encounters a `def` statement, it knows that it is not supposed to actually execute the code. You can think of the function definition as a "template" (not in the standard programming terminology, but rather in the English usage) for code that will be executed only when it is needed. You can have as many functions in a given application as you like, but only the ones that are called (or "invoked") will ever use up any processing time in the computer.

As for using a function, you've been using quite a few of them in this book already. Some of them are built-in functions, like the `print` statement or the `raw_input` function. The difference between statements and functions is somewhat arbitrary. A statement is a part of the language that requires no parentheses or other syntax elements, but it is treated exactly the same way as any other function. Put in its simplest terms, a statement is a part of the language, whereas a function is an extension to the language implemented by the programmer.

For an example of using a function, let's consider the `raw_input` function that we have been using in the past few chapters to receive information from the user via the console. The `raw_input` function looks like this:

```
value = raw_input(prompt_string)
```

The function takes one (optional) argument, a prompt string that is displayed for the end user to tell him what sort of information the program is expecting. It returns a single value, the input string, which the end user typed into the program. We'll be looking at arguments in just a moment, but for now, let's consider what the definition of the `raw_input` function would be, if we were writing it.

```
def raw_input( prompt ) :
        # Output the prompt
        # Do something to get some text from the user
        # Return the text entered.
```

As you can see in the above function pseudo-code, a function can return values to the calling program. It does not have to, of course. You can have a function that performs an action, such as printing out a string. For example, suppose that you wanted to have a function that you could use to print out the copyright information for a program. It might look something like this:

```
def print_copyright() :
    print "This program is copyright © 2007 Matt Telles Enterprises"
```

Notice that the function does not take any arguments, nor does it return any values. However, it does execute one statement, the `print` statement, to present some information to the user. A function's scope is from the starting `def` statement to the last blank line, indicated by the end of the indentation block. Just like `if` statements, `for` loops, and any other Python construct, the function definition is defined by indentation. Remember, way back in

Chapter 1, you were told that indentation was an important part of the language of Python. Well, here's yet one more example of this.

You might also notice, going back to the `raw_input` example, that there is no way to define whether or not a function returns a value, or what type that value might be. If you are used to working with strongly typed programming languages, such as C, Java, or Pascal, this might seem rather odd to you. In C, for example, you indicate a function by writing something like this:

```
type funcname( argtype argname, .. )
```

where:

❋ `type` is the type of return value for the function. This may be void if nothing is returned from the function.

❋ `funcname` is simply the name of the function, much as we have used `func`, or `print_copyright`, above.

❋ `argtype` is the type of each argument to the function. Python does not use types for arguments; it simply lists them by name.

❋ `argname` is the name of each argument. There may be multiple `argtype` and `argname` pairs for a given function.

Let's create a simple function in Python and look at how you call it in the interpreter. Our function isn't going to take any arguments, nor is it going to return any values. The purpose of this function shall be to print out the current working directory for our application. The current working directory is where all files will be created and read, unless a path is specifically defined for the file name. For example, if I create a file called "`foo.dat`" without specifying a path for it, it will be created in the current working directory. If I create a file called "`c:\foo.dat`", it will be created in the root directory of the c: drive on my machine.

1. Create a new file, using your favorite editor or the IDLE editor that ships with Python. Call the new file `ch7_1.py`.

2. Enter the following code into the `ch7_1.py file`:
```
import os
import os.path

def print_current_working_directory() :
    s = os.getcwd()
    print "Current Working Directory: " + s
```

3. Save the file to a location of your choice, by using the File | Save command.

4. Run the file in the interpreter by either selecting Run | Run Module in the Editor window or by pressing the F5 key on Windows.

5. Notice that nothing happens in the IDLE console window. This is because a function definition does nothing until the function itself is invoked.

6. Run the function in the IDLE interpreter by entering the following line at the command prompt.

```
>>> print_current_working_directory()
```

7. You should see something like the following displayed (note that your directory and drive is likely to be very different than mine):

```
Current Working Directory: E:\Python
```

You can call the function as many times as you want, and it will return the same value, at least until you change the current working directory. The code executed will remain the same. This is the advantage to a function—you can keep calling it and getting the same expected result without worrying about how to implement the functionality or being concerned with typos in your code.

What Are Arguments?

An argument is a bit of data that is passed into a function to provide a way to customize the functionality (if you will excuse the description) of the function. For example, you might pass in the current name of the user to a function used to greet people so that you can greet each user differently. Arguments can be any valid Python type, from strings to numbers, to tuples, dictionaries, or lists. The advantage to being able to pass in a function argument, rather than simply having functions use the same values over and over, is that you can easily change the behavior of an application by modifying the arguments that you pass to the functions in that application.

If you are accustomed to other programming languages, you might be used to the idea of passing arguments by reference and by value. Python has no notion of passing simple data types by reference, because all simple data type arguments are immutable. That is, you can't pass in an argument to a function and have that argument modified and returned to the calling program directly. This does not apply to mutable complex types, such as lists or dictionaries. We'll look at just how this works in a moment.

You cannot change the type of an argument in a function either, except through direct conversion. For example, if the user passes in a list, you can't treat it as a single value. Likewise, you cannot treat a single value as a list. You are stuck with whatever the user passes in. Arguments are not strongly typed in Python. For example, if you do not actually check to see if something is of an expected type before you operate on it, you will find that you get runtime errors.

How Do You Pass an Argument to a Function?

When you have a function defined, you list the names of the arguments you want the user to pass to the function. As you'll see in just a bit, they don't always have to pass in all of the arguments, but it is a good assumption to begin with. Arguments can be mutable, meaning that they can be modified within the function and returned changed to the caller. However, only some arguments can be mutable. Simple data types cannot be changed in a function. To illustrate this, let's look at some real code.

1. Create a new file, using your favorite editor or the IDLE editor that ships with Python. Call the new file `ch7_2.py`.

2. Enter the following code into the `ch7_2.py` file:

```
def func_immutable( a ) :
    a = a + 1

def func_mutable ( l ) :
    l.append( 4 );

a = 10
print "A starts as: ", a
func_immutable(a)
print "A ends as: ", a
l = [1,2,3]
print "L starts as: ", l
func_mutable(l)
print "L ends as: ", l
```

3. Save the file to a location of your choice by using the File | Save command.

4. Run the file in the interpreter by either selecting Run | Run Module in the Editor window or by pressing the F5 key on Windows.

5. You should see the following output in the IDLE interpreter:

```
A starts as:   10
A ends as:   10
L starts as:   [1, 2, 3]
L ends as:   [1, 2, 3, 4]
```

Even though you modify the value of the variable `a` in the `func_immutable` function code, the value once the function has finished is the same as it was in the main program before it starts. This shows you that simple data types, such as numbers (int, float, etc.), are immutable in functions. On the other hand, data types that are containers, such as lists and arrays, can be modified within a function, as you see in `func_mutable`. The list that is passed in contains only three elements. In our function, we modify the list to contain a fourth element. When the function has completed execution, you can see that the list now contains a fourth element in the main program, too.

Any type of variable can be used as an argument, but the arguments must be used properly in the function. For example, if you tried to pass a single integer to the `func_mutable` method, you would get an error from the interpreter when it tried to execute the code. The entire process would look something like this:

```
>>> func_mutable(3)


Traceback (most recent call last):
  File "<pyshell#3>", line 1, in <module>
    func_mutable(3)
  File "E:/Python/ch7_2", line 5, in func_mutable
    l.append( 4 );
AttributeError: 'int' object has no attribute 'append'
```

Because Python is interpreted, and not compiled, some things have odd side effects. For example, if you had a class object that had an `append` method defined for it, you could pass that object to the `func_mutable` function, and it would work fine. The interpreter only cares that the usage of the argument matches something that it knows how to do with the argument you pass into the function. It does not care that you meant for the object to be a list, or an array, or some user-defined class.

You are not restricted to a single argument in a function. In fact, you can have as many as you like. The only restriction is that arguments need to be passed to the function in the same order as they were defined. The naming convention does not matter (there is an exception to this, as you'll see in just a minute); it is the order that is important. So, if I have a function that defines four arguments:

```
>>> def func4(a,b,c,d) :
        print "a = ", a
        print "b = ", b
        print "c = ", c
        print "d = ", d
```

And then I call this function with some variables that I define in the interpreter, external to the function, like this:

```
>>> a = 10
>>> b = 20
>>> c = 30
>>> d = 40
>>> func4(d,b,c,a)
a =   40
b =   20
c =   30
d =   10
```

As you can see, the names of the variables in the interpreter bear no relationship whatsoever to the names of the arguments in a function. The arguments have a scope of the function itself. You can't use the variable a, for example, outside the lines starting with the def statement and ending with the end of the indentation block of the function, and expect to see the same value as in the function. We say that the arguments are scoped to the function itself.

Please notice that the order in which you pass arguments is important. If you define a function to accept four arguments, such as we did in func4, you have to pass in four arguments (although, as we will see later, you can allow some of them to be default values). If you try to pass in three, or five, or some other number, you will get a runtime error from the interpreter:

```
>>> func4(1,2,3)

Traceback (most recent call last):
  File "<pyshell#19>", line 1, in <module>
    func4(1,2,3)
TypeError: func4() takes exactly 4 arguments (3 given)
>>> func4(1,2,3,5,6)

Traceback (most recent call last):
  File "<pyshell#20>", line 1, in <module>
    func4(1,2,3,5,6)
TypeError: func4() takes exactly 4 arguments (5 given)
```

So, those are the rules for arguments. As with any rule, there are also exceptions. Let's look at two of the exceptions to the rules I just mentioned.

Default Arguments

So, we just got finished saying that if you define a function that takes four arguments, you need to pass in four arguments at all times. This isn't exactly true, although it is true that a function with four arguments will always receive four arguments. How can these two statements both be true? The answer lies in something called a *default argument*. A default argument is one that the writer of a function defines to have a default value if the user does not specify a value. For example, let's say that I wanted to print out the copyright date for my application. The copyright date is a string containing some boilerplate legal text and a year from which that copyright is valid. Now, it would make sense to have a default year that happened to be the current year, wouldn't it? So, we could write a function like this:

```
def print_copyright() :
    print "This application is copyright 2007, Matt Telles Enterprises"
    print "All rights reserved"
```

Then, in my main program, I could call it the same way that I call any other function:

```
print_copyright()
```

Imagine, however, that a few years go by, and it is now 2010. If the program were new, I would need to go track down all of the instances of the `print_copyright` function in any libraries I was using and change the function to read 2010 instead of 2007. But why not just pass in the date as an argument? Good idea. Let's rewrite the function to accept an argument instead of a hard-coded number:

```
def print_copyright(year) :
    print "This application is copyright ",year,", Matt Telles Enterprises"
    print "All rights reserved"
```

Now, I can call the function with an argument to indicate what year the copyright is valid for:

```
>>> print_copyright(2007)
This application is copyright 2007 , Matt Telles Enterprises
All rights reserved
>>> print_copyright(2010)
This application is copyright 2010 , Matt Telles Enterprises
All rights reserved
```

This does get a bit annoying, however, especially when you realize that the majority of the time, I'm going to be using the function this year. So, we can make the year argument into a default argument, by assigning it a default value:

```
>>> def print_copyright(year=2007) :
        print "This application is copyright", year, ", Matt Telles Enterprises"
        print "All rights reserved"
```

After I've create a default argument, I can either pass in a value or not, as I choose:

```
>>> print_copyright(2010)
This application is copyright 2010 , Matt Telles Enterprises
All rights reserved
>>> print_copyright()
This application is copyright 2007 , Matt Telles Enterprises
All rights reserved
```

If the user does not pass in a value, and the argument has a default value, then the value used for the function will be the default. If the user specifies a value, the value that they specify will be used. Not all of the arguments in a function must be the same. You can have some default values and some non-default values. As you'll see in just a moment, it is possible to have the default parameters and non-default parameters in any order; however, in general, you must specify default parameters at the end of the function list. That is, you cannot define a function that looks like this:

```
def func_test(i=10, j)
```

Why is that? Because there is no way for the interpreter to know which value you want a default value for and which value you are passing in. When you are defining default value arguments, you must start at the right-hand side and work your way backward. That is, you can do this:

```
def func_test(i, j=10)
```

or even this:

```
def func_test(i, j=10, k=20)
```

In any case, the end user of the function can always override the default value of an argument, something that is important for you to realize. Default arguments, by the way, are also known as *optional arguments* because the user doesn't have to specify them.

Variable Default Arguments

You might wonder if you could specify variables for default arguments in Python. The answer, sadly, is no. That is, you can't do something like this:

```
def func( a, b, c=a+b )
```

Unfortunately, the way the interpreter works, the variables are processed from right to left. So, when the interpreter is trying to define variable c, variables a and b do not yet exist. As a result, there is no way to accomplish this in the definition of the function. All is not lost, however. You can use signal values to accomplish this. For example, let's imagine that you have the function just mentioned, with a, b, and c passed in as arguments.

Now, let's assume that you want the value of c to be the values of a and b multiplied, but only if the user didn't specify a value of c. We could do this in a slightly roundabout fashion:

```
def func(a, b, c=-1) :
    if c == -1 :
        c = a * b
    # more code follows
```

This will accomplish the same task, without having to bend or break the language to make it happen. In Python, the common default value when you don't want to use a variable is "None," rather than -1 as in most other languages

Keyword Arguments

One of the problems with default arguments is the order in which they are processed. Suppose, for example, you have a function like this:

```
def print_stuff( name="Me", date="01/01/99", stuff=stuff to print")
```

You can call this function in any of the following ways, with no problems at all in your own applications:

```
>>> print_stuff("fred")
fred
01/01/99
stuff to print
>>> print_stuff("fred", "01/02/03")
fred
01/02/03
stuff to print
>>> print_stuff("fred", "01/02/03", "other stuff to print")
fred
01/02/03
other stuff to print
```

What happens, however, if you want to print out something like fred, 01/01/99, "other stuff to print." Well, obviously, you would have to duplicate the two beginning arguments and pass them to the function, like this:

```
>>> print_stuff("Me", "01/01/99", "other stuff to print")
Me
01/01/99
other stuff to print
```

That seems rather obvious, because you can't just ignore the first two arguments and use the defaults, since the interpreter wouldn't know which argument you were referring to. It turns out that there is a way to do exactly this. The answer to this little conundrum is the keyword argument. Python allows you to send a name with the argument to a function, like this:

```
>>> print_stuff(stuff="other stuff to print")
Me
01/01/99
other stuff to print
```

When Python passes a set of arguments to a function, it is actually creating a set of name-value pairs that are then expanded out into the arguments in the order specified in the function signature. In fact, Python provides a very special syntax for retrieving all of the parameters of a function along with their names, the "**" syntax. While it is somewhat unusual to use this particular syntax in a normal function, you certainly are permitted to use it if you like:

```
def print_params( **params ) :
    for p in params :
        print p, params[p]
>>> print_params( a="1", b="2", c=3, d=123.45)
a 1
c 3
b 2
d 123.45
```

This rather odd syntax allows you to retrieve all of the named parameters to a function. You might want to do something like this if you were constructing some sort of a parameterized function that was called from an external source. Otherwise, honestly, it is just a curiosity of the language.

Returning Values from Functions

If you are accustomed to other languages, one of the things you are probably most used to with respect to functions is the ability to return a value. For example, consider the find function of the string module. This function returns the position of a given substring within a specified string. The usage of a function like this is:

```
idx = string-object.find(substring)
```

This particular type of function is actually a class method, which means that it operates on an object of type string. There is no reason, however, that you have to implement it that way. Suppose, for example, you wanted to write a function that found the first instance of a character within a string. To do this, you have to take two arguments, a string to search and a character to find. However, you also need a third piece, which is the return value of the index of the character within the string. To do this, you use the return keyword in Python. Let's look at a possible implementation of our function.

```
def find( s, c ) :
    idx = 0
    for c in s :
        if c == c :
            return idx
        idx = idx + 1
    # If we get to here, the value wasn't found
    return -1
```

You can now use this function in your own code by just calling it directly in the interpreter in IDLE:

```
>>> idx = find( "This is an examination", 'x' )
>>> print idx
12
```

As you can see, the index was properly computed, and the result was returned to the calling program and stored in the assigned variable (in this case, idx). You could also implement a math function using input and returned values.

```
>>> def square(x) :
        return x * x

>>> square(10)
100
```

Note that you haven't modified the input value at all; you've just returned it. You can modify the value in the calling program, however:

```
x = 10
x = square(x)
print x
100
```

Returning Multiple Values from Functions

Sometimes, there are ways in which Python shines in ways that no other language can quite match. Returning values from a function is one of those ways, where Python does things that more conventional languages cannot do at all. In a conventional language, if you want to return more than one value from a function, you have to either return some compound object type or return values by reference, or just give up entirely. Python makes it easy to return multiple values from a single function.

Imagine, for a moment, that you want to write a function that computes the first three powers of a value. That is, you want to pass in a single number and return three values, representing the number, the number squared, and the number cubed. In a conventional language, this would be difficult, if not impossible. For example, in a language like C++, you would have to do something like this:

```
void compute_multi(int inval, int& outval, int& outval1, int& outval2);
```

This is confusing, to say the least. Am I sending a value into those values, or are they just being returned? Do I need to initialize the values or not? All of these questions have to be answered by either studying the code or digging up the documentation for the function. Eventually, you would have an answer, but even then someone reading the code later on would have the same questions.

In Python, however, you would do something like this:

```
>>> def multi_return(x) :
        return x, x*x, x*x*x

>>> a,b,c = multi_return(3)
>>> print a
3
>>> print b
9
>>> print c
27
```

All that is really happening here is that you are defining a tuple within the function and returning it, and then unpacking it into its component parts upon the exit from the function. But, to the user, it looks as if you are really returning multiple values from the function. In essence, you actually are returning multiple values from a single statement. Now that is pretty cool.

By the way, you aren't restricted to just three values; you could return any number. Nor are you restricted to a single type. Since a tuple can contain a heterogeneous mixture of data types, you could easily return different values:

```
>>> def multi_return_1() :
        return 1, "Hello", 45.67
>>> a,b,c = multi_return_1()
>>> print a
1
>>> print b
Hello
>>> print c
45.67
```

Recursive Functions

One of the more interesting things in the software development world is the notion of a recursive function. Recursive functions are those that call themselves, or "recur," over and over, until a given problem has been solved. There are no problems that absolutely require a recursive function, but there are quite a few that are a lot easier to solve with the ability to recurse. To give you an idea of how this works, consider the concept of a factorial function, which is pretty much the classic example of how a recursive function works.

A factorial is defined as all of the numbers between 1 and a given number multiplied together. So, the factorial of four, for example, is equal to:

```
Fact(4) = 1 * 2 * 3 * 4
```

or

```
24
```

To compute a factorial, you start with the number you want the factorial of. Then you multiply that by the factorial of the number one less than that number. This continues, until you get to the value one, at which point you start adding things together. Believe it or not, it is actually easier to look at the code than it is to explain the math.

1. Create a new file, using your favorite editor or the IDLE editor that ships with Python. Call the new file ch7_4.py.

2. Enter the following code into the ch7_4.py file:

```
def fact( value ):

    # Terminating condition:
```

```
    # If the number is 1 or less, the factorial is, by definition 1.
    if value <= 1 :
        return 1
    else :
        # The factorial of any other number is the number * all of the
        # numbers leading up to it.
        return value * fact( value-1 )
```

3. Save the file to a location of your choice by using the File | Save command.

4. Run the file in the interpreter by either selecting Run | Run Module in the Editor window or by pressing the F5 key on Windows.

5. Notice that nothing happens in the IDLE console window. This is because a function definition does nothing until the function itself is invoked.

6. Run the function in the IDLE interpreter by entering the following line at the command prompt.

```
>>> fact(4)
24
>>> fact(6)
720
>>> fact(10)
3628800
>>> fact(12)
479001600
>>> fact(1)
1
```

One very important point about recursive functions: You must be absolutely sure that the function has a valid terminating condition that will be executed under all circumstances. If you do not, the recursive loop becomes an infinite loop, and your program eventually crashes. This is equivalent to writing a function like this:

```
def bad_loop(i) :
    if ( i == 0 ) :
        return 0
    return bad_loop(i)
```

This appears to be a similar function to the factorial one, but contains a deadly error. Note that at no time do we modify the value of the variable "" that controls whether or not the function terminates. In this case, we have created a disaster of an infinite loop, certain to crash whenever it is called. In Python, we will get the error "RuntimeError: maximum recursion depth exceeded" and the program will terminate.

While we are on the subject of errors, there is actually a slight error in the factorial function. Can you see it? It isn't a programming error, per se; it is a logic error (which are the hardest ones to find). In the factorial function, if you pass in the value -1, or any other negative value, you get back 1 as a result. Factorials are somewhat undefined for negative values (or zero, for that matter), and thus we have to return something. However, under certain circumstances, this can cause other program logic errors to appear. It would probably be better to raise an exception for a zero or negative number, as you will see in the next chapter.

Passing Functions as Arguments

You can pass all sorts of things as arguments to functions. Simple variables, dictionaries, tuples, and even your own class objects can be passed into and used by functions that you write. However, there is one other thing that can be used as an argument that we haven't discussed yet, and that is using another function as an argument. In Python, a function is really just a "pointer" to a block of memory containing code. This code is jumped to and executed when a function invocation is used within the calling application. There is no reason that you can't use a function as an argument, or to store in a dictionary (as we saw in Chapter 3), or in any other format.

Suppose, for example, that you wanted to parse through a string and call a function each time that a given character, or string, was encountered. Such functionality might be used to implement an XML parser, or some such thing. Let's write a simple function that simply scans through an input string and calls a function when an angle bracket ('<' or '>') is encountered.

```
def find_angle_brackets( s, func ) :
    idx = 0
    for c in s :
        if c == '<' or c == '>' :
            func(s, idx)
        idx = idx + 1
```

Now, to use this function, you need a string and a function to call. The string is easy to come by: you just create one and pass it in. The function, on the other hand, you will need to create in the IDLE editor, and pre-compile it by entering the text and allowing IDLE to know it exists. Let's type one into the editor now:

```
>>> def func_print( str, idx ) :
        print "Found bracket in ["+str+"] at position", idx
```

There is nothing special about this function; it simply prints out information whenever it is called. If you call it with a string like this `"This is <b>a test!</b>"`, you would expect to see four calls of your function. Let's try it out! Enter the following line into the IDLE interpreter and observe the output, it should look like what I have shown following the line:

```
>>> find_angle_brackets( "This is <b>a test!</b>", func_print)
Found bracket in [This is <b>a test!</b>] at position 8
Found bracket in [This is <b>a test!</b>] at position 10
Found bracket in [This is <b>a test!</b>] at position 18
Found bracket in [This is <b>a test!</b>] at position 21
```

So, there you are, four angle brackets, four calls of your function, and four messages displayed to the console window. As mentioned, this isn't exactly rocket science. A function name is like anything else in Python. There is no reason to expect you would have to do something strange to make it work as an argument to a function. As you can see from this example, that is the case.

Lambda Functions

Lambda functions, named for the Greek letter, are also known as *anonymous functions*. The reason for this is that a lambda function doesn't have a name; it only has code to execute associated with it. Normally, a lambda function is implemented to do something very trivial, such as multiplying a number or extracting a section of a string. If you are using the same basic statement over and over in your code, you might consider making it a lambda function.

The basic syntax of a lambda function is as follows:

```
name = lambda (variables) : code
```

Note that you cannot place statements in a lambda expression. This means that you can't have an embedded `if` statement in the lambda expression, or a variable declaration. Aside from that restriction, a lambda expression is really just a very trivial function that avoids having to do all the `def funcname`(variables): stuff that you would normally have to do to implement a function. Let's look at two examples of lambda functions to show you how they work:

```
>>> double = lambda x : x * 2
```

This statement creates a lambda function called *double*, which takes a single argument and doubles it. You can use it as a function in your code:

```
>>> double(2)
4
>>> double(4)
8
```

You can pass it as an argument to a function:

```
>>> print double(6)
12
```

In fact, you can use this function anywhere that you would use any other Python statement or function. Lambda functions are not at all restricted to one variable; you can write them with more than one:

```
>>> combine = lambda x, y, z : x*y*z
>>> combine(1,2,3)
6
```

Where lambda functions are most useful is when combined with the map function that is built into Python. The map function takes two arguments, a function to execute and a list of values to apply the function to, and generates a list of values that are the list values applied to the function. So you could write this:

```
def double_it(x) :
    return x * x


retList = map( double_it, range(1,5) )
```

This bit of code produces the following output when you type it into the IDLE interpreter:

```
>>> retList = map( double_it, range(1,5) )
>>> print retList
[2, 4, 6, 8]
```

Now, this little code is only a few lines. However, it is nice to know that you can implement this exact bit of functionality in only a single line of code:

```
>>> l = map( lambda x : x * 2, range(1,5) )
>>> print l
[2, 4, 6, 8]
```

Personally, I consider lambda functions to be more of a curiosity than anything else. They make the code a bit harder to read, and make the intent a bit harder to understand. Unless you have a compelling reason to use lambda functions, it is probably best to simply use regular ones in Python.

Variable Numbers of Arguments to a Function

Every now and then, you run into a situation where the writer of a function has decided that you should have "n" arguments to the function. If you are using a function to open a file, and the arguments are the name and the mode, this makes sense. If, on the other hand, you are writing a function to determine the average of a group of numbers, it really doesn't. Python provides a method for writing a function that accepts a variable number of arguments. For example, rather than having to do this:

```
>>> def avg( l ) :
        total = 0
        count = 0
        for i in l :
                total = total + i
                count = count + 1
        return total / count

>>> print avg([1,2,3,4,5,6])
3
```

Wouldn't it be nicer to simply be able to do something like this?

```
print avg(1,3,5,7,9,11,13)
```

Yes, I realize that this is only a few characters less in typing, but the ideas behind the two are quite different. In one case, I need to write a function to deal with a list. In the second example, I am just processing numbers directly. To accomplish this in Python, you use a variable name with an asterisk (*) in front of it as the name of the argument for the function:

```
def average( *args ) :
    total = 0
    count = 0
    for i in args :
        total = total + i
        count = count + 1
    return total / count
```

This syntax doesn't look any different from what you did before, but it really is. You can also accept a variable number of arguments of different types. To do this, you might write a function that looks like this:

```
def var_func(*args) :
    for a in args :
        print "Argument: " + repr(a)
        print "Type of argument: ", type(a)
        if type(a) == int :
            print "It is an integer!"
```

Note in this example, you actually test the type of the arguments to see if you are getting what you expect. By comparing the value to a known quantity type, you can identify the type of variable and process it properly.

Variable arguments are less common than you might think in Python, simply because of the availability to dynamic lists and tuples. However, there are definite times when they come in handy, so they are a good addition to your arsenal of coding techniques.

Variable Scope in Functions

Before we leave the discussion of functions, it is really worth taking a moment to talk about the scope of variables in applications and in functions. As mentioned previously, a variable in Python exists from the moment of its first usage until the end of the scope in which it is defined. For functions, however, there are two types of variables. First, there are *local* variables. Local variables are those defined and used within the function. The second type of variable is known as a *global* variable. Global variables are those that are defined externally to any function, but used within the function at runtime. This sounds kind of confusing, so let's look at an example here:

In a new Editor window in IDLE, enter the following:

```
x = 10
def func() :
    x = 20
    print "in function func, x = ", x

def gfunc() :
    global x
    x = 20
    print "in function gfunc, x = ", x

print "Initially, x = ", x
func()
print "After func, x = ", x
```

```
gfunc()
print "After gfunc, x = ", x
```

Normally, when you use a variable in a function, it must be defined in that function. If you do not, and try to access it before it is assigned a value, you will get an error. For example:

```
>>> def func() :
        print i
        i = 10
        print i


>>> func()

Traceback (most recent call last):
  File "<pyshell#46>", line 1, in <module>
    func()
  File "<pyshell#45>", line 2, in func
    print i
UnboundLocalError: local variable 'i' referenced before assignment
```

Python, however, provides a way to get at variables that are defined in the main program, external to the function itself. This method is the global keyword, which permits you to define a variable as external to the function and use the global version of the variable. In our first example, the func() function assigns a variable called x the value 20. This variable is defined within the func() function, and is not accessible outside of the function in the same way. That is why when you change the value of x in the function, it does not affect the variable x defined in the main program. They are completely different variables. You can think of the main program variable as global.x, while the variable x in the function func() is func.x. That isn't really the name assigned to each of them, but it will work for discussion purposes. In func(), when you change func.x, you are working on a local variable. The global.x value is not affected, and you see this when you print it out after calling the function in your main program.

On the other hand, the gfunc() function references the variable x using the global statement. This forces the interpreter to go out and look for a variable that was defined before gfunc() was called that has the name "x." You can think of the gfunc() function as using the global.x variable, rather than the gfunc.x variable. When you then change this value inside the function, the value is also changed in the main program, as you see in the output.

Remember, if you don't explicitly tell Python that you want to use the global version of a variable, while in a function, a local variable will be used. This can lead to some strange errors, so pay attention to your variable scope. For example, you might expect a variable to change in your main program, but it doesn't because you defined a local version of the same name. This is referred to as "shadowing" a global variable.

Using Modules

A module is essentially a file that can be included in your Python application that contains a series of variables, functions, and even classes. We've been using modules all throughout this book, but you may not have realized it before. For example, every time that you write some code that starts with:

```
import os
```

or any other sort of import statement, you are using a module. The os module is simply a Python file (os.py) that you can bring up and look at in the IDLE editor, or any other editor of your choice. Modules are loaded by applying their name and the Python path variable to search for anything of that name within the path. The order of the search is the same as the order of the entries in the Python path variable, so if there are multiple modules by the same name in the path, the first one found will be used.

You can write your own modules in Python, and have been doing that all along. If you create a new file and save it within the Python path, the system will allow you to use it as a module.

1. Create a new file, using your favorite editor or the IDLE editor that ships with Python. Call the new file ch7_6.py.

2. Enter the following code into the ch7_6.py file:
```
def myprint(str) :
    print str
def mycopy( str1, str2 ) :
    return str1 + str2
```

3. Save the file in the IDLE editor, in the lib directory of your Python installation (this is guaranteed to be in the Python path). For example, if you installed Python into the directory c:\Python25, place the file in c:\Python25\lib.

4 . Do not run the file within the IDLE environment. Instead, go into the interpreter, and enter the following lines:
```
>>> import ch7_6
>>> ch7_6.myprint('hello world')
hello world
```

As you can see, the import statement properly picks up your module. Because the module is not "run" in the interpreter, you have to specify the name of the module for the interpreter to pick up the function that you want to call. If you simply called the `myprint` function directly, you would get an error:

```
>>> myprint('hello world')

Traceback (most recent call last):
  File "<pyshell#51>", line 1, in <module>
    myprint('hello world')
NameError: name 'myprint' is not defined
```

Just one last note on modules. You will notice, if you look through the directories in the Python `lib` directory, that there are two kinds of files located here. Most are of the form `name.py`, which is just a Python script file that we've been looking at all along. However, there are a number of files of the form `name.pyc`. In fact, after running the code above, if you look in the `lib` directory, you will see a file called "`ch7_6.pyc`." What are these files? The `pyc` file is a compiled Python file. Importing and processing a module is an expensive operation, since the interpreter has to load the file, check it for valid syntax, and create the appropriate structures in memory to store the functions and variables it encounters. If it had to do this for every script you wrote, it would take a long time to execute complicated scripts. To avoid this, the interpreter stores a "tokenized" version of the file that is very quick to load. This file contains the same data as the original script file, but is in a binary format that requires no tokenizing, just loading.

In Conclusion

This chapter has been a fairly low-key tour of a major component of the Python programming language: functions. As you have learned, functions are a great way to encapsulate code and hide the implementation of algorithms from the user, allowing them access to functionality without needing to understand how it works. We will be using functions and modules quite a bit in the remainder of the book, so it is important that you understand them now.

In the next chapter, we'll be talking about a form of error handling often used in conjunction with functions, that of exception handling.

8 } Exception Handling

They say that nothing is certain except death and taxes. Of course, in the software development world, we know that there are other things that are true. One of the certain things in the software development world is the existence of bugs in software. Bugs have existed since the beginning of the programming era, and will continue to exist long after you and I have disappeared from this world. Bugs are caused by a lot of different things but one of the most egregious is the mishandling or lack of handling of errors.

In any non-trivial application, there will be errors. Some of those errors are caused by a lack of understanding by the end user. Some are caused by hardware or software failures on the user's machine. Yet more errors are caused by bad or malformed input that is needed by the application. Whatever the case, it is a given that your application will have to handle errors while it is running.

There are two kinds of errors in Python. The first, most basic, type is the error code. For example, the `find()` function in the string module will return an error code, -1, to indicate that it could not find the requested substring within a given string. Error codes are easy to deal with, because you just check for them and do the appropriate thing. Sometimes, that means printing out an error message, and sometimes it is just a normal event flow within the application that indicates the end of a processing loop (such as the aforementioned `find()` function). Whatever the case, there is really no reason to discuss the handling of error codes in this chapter. As an experienced programmer, you are well aware that you need to check the return value of any function that can conceivably return an error code. If you don't already know this, and do this in your applications, nothing I can say will change your mind and make you do so. Really, do us all a favor and handle them, okay?

The second type of error that can occur in a Python application is the exception. An exception is really intended (as its name implies) to handle an exceptional situation. Something bad has happened, and the program needs to handle it. Imagine, for example, that you are writing an interpreter for a programming language such as Python. If the user were to enter a statement that was obviously malformed, you would need to handle that problem. In Python, the way in which errors are handled by the interpreter is generally by raising an exception and allowing that exception to be handled.

Exceptions have three basic components. First, there is the exception itself. The exception consists of an error, and may optionally contain information about the exception. Second, the exception must be "raised" within the application. Raising an application stops the processing at the point it occurs, and throws control back to the application. If the application does not process the exception, which is called "catching the exception," control eventually returns to the interpreter, and finally to the operating system. Finally, the exception may have "arguments," that is, information about what went wrong. Arguments are an optional part of the process.

Looking at Exceptions in Python

There are, unfortunately, a lot of ways to generate an exception easily in Python. Let's look at the simplest one, which is a syntax error in your Python code. You can generate one of these directly from the IDLE interpreter:

```
>>> fro i in range(1,20) :

SyntaxError: invalid syntax
```

Obviously, I didn't mean to type *fro*, I meant to type *for* and generate a `for` loop that I could use to loop through the values 1 through 19. Unfortunately, that's not what I typed, and the Python IDLE editor has not yet become advanced enough to know what I meant. It has to go with what I said, instead.

An exception consists of three elements: the error message, the position at which the error occurred, and any information that goes along with the exception. For example, in our previous example, the error message would be `SyntaxError`, which is a type of exception. The position is shown in the editor itself, pointing at the *fro* entry in the code. The information that went along with the error was the descriptive text "invalid syntax," indicating that the Python interpreter did not understand what we were trying to do with the `fro` statement. It probably thought we were trying to create a variable called `fro` in the interpreter, and since the remainder of the line did not properly follow the assignment syntax, it complained.

You might wonder why you should worry about trapping things like syntax errors. After all, in Immediate mode, the interpreter shows you what went wrong. When you try to load a module with a function or statement that contains an error, the interpreter will complain at load time, telling you that there was an invalid syntax problem. However, consider the following example.

1. Create a new file, using your favorite editor or the IDLE editor that ships with Python. Call the new file `ch8_1.py`.

2. Enter the following code into the `ch8_1.py` file:

```
for i in range(1,20) :/
    pritn "Hello world"
```

Note that the `print` statement is intentionally misspelled here.

3. Save the file and exit the IDLE editor (or whatever editor you used to create the file).

4. Open a command prompt in Windows and run the following command at the prompt, in the directory in which you saved the file.

```
E:\Python>c:\Python25\python.exe ch8_1.py
```

5. Observe the following output in the command prompt:

```
  File "ch8_1.py", line 2
    pritn "Hello world"
                     ^
SyntaxError: invalid syntax
```

Now, you realize that the script might never have been tested. Naturally, none of the "real" programmers among us would do such a thing, but these things have been known to sneak in from one of those "fake" programmers. Seriously, if a last-minute change were made to a file, you could end up with a syntax error like this that was never shown in the interpreter.

Traceback Example

When an exception occurs in code that is running, whether in the IDLE environment or via the Command Line interpreter, a traceback is generated and displayed, showing you where the problem occurred. For example, if you had a little script like this:

```
>>> for i in 1,3,5,7,9,0 :
x = 100 / i
 print x
```

There is a problem with this piece of code. If you run the code in the interpreter, you get the following display:

```
100
33
20
```

```
14
11


Traceback (most recent call last):
  File "<pyshell#38>", line 2, in <module>
    x = 100 / i
ZeroDivisionError: integer division or modulo by zero
```

In this case, the error is a division by zero that occurs when the value of i becomes zero at the last entry in the for loop. This is likely to be a typographical error in this case; at least, it seems likely (especially since you just wrote it) that the last value should have been 10 and not zero. Still, you generated an error. What do you do about it?

Understanding Tracebacks

The information available to you in the traceback shows you the problem that was encountered and, if possible, where the problem occurred. When a traceback is displayed, you will see the name of the file that the interpreter was processing when the error was encountered, as well as the line in which it happened. It will also attempt to tell you what module and function the error was found in.

In the example above, the problem happened while you were running in Immediate mode. We can tell this because the error file is called pyshell#38. In this case, the name pyshell indicates that the temporary file that represents the Python shell was the culprit. The #38 really isn't a useful thing to know, because it represents some sort of an internal descriptor for the current run within the shell. The line number will represent the line on which the problem happened. Note that lines begin at 1, so looking at your code, it must be the line that reads:

```
x = 100/i
```

In fact, this is the information that is displayed in the traceback description as well. If the interpreter is unable to determine exactly what the code was that caused the problem, it will not display anything here.

The final bit of information that you get from a traceback is what the error was that the interpreter encountered. If you look at the description, it is telling you that there was an integer division (or modulo) by zero. Looking at the line that is indicated, it is quite clear that the only way this could happen would be if the value of i were zero. Let's add a single print statement to the code, to see what is going on. This is probably the process you would follow if you were debugging this module on your own:

```
>>> for i in 1,3,6,7,9,0 :
        print "i = ", i
```

```
        x = 100 / i
        print x


i =   1
100
i =   3
33
i =   6
16
i =   7
14
i =   9
11
i =   0
```

From the output, it is quite clear that the value of i becomes zero just before the program halted. Thus, you can use the traceback information, combined with debugging information, to figure out what the problem was. Of course, it would be nicer if you simply stopped the application from halting in the first place, right?

Exceptions

The division by zero problem is called an *exception* in Python parlance. Not all errors can be considered exceptions, but the majority can. In order to stop the program from crashing, you need to do one of two things:

1. Stop the error condition from occurring
2. Capture the error and deal with it, continuing if possible.

The first solution, in this case, would be to modify your loop as follows:

```
>>> for i in 1,3,5,7,9,0 :
        print "i = ", i
        if i != 0 :
                x = 100/i
         else :
                print "Error, cannot divide by zero!"
                x = 0
        print x
```

If you do this, the new output from your script will be:

```
i  =   1
100
i  =   3
33
i  =   5
20
i  =   7
14
i  =   9
11
i  =   0
```

Error cannot divide by zero!

Unfortunately, it is not always possible to anticipate what the problem might be. For this reason, Python provides the `try` and `except` statements.

Catching Exceptions with `try..except`

The purpose of the `try` statement is to tell Python that you think that the code you are about to run might raise an exception. When you use a `try` statement, you are telling the interpreter that you will handle errors that come up in the code, rather than allowing the generic handler to end the program and display an error message. The basic format of the `try` and `except` statements is as follows:

```
try:
    # some python statements
except [ExceptionName]:
    # some error handling
else:
    # some other statement
finally:
    # do something when all is done.
```

Let's look at each part separately. First, we have the `try` statement. The `try` statement has no arguments and no other forms. You simply place a `try` statement in your code, and the interpreter knows that you want to handle an error. The `try` statement must be followed by, at a minimum, a single `except` statement. The other statements, `else` and `finally`, are completely optional during error handling. The assumption is that the code within the `try` block is the code that is likely to raise an exception! Otherwise, what would be the point?

The `except` statement may contain zero or more exception types that may follow it. These may either be system exception types, which are predefined, or they may be user-defined exception types that are defined in your application. Table 8-1 shows the predefined system exception types in Python.

Table 8-1   Standard Python Error Types

Error Name	Meaning
Exception	The basic Python exception, the base for all other exception types.
StandardError	The base class for all standard exceptions in Python
ArithmeticError	The base class for all arithmetic errors, such as overflows.
LookupError	Errors related to containers, trying to find things that aren't in dictionaries, for example.
AssertionError	An assertion failed, generating an exception in the code.
AttributeError	An attribute is invalid, illegal, or out of range.
EOFError	End of file error.
EnvironmentError	The base class for all errors, which occur outside of the Python environment, such as IO errors.
FloatingPointError	Raised whenever an error occurs in processing a floating point value.
GeneratorExit	Raised when the `close()` method of a generator object is called.
IOError	Raised whenever an error occurs in an input/output operation.
ImportError	Raised when the system is unable to locate or load the target of an import statement in the code.
IndexError	Raised when the index value used to access an array or list element is out of range.
KeyError	Raised when a key in a dictionary is not found.
KeyboardInterrupt	Raised whenever the user terminates input in a nonstandard way, such as pressing Ctrl-C during an `input` statement.
MemoryError	Raised when the system runs out of memory while running, but can still be rescued. This is a nonfatal memory error.
NameError	Raised when a name or scope cannot be found by the interpreter.
NotImplementedError	Normally not raised by the system, this error should be raised by the implementer of a derived class when functionality is not implemented in their class.
OsError	Raised any time an operating system error occurs.
OverflowError	Raised whenever an overflow occurs in a mathematical statement, such as when a number cannot be represented by the types it is using.
ReferenceError	Called when a reference to a garbage collected object is used.
StopIteration	Raised when an iterator's `next()` method is called, and there are no further values to be processed.
SyntaxError	Raised by the interpreter when a syntax error is encountered while parsing the code.

Table 8-1   Standard Python Error Types (Cont.)

Error Name	Meaning
SystemError	Raised by the interpreter when an internal error occurs, but the system can be restarted and continued.
TypeError	Raised when a given type is invalid, or a value is assigned that is inappropriate for a given type.
UnboundLocalError	Raised when a local variable is used without having been assigned a value.
ValueError	Raised when a given type is valid, but the value assigned to it is not appropriate or valid.
WindowsError	Generic error class for all Windows-specific errors.
ZeroDivisionError	Raised when a division by zero would occur in the code.

Let's look at a real example of using the `try..except` statements to catch an exception in a Python class. In the IDLE interpreter, enter the following code:

```
try:
    name = raw_input("Enter your name: ")
    print "You entered: " + name
except KeyboardInterrupt:
    print "You hit control-c"
```

Now run the program. If you enter a name and press Enter, you will see the following output in the console window of IDLE:

```
>>>
Enter your name: matt
You entered: matt
```

On the other hand, if you press the Ctrl-C keyboard combination while you are entering your name, you will see the following output in the IDLE console window instead:

```
>>>
Enter your name:
You hit control-c
```

As you can see, the interpreter properly caught the exception generated by the pressing of the Ctrl-C combination and notified the application. Since we had installed a handler by placing the code within a `try..except` block, the code was able to recover from the error and continue processing properly. This is the real purpose of exception handling, to allow your program to continue processing and, if possible, to accomplish its task. Whether or not the error is something you can deal with, you can at the very least do a clean shutdown of your application if you use exception handling.

Multiple `except` Clauses

The problem with errors isn't that they occur, but that they occur in such varied ways. For example, imagine that you are going to ask the user to enter a number and then use that number for a mathematical calculation. How many things can go wrong in this simple little exercise? Quite a few, really. First, the user could interrupt the input, as we saw in the previous example. Next, he could enter a value that isn't a valid number, generating a `ValueError` that would crash your program. We could divide by the input number and somehow generate a `DivisionByZero` exception. How can you possibly handle all of these possibilities in a single application?

One possibility you might consider would be a series of `try..except` blocks. For example, you might try something like this:

```
try:
   try :
      v = int( raw_input("Enter a value: "))
   except ValueError:
      print "Invalid input, please enter a value"
except KeyboardInterrupt:
   print "Please don't hit ctrl-c"
```

This certainly works, and will accomplish what you want. However, if you have even more possible errors, the code will quickly become unreadable, with too many levels of indentation and too many nested blocks of `try` statements. There really does have to be a better way. Since Python is all about making things easier for you, there naturally is an easier way. In fact, there are three easier ways. Let's look at two of them first, and then discuss the third, since they are slightly different.

First, you can have multiple `except` clauses for a given `try` statement. For example, let's consider the two cases of `KeyboardInterrupt` and `ValueError` that we looked at in the previous code. We could rewrite this code as follows:

```
try:
   v = int( raw_input("Enter a value: "))
   print "We got some valid input!"
except ValueError:
   print "Invalid input, please enter a value"
except KeyboardInterrupt:
   print "Please don't hit ctrl-c"
```

The Python interpreter understands that multiple except clauses may follow a single try statement. Until the indentation level changes, it will process each of the except clauses until it finds one that matches the exception type. Now, if none of the except clauses matches the kind of error we get, then bad things will happen. Let's modify the code above slightly, and see what I mean:

```
try:
    v = int( raw_input("Enter a value: "))
    print "We got some valid input!"
    x = 100 / v
except ValueError:
    print "Invalid input, please enter a value"
except KeyboardInterrupt:
    print "Please don't hit ctrl-c"
```

Now, run the above code, but enter 0 for the value:

```
>>>
Enter a value: 0
We got some valid input!

Traceback (most recent call last):
  File "C:/Python25/ex.py", line 4, in <module>
    x = 100 / v
ZeroDivisionError: integer division or modulo by zero
```

Notice that the input works fine, but when the value is used to divide, a division by zero occurs, generating an error. We could add a third except clause to the list, but the problem would get out of hand quickly. Obviously, what we really want are categories of exceptions, so that invalid input types are handled one way, and math errors and the like are handled in another. This brings us to the second form of the except clause that we need to consider, multiple exception types for a single except clause. Here is how you do them:

```
try:
    v = int( raw_input("Enter a value: "))
    print "We got some valid input!"
    x = 100 / v
except (ValueError, KeyboardInterrupt):
    print "Invalid input, please enter a value"
except ZeroDivisionError:
    print "You can't divide by ZERO!"
```

As you can see from the above example, it is possible to handle multiple exception types with a single `except` clause. Placing the exception list that you want within parentheses, separated by commas, permits the interpreter to know that you want to look at all of those exceptions as a single kind of error. Thus, the `ValueError` and `KeyboardInterrupt` exceptions are treated the same way, allowing you to combine all of the code for bad input types in a single block. Meanwhile, the division by zero error is handled on its own, although you could combine it with other math errors and process them all the same way.

Blank `except` Clauses

You might wonder what you do when you know there are possible exceptions out there, but really don't know what they might be. For example, as we've seen, there are numerous exceptions that can be thrown for a simple input statement. There are probably dozens of other possible errors that could occur for a single Python statement. How can you possibly write enough exception handling code to deal with them all? Do you really have to list every single error that can occur and deal with each one individually? That would be pretty horrifying, wouldn't it? The answer to this is that you never have to do something like that. If all you want is to deal with any potential errors you didn't think about, Python provides the `except` clause with no exception handlers defined:

Let's imagine that we want to input a number from the user. If the user presses the Ctrl-C combination, we want him to exit the application. If the user enters 0, we want to warn him about division by zero and prompt him again. Any other errors should simply tell the user that he gave us bad input and try again. To do this, we use the blank `except` clause:

```
while True :
    try:
        v = int( raw_input("Enter a value: "))
        print "We got some valid input!"
        x = 100 / v
        break
    except (KeyboardInterrupt):
        print "well, ok, if you don't really want to.."
        break
    except ZeroDivisionError:
        print "You can't divide by ZERO!"
    except:
         print "Some other error happened here"
```

Now, when we run the program, it will continue to request input from the user until we either enter something valid or press the Ctrl-C combination at the keyboard. Here is a typical set of input and the resulting conditions from the previous code.

```
>>>
Enter a value: abc
Some other error happened here
Enter a value: 0
We got some valid input!
You can't divide by ZERO!
Enter a value: 1
We got some valid input!
>>>
Enter a value:  [ Control-C was pressed ]
well, ok, if you don't really want to..
```

The blank `except` clause catches any exception. If you want to simply handle errors and make sure that the program does not terminate abnormally, each `try` statement that you use should contain a blank `except` clause to handle anything you didn't think of. That doesn't absolve you from catching exceptions that you do know about and handling them properly.

The `else` Clauses

The exception handling system in Python provides ways to try one or more statements and to catch any exceptions that are generated as the result of those statements. As we've looked at the process so far, it looks like this in a generalized way:

```
try:
    statement-that-may-generate-exception
except:
    statements to handle exceptions
# Continue down here somehow.
    statements-to-process-if-no-exception
except:
    exception-handling-code
```

There is a problem here, however. While we assume that the original statement may generate an exception, we do not worry about what might happen in the statements to process after that, which might also generate exceptions. To avoid this problem, Python provides the `else` statement. Yes, we have looked at the `else` statement with respect to `if` statements, and with for loops. It turns out that the versatile else can also be used with respect to the try statement as well.

The purpose of the else statement in exception handling is to provide a path to execute if no exceptions occur during the try block. For example, if we are processing a file, reading in and doing something with the data from the file, we might worry about exceptions occurring during the processing. Maybe we want to warn the user if not all of the data could be processed. All of that is easy enough to do in the scope of a try..except block. However, what happens if all went fine? We want a way in which to let the user know that everything went as expected. This is the idea behind the else clause. Take a look at the following example to get an idea of how it all works.

```
try:
    v = int( raw_input("Enter a value: "))
    print "We got some valid input!"
    x = 100 / v
except (KeyboardInterrupt):
    print "well, ok, if you don't really want to.."
except ZeroDivisionError:
    print "You can't divide by ZERO!"
except:
    print "Some other error happened here"
else:
    print "All went well, x = ", x
```

Now, when we run this script in the interpreter, we can either generate an error or get through the code properly. Let's look at both cases:

```
Enter a value: 10
We got some valid input!
All went well, x =  10
>>>
Enter a value: 0
We got some valid input!
You can't divide by ZERO!
```

When we process a block of potential exception generating code properly, it is important to care about the "happy path" case, as well as all of the error cases. The else clause is an important weapon in creating exception free code. Note, however, that code within an else clause can generate exceptions and that those exceptions will not be caught by the try block above them.

233

Only place code within the else block that you know to be safe, or encase it in its own try block for safety.

The finally Clause

The else clause handles the case where everything worked fine in an exception handling block. What do you do, however, when you want to process some code, regardless of whether or not something worked properly? The answer is the finally clause in Python. The finally clause, used for cleanup and final processing, will be executed at the end of a block of exception handling code, whether there was an error encountered or not. You can think of it as your last chance to clean things up before the program moves on from its problem state.

In order to use the finally clause, you simply place a finally statement as the last thing to do in your try block. For example, in our example that we have been using so far in this chapter, we would modify it to look like this:

```
try:
    v = int( raw_input("Enter a value: "))
    print "We got some valid input!"
    x = 100 / v
except (KeyboardInterrupt):
    print "well, ok, if you don't really want to.."
except ZeroDivisionError:
    print "You can't divide by ZERO!"
except:
    print "Some other error happened here"
else:
    print "All went well, x = ", x
finally:
    print "This is executed no matter what!"
```

So what happens when we run the code above? We'll consider three cases. First, we'll look at the case where everything went just fine. Second, we will consider the case where the user presses the Control-C combination while entering a value. Finally, we will consider the case of a division by zero error from valid numeric input. If you try all three of these in the interpreter, you will see the following output.

```
Enter a value: 10
We got some valid input!
All went well, x =   10
This is executed no matter what!
```

```
>>> ============================ RESTART ============================
>>>
Enter a value:
Some other error happened here
This is executed no matter what!
>>> ============================ RESTART ============================
>>>
Enter a value: 0
We got some valid input!
You can't divide by ZERO!
This is executed no matter what!
```

Notice that in all three cases, you see the code that is listed in the `finally` clause executed. Naturally, you can have as many statements in this clause as you want, always bearing in mind that exceptions could be generated in this block as well as any other.

Raising Your Own Exceptions

Obviously, if exceptions are such an integrated part of the Python environment, it would make sense that you should be able to launch your own exceptions when something goes wrong in code that you've written. Naturally, that capability does exist. The function of creating a new exception and propagating it across the running application is called *raising an exception*. It's called *raising* because the keyword that is used to accomplish the task is named *raise*.

Suppose that you are writing a simple function that computes the factorial of a number. You may remember that in the last chapter, we wrote a recursive Python function that did exactly that. At the time, I said there was a minor bug in the logic of the code. The function looks like this:

```python
def fact( value ):

    # Terminating condition:
    # If the number is 1 or less, the factorial is, by definition 1.
    if value <= 1 :
        return 1
    else :
        # The factorial of any other number is the number * all of the
        # numbers leading up to it.
        return value * fact( value-1 )
```

As mentioned back in Chapter 7, the factorial program has a problem. The factorial of a negative number is defined, at least here, as 1. That's not correct; in fact, the factorial of a negative number is undefined. An undefined situation seems like an absolutely ideal time to raise an exception, so let's modify our function to do just that.

```
def fact( value ):
    # Sanity check. Negative numbers are not valid
    if value < 0 :
        raise ValueError

    # Terminating condition:
    # If the number is 1 or less, the factorial is, by definition 1.
    if value <= 1 :
        return 1
    else :
        # The factorial of any other number is the number * all of the
        # numbers leading up to it.
        return value * fact( value-1 )
```

Now, if we try to pass the negative number to the `fact()` function, you should see an exception raised. Let's try it in the IDLE interpreter:

```
>>> print fact(-1)

Traceback (most recent call last):
  File "<pyshell#5>", line 1, in <module>
    print fact(-1)
  File "E:/Python/ch8_2.py", line 4, in fact
    raise ValueError
ValueError
```

Can we catch this error and have it not propagate into the interpreter? You better believe we can:

```
>>> try :
        fact(-1)
except ValueError:
        print "It is invalid to take the factorial of a negative number"
else:
```

```
     print "Looks good"
```

```
It is invalid to take the factorial of a negative number
```

Finally, we could have rewritten our statement checking the value of the variable by using the assert statement in Python, rather than an `if` statement. In this case, we would have:

```
assert value >= 0
```

Then instead of checking for a `ValueError` in our exception handler, we would check for an `AssertionError`.

Exception Arguments

Sometimes, it is rather nice to tell someone not only what went wrong, but why it happened. For example, it is all very well and good to tell the programmer that he passed an invalid argument to a function, but it would certainly be a lot better to tell him which argument it was and what a valid range would be for that argument. That saves the programmer a lot of time tracking down the documentation for a function, which nobody reads anyway, and then seeing what values he passed to it and what were expected. Programming really shouldn't be all that hard, and Python strives to make it as easy as possible.

Let's imagine that you have a function that takes a few arguments. The arguments are all numeric and have various allowable ranges. In fact, the function might look something like this:

```
def myFunction( a, b, c ) :
    if a < 0 or a > 10 :
        raise ValueError, "a must be between 0 and 10"
    if b > 50 :
        raise ValueError, "b must be less than 50"
    return a*b + c
```

The function listed above raises an exception (`ValueError`) if one of the arguments passed to it is out of range. This is normal for Python, and the programmer can easily trap for it. If you were to call the function in IDLE, passing it invalid numbers, you might see something like this:

```
>>> myFunction(-1,5,3)

Traceback (most recent call last):
  File "<pyshell#1>", line 1, in <module>
    myFunction(-1,5,3)
  File "G:/Python/ch8_3.py", line 3, in myFunction
```

```
      raise ValueError, "a must be between 0 and 10"
ValueError: a must be between 0 and 10
```

Likewise, you might pass in an invalid value for the second argument "b" into the function. In that case, you would see the following output in the IDLE interpreter:

```
>>> myFunction(5,100,2)

Traceback (most recent call last):
  File "<pyshell#2>", line 1, in <module>
    myFunction(5,100,2)
  File "G:/Python/ch8_3.py", line 5, in myFunction
    raise ValueError, "b must be less than 50"
ValueError: b must be less than 50
```

Hopefully, you can see how it is a lot easier to find and fix the problem when you see errors like this instead of an error like `ValueError at line 5`. If you make it easy for people to understand what the problem they are causing is, they will fix it faster, and make everyone's life easier.

Exception arguments are somewhat limited, depending on the exception type. For the exception `ValueError`, for example, you can only specify a single argument, and then a traceback argument if you want. The traceback functionality is provided in case the function you are calling calls other functions that cause the exception to be generated.

Of course, you may want to actually see what the exception arguments are in your code. In this case, you do something like this:

```
# get an exception's argument
try:
    num = float(raw_input("\nEnter a number: "))
except(ValueError), e:
    print "Not a number!  Or as Python would say:\n", e
```

User-Defined Exceptions

You can define your own exception types in Python. These exceptions can work just like "built-in" exceptions and can contain traceback information and arguments that can be used by the programmer catching them. Naturally, a user-defined exception can be caught with the `try..except` logic, exactly the same as with "normal" exceptions. We will discuss how to create user-defined exceptions in Chapter 10, when we talk about how to define your own classes, and how to derive your classes from existing ones.

Working with the Exception Information

When you are programming in Python and working with exceptions, there is information available to you that will allow you to print out things you want the end user to see, while permitting you to ignore showing the user things that really won't mean anything to them. There are three basic variables that you need to know about when you are working with Python exception handling, which are `exc_type`, `exc_value`, and `exc_traceback`. Let's take a brief look at each one and see what they are and why you might care about them. Note that these values are all a component of the system package (`sys`), and you will need to import `sys` to use them in your own modules.

exc_type

The `exc_type` value represents the type of the exception that was last generated. Normally, you use these values within the exception handler, but there is actually no particular reason you need to. Until another exception is generated, the values will contain the last value that was set for them, so if you want to log exceptions or such, you can do so at any time, up until the next exception comes along. To see an example of how the `exc_type` value works, consider the following code:

```
>>> import sys
>>> try :
        raise ValueError, "Got an error"
except :
        print sys.exc_type



<type 'exceptions.ValueError'>
```

You can compare type values, if you want to. For example:

```
>>> try :
        raise ValueError, "Got an error"
except :
        if sys.exc_type == ValueError :
                print "Value Error"
        else :
                print "Something else"



Value Error
```

The ability to compare the error types is particularly useful when we start talking about derived types and user exceptions, which we will do in Chapter 10. Until then, you can just consider the ability to look at the type of the exception to be a useful way in which to handle them. For example, the exception types could be stored in a global dictionary along with global handlers for those types. The Python system is amazingly flexible, so you can write code that does things like this:

```
import sys

dict = {}
dict[ValueError] = "Enter a valid value"
dict[IOError] = "An error occurred in the IO system"
try :
    raise ValueError
except :
    if dict.has_key(sys.exc_type) :
        print dict[sys.exc_type]
```

In this case, we have a dictionary that contains a list of potential exception types, along with some text to output when that exception is raised. It would be just as simple to replace the text with a function to call when the exception is raised, and call that function from anywhere in the program. This is a very useful technique, particularly for generalized errors like input/output or memory problems.

exc_value

The exc_value argument of the system exception subsystem is an object that represents parts of an exception's state. When you pass an argument to an exception via the raise statement, you can retrieve this argument via the exc_value variable. This can be particularly useful for user-defined errors, since you can print out a much more meaningful message to the user than "exception <blah> occurred" in your error handling functions. The type is not really what you expect of a value. For example, if you look at this:

```
>>> try :
        raise ValueError, 123
except:
        print sys.exc_value
```

123

It would appear that the value here is the integer 123, and it is, sort of. However, if you print it out in string format, using the `repr()` function, you will see that it isn't.

```
>>> try :
        raise ValueError, 123
except:
        print "The error argument was"+repr(sys.exc_value)
```

```
The error argument wasValueError(123,)
```

What you are actually getting here is a representation of the error argument as an object, which is correct from the perspective of the Python interpreter. It is easier to use the `str()` function, which will convert the value to a string properly:

```
        print "The error argument was "+str(sys.exc_value)
```

```
The error argument was 123
```

Values are useful for comparison, for logging, or just for telling the user what was going on at the time of the exception.

exc_traceback

In older versions of Python, before 2.4, the `exc_traceback` variable was used to store traceback information for showing the call stack that led to the error. In current versions, this variable is still available but considered deprecated (that is, don't use it, it may go away in the next release). You are supposed to use the `exc_info()` function instead. This function prints out a traceback of the call stack, which shows how you got to a given point. If you get an exception in a function that you call, for example, you will see the function and line that generated the exception.

```
import sys

def excFunc() :
    raise ValueError

try:
    excFunc()
except:
    print "Got an exception"
    print sys.exc_info()
```

This code generates the following output to the console:

```
Got an exception
(<type 'exceptions.ValueError'>, ValueError(), <traceback object at 0x00C455F8>)
```

> **Note about the Address**
>
> The address shown, 0x00C455F8, is likely to be different on your system.

The last bit there, the traceback object, can be used to print out information about the exception. By importing the traceback module, you have access to a whole host of functions that work with traceback objects. For example:

```python
import sys
import traceback

def excFunc() :
    raise ValueError

try:
    excFunc()
except:
    print "Got an exception"
    print traceback.print_stack(sys.exc_info()[2])
```

This function call results in a printout of the stack, indicating how you got to this stage. In this case, the actual stack trace will look like this:

```
Traceback (most recent call last):
  File "C:/Python25/temp1.py", line 11, in <module>
    print traceback.print_stack(sys.exc_info()[2])
  File "C:\Python25\lib\traceback.py", line 262, in print_stack
    print_list(extract_stack(f, limit), file)
  File "C:\Python25\lib\traceback.py", line 293, in extract_stack
    lineno = f.f_lineno
AttributeError: f_lineno
```

Which shows where you are at this point and how you got there.

In general, using the exception variables is frowned upon, with the exception of printing out the exception argument. You really should not have to know a great deal about the internals of the exception handling system in order to use exceptions. Just knowing that an exception occurred is usually enough, and then knowing what sort of exception it was will complete the picture.

Using the `with` Clause for Files

One of the most common problems with using exceptions is cleaning up after yourself when something really bad happens. The most common problem is that files are not closed and flushed to disk when you encounter an error in processing them. For this purpose, Python provides a special form of error handling, which is the `with` clause. The `with` clause allows you to free up any form of object in a specific block if an error occurs.

The basic format of the `with` clause is as follows:

```
with var = expression :
    block
```

Where `var` is simply the name of a variable, `expression` is a valid Python statement or function call that returns a value, and `block` is a set of Python statements for which you want the variable `var` to be supported. An example might be useful at this stage.

Let's imagine that you are opening a file, writing some data to the file, and then closing it down. You want to make sure that when the file is done being written to, all of the data is flushed to disk, and the file object is freed from memory. Suppose that you have a block of code that looks like this:

```
fObj = open('output.txt', 'w')
for i in range(1,10) :
    value = call_func(i)
    fObj.write(value)
```

If the `call_func()` function were to throw an exception, the file would eventually be closed by the Python interpreter, but not necessarily flushed to disk. In addition, it is very possible that when the Python script terminated due to the exception, some other process would kick in and try to read the file. Since the file has not been flushed, nor closed, the other process could easily fail. What you really want to have happen is for the file to be closed no matter what, as soon as your processing is complete. If there is some sort of error, you want the file closed immediately. This is where the `with` statement comes into play.

```
from __future__ import with_statement
with open('output.txt','w') as fObj :
    for i in range(1,10) :
        value = call_func(i)
        fObj.write(value)
```

This slight rewrite, using the `with` clause, changes the dynamics of the script dramatically. Now, no matter what goes wrong within the scope of the `with` statement, the file will automatically be closed, and the data flushed to disk. You don't have to use the `with` statement as an error handler. It is really more of a generic way to make sure that objects are removed from memory, but it makes sense to consider it when thinking about possible errors, exceptions, and handling.

Re-throwing Exceptions

The final topic of discussion with respect to exceptions and exception handling is how to "re-throw" an exception. Suppose, for example, that you want to handle certain errors in a function, but you want to allow the calling function to handle them as well. Examples might include simply logging the error and then allowing the calling program to handle it, or perhaps doing some cleanup before letting the caller know things went wrong. In either case, Python permits you to pass an exception back up the chain even after you have handled the problem in your code. This process of delegating an exception to a higher level for further processing is known as *re-throwing the exception*, and is handled by a simpler version of the `raise` statement.

Normally, if you raise an exception, you use the `raise` statement as follows:

```
raise exception-type
```

where exception type, obviously, is the type of exception you want to raise to the calling program or function. However, there is another form of the `raise` statement that is simpler:

```
raise
```

In this case, the exception that was caught by your `try` block will be raised again. Let's look at a simple example of this. Suppose that you had a function that does some mathematical operation and catches exceptions generated during those operations:

```
import sys

def exc_thrower(x) :
    z = 0
    try :
        z = 100 / x
    except :
        # We got an exception. Make sure that it is logged
        print "Error encountered in exc_thrower: "+repr(sys.exc_type)
```

If you pass in a non-zero value to this function, you would expect to have it work properly and compute the number of times that 100 can be divided by that value. However, if the value zero is specified for the input argument, you will get a division by zero error. Because you do not simply want to have the program crash with no processing, you handle that exception. At the same time, however, you want to let the caller know that the error occurred so that it can deal with it and reprocess if necessary. The above function "swallows" the error so that the caller never knows about it. In fact, if you run the function from the interpreter, you will see this output:

```
>>> exc_thrower(0)
Error encountered in exc_thrower: <type 'exceptions.ZeroDivisionError'>
```

How do you do the error handling to log your error, while still letting the calling function handle the error properly? You could add something like this to the function after the print statement:

```
raise ZeroDivisionError
```

This would handle the case where the error is division by zero, but won't handle other cases, such as where "x" is not a legitimate numeric value. Instead, you do this:

```
import sys

def exc_thrower(x) :
    z = 0
    try :
        z = 100 / x
    except :
        # We got an exception. Make sure that it is logged
        print "Error encountered in exc_thrower: "+repr(sys.exc_type)
        raise
```

Now, if you call the function with a value of 0, you get:

```
>>> exc_thrower(0)
Error encountered in exc_thrower: <type 'exceptions.ZeroDivisionError'>

Traceback (most recent call last):
  File "<pyshell#74>", line 1, in <module>
    exc_thrower(0)
  File "C:/Python25/temp3.py", line 6, in exc_thrower
    z = 100 / x
ZeroDivisionError: integer division or modulo by zero
```

At the same time, passing an invalid argument, or another type of exception that you didn't think about can be handled as well:

```
>>> exc_thrower("Hello")
Error encountered in exc_thrower: <type 'exceptions.TypeError'>

Traceback (most recent call last):
  File "<pyshell#75>", line 1, in <module>
    exc_thrower("Hello")
  File "C:/Python25/temp3.py", line 6, in exc_thrower
    z = 100 / x
TypeError: unsupported operand type(s) for /: 'int' and 'str'
```

Note that, in any case, your function properly logs the error, so that even if the caller does not handle the exception, you still know what happened. This can be very useful, especially if you are concerned about callers not handling errors properly when using your functionality.

In Conclusion

Errors and error handling are one of the most important parts of the user experience in any language. Python provides a rich set of error handling routines, especially exception handling, which allows you not only to handle errors before they reach the user, but also to let the user know exactly where they went wrong. Exception handling is not something you can just "bolt on" to an existing application. It has to be designed into the original system and programmed in at every level. You should always consider exceptions and exception handling with your own Python applications, and make sure that, at the very least, your program catches all exceptions to avoid an unfriendly and unclean shutdown.

This also completes the first section of this book, where we discuss all of the low-level building blocks of the Python programming language. At this point, it is time to move on and start using those building blocks to create more complicated structures and code. In our next chapter, we will explore the concepts and language of object-oriented programming, before we move on to the most exciting part of Python, classes and objects.

9 } Object-Oriented Programming

Python, it has been mentioned, is an object-oriented programming language. Of course, that begs the question, "What is object-oriented programming?" After all, it would be nice to know what it meant to be object-oriented, in order to understand what that buys you as a programmer. What are objects, and why are they important to us as programmers? Although we will not specifically look at Python here, the basic concepts you will learn in this chapter will apply directly to the next chapter as we talk about how Python implements all of these concepts. If you have a good background in object-oriented programming (often abbreviated OOP), please feel free to skip to the next chapter and learn how Python does it all.

A Brief History of OOP

The idea of computer programming as a simulation platform has been around for a very long time. In the 1960s, the SIMULA I and SIMULA 67 programming languages were created for that express purpose. The idea behind OOP is really simple enough: model real-world entities in computer languages.

In the 1970s, the language of choice for OOP was *Smalltalk*. It was a "pure" object-oriented language, and had most of the concepts that we take for granted in a programming language today. Unfortunately, Smalltalk had some rather strange syntax and compiler issues that made it less than ideal in the corporate programming world. More importantly, probably, was the fact that the world was simply not ready for a true object-oriented language at that point.

By the 1980s, there were two serious contenders for the crown of OOP king. Modula-2 was Niklaus Wirth's foray into the serious language world, while Bjarne Stroustrup was lighting up the programming community with his C++ offering. In the end, C++ "won" the battle, primarily because it was an offshoot of the massively popular "C" programming language. The C++ language, however, suffered from a number of deficiencies that made it sub-optimal for object-oriented purists. First, the original versions of C++ were not compilers or interpreters at all, but rather converters. They took C++ source code input and translated it into C code that could then be compiled by existing C compilers. This had a number of problems associated with it: Error messages were rather odd, line numbers were often wrong, and code that seemed syntactically correct could be mangled by the interpreter into invalid C code.

Later versions of C++ fixed many of these deficiencies, but the underlying problem remained. C++ was really a "better C," and not a new language, or a pure object-oriented language. At best, it was a stepping stone between second-generation programming languages and later, true object-oriented, languages. These problems did not stop the language from becoming amazingly popular, and they really aren't "problems" at all, except to the purists.

The 1990s and early 2000s saw a rise of a number of object-oriented programming languages. Some of these languages were new, experimental concepts that sought to make it easier and more "pure" to implement object-oriented code. Others were really renovations of existing languages with new twists to permit the use of techniques that had been discovered over the years in the search for object-orientation. Yet other languages were along the lines of "lipstick on a pig," that is, languages that had a thin layer applied to the top of them to make them appear more object-oriented. Visual Basic™, for example, had classes and objects added to it to make it fit the object paradigm and appeal to a younger and more schooled generation of programmers. In addition, we had extensions to C++, the rise of Java as a programming language and environment, and languages such as Perl, PHP, Ruby, and Python, which rose with the increase in popularity of the Internet.

Why has the number of object-oriented languages increased? The underlying reason is that none of the languages is the "right answer" to the problem of modelling the real world in software. Some do parts very well, and others very poorly. Some languages implement all of the features they offer very well, but lack support for some features completely. The programming "war" to determine the perfect language is one that is likely to never really end, as the preference for a given programming language is almost as unique as the preference for a given type of food or drink.

In spite of the almost religious nature surrounding programming languages, there are some things that all programmers can agree upon. There are certain aspects of object-oriented programming languages that make it easier to create high-quality code. To understand what they are, you need to understand a little more about the concepts and components of object-oriented programming. To do this, we have to start with the basic question: What is an object?

What Is an Object?

In the real world, an object is a "real" thing. A car, a horse, a tree, and a light socket are good examples of "real" objects. The notion of an object also brings to mind certain descriptive attributes, behaviors, and capabilities. For example, a dog has four legs, a human has two legs, a car has no legs. Yet all of them share the ability to move around. On the other hand, a table has legs, but can't move at all. The concept of an object allows us to model similar attributes and similar behaviors.

The primary purpose of objects in software development is to attempt to model things that occur in the real world. We might have an "object" in our application that models a user in the real world, for example. Alternatively, we might have an object that models something less concrete, such as a bank account. Whatever the real-world model is, the purpose of the software model is to allow us to develop code that simulates the behavior of things and actions in the non-electronic world, or the world around us. By doing so, we give the end users a more familiar place in which to do their jobs and a better way in which to interact with the computer.

There is no real need for an object to be a physical, or tangible, thing. Objects in software development can model things within the software world as well. For example, it is not at all uncommon to use object-oriented programming to model a windowing environment, where individual windows represent different applications for the user to interact with. Menus, processes, files, all of these computer concepts are often "wrapped" by software object models that allow us to work with them as packages. The underlying reason for using object-oriented technology is that it removes the need for the programmer of the "concept" (or object) to know the rules for working with it. The programmer understands the properties and functionality associated with the object, and works through those things to accomplish whatever it is they want to do in the software world.

Why Do We Use Objects?

It might seem that, by taking a step back from the "bare metal" of the programming world, we are making things more complicated for the programmer. However, the user of objects and object-oriented programming really has a number of huge benefits that are not immediately apparent to the user. Let's look at some of the reasons you might want to use objects in your own programs.

Reuse

By far and away, the most important reason to use objects is that of reuse. When code is encapsulated into objects and single components, it is trivial to move a given set of code from one project to another. In addition, you have a standard interface that you can use in multiple projects easily. As projects grow in complexity and scope, it becomes more and more important to stop writing everything from scratch. One of the reasons that programmers choose a programming language is because of the body of code that exists in that language for their use. When that code is embodied in discrete containers, which is what objects really are, it is easier to use than if you have to copy individual lines of code into your project.

Consider two cases of reuse. In the first case, you have, say, a hundred lines of code that you want to copy into a project. The code is copied into a file, the file added to the project, and then the process of rebuilding begins. That's when you discover that you really needed some other bit of code, and have to go back and paste that into the file. This process continues until you have found all of the pieces and added them to the file. Of course, the next time that you want to reuse that code, the same process must be followed as well. Contrast that with the object-based approach. In this case, the code is all in one file, and more importantly, in one block. You either copy the file, or just the block, into your own project and move on. Now, which one do you want to do on a daily basis—the first or the second case? This is not to say that a procedural project cannot be organized in such a fashion as to make it easy to separate and move. It can be, but it is much harder to accomplish.

Ease in Debugging

When code is scattered all over a project, it becomes rather difficult to debug a problem. Is it happening in the function you are stepping into right now, or that function over there? If you fix a problem in one place, do you have to find each and every case where that line of code was copied and fix it, or is there only a single place to fix everything? Once a class of object has been written, tested, and debugged, that class is "safe" to use in a variety of projects and places without having to worry about all of the things that might go wrong with it each and every time you use it.

The other big advantage to objects is that they encapsulate the access to and modifying of data within the object. This means that it is harder to make a mistake. The harder it is to do something wrong, of course, the easier it is to do it right. Every time it is easy to do something right, and that things actually get done right, it is one less time you are going to have to dig in and debug something. The less time you spend debugging code, the more time you can spend writing new code, which is something programmers prefer to do anyway.

Maintainability

If you are like me, you have spent a good portion of your career fixing other people's code, rather than simply spending all of your time writing your own. Whether that means fixing bugs, or adding new features to existing applications, maintenance is a basic part of the developer's life. Wouldn't it be nice then, if someone made it easier to maintain applications, rather than creating more messes for us to clean up? Object-oriented programming naturally lends itself to more well designed, well-implemented code that is self-contained. That means no more searching through the code for global variables that are set in a half-dozen places. That means no more spaghetti code that loops back on itself a half-dozen times and has no rhyme or reason to its layout. Mostly, it means that the code is easier to read, easier to understand, and easier to maintain.

As we will see shortly, the entire purpose of object-oriented programming is to restrict the number of places you have to modify code to change the actions of an object. This limits the number of places you need to modify to enhance code or search for problems. These restrictions make it easier to maintain code, which cuts down on the amount of time you need to spend in fruitless searching of source code files, which makes life easier on the programmer. Since we are usually the people who suffer when a bug is found in code, it makes sense to do everything possible to limit the severity of bugs or the area that must be searched to find that bug.

The Attributes of Object-Oriented Development

The object-oriented paradigm consists of several important aspects that you should be aware of when writing code. These terms define the most important parts of the object-oriented system, and are things you will need to understand before you can really understand how it all works. In addition, these words are always coming up in interviews and in literature on the subject, so knowing them isn't going to hurt you any.

Abstraction

In the beginning, there was the code. The code was all that mattered, because in the end, the code was all that the computer understood. The programmer worked directly with the code, moving data into registers and invoking machine level instructions and worrying about bits and bytes and all of those wonderful low-level data types that computers need to deal with.

The problem with working at the computer level is that it is difficult. Computers think in terms of ones and zeroes and of single operations and moving data into and out of memory locations. People do not think in those terms, at least not the people who you encounter outside of small dark caves. We think in terms of user interfaces, and databases, and variable names, and other high-level concepts. The idea of moving things from the low-level "bare metal" programming to higher level concepts of loops and conditionals and variables is called *abstraction*.

The dictionary defines *abstraction* as "the act of considering something as a general quality or characteristic, apart from concrete realities, specific objects, or actual instances." In the object-oriented world, you want to think in terms of the entities that you are modelling, not the bits and bytes of how the computer implements those entities. When you think of a window, in the computer context, you think in terms of an area of the screen in which you can output text and graphics, or input things via widgets and mouse clicks. You don't want to think in terms of a set of pixels and z-orders and drawing outlines and worry about what area is covered up by what other area. You think in abstract terms, not concrete ones.

The better you model something, the more abstract it can be. You can think in terms of levels of abstraction. For example, suppose that you are modelling a dog. You can model all of the pieces of a dog: the legs, the tail, the nose, and so forth. However, most of those pieces also apply to cats, or hamsters, or mice. In fact, we think of them all as "animals." As you will see, it is this kind of thinking that is core to the object-oriented approach. Think in the most abstract way you can, and then add the specifics afterward.

Data Hiding

One of the biggest problems in software is invalid data. Data forms the backbone of most software applications, allowing the user to define the flow and use of the functionality, based on choices and input. If the data is invalid, the program is likely to veer off into uncharted waters of code and do odd things. For example, if you have a function that expects a number between one and 10, and you pass that function an 11, it obviously is not going to do what you want it to do.

In the object-oriented approach to software, we don't allow you to directly modify data. Instead, you use "accessor" functions to change a value. If the value is acceptable for the data type, it is modified. If the value is not acceptable, the value will not change and an error may be generated. For example, imagine that you are writing one of these accessors for a date value. You might have an object that represented a date in memory. The pseudo-code for this object's date accessor might look something like this:

```
Set-Date month, day, year
    # Sanity checks.
    If  Month < 1 or Month > 12 then
        Error "Invalid Month Value, must be between 1 and 12"
    If Day < 1 or Day > 31 Then
        Error "Invalid Day value, cannot be less than 1 or greater than 31"
    # See if the day is valid for this month
    If IsLeapYear year then
        If Month == 2 Then # February
            If Day > 29 Then
                Error "Invalid Day Value!"
            Else
                If Day > 28 Then
                    Error "Invalid Day Value!"
            End If
        Else
            If Day > DaysPerMonth month Then
                Error "Invalid Day Value!"
        End If
OurMonth = month
OurDay = day
OurYear = year
```

Now, in our application, if we try to set the date with any invalid values, such as 2/30/2007 or 13/13/2005, we will automatically generate an error. We don't need to worry about the date "object" containing invalid values for the month or day, because they can never be set to those invalid values.

The idea of "hiding" data behind accessors for setting and getting the values is a core component of object-oriented programming. You should never allow the user to directly change values that require validation.

Inheritance

If we go back to the previous example of the dog as an animal, you will begin to understand the concept of inheritance in object-oriented programming. Inheritance allows an object type to "inherit" data and functionality from a base class. You can think of this, in a lot of ways, as the same as genetics in our own human development. We inherit certain things from our parents. For example, our height, our eye color, our hair color—all of these attributes come from the genetics of our parents. Our functional abilities often come from our parentage as well. For example, the children of athletes are often athletic in their own right. On a more basic level, however, we have two legs because our parents had two legs. We can talk because our parents could talk, and so forth and so on.

In the programming world, we often use the idea of inheritance without even thinking about it. If we have a function that allows us to set 12 values in a given application, and we want to make life easier for the user, we might wrap that function up in another function that defaulted most of the arguments to reasonable values for our application. In so doing, we "inherit" the functionality of the original function and extend it in our application. The purpose of inheritance is really to write as little code as possible while using as much as possible from previous instances.

How does inheritance work? When you inherit from a base type of object, you gain all of the data and all of the functionality of that base type. Let's look at a real-world example in the software development field to understand what this is all about. Imagine, for a moment, that you have a base type called *Vehicle*. The Vehicle type looks like this:

Features:

- ❋ Number of Wheels
- ❋ Type of Engine
- ❋ Type of Fuel
- ❋ Range

Functionality:

- ❋ Move
- ❋ Stop
- ❋ Turn
- ❋ Add Fuel
- ❋ Check Fuel
- ❋ Change Tire

A vehicle type, of course, represents any sort of system that allows you to move. It would not apply to walking from place to place, obviously, because that does not involve a number of wheels. However, it might apply to a bicycle. A bicycle allows you to move from place to place, and it has wheels. However, it has no engine and no fuel. Is this a problem? Not really, since we can consider the fuel type to be None and the engine type to be Human Powered. This might be considered a stretch, however, and points out one of the pitfalls of object-oriented design and programming, which is making things fit a mold that they aren't really a part of.

Now, suppose that we have a new sort of type, called a *Car*. A car is a kind of vehicle, so we can say that a car "inherits" the functionality of a vehicle:

Car: Vehicle

This inheritance means that the car automatically has all of the features and functionality of a vehicle, while potentially adding its own customizations to those features and functionality, or adding its own to the list. For example, we might add the following features and functionality for the car type:

Features:

- ❋ Color
- ❋ Number of Passengers
- ❋ Windshield Wipers

Functionality:

- ❋ Start Wipers
- ❋ Stop Wipers
- ❋ Paint Car

When we talk about the features of a car, we really mean the list above plus the list of features that are already defined in the vehicle type. This is the purpose of inheritance. What does this gain you as a programmer? You get all of that functionality for free. In addition, because you know that your vehicle implementation already has functionality in place to verify the setting of the various features of the type, you don't need to worry about doing any of that. In short, you actually get something for free! How often does that happen in the real world?

Polymorphism

Going back to the dictionary, we find that the definition of polymorphism is "the quality or state of existing in or assuming different forms." How does that apply to software, and specifically to object-oriented programming? The answer lies in the way in which something exists in a different form. As mentioned previously, we can "inherit" functionality from a base type. What wasn't clear during that discussion is that the new type (we called it *Car*, the base type was *Vehicle*) really is an object of the base type. So a *Car* is a *Vehicle*. The reverse, by the way, is not true. A *Vehicle* does not have to be a *Car*; it can be any sort of vehicle or derived (that is, inherited) type.

This is important because if a Car is a vehicle, then any functionality that is written that expects to have an object of type Vehicle will work with an object of type Car. We have modified the functionality of the old function without changing it in the least. For example, consider the following problem.

Let's imagine that we have a bit of functionality that is defined for the Vehicle type that rotates the tires. We will call this bit of functionality the "RotateTire" function, in a rare bit of originality. This function is intended to move each tire around, so that tire number one becomes tire number two, tire number two becomes tire number three and so forth, until the final tire becomes tire number one again.

We might implement a function like this to accomplish the rotate tire task, at least in pseudo-code:

Rotate Tires:

```
For tireNumber = 2 to NumberOfTires - 1 :
       SetTire ( tireNumber, tireNumber+1 )
SetTire( 1, NumberOfTires )
```

This particular routine is nothing spectacular. It moves the tires around, replacing the first tire with the last one and all the rest in order. There is one important point about the routine, however, and that is that it works with one of the "features" we defined a bit earlier, NumberOfTires. This feature can be overridden in inherited classes (also called *derived classes*) to return a different number of tires. So, for a motorcycle or bicycle, the function would return two, whereas for a car it would return four and for a truck, perhaps, six or eight. Whatever the number, the functionality of this routine does not change. This does assume, by the way, that the vehicle has at least one tire. It would break for a vehicle with no tires, but would work for a vehicle with one (a unicycle?). By changing the number of tires, we change the functionality of the routine, without having to change the actual code of the routine. This is what is meant by *polymorphism,* and it is a very powerful capability in object-oriented programming.

Terminology

Any time you are talking about a new concept, such as object-oriented programming, it is important to get the terminology correct. Object-oriented purists have a tendency to sneer at those who use the wrong words for a concept, even if the idea itself is quite clear. With that understanding, let's look at some of the words that you will need to understand if you are working with OOP.

Class

To this point, we have been using the terms object, type, and class interchangeably. We need to stop that or the OOP Police will come get us and take us away. In object-oriented parlance, the term "class" means the template for a type of object. A class does not exist within an application as any sort of entity, but rather it is a substitute for a type of object.

When we refer to a class, we are referring to a specific name for a set of data and functionality. Going back to our previous examples, a Vehicle would be a class name. A Car would be a class name. A specific car, such as a Red Volvo, would not be a class. Instead, it would be called an *instance*. An instance always has a type associate with it, and when we are talking about objects, the type is always a class.

A class has certain built-in bits of functionality. For example, when you create a new instance of a class (a process called *instantiation*), the system will automatically allocate a block of memory of the proper size, and initialize all of the features (called *attributes*) within the block to a preset value, depending on their type. This process is called *initialization*. In most object-oriented languages, including Python, you can define a special method that is built into the class to do the initialization according to your preferences.

Remember, a class is just a template. It is much akin to having a stencil for drawing letters on a painting. The stencil itself contains information about what will be produced (the specific letter you are creating), but it does nothing by itself. You only have one stencil for each letter, but each stencil can be used to create as many letters as you want. In the object-oriented world, the stencil is a class, and the letter is an object. We will spend a fair amount of time in the next chapter discussing classes and how they are implemented, so it is important for you to understand the difference between classes and their objects.

Object

Going back to our example in the class terminology section, if a stencil is a class, then the letters the stencil produces are objects. Objects are specific instantiations of a given class. If a class is a template that defines what features a given entity will contain, such as color, size, and such, then the object is the container that has the actual values for the color, size and so forth.

Objects can be created, used, and destroyed. The process of creating an object is called *instantiation*, which is quickly followed by *initialization*. Instantiation allocates the block of memory that will contain the values for the object. For example, if you had a class that had four bits of data associated with it:

Car:

❋ Name

❋ Color

❋ Number of Tires

❋ Miles Per Gallon

We could then create two separate objects of this class. They might look like this:

Car #1:

❋ Name = Volvo

❋ Color = Red

❋ Number of Tires = 4

❋ Miles Per Gallon = 30

Car #2:

❋ Name = Ferarri

❋ Color = White

❋ Number of Tires = 4

❋ Miles Per Gallon = 20

Obviously, the first listing (Car) is a class definition, since it has only the names of the variables that make up the entity. The second and third listings (Car #1 and Car #2) on the other hand, are instances of the car type, since they contain values for each of the variables.

Attribute

An attribute is what we have been calling a "feature" in this section. Attributes, also known as *properties* or *members*, are the components that make up the data section of the class. Attributes will have types, and may be classes themselves. For example, if we go back to our car example, the attributes for the car are the following:

❋ Name

❋ Color

❋ Number of Tires

❋ Miles Per Gallon

The name is probably a string, the color might be some sort of system value, and the other two values are likely to be numeric values. Attributes are normally assigned via some sort of accessor function. An accessor is simple a function that either gets (read) or sets (write) the value of a property/attribute in an object.

Remember that while the definition of an attribute is a part of the class, the implementation of the attribute is a part of the object. That means that the color attribute is a part of the class, while the value of the color (i.e., "white") is a part of the object to which that attribute is assigned. Different objects may contain different color values, but they will all contain an attribute called *color*.

As you will see in Python, attributes do not have to be strongly typecast, although in most compiled languages, they will be. Attributes in some languages can have "access levels," in which they are described as public or private, limiting the access to those attributes to either the functions declared in the class, or to everyone. Python does not support this particular restriction directly, although it does have some notion of privacy

Method

If an attribute is the data side of a class definition, then a method is the functionality side of the class. Methods are functions that are defined for a given class. The primary difference between a method and a function is the availability of the actual object within the method. In a method, you can simply refer to the object you are working on, rather than having to pass that object in. The object has different names in different languages; For example, in C++ and Java, it is referred to as a "this" pointer, meaning this object that I am working on. In Python, the object is referred to as the "self" object, meaning that I am operating on myself.

The purpose of methods within a class is to define a set of functionality that makes sense for the type of object you are working with. For example, going back to our car class, we might have methods that include the following:

* Start
* Stop
* Number of Tires
* Turn
* Rotate Tires
* Open Door
* Close Door
* Change Oil

Obviously, this is only a partial list of possible methods for cars. However, they all share the idea that they work on a given car object. Methods have a few general types:

❋ **Accessors** : An accessor method sets or gets the current value for a property or attribute of the class. Accessors normally check the value that is being passed in to make sure it is valid for the object. In our list above, the "Number of Tires" method falls into this category. In addition, some accessors are written to convert the data going out into a type that the user of the method prefers, such as converting a time value into a time string.

❋ **State Changing**: Many objects have a state associated with them, which is why they are objects and not simple sets of functions. For example, our car object might be running, or parked, or stopped at a traffic light. It might have a flat tire or need an oil change. All of these states can be impacted by specific methods in the class. In our previous list, the Start and Stop methods fall into this category.

❋ **Computations**: Methods that do not change the internal state of the object, but do some sort of computation or manipulation of data will fall under this category. For example, for the car object, turning would come under this category. It changes the position of the car, but since we are unlikely to track that in the object itself, it doesn't affect the state of the car object. Computational methods may accept arguments, or may not, but they will always do some sort of calculation without changing the internal representation of the object.

❋ **Initialization**: Methods in this category initialize values. They may do it once, such as when the object is first created. The methods may be invoked numerous times, such as a "return to default values" method. Initialization methods usually set the attributes that they affect to a single known good state.

❋ **Termination**: Methods in the termination category are called when a process ends. That can be the object being destroyed, or when a given state changes, or simply when the user indicates that he is done with a specific action.

Message Passing

Objects need to be able to talk to each other for an object-oriented system to stand any change of doing anything useful. For example, you might have a Car object and a Road object. The car needs to know what sort of road (gravel, dirt, paved) it is travelling on, to determine the wear on tires and how far it has gone within a given period of time. As a simple example, the speed limit on the road might be used to determine how far you have gone, and how long it will take you to reach a given place. The road, of course, needs to know how many cars are on it so that it can determine the wear and tear and the likely number of accidents and such.

There are a number of ways in which message passing is done in object-oriented languages. The primary one, and the one we will focus on for most of this book, is via method calls between objects. For a given state, you have one object "notify" another object that something happened. Other languages use event handling to accomplish the same thing, and we will see examples of this sort of thing when we talk about the Tk GUI system in Chapter 12 of this book.

Event Handling

Similar to the notion of messages, events are notifications from a given object that something has happened. It might be a change of state, such as the object having a given attribute change. It might be the initialization or termination of the object within the system. Whatever the event, the object needs a way in which to tell "subscribed" objects that it has changed a value.

A good example of this would be in the GUI world. Suppose, for example, that we have a list box on a dialog window. When the user selects an entry in the list box, the dialog window wants to know what the new selection might be, so that it can update other GUI elements in the dialog. The way in which this happens is that the list box "publishes" an event that the dialog window "listens" for, indicating a change. When the event occurs, a method in the dialog is invoked, and the information is passed to that method, indicating the new selection.

Derivation

As mentioned a bit earlier, the process of creating new classes from existing ones is called *derivation*. What this really means, however, is that you are taking all of the existing functionality of an existing class and adding new functionality to it that only applies to a new class. As an example, consider our Car class that we have been working with to this point. Suppose that we had a new kind of car, called a *HybridCar*. This car would have functionality that existed in the car class, and it would have wheels and doors and oil to change and so forth. It would also have new functionality that would be specific to the HybridCar type.

Let's assume that our hybrid had two new attributes, called *Battery Life* and *Recharging Time*. These two functions apply only to electric-type cars, and would not be applicable to a normal car, so it makes sense to have them in their own class. If we looked at the new class, we would see the following:

Car:

* Name
* Color
* Number of Tires
* Miles Per Gallon

Hybrid Car:

* Battery Life
* Recharging Time

Why are things broken out this way? The reason is the underlying fact that the hybrid variety really is a car, and can be used as a car. Suppose further that we had a function that accepted a car object as a parameter. We can pass a HybridCar object as a parameter to that function and have everything work in exactly the same way.

Coupling

While coupling might sound like some British way of having people go out on a date, the term actually means something in object-oriented programming. Coupling is the degree to which two or more modules depend on each other. Coupling can either be strong, in which case the two modules cannot exist without each other around, or it can be weak, in which case there is some interaction, but the interaction can be easily removed or ignored.

The best way to look at coupling is in this manner. If changes to one module force changes to another module, there is very strong coupling between the two modules. If, on the other hand, changes to one module cause little or no change to another module, we say those two modules are weakly coupled.

Consider the case of the car and the road. The car needs a road to run on, and the road needs cars to drive upon it. However, if we change the surface of the road, or the speed limit for that road, we do not really change the car object at all. We impact how far the car can go in a given time period, but the car doesn't really care. It just wants to know there is something there to drive on. These two objects, therefore, are weakly coupled.

On the other hand, consider the case of a car object and a tire object. If we change the interface to a tire, how it is removed from the car, for example, we need to change the code in the car object to reflect this functionality. Suppose that you had to take off tires in twos, rather than one at a time. This would impact the way in which tire rotation happened. This is a case of strong coupling between objects.

The weakest form of coupling is known as *message coupling*, in which messages are sent from one class and received in another. The sending class does not care who receives its messages, and the receiving class does not care who sends a message, so long as it receives one.

Cohesion

Cohesion is defined as the way in which the lines of a module work together to accomplish a task. In object-oriented programming, cohesion is primarily identifying overlap between different methods and redundant attributes. We really won't be talking about cohesion at all in this book. Instead, please refer to a really good object-oriented programming and design book (such as ones in this series) to get a better understanding of concepts like this. For our purposes, we will simply say that cohesion is concerned with whether or not a function or module does a single task or multiple tasks.

Constants

It is natural, in any programming language, to have values that do not change. We refer to these values as *constants*. Constants are simply names for things in programs, rather than using magic numbers. For example, I might refer to the constant "pi," rather than using the numeric value 3.14 (approximately). Constants are also useful for storing data in programs that is used in more than one place, in case that value needs to change in the future. A good example of this might be the number of log files that the program creates before deleting old files. We could simply hard-code the value 10 (as an example) everywhere that the number of current log files is needed, or we could use a symbolic name such as `NumberOfCurrentLogFiles` everywhere and then define it in one place. This is a good technique and one you should pay attention to in your own programs. Avoid magic numbers in your code!

Other Concepts

There are only a few other concepts that you really need to know anything about at this point in object-oriented software development. First, we have the difference between "is-a" and "has-a." In object-oriented terms, this is the difference between inheritance and composition. Inheritance, as we have seen, is the ability to reuse all of the functionality of a class and extend it in the process. This ability, however, comes at a price. You cannot remove any of the functionality that is available to the user of the original class via your derived class. This can cause problems, especially if the derived class is more specific and has more restrictions on its abilities.

The "has-a" relationship, also known as *composition*, is the ability to embed existing class structures within new classes. For example, we could have a class called *Tire* that represents a single tire in a car, truck, or airplane. Within the Car class, we could embed an array of Tire objects, which would represent the tires on the car. We could then allow the user to get at whatever portions of the Tire class we want to provide accessibility to, without necessarily allowing them to change anything they want. Of course, there is a price here, too: You need to write your own accessor functions to provide access to the pieces of the Tire class you want to allow the user to use. This is a bit more work, but more importantly, it means that if things change in the Tire class, and you want to provide access to those new changes, you need to add methods to the Car class to do so. Obviously, this is a case of high-degree coupling.

The last concept we want to talk about, very briefly, in this chapter is that of patterns. Patterns are an important part of object-oriented programming, although they are not one you are required to follow. The concept of patterns is really quite simple. Over the years, it has been observed that there are certain ways of doing things that work out very well. These methods of implementing specific types of functionality in a given way are called *patterns*. We will not really be using patterns in Python in this book, but you will certainly want to review the concepts and patterns available when you are writing your own object-oriented code.

In Conclusion

Well, that was certainly a very fast introduction to the ideas and terminology involved in object-oriented software development. This book was not intended to be a primer on object-oriented concepts, nor was it meant to follow them to the letter. Instead, what this chapter has attempted to do is to introduce you to the ideas that we will be implementing in Python in the next few chapters. Without at least a passing knowledge of why things are the way they are, it is very hard to understand why Python makes the choices that it does for implementation purposes. Hopefully, you will understand enough to look at the Python code that follows and see where it comes from. At the same time, however, you will not have just enough knowledge to be dangerous. Object-oriented programming is neither a science nor a law book. You can feel free to choose what you want to use in your own applications, based on your own abilities and needs.

In the next chapter, we will explore how many of these concepts are implemented in Python. When you are done with that chapter, you will have nearly all of the fundamentals in place for writing complete Python applications.

10 } Classes and Objects in Python

In our last chapter, we explored the theoretical concepts involved in object-oriented programming. In this chapter, it is time to apply those theoretical concepts to the world of Python programming. The idea of a "class" in Python is simply defining your own kind of object. As you've seen so far, pretty much everything you work with in Python is already an object, so it makes sense that you can create your own object types to work with.

Python Classes

The Python class construct is created with the keyword *class*. The basic structure of a class looks like this:

```
class <classname> :
    # Definition goes here
```

In the example above, the `<classname>` is any valid name that you want to create. Python class names are restricted to the same sets of rules as variables. So you can create a class name with letters and numbers, as well as underscores, so long as it starts with either an underscore or a letter. Because most reserved words in Python begin with an underscore in the class world, it is better if you do not use that character unless you have a particularly good reason to. Here are some simple examples of class names that work just fine in Python:

* Foo
* Bar
* Foo_bar
* Class22

Note that you cannot define a class name that is a reserved word. So writing something like this:

```
class for:
```

will result in an error message within the interpreter:

```
>>> class for :
```

```
SyntaxError: invalid syntax
```

Normally, this is not much of a problem. There aren't that many reserved words, and they don't tend to be the sort of thing that you would want to name a class anyway. In general, your class name should be descriptive enough so that the user will understand what it is trying to accomplish.

The simplest form of a class is the "empty" class. This class definition looks like this:

```
>>> class Foo :
        pass
```

It might not be apparent why you would want to create such a class. As you will see when we get to defining class attributes, it can make a lot of sense when you simply want a storage mechanism for keeping track of related entries. For example, if you had the need for a Pascal-style "record" that simply stored a bunch of data about a given topic, this would be the ideal structure for it.

If you are accustomed to working with other languages, such as Visual Basic, C++, or Java, you are probably wondering how such a class can do any good. After all, you need to define the data variables within the class that will store the information for the class. In Python, because it is an interpreted language, it is not necessary to predefine either the name, or type, of a class attribute (called an *instance variable*, in object-oriented parlance).

Now that you have a class defined, what can you do with the class definition, other than look at it? Obviously, you can create an object of the type that you just defined. For example, given our Foo class that was defined previously, you can create a new instance of the Foo class in the interpreter by using this sort of syntax:

```
f = Foo()
```

This syntax might look like a function call, but when the interpreter recognizes that Foo is a class, and not a function, you get an object of type Foo defined, rather than invoking a function called Foo and putting the return value into the variable f.

You might be wondering what happens if you have a class named `Foo` and a function called `Foo` defined in the same program. Good question—let's try that out and see. Enter the following lines into the interpreter:

```
>>> def Foo() :
        print "This is a test"
        return 1

>>> f = Foo()
This is a test
>>> class Foo :
        pass


>>> f=Foo()
```

The interpreter does not care which of the definitions you use, with the following exception. The last one defined "wins." That is, if you define a function and a class of the same name, the last one defined is the current "value" of that name in the system. This might seem a bit odd, especially if you happen to use common names a lot for functions and classes, but it is just the way that Python works. If you wonder, it makes no difference whether the classes and functions are defined directly in the interpreter or whether they are stored in a module file and loaded into the interpreter later, because the rules are the same. When we talk about scopes and namespaces just a little later in this chapter, you will understand how you can avoid name collisions like this so that you can have your own functions and classes with the same name as things already defined in Python or by other users in your system.

> ❋ **Capping Conventions**
>
> One final note on conventions in Python classes: By convention, we capitalize the first letter of a class to indicate that it is a class and not a function. In this way, you know that when you see "Foo" it is a class and when you see "foo" it is a function.

Properties

Python classes would be of very little use as data collections if there were no way to store data in one, so Python provides a way to store data in classes. This is called a *property definition* (or, in *Pythonese*, an "attribute") for a class. Unlike some other languages, Python provides no way to predefine a property for a class. Instead, property definitions simple come into being as soon as they are used. For example, you could define a class with a property called *name* like this:

```
>>> class MyClass :
        name = "MyClass"
```

You access the properties of a class by using the dot ('.') notation for an object of the type of class you have defined. You can access the name object by writing code that looks like this:

```
>>> me = MyClass()
>>> print me.name
MyClass
```

Naturally, you can set the value of an attribute in a class directly:

```
>>> me.name = "fred"
>>> print me.name
fred
```

Python does not have the direct concept of read only and writeable properties. Once you have exposed a property in the class, it is available to anyone who knows about it (or can read the code). This is in keeping with the Python philosophy of "trust the user," which is quite different than most strongly typed languages, which operate on the "trust no one" philosophy. This can lead to some problems, but in general is a lot easier to work with than the reverse philosophy. If you are accustomed to programming in Java, C++, or Visual Basic, you might have some issues with this concept. Yes, there are ways around it, but it is a lot easier overall if you just get used to it.

Python properties (or attributes) are dynamic. That is, you can add one any time you want in your code. What might not be quite so straightforward, however, is the fact that anyone can add an attribute to an object of a class at runtime. Consider the following example of code:

```
>>> class MyClass :
        x = 1


>>> me = MyClass()
>>> print me.x
1
>>> me.y = 2
>>> print me.x
1
>>> print me.y
2
```

As you can see in the above code, we defined a class called MyClass. This class defined a single attribute called "x" by setting the variable x within the class to a value. Once you define an instance of the MyClass class, you can then look at the current value of x, or modify it, in your own code. You can also add a new attribute to the object me of type MyClass, as shown by creating the attribute "y." However, and this is quite important, while "y" is an attribute of the object me, it is not a generalized attribute of the class MyClass. That is, you can't expect the MyClass methods (something we will learn about in just a moment) to know anything about the attribute "y." You can use the value in your own code, but it is more of an appendage to the class than a formal part of it. Creating attributes outside of a class method is allowed, but a poor programming practice, and really it should be avoided.

How do you find out what attributes and methods a given class supports? For this, Python offers us the dir() function. The dir() function gives you back a list of the entities stored within a Python object. This is object-based, rather than class-based, so you can get all of the user defined attributes, as well as all of the class attributes:

```
>>> class MyClass :
        name = "MyClass"


>>> me = MyClass()
>>> me.color = "red"
>>> print dir(me)
['__doc__', '__module__', 'color', 'name']
```

The returned value from the dir() function is a list, so you can actually use it if you want:

```
>>> d = dir(me)
>>> for a in d :
        print a


__doc__
__module__
color
name
```

We aren't going to worry about the __doc__ or __module__ entries quite yet. However, you can see that the values for color and name are listed there. Naturally, you can apply the dir() function to a type as well as a variable. For our MyClass definition, we could look at the various elements defined there by writing:

```
>>> dir(MyClass)
['__doc__', '__module__', 'name']
```

Notice that the name attribute is defined for both the class definition and the variable definition, but that the name attribute is only defined for the specific variable definition that included it (the me variable we defined above).

This all seems like magic, but it really isn't at all. Python implements an internal data structure for things, using a hidden variable called __dict__ for the type or variable. For example, you can look at the __dict__ (let's just call it the dictionary) for the class MyClass:

```
>>> print MyClass.__dict__
{'__module__': '__main__', 'name': 'MyClass', '__doc__': None}
```

Then you can look at the dictionary for the variable "me" of type MyClass:

```
>>> print me.__dict__
{'color': 'red'}
```

Note that the dictionary for the class contains all of the variables defined for all instances of the class, whereas the dictionary for the variable me only contains the entries that you defined for the variable itself. The dir() function simply combines the two dictionaries to produce a single, cohesive list of the attributes of the class. The dictionary object, by the way, is a writeable entity, so you can change the values of a class indirectly at runtime, without really knowing the object name within the class for an attribute. You can write something like this:

```
me.__dict__['name'] = 'newname'
```

This will change the value of the name attribute of the me variable to be the new value newname. If you are wondering, there is another hidden variable within the Python class architecture, called __class__. This attribute allows you to change values within the actual class definition for a given instance of that class. This might not seem obvious, so let's take a look at this:

```
>>> class Foo :
        x = 1


>>> f1 = Foo()
>>> f2 = Foo()
>>> print f1.x
1
>>> print f2.x
```

```
1
>>> f1.__class__.__dict__['x'] = 2
>>> print f1.x
2
>>> print f2.x
2
```

Okay, now you know how to change the attribute for all of the instances of a given class at once. Please don't do things like this. It is amazingly hard to figure out why your values suddenly change all over the place, thanks to a single line of code. It is a by-product of Python namespaces and the way in which the interpreter works, and a curiosity, but that is all it should be considered. However, one very nice side-effect of this horrible syntax curiosity is that you can look at not only the instance value of an attribute, but also whether or not the attribute is the same value as the default value of the attribute in the class:

```
>>> f3 = Foo()
>>> print f3.x
2
>>> f3.x = 3
>>> print f2.x
2
>>> print f3.x
3
>>> if f2.x == f2.__class__.__dict__['x'] :
        print "No change"


No change
>>> if f3.x == f3.__class__.__dict__['x'] :
        print "No change"
else :
        print "Value changed"

Value changed
```

Imagine how useful something like that could be for keeping track of "dirty" values for a database or other persistent storage mechanism for Python class instances. In fact, there are quite a number of systems that work in exactly that way.

Attribute Modifying Functions

The whole method of setting attributes by using the internal __dict__ variable within a class or variable works, but it is definitely somewhat messy. Fortunately, Python developers recognized this, and offered up several functions that would do the same job, without the messy syntax. The two functions are called getattr() and setattr().

The getattr function, which is a built-in function, accepts two standard arguments and one optional argument. The standard arguments are the object you want to retrieve the attribute from, and the name of the attribute that you want to retrieve. The optional argument is the default value if the attribute is not found in the object. For example, using our previous example, we could write:

```
>>> print getattr(f3, 'x')
3
```

The usage here retrieves the value of the attribute called "x" from the object named "f3" and prints it out to the standard console. Note, however, that if the attribute does not exist, an exception will be generated for the function call:

```
>>> print getattr(f3, 'fred')


Traceback (most recent call last):
  File "<pyshell#97>", line 1, in <module>
    print getattr(f3, 'fred')
AttributeError: Foo instance has no attribute 'fred'
```

To get around this problem, the optional third argument can be used to return a value if no attribute can be found in the given object for the given attribute name you have selected. You can therefore modify the above statement to provide a default value, which will be returned if the attribute isn't found. In this case, you get no exception generated:

```
>>> print getattr(f3, 'fred', 1)
1
```

An important note about the default attribute value: If the attribute does not exist, it is not added to the variable or the class. That is, after using the above statement, you cannot use f3.fred or do a getattr() function call to retrieve the fred attribute without a default. It is only a way around the error return.

Similarly, Python provides a companion function called setattr(), which will set an arbitrary attribute in a given object, given the object, the name of the attribute you want to set, and the value of the attribute you want to set the attribute name to. If the attribute does not already exist, it will be created in the object and can be referred to either by name directly or via the getattr() function:

```
>>> setattr(f3, 'fred', 3)
>>> print f3.fred
3
>>> print getattr(f3, 'fred')
3
```

For completeness, there is a third function, called delattr(), which will remove a given attribute from a variable. This one is a little bit confusing in behavior, although the syntax is simple enough:

```
delattr( object, attribute)
```

When you invoke delattr() on an object, one of two things will happen. If the attribute is one that has been added at the object level (that is, it does not exist in the class definition), then it will be removed completely:

```
>>> f1 = Foo()
>>> f1.newvar = 1
>>> print f1.newvar
1
>>> delattr(f1, 'newvar')
>>> print f1.newvar

Traceback (most recent call last):
  File "<pyshell#114>", line 1, in <module>
    print f1.newvar
AttributeError: Foo instance has no attribute 'newvar'
```

This seems obvious and straightforward enough. The problem comes in, however, when you try to delete an attribute that exists within the class definition for a given variable. For example, in the Foo class above, you have a variable named x, as you can see by doing a dir() function call on the variable:

```
>>> dir(f1)
['__doc__', '__module__', 'x']
```

What happens if you delete the value of "x" in the variable f1? You get an error, that's what. The error occurs because you haven't defined any instance attribute called x for f1. The only value of "x" in the variable is assigned at the class level. So, if you try to delattr() the value of "x," you get:

```
>>> delattr(f1, 'x')

Traceback (most recent call last):
  File "<pyshell#116>", line 1, in <module>
    delattr(f1, 'x')
AttributeError: Foo instance has no attribute 'x'
```

That seems simple enough and makes some sense. However, there is a twist. If you have defined a value for the variable in the instance, rather than the class, and it overrides the values in the class, you can delete it:

```
>>> f1.x = 12
>>> print f1.x
12
>>> delattr(f1, 'x')
>>> print f1.x
2
```

Calling `delattr()` will remove the instance value of the variable x, but since there is a class value for the same attribute name, you can still refer to it. This doesn't seem very obvious, but it explains a lot about the way in which Python uses class attributes. Attributes at the instance level automatically add to, and replace, attributes at the class level.

Private Attributes

In many programming languages, there is the concept of "private" and "public" attributes. Public attributes are those that can be modified by functions and code outside of the class definition. Private attributes can only be used by code that exists within the scope of a class, methods, or direct code executed when the class is created. Python does not really support the latter form of attribute; only public accessible attributes exist. However, there is a way to sort of create a private variable in Python, even if it is just a syntactic kind of variable hiding. To accomplish this, you pre-pend two underscore characters to the front of the variable name:

```
>>> class Private :
        __internal = 1
        x = 2



>>>
>>> p = Private()
```

```
>>> print p.x
2
>>> print p.__internal

Traceback (most recent call last):
  File "<pyshell#138>", line 1, in <module>
    print p.__internal
AttributeError: Private instance has no attribute '__internal'
```

It certainly appears that you cannot get at the variable __internal. Unfortunately, this is not really the case. If you look at the available data for the class, you get:

```
>>> dir(p)
['__doc__', '__module__', '_private__internal', 'x']
```

That odd looking thing, private__internal, is what we are referring to in our code as __internal. When you use the double underscore in front of a variable name, the interpreter automatically adds the name of the class to the front of the variable name, making it harder for someone just scanning the code to realize that it is there. Of course, this is only a convention, and it doesn't stop anyone from changing the value of your private variable:

```
>>> print p._private__internal
1
>>> p._private__internal = 3;
>>> print p._private__internal
3
```

Doc Strings

While doc strings are not really a part of the process of writing and defining classes, they do fit in nicely here, so let's take a moment to talk about them. One of the problems with choosing class and method names is that something that makes sense to you doesn't necessarily make sense to others reading the same code. Imagine, for example, that you are writing a function to copy an object from one place to another. You might call that routine, StarWarsII, because it reminds you of the whole "Clone War" thing. Now, that seems rather obvious to me and you, but there is this outside chance that there is someone on the planet who didn't see the movie. For this purpose, you need to document things so that those who have a lack of basic education don't feel left out.

The concept of doc strings allows the programmer to place comments directly inline for the end user to view and for the editor and compiler to read. There are quite a few tools for taking doc strings and converting them into end-user documentation automatically, which certainly beats sitting down and writing about all the stuff.

The basic form of a doc string is:

```
def func(params):
    """Do something with a dictionary of parameters.
    """ Parameter 1 is blah
    """ Parameter 2 is blah
    """
```

The triple quotes indicate to the interpreter that this is a block of text and should be treated as a doc string. The fact that the comment is the very first thing in a function or method indicates to the interpreter that this is a doc string. Doc strings can be any length, but must appear as the first thing following the opening colon (:) of a function or method.

Many editors, including the IDLE editor, use the doc string as documentation for a given function in the form of context sensitive help while you are working in the editor. Of course, the documentation is only as good as the text you write, so try to be as complete and concise as possible, indicating the purpose of the function, any return values from the function, and any arguments that should be passed in as parameters. The better your documentation, the less likely it is that someone will come knocking on your door (or cube wall) asking how things work while you are in the middle of a crucial solitaire game.

One last note about doc strings: If you define a doc string for a given class, it will become the __doc__ property of the class. When we looked at the dir() function, you probably noticed that the __doc__ property was one of the things that was automatically defined for a given class. We can look at a class that has a doc string like this:

```
>>> class Foo :
        """ This is a document string for the Foo class.
        """
        x = 1



>>> dir(Foo)
['__doc__', '__module__', 'x']
>>> print Foo.__doc__
 This is a document string for the Foo class.
```

As you may realize, Python is doing a lot for you behind the scenes as you type and enter text into the editor. A lot of what the editor and the interpreter do for you is not appreciated until much later, when you really need it.

Properties

While it is true that Python has no concept of private variables, it does have something almost as good. Newer versions of Python come complete with a wonderful feature called a *property*. Properties are variables in classes that can have their own dedicated functions for getting and setting values. For example, if you have a property that implemented the number of minutes past the hour, you could have a "set" function that screened out any values outside of the range 0 to 59, since those are the only valid values for a minute.

Python implements properties through a function called, appropriately enough, *property*. You can indicate the internal variable that you want to wrap accessor functions around and the functions that you want assigned to that variable. In addition, you can specify an optional document string that will appear for the property value in editors that support such things. The signature for the property function is as follows:

```
property([fget[, fset[, fdel[, doc]]]])
```

Where:

fget: is the name of a function assigned to returning the value of the property.

fset: is the name of a function assigned to setting the value of the property.

fdel: is the name of a function assigned to dealing with the deletion (del) of the property.

doc: is the optional documentation string to assign to the property.

The return value from the property function is the managed variable you want to work with in your code. Let's take a look at a simple example of a property in a class called Foo, with a property called x:

```
class C(object):
    def __init__(self): self._x = None
    # Return the value of x
    def getx(self): return self._x
  # Set the value of x
  def setx(self, value):
      print "setx called"
      self._x = value
  def delx(self): del self._x
  # Define the property 'x'
  x = property(getx, setx, delx, "I'm the 'x' property.")
```

277
❊ ❊ ❊

Now, let's take a look at the pieces here and see what is involved in the process., We have a property in our class called "x." That one is assigned in the __init__ function (don't worry about this, we'll talk about it in a minute). The self.x statement creates a class property called "x." However, creating it as a normal property will allow the end user to modify it directly. We don't want that; instead, we want to have an indirect method using accessors. This is where the property() function comes in.

In the property() function, you pass it your get, set, and del functions. When the end user tries to change the value of the x variable, your functions will be called instead. If you enter the above code into the editor and then enter the following statement, you will see the output from the set function:

```
>>> c = C()
>>> c.x = 1
setx called
```

As you can see, even though it looks as if you are simply setting a variable in the code, you are actually calling a function indirectly. Is it possible to check the value and not set it, if necessary? You can modify the code to find out. Change the set function to read as follows in your code:

```
def setx(self, value):
    print "setx called"
    if value > 0 and value < 60 :
        self._x = value
```

Now you can test the function in the IDLE interpreter:

```
>>> c = C()
>>> c.x = 5
setx called
>>> print c.x
5
>>> c.x = 100
setx called
>>> print c.x
5
```

In the first case, you assign the variable x to be a legal value, which is one between one and 59. The output from the print statement (which is calling your get function) shows that the set function worked as we expected. Now try assigning the value to something invalid, in this case 100. Once again, you can print out the value of the variable. The output clearly shows that the value was not changed, indicating that the set function properly screened out values outside of the allowed range. This sort of programming concept is a best practice scenario that you should seriously consider in your own code. It is a lot easier to figure out what is going on in code when you know that the values you are working with are always valid.

Here is one very important note about properties you will need to know if you want to use them. To use properties and have them work properly, you must derive your class from "object." You'll learn about this a bit later in the chapter.

The `self` Object

We briefly looked at an example, while looking at properties, of the `self` object. Put simply, the `self` object is the instance of the class that you are presently working upon within a class method. This isn't always clear, so let's look at a few very simple examples of what `self` means:

```
a1 = Foo()
a2 = Foo()
a3 = Foo()
```

Assuming, in this code, that `Foo` is a class, then `a1`, `a2`, and `a3` are all instances of the `Foo` class. When you create them, you get a variable that you can use. Now, again assuming that the `print_me` method below is a method of the `Foo` class:

```
a1.print_me()
```

This line of code indicates that you are calling a method, `print_me`, on an object, `a1`. The actual method signature for the `print_me` method probably looks something like this:

```
def print_me(self) :
    # do something
```

As you can see in the calling example, however, you are not passing any arguments to the method, yet it expects a single argument called `self`. How does that work, exactly? The answer is a bit of behind-the-scenes magic by the Python interpreter. When the interpreter encounters a line like this:

```
a1.print_me()
```

It translates that line, behind your back, into something that looks like this:

```
Foo.print_me(a1)
```

Note that the line shown here is for illustrative purposes only. This line of Python code never really exists in your application.

The `Foo` part is simply the name of the class, so that the interpreter knows which version of a function called `print_me` to call. The `print_me` part, obviously, is the method name within that class. The `a1` part, on the other hand, represents the `self` argument. Since an instance of a class can have its own values for all of the attributes and properties defined within the class, it makes sense that you want to differentiate between the instances in your methods. Let's look at a simple example of what we are talking about:

```
>>> class Foo :
        def __init__(self) :
            self.x = 1

        def print_me(self) :
            print "x = ", self.x

>>> f = Foo()
>>> f.print_me()
x =  1
```

Don't worry about the __init__ method quite yet. The class `Foo` defines a method called `print_me`. This method refers to an instance of the `Foo` class and prints out the variable `x` in that instance. If you had several instances and changed their `x` values, you would get different outputs from the method:

```
>>> f1 = Foo()
>>> f1.x = 2
>>> f2 = Foo()
>>> f1.x = 3
>>> f3 = Foo()
>>> f1.x = 2
>>> f3.x = 3
>>> f1.print_me()
x =  2
>>> f2.print_me()
x =  1
>>> f3.print_me()
x =  3
```

The important thing to remember is that the `self` argument refers to the instance of the class that you are working with. If you do not use the instance value within a method, you will get the class value of a variable, which may or may not be the same thing. Any method that is called for a given instance (that is, any method that has an object and a dot on the left-hand side of it) must have `self` as the first argument to the method.

You might wonder if you can create a method that does not accept a `self` argument and then use it without any sort of instance variable. The answer is "not really." If you are accustomed to C++ and its static methods, you will find there is nothing directly comparable in Python. This isn't really a bad thing, as consistency in usage more than makes up for the lack of the feature.

Obviously, the `self` parameter is a reserved word in Python. You cannot use `self` as a secondary parameter in a method call. However, it is perfectly acceptable to use `self` in a non-class function, as you can see in this simple example:

```
>>> def func(self) :
        print "Self = ", self
```

```
>>> func(1)
Self =  1
```

This is a bad habit to get into, however, as you should think of `self` as a reserved keyword for class methods only. Once you get used to it, working with the `self` variable will be as natural as writing code.

Methods

We have briefly looked at the concept of methods previously in this chapter. A method is no more than a function that is defined within a class scope. Methods do, as previously mentioned, have a special parameter called `self`, which identifies the instance of the class that is being operated on by the method. Methods can only be called for class instances in Python, with the exception of the aforementioned static method

As with any other sort of function, methods may take arguments. These arguments may interact with, and even replace, what instance variables in the object refer to, that the method is operating upon. For example, let's consider a simple class that has an instance variable called `cost`. You can retrieve the cost by using a method called `get_cost` that allows you to pass in a multiplier. You can set the cost by using a method called `set_cost` that allows you to set the cost from an input value. How would you accomplish these tasks? The following code will do it:

```
class Cost_example :
    def __init__(self) :
        self.cost = 0

    def get_cost(self, multiplier=1.0) :
```

```
        return self.cost * multiplier

    def set_cost(self, value) :
        """ This method allows you to set the cost to a given value.
            Value must be a numeric.
        """
        self.cost = value
```

Note the use of a doc string in the `set_cost` method. This allows you to display some information for the programmer when he starts to call the `set_cost` method in code. You might use this class in the following manner in the interpreter:

```
>>> ce = Cost_example()
>>> ce.set_cost(10.0)
>>> print ce.get_cost(2.0)
20.0
```

There are a few important things to note about this set of methods. First, note the use of the `self` parameter. You are using the instance (`self`) to store a variable (`cost`) for use in other methods. Once the `cost` variable has been assigned within the instance, it is available to any method of the class. Secondly, notice that you can pass arguments to the methods of a class other than the `self` parameter. The parameters all come after the `self` argument. When you are actually calling the method, you omit the `self` argument, since it is automatically passed by the interpreter. For example, in your `get_cost` call, you pass a single argument, 10.0, to the method, but the method signature indicates that there are two arguments: `self` and `cost`. This all works itself out in the interpreter, and you don't need to worry about it, but it can be a bit confusing the first few times you work with classes and methods.

Two other things immediately leap out when you study the code. Methods can take default values for arguments just like normal functions. In fact, for the most part, you can do anything with a method that you can do with a function. As you can see in the `get_cost` method, you can return values, just as you can with functions.

The primary difference between ordinary functions and methods is less in the functionality provided by each, and more by the way in which they can be invoked. Methods are invoked for a given instance object, whereas functions are invoked in ordinary code with no restrictions. However, more importantly, there are a number of special methods that you need to be aware of. Some of these we have looked at briefly in this chapter, and we will look at the rest of them now.

Special Methods

When you create a class in Python, there are certain methods that are automatically defined for the class, whether or not you ever write any code for them. These methods can be overridden in your own code to perform some special processing if the need arises. There are three basic methods that are auto-generated (although others exist). For now, we will consider only the three cases of initialization, termination, and string conversion for an object.

Initialization

If I have a class named Foo, and I create an instance of that class using the code "f = Foo()" then what really happens? First, the interpreter allocates a block of memory for use with the "f" object. Next, the object receives the type Foo. Finally, the object is initialized. By default, the initialization process does nothing except allocate the object. You can, however, modify the initialization process to do pretty much anything you want to do in your own code.

The special name of the initialization function is __init__. Remember that private members of a class are defined using two underscores in front of them. Private methods of a class are done the same way. You cannot directly invoke the __init__ method of a class, but the interpreter will do that for you when you create an instance of the class. The signature of the __init__ method, surprisingly, is not fixed. You are allowed to pass values to the initialization method so that they can be used in your own code. However, unlike other programming languages, such as Java or C++, you cannot have multiple initialization functions (they are called *constructors* in those languages). You can have only one __init__ method defined for each class. If you define more than one method of a name, the code will load properly, but only the last implementation of the method will be used. This is, of course, true of all methods, not simply the __init__ method.

So what can you do in an initialization method? The most common use of the method is to create and assign values to the instance variables that you want to use across all instances of the class. For example, let's consider a very simply class that maintains an instance variable called value. You can make sure that the value is assigned and exists in every instance of the class by placing an assignment to the variable in the initialization method of the class:

```
class Constr :
    def init (self, v) :
        self.value = v


    def get_value(self) :
        return self.value
```

It can be annoying to have to remember to pass in values to the initialization function, so Python allows you to have a default value for the arguments:

```
    def init (self, v=0) :
```

This way, you can write either of the following two lines and accomplish the same thing in terms of initialization:

```
c = Constr(0)
c = Constr()
```

Naturally, you can always pass in a non-zero value if you want to use that value for the initialization of the value class variable. In addition to assigning passed-in values to instance variables, you can define any of the instance variables you want to exist in all members of the class in the __init__ method. You can even use properties in the method if you like and the proper handling will be done for them.

One of the most common things to do with initialization methods is to keep a reference count of the number of objects created and destroyed. This is particularly easy when you know exactly when the object is created. How do you know when the object is destroyed? That is taken care of in the termination method.

Termination

It only makes sense that if there is a specialized method that is called when an object is created and initialized, there should be a specialized method that should be called when the object goes out of scope and is destroyed. In Python, this termination method is called __del__. By default, all this method ever does is to remove the reference to the object. However, you can override the method to do pretty much anything you want it to do.

Unlike the initialization method, the termination method does not take any arguments aside from the self parameter. You cannot pass in arguments, simply because there is no specific way in which to remove the object (other than explicitly calling del() on the object, which takes no arguments either).

One important note: Termination takes place at the discretion of the garbage collection system in Python. There is no particular definition for when your __del__ method will be called, other than the guarantee that the object will eventually be destroyed, and your method will eventually be called.

To look at the usage of the __del__ method, let's create a simple object that implements an initialization and a termination method, create a few objects, and see what happens.

```
class Test_init_term :

    refCount = 0
    def __init__(self) :
        test_init_term.refCount = test_init_term.refCount + 1
        print "init: RefCount is now: ", test_init_term.refCount
```

```
    def __del__(self) :
        test_init_term.refCount = test_init_term.refCount - 1
        print "del: RefCount is now: ", test_init_term.refCount


def test_function() :
    t1 = Test_init_term()
    t2 = Test_init_term()
    t3 = Test_init_term()
```

Why did we place the object creation in a function? Primarily because that way the objects would go out of scope faster, and you could watch the process occur in the interpreter. Running the function in the interpreter results in the following output:

```
>>> test_function()
init: RefCount is now:   1
init: RefCount is now:   2
init: RefCount is now:   3
del: RefCount is now:   2
del: RefCount is now:   1
del: RefCount is now:   0
```

One last note about the above class definition: In addition to its overriding of the initialization and termination methods, there is one more little thing to observe. You will notice the use of a static (or class level) variable to maintain the reference count. Class instance variables are unique across all instances of the class. That is, no matter how many objects of the class you create, there will only be a single refCount variable shared among them. This is a handy little trick you can use for a lot of uses, including reference counting.

String Conversion

Have you ever wondered how Python is able to convert types into strings with the str() and repr() functions? The answer lies in another special method that can be overridden for classes, called the stringify, or __str__ method. This method is used to convert the internal values of a class into a string representation for display to the end user. Normally, this method is generated for you automatically by using the internal components of your class to create a set of string outputs, which are combined into a single string for display. However, it is possible to override this method to create your own specialized string display. If you are wondering, there is also a __repr__ method that can be overridden to allow that particular function to work. The difference is, the __str__ method does not have to produce a valid Python expression, which the __repr__ method does. Otherwise, they are exactly the same.

To illustrate the __str__ method, let's create a class that represents money. The class will have two attributes: dollars and cents. The string method will produce an output using the dollars and cents to create a monetary display that we are accustomed to seeing.

1. Create a new file, using either the IDLE editor or the editor of your choice. Give the file the name ch10_4.py.

2. Enter the following text into the ch10_4.py file:

```python
class Money(object) :
    def __init__(self) :
        # Set dollars and cents to 0 initially
        self.dollars = 0
        self.cents = 0

    def __str__(self) :
        return "$" + str(self.dollars) + "." + str(self.cents)

    def get_dollars(self) :
        return self.dollars

    def get_cents(self) :
        return self.cents

    def set_dollars(self, d) :
        self.dollars = d

    def set_cents(self, c ) :
        self.cents = c
```

> ❄ **Note on File Naming**
>
> If you have chosen another name, or location, for the file, substitute the file name of your choice in the line marked with the comment "#1."

3. Save the file to a location of your choice by using the File | Save command.

4. Run the file in the interpreter by either selecting Run | Run Module in the editor window or by pressing the F5 key on Windows.

❄ ❄ ❄

5. Now enter the following code into the IDLE interpreter and observe the results. You should see something that looks like this:

```
>>> m = Money()
>>> print str(m)
$0.0
>>> m.set_dollars(10)
>>> m.set_cents(50)
>>> print str(m)
$10.50
```

As you can see, the output is exactly what you would have expected from the Python `str()` function for a monetary value. This shows you that it is possible not only to define functionality for your class so that it works properly for the user, but also to make it easier for the user to display your object values properly. You could easily add additional functionality to the class, such as defining the output format, or setting the dollar character to something other than the dollar sign ('$').

Inheritance

In several of the examples we've looked at so far in this chapter, you have seen a class defined in the following way:

```
class <classname>(object) :
```

Up to this point, we've pretty much ignored this part of the class definition, with the exception of the class name field itself. However, that little area within the parentheses is rather interesting. When you create a class and place the name of another class in the parentheses, you are inheriting from the parenthetical class. That is, your class name is really of type "object." You do not, however, have to derive things from object; you can derive them from anything that you like.

Let's imagine, for example, that you have a class called `Car`. If this sounds familiar, it probably is, since we talked about this example in the last chapter. The `Car` class has a number of attributes, such as a name, a color, the number of tires, and the miles per gallon it gets on the highway. You might implement such a class like this:

```
class Car :
    def __init__(self) :
        self.color = "black"
        self.number_of_tires = 4
        self.miles_per_gallon = 20

    def __str__(self) :
```

```
        return "Car { Color: "+self.color+" Tires: "+str(self.number_of_tires) \
              +" MPG: " + str(self.miles_per_gallon) + " }"

    def set_color( self, clr ) :
        self.color = clr

    def get_color( self ) :
        return self.color

    def set_number_of_tires( self, nt ) :
        self.number_of_tires = nt

    def get_number_of_tires( self ) :
        return self.number_of_tires

    def set_miles_per_gallon( self, mpg ) :
        self.miles_per_gallon = mpg

    def get_miles_per_gallon( self ) :
        return self.miles_per_gallon
```

Now, let's imagine that you have a new kind of car, called a Hybrid. This car has all of the attributes of a normal car, but also has a new attribute, called battery life. You could simply create an entirely new class called Hybrid and copy all of the functionality that you implemented for Car into it, but that would be rather wasteful. In addition, if you changed the interface for Car, you would need to change it for Hybrid as well, adding the possibility that someone will forget to make the change and introduce error into the system. This is bad enough for a single class, but imagine if you had a dozen such forms of car-like classes! You could be changing things until the cows came home.

A better approach, therefore, is to inherit the functionality of the Car class in your new Hybrid class. That way, you only change, or add to, the functionality that you need for your new class, leaving all of the existing functionality alone. You could do this in a number of ways, but let's look at the easiest. You will simply derive from the existing Car class and add your single new attribute.

```
class Hybrid(Car) : #1
    def __init__(self) :
        Car.__init__(self) #2
```

```
        self.battery_life = 20

    def __str__(self) :
        s = Car.__str__(self) #3
        s = s + " Battery Life: " + str(self.battery_life)
        return s

    def set_battery_life(self, bl ) :
        self.battery_life = bl

    def get_battery_life(self) :
        return self.battery_life
```

There are some interesting aspects to this little code listing, so let's take a look at a few of them. First, notice how you can derive your class from an existing class called Car. This is done on the line marked with the comment #1. Once you do this, Python knows that your class really *is* a Car with some additional features. This is called an "is-a" relationship.

Next, take a look at the line marked with the comment #2. This line might not be as obvious to you in terms of functionality. The easiest way to see what is going on here is to remove the line and then run the program. If you comment out the line containing the comment #2 and then run the thing, you will still load properly in the interpreter. However, when you create an instance of the Hybrid class and try to print it out, something interesting happens. Let's try it:

```
>>> c = Car()
>>> h = Hybrid()
>>> print h

Traceback (most recent call last):
  File "<pyshell#16>", line 1, in <module>
    print h
  File "E:/Python/ch10_5.py", line 36, in __str__
    s = Car.__str__(self)
  File "E:/Python/ch10_5.py", line 10, in __str__
    +" MPG: " + str(self.miles_per_gallon) + " }"
AttributeError: Hybrid instance has no attribute 'color'
```

You get an error in the base class routine that *stringifies* the class. Why? The answer is, the base constructor __init__ routine was never called, so the instance variables for the base class were never created properly, and thus cannot be used. When you put the line marked #1 back in, you get a very different result from the same code:

```
>>> c = Car()
>>> h = Hybrid()
>>> print c
Car { Color: black Tires: 4 MPG: 20 }
>>> print h
Car { Color: black Tires: 4 MPG: 20 } Battery Life: 20
```

It is extremely important that you remember to "chain down" the list of inherited classes. Since Python will permit you to inherit from a class which it itself inherited from other classes, you can see where this chain could become quite long in theory. However, as long as each class calls its "parent" class (that is, the class from which it is derived), then the chain remains unbroken and everything works fine.

Going back a bit, look at the line marked with the comment #3. This line is calling the base class __str__() function to build a car string, and then appending more information to it. This is the entire purpose of inheritance, using the base class functionality and adding to it.

Just one last comment about inheritance, and we will move on. The best part of inheritance is the ability to change the functionality of the base class without having it be aware of what you are doing. For example, consider the following example of a new kind of Car class:

```
class ThreeWheelCar(Car) :
    def __init__(self) :
        Car.__init__(self)
        self.number_of_tires = 3
>>> c = Car()
>>> t = ThreeWheelCar()
>>> print c
Car { Color: black Tires: 4 MPG: 20 }
>>> print t
Car { Color: black Tires: 3 MPG: 20 }
```

In this example, you create a new kind of Car that only has three wheels. Rather than modify the attribute of the Car class to support three wheels, you simply create a new class and modify the attribute within the constructor for your new class. The Car class is not modified, but rather a new class is created, When you print the car out, it has the proper number of wheels.

Multiple Inheritance

Python supports multiple inheritance, allowing you to derive from more than one base class at a time. This is different than chaining up from a single base class along a specific route of inherited classes. In multiple inheritance, you combine separate base classes that are not involved with each other to form a group of classes from which a derived class is "'built."

Before we discuss multiple inheritance, a few warnings are in order. First, there are those in the object-oriented community who consider multiple inheritance "bad." It is true that it makes the code more complicated and confusing, and can lead to some very strange errors. However, there is nothing inherently wrong with a language feature, only how it is used and abused. If you have a valid case where multiple inheritance will work best, you should use it. Now, with that said, how do you implement inheriting from multiple classes in Python?

To inherit from more than one class, you simply list the classes individually on the class definition line for your derived class. Let's assume that you have three base classes: A, B, and C, and want a fourth class D that inherits from all three. Let's look at an example of this, and what is required to make it all work.

```
class A :
    def __init__(self) :
        self.a = 1

    def print_me(self) :
        print "A: " + str(self.a)

class B :
    def __init__(self) :
        self.b = 2

    def print_me(self) :
        print "B: " + str(self.b)

class C :
    def __init__(self) :
        self.c = 3

    def print_me(self) :
```

```
        print "C: " + str(self.c)



class D(A,B,C) :
    def __init__(self) :
        A.__init__(self)
        B.__init__(self)
        C.__init__(self)
        self.d = 4


    def printme(self) :
        A.print_me(self)
        B.print_me(self)
        C.print_me(self)
        print "D: "+str(self.d)
```

You can now create instances of the D class and print them, so let's do that in the interpreter:

```
>>> d = D()
>>> d.print_me()
A: 1
```

Wait a second, what happened here? The `print_me` method should have called your `print` method, which should have printed out all of the base classes, right? Ah, but looking back at the code, you can see that you misspelled the `print_me` method as `printme` in the D class. This points out one of the problems with inheritance. When you re-implement methods in derived classes, you have to make sure that the name and arguments match exactly. After changing `printme` to `print_me` in the D class, you get the following output:

```
>>> d = D()
>>> d.print_me()
A: 1
B: 2
C: 3
D: 4
```

Inheritance works fine, whether singly or multiply inheriting from base classes. However, you must call each of the base classes that you want to work with, as shown in the `__init__` method for class D. Also, as we have seen, if you call a method that does not exist in the derived class, the base class version will be used. So how does it know which one to call? If you look at the class tree, it is obvious that there are three choices in the base class hierarchy that are called "print_me." But Python has no clue which version of the print_me method you want to call, so it applies a search to find one. The search for derived classes is done by searching from left to right, based on the order in which the classes were added to the definition of the derived class. Since our definition of "D" is "A, B, C," the order is exactly that. So, first the A class will be searched for a method matching the name, then B, and then C. This assumes, of course, that the method name was not found in the D class. If so, it will always be used first. Otherwise, multiple inheritance works just the way single inheritance does.

Using super

One last note about using inheritance in Python, sometimes you will need to override the functionality of a base class, but still use that information in the derived class. We've seen how you can call the base class method directly previously. However, there may be times when you don't exactly know which base class implements the functionality you want. For cases like this, the super() function was invented. In order to use the super() function, you need to derive all of your classes from object, but this really isn't much of a problem, since you should really be doing that anyway. The object class is the fundamental class in Python, and gives you a lot of functionality (like super() and property()) that you want anyway.

Let's look at an example of using the super() function, as well as a pretty cool way to implement saving an object in a generic fashion:

```
class A(object) :
    def __init__(self) :
        self.a = 1

    def multiply(self, v) :
        return self.a * v

class B(object) :
    def __init__(self) :
        self.b = 2

    def save(self) :
        print "Saving Object.."
        for a in vars(self) :
            print "Saving " + a

class C(A,B) :
```

```
def __init__(self) :
    A.__init__(self)
    B.__init__(self)

def multiply_and_save(self, v) :
    super(C,self).multiply(v)
    super(C,self).save()
```

The first two classes are just average everyday implementations of Python classes, both of which are derived from object. The first class implements a `multiply()` method, while the second one implements a `save()` method. You then have a third class, C, which inherits from the first two and implements a method that combines the functionality of the first two classes. You initialize all of the classes properly in the C class and add nothing new to the equation here. It is in the `multiply_and_save` method that things get interesting. First, look at the way in which you call the base class methods. Rather than referring directly to the class that implements them, you use the `super()` function to find the right class in the inheritance tree that implements the method you want. Note that you don't have to pass the self parameter to the base classes, it is found via the `super()` function call. Also note that the function properly finds the base class that first implements the method, just as if you had called it from the derived class.

The really cool thing, however, is in the `save` method of the B class. Note the use of the `vars()` function. This method returns all of the variables in the variable dictionary for the instance object that is passed to it. Because the instance is of type C, however, rather than type B, both the variables defined in A and B are found and saved. If you run this little script, you will see that this is the case:

```
>>> c = C()
>>> c.multiply_and_save(3)
Saving Object..
Saving a
Saving b
```

Hopefully, you can see the benefits of doing things this way. You can create a single `save()` interface for a class and inherit it in all of the other classes. For example, you might implement a class like this:

```
class Save(object) :
    def __init__(self) :
        self.filename = "save.txt"

    def save(self) :
```

```
        fH = open(self.filename, "w")
        for a in vars(self) :
            fH.write( a )
            fH.write( "=" )
            fH.write( str(self.__dict__[a]) )
            fH.write("\n")
        fH.close()


class D(Save) :
    def __init__(self) :
        Save.__init__(self)
        self.name = "D"
        self.value = 3
        self.color = "blue"

    def __del__(self) :
        super(D, self).save()
```

The `save()` method can be called from any derived class, and will save all of the components of the class to a file whose name can be changed at runtime. For example, if you try this little snippet in the interpreter:

```
>>> d = D()
>>> del d
```

Nothing appears to happen in this case, but a file is created in the current directory, called `save.txt`. If you look at this file, you will see that it contains the following text:

```
C:\Python>type save.txt
color=blue
name=D
value=3
filename=save.txt
```

Polymorphism

In the previous chapter, we discussed the concept of polymorphism. This is the ability to change the behavior of a function without having to change the code. Python most certainly supports this object-oriented concept, without a whole lot of work on your part. Let's say, for example, that you wanted a function that would rotate the tires on your car, putting the first tire on the second position, the second on the third, and so forth until the last tire went onto the first position. You could write such a function like this:

```python
def rotate_tires( car ) :
    for i in range(1, car.tire_count()) :
        print "Moving tire from " + str(i)
        car.set_tire( i+1 )
    print "Moving tire from " + str(car.tire_count())
    car.set_tire( 1 )
```

This function assumes that it is receiving an object which supports two methods: tire_count and set_tire. Any class that supports those two methods will work fine for rotation. Now, you might have two classes:

```python
class Car(object) :
    def __init__(self) :
        self.number_of_tires = 4

    def set_tire( self, nPos ) :
        print "Setting tire into position: " + str(nPos )

    def tire_count(self) :
        return self.number_of_tires


class Hybrid(Car) :
    def __init__(self) :
        self.number_of_tires = 3
```

If you run the function with the two different sorts of car objects, you get different outputs, just as you would expect:

```
>>> c = Car()
>>> rotate_tires(c)
Moving tire from 1
Setting tire into position: 2
Moving tire from 2
Setting tire into position: 3
Moving tire from 3
Setting tire into position: 4
Moving tire from 4
```

```
Setting tire into position: 1
>>> h = Hybrid()
>>> rotate_tires(h)
Moving tire from 1
Setting tire into position: 2
Moving tire from 2
Setting tire into position: 3
Moving tire from 3
Setting tire into position: 1
```

As you can see, it can be useful to have polymorphic functions in a programming language. Python does this as well, if not better, than any other language. The ability to write code that can be reused with completely different types of objects that share only a common set of functions is very powerful. You could, for example, write a `save()` function that worked with any sort of object, as was illustrated previously in the multiple inheritance case. That would certainly be impressive.

Exception Classes

Back in Chapter 8, we talked about exceptions and exception handling in Python. During that discussion, it was mentioned that you could develop your own personalized exceptions, but that it could only be done by implementing your own exception class derived from the basic exception class in Python. Since you now have enough background to understand exactly what all that means, it is time to actually approach the problem of deriving your own exception classes.

Let's imagine that you are writing a program and need to check an input value. You could put the same basic code everywhere to check a given value to be within a given range, but wouldn't it be easier to just check that stuff in a single function? Sure, and while you are at it, why not define a standard way in which to report errors? Let's use a user-defined exception to tell the users when they enter something invalid.

```python
class RangeException(Exception) :
    def __init__(self, low, high) :
        self.low = low
        self.high = high
    def __str__(self) :
        s = "Expected value in range "+str(self.low)
        s = s + " to "
        s = s + str(self.high)
```

```
        return s

def CheckValue( inV ) :
    if ( inV < 0 or inV > 10 ) :
        raise RangeException(0,10)
    return True
```

The `RangeException` class, which is derived from the basic Exception type, will do the work of storing the expected range and letting the user know what they did wrong. Because the *stringify* function of the class is defined, the exception will be printed out normally in the interpreter, and can be caught in user code. To show you what we mean, first, let's try it in the interpreter:

```
>>> CheckValue(12)

Traceback (most recent call last):
  File "<pyshell#2>", line 1, in <module>
    CheckValue(12)
  File "E:/Python/ch10_9.py", line 14, in CheckValue
    raise RangeException(0,10)
RangeException: Expected value in range 0 to 10
```

As expected, when the user enters a value that is outside of the range, the function raises your custom exception and the interpreter prints out an error. If you wanted to catch this error in code of your own, you would use a `try..catch` block to do so. Because your `RangeException` class is derived from the basic `Exception` class, you can catch it properly.

```
>>> import sys

>>> try :
        CheckValue(12)
except Exception:
        print sys.exc_info()


(<class '__main__.RangeException'>, RangeException(), <traceback object
at 0x00C4B558>)
```

In fact, if you wanted to work with the "real" exception that was generated, you could do that as well:

```
>>> try :
        CheckValue(12)
except RangeException, re:
        print "You didn't enter a value between: "+str(re.low)+", and
"+str(re.high)
```

```
You didn't enter a value between: 0, and 10
```

That's really about all you need to know about custom defined exceptions. If you can create a class, derive from a base class, and implement a few simple methods, you can create whatever sorts of exception classes you want in your own applications.

Iterators

As we learned about various parts of the Python language, one of the more interesting and useful features was that of the `for` loop. The looping construct in Python is really just an iterator, stepping through the various pieces of a collection. Wouldn't it be nice if you could define a collection class that could be used in the same sort of loop? For example, imagine being able to define a collection that was a list of files and being able to step through them the same way that you are able to step through a list, or array, or dictionary. Well, as it happens, you can do just this with Python.

There is nothing magic about iteration. The Python interpreter looks for certain special methods within a class to indicate whether or not the class supports iteration. If those methods are found, you can use the class with an iterator. If they are not found, you cannot—it is really that easy. The two methods you are required to implement are `__iter__` and `__next__`. All you really need to know is that when the `next` method is called, and there are no more items to iterate over, you should raise a `StopIteration` exception. Otherwise, what you return and how you choose to return your data is completely up to you.

Let's look at a simple example of iteration. In this case, you will implement a class that contains a list of files. For simplicity, the files will be hard-coded into the class, to avoid making the code more complicated than it needs to be.

1. Create a new file, using either the IDLE editor or the editor of your choice. Give the file the name `ch10_10.py`.
2. Enter the following text into the `ch10_10.py` file:

```
class FileList:
    "Implement a collection of files as an iterated list"
    def __init__(self):
        self.ptr = 0
        self.file_list = ["file1", "file2", "file3", "file4" ]
    def __iter__(self):
        self.ptr = 0
        # Indicate we support iteration
        return self
    def next(self):
        # See if we are at the end of the list
        if self.ptr == len(self.file_list):
            raise StopIteration
        # No, go ahead and store the current item
        s = self.file_list[self.ptr]
        # No, increment the pointer
        self.ptr = self.ptr + 1
        # And give them back an item.
        return s
```

❄ **Note on File Naming**

If you have chosen another name or location for the file, substitute the file name of your choice in the line marked with the comment "#1."

3. Save the file to a location of your choice by using the File | Save command.

4. Run the file in the interpreter by either selecting Run | Run Module in the editor window or by pressing the F5 key on Windows.

5. Now enter the following code into the IDLE interpreter and observe the results. You should see something that looks like this:
```
>>> fl = FileList()
>>> for f in fl :
        print f
```

```
file1
```

```
file2
file3
file4
```

Remember, there is nothing sacred about the way in which iteration works. If you wanted to, you could return the file list in reverse order, or even in a completely random order. The only important part is that you start and end the process in a reasonable manner. By the way, note the reset of the `self.ptr` variable in the `__iter__` method. This is very important. The `__iter__` method is called when the iteration process begins (that is, when you say "for f in fl"). If you do not reset the pointer when you begin the process, you will only be able to iterate over the collection once. In some cases, this may actually make sense, such as when you are removing items from a collection as you process them. For most static collections, however, you will want to give the user the capability to go back over them as many times as necessary.

Operator Overloading

The final topic we are going to discuss in this chapter is that of operator overloading. The idea of overloading various operators is not a new one; it has been used in a multitude of languages, from C++ to C# and others. The concept is simple: If you can define a new type (which is what a class really is), you should be able to define how the operators for that class work. For example, consider the string class. You can "add" strings using the "+" operator, to concatenate them. It would be kind of nice if you could "subtract" strings using the "-" operator, but the implementers of the class chose not to give you that functionality. This tells you a lot about the power and flexibility of Python—you can choose to implement the pieces of the language that you want to, without being hemmed in by other people's idea of what is right or wrong in terms of functionality.

The four basic functions for operators are:

❋ `__add__` : Implements the plus "+" operator.

❋ `__sub__` : Implements the minus "-" operator.

❋ `__mul__` : Implements the multiplication "*" operator.

❋ `__div__` : Implements the division "/" operator.

To show you how this works, here's a very simple and very dumb example. This example creates a class whose internal value is always modified by two times the value you use to modify it. This means that if you add two to the value of the class instance, you will really be adding four. If you multiply by four, you are really multiplying by eight, and so forth. Finally, if you compare the value to a known value, the internal value will really be compared to the value times two, just for completeness. No, it isn't a realistic example, and you are unlikely to ever use it, but it does illustrate how to work with operator overloading without overloading you with code.

Here's the class definition:

```
class Double(object) :

    def __init__(self) :
        self.value = 0

    def __add__(self, value) :
        return self.value + 2 * value

    def __sub__(self, value) :
        return self.value - 2 * value

    def __mul__(self, value) :
        return self.value * (2*value)

    def __div__(self, value) :
        return self.value / (2*value)

    def __cmp__(self, value) :
        if self.value < (value*2) :
            return -1
        elif self.value == value*2 :
            return 0
        else :
            return 1
```

To use the class, you just instantiate an object of type `Double` and assign a value to the internal member containing the number value of the class:

```
>>> d = Double()
>>> d.value = 10
```

At this point, you have a `Double` instance that contains the value 10. As mentioned, you should be able to add, multiply, divide, and subtract from the class instance. Looking at this simple output in the IDLE interpreter, you will find this to be true:

```
>>> print d + 2
14
>>> print d - 2
```

```
6
>>> print d * 2
40
>>> print d / 1
5
```

Note one very important point here. The operators return a value based on the internal representation of the object. They do not modify the object value. That is, when you multiply a Double object by two, you get back the result in a new variable, without changing the internal value of the Double object. This is important, and a common mistake among new users of operator overloading. Wouldn't it be a bit strange to say "a+2" and have the value of "a" change? Of course, it would; it would be silly. That's why the operator methods in the class return a value, but do not assign it to the self.value variable.

Finally, we can compare values, as we've seen in the class definition. Here's a simple example of using that code in the interpreter:

```
>>> if d < 5 : print "Less than 5"
else : print "Not less than 5"


Not less than 5
```

Since the assigned value of "d" is 10, and you compare it to twice the value that is shown on the less than line (5, in this case), the two values are actually equal. Can you therefore compare the values and get a correct result?

```
>>> d.value = 10
>>> if d == 5 :
        print "Yes!"
else :
        print "no..."



Yes!
```

The __cmp__ method is called for all comparisons, whether they are less than, greater than, equal to, not equal to, and so forth and so on. The result of the __cmp__ method is used to determine how the values compare, and the interpreter uses that result based on the operator invoked. The return from the __cmp__ method should always be less than zero (doesn't matter what, as long as it is negative) if the internal value is less than the compared value. It should be greater than zero if the internal value is greater than the compared value, and zero if the two values are the same. By using those three "signal" values, the interpreter knows how to do the comparisons.

In Conclusion

That concludes our tour of classes in Python. At this point, you know all of the basics of the language and its syntax. In the next chapter, we will take some time to explore the core of the Python library and show how to use the various classes, methods, and functions that work with Python code. After that, the remainder of the book will illustrate how to use Python in real-world environments. Congratulations! You are now a Python programmer!

11} The Python Library

The heart and soul of any programming language, from the perspective of the programmer, is the composition of the libraries that it ships with. After all, if you have a wonderful programming syntax and marvelous constructs, but you can't use the language for anything, it makes no sense at all to try to use it in a production environment. Fortunately for the Python programmer, the Python environment that ships with version 2.5 is one of the richest available to any programmer.

In this chapter, we are going to explore many of the modules available to you in the standard version of the 2.5 Python library. This will not include user interface or database elements, since we are going to discuss those in future sections of the book. Instead, it includes the kinds of modules that you are most likely to need in the development of the majority of your scripts.

Python is, at its heart, a language that is used for utility programming. Simple scripts, quick and dirty applications, and the like are the core of what Python programmers spend the majority of their time doing. This is not to say that the language cannot be used for more complex and lengthy tasks, but it is much more common to write a Python script to accomplish a single, one-off task than to develop a full-blown application in it. The library components that ship with the system, therefore, are optimized for quick and dirty jobs, and they do that job very well.

Let's take a look at some of the modules that ship with Python and how you can integrate them into your application scripts.

Containers

The first module we are going to look at is one that is fairly new to the Python library system: the containers module. As you might guess, the containers module contains classes that extend the default container objects in Python. We've looked at the simple containers in Python: the tuple, list, array, and dictionary. In the containers module, you will find more complex classes that are slightly more special purpose.

The first class in the containers module is the deque class. This class, pronounced like a "deck" of cards, is a double-ended queue (hence the de-queue name). You can add or remove elements from either end of a deque, making it ideal for uses in implementations like stacks.

The deque class works with any iterable object or set of objects. As you saw in the last chapter, an iterable object is one that implements the __iter__ and __next__ methods internally. Any string can be iterated over, so they are certainly candidates. Arrays, lists, and dictionaries can all be iterated, and thus can be targets for a deque.

Table 11-1 lists all of the methods of the deque class, with a short explanation of what they do. Take a look at the table, and then we will look at some examples of creating and using instances of the class to accomplish certain tasks.

Table 11-1 The Deque Class

Method	Purpose
deque([iterable])	Creates a new deque object using an optional iterable as the starting point. If no input is given, the initial queue is empty.
append(x)	Adds a new object, x, to the right-hand end of a deque object.
appendleft(x)	Adds a new object, x, to the left-hand end of a deque object.
clear	Removes all objects from a given deque object.
extend(iterable)	Adds the items in an iterable object to the right-hand side of a deque object.
extendleft(iterable)	Adds the items in an iterable object to the left-hand side of a deque object.
pop	Removes the "top" item from the right-hand side of the deque.
popleft	Removes the "top" item form the left-hand side of the deque.
remove(value)	Removes the first occurrence of a given value in the deque. If the item is not found, an exception is raised.
rotate	Removes items from the right-hand side of the deque and appends them to the left-hand side.

Working with the deque Class

The first step to working with deque objects is to create one. In reality, there are three basic use cases for working with a deque. First, you can create an empty one. Second, you can create one from some external collection object, such as a string or list. Finally, you can create one from another deque object. Let's take a look at all three possibilities and see how they work out. Consider the following examples, shown in the IDLE interpreter:

```
>>> from collections import deque
>>> dq = deque()
```

```
>>> for e in dq :
        print e


>>> dq1 = deque(['a','b','c'])
>>> for e in dq1 :
        print e


a
b
c
>>> dq2 = deque({1:"a", 2:"b", 3:"c"})
>>> for e in dq2 :
        print e


1
2
3
>>> dq3 = deque(dq1)
>>> for e in dq3 :
        print e


a
b
c
```

Example 1 simply creates an empty `deque`. It is no real surprise that such a collection would contain no elements, and iterating through it shows this to be true. The next two examples show different ways to create a `deque` from a set of collection objects. The first is a list, while the second is a dictionary. Note that the elements stored in the `deque` are the same as you would get if you iterated over the selected collection. For example, if you had a dictionary defined as an object, as you do in the Python shell in the second example, you might try to iterate over it like this:

```
>>> dict = {1:"a", 2:"b", 3:"c"}
>>> for d in dict :
        print d


1
2
3
```

As you can see, the result of a dictionary iteration (iterating over the keys of a dictionary) is exactly the same as a deque iteration, which is what you would expect. The final example, using a deque as input to another deque, also works as expected. Now, once you have defined a deque, what can you do with it?

Let's write a simple program that lets you see the effect that various actions have on a deque. By watching the output of a given action, you will have a much better idea of how things work.

1. Create a new file, using either the IDLE editor or the editor of your choice. Give the file the name ch11_1.py.

2. Enter the following text into the ch11_1.py file:

```
from collections import deque
done = False
dq = deque()
while not done :
    cmd = raw_input("Enter a command (or help): ")
    if cmd == "help" :
        print "The following commands are available: "
        print "add : add a new entry to the deque"
        print "remove : remove an entry from the deque"
        print "print : display the current state of the deque"
        print "rotate: rotate the deque one position"
        print "clear: remove all entries from the deque"
        print "str : insert a new string of characters"
        print "done: exit the program"
    elif cmd == "add" :
        d = raw_input("Add at the (l)eft or (r)ight of the deque: ")
        val = raw_input("Enter value to add: ")
        if d[0] == 'l' or d[0] == 'L' :
            dq.appendleft(val)
```

```
        else :
            dq.append(val)
    elif cmd == "remove" :
        val = raw_input("Enter value to remove: ")
        try :
            dq.remove(val)
        except :
            print "Error: Value not found!"
    elif cmd == "print" :
        print "Current contents of deque: "
        for e in dq :
            print e
    elif cmd == "rotate" :
        dq.rotate()
    elif cmd == "clear" :
        dq.clear()
    elif cmd == "str" :
        dir = raw_input("Add at the (l)eft or (r)ight of the deque: ")
        val = raw_input("Enter string to add: ")
        if dir[0] == 'l' or dir[0] == 'L' :
            dq.extendleft(val)
        else :
            dq.extend(val)
    elif cmd == "done" :
        done = True
    else :
        print "I don't understand the command "+cmd
```

3. Run the program by selecting Run from the Debug menu or by pressing F5 in the editor window.

4. Enter some commands when prompted, and you should see something along the lines of the following conversation in the IDLE interpreter:

```
Enter a command (or help): help
The following commands are available:
add : add a new entry to the deque
remove : remove an entry from the deque
print : display the current state of the deque
```

```
    rotate: rotate the deque one position
    clear: remove all entries from the deque
    str : insert a new string of characters
    done: exit the program
    Enter a command (or help): add
    Add at the (l)eft or (r)ight of the deque: l
    Enter value to add: 1
    Enter a command (or help): print
    Current contents of deque:
    1
    Enter a command (or help): add
    Add at the (l)eft or (r)ight of the deque: r
    Enter value to add: 2
    Enter a command (or help): print
    Current contents of deque:
    1
    2
    Enter a command (or help): add
    Add at the (l)eft or (r)ight of the deque: l
    Enter value to add: 3
    Enter a command (or help): print
    Current contents of deque:
    3
    1
    2
    Enter a command (or help): rotate
    Enter a command (or help): print
    Current contents of deque:
    2
    3
    1
    Enter a command (or help): str
    Add at the (l)eft or (r)ight of the deque: hello world
    Enter string to add:
    Enter a command (or help): str
    Add at the (l)eft or (r)ight of the deque: l
    Enter string to add: hello
```

```
Enter a command (or help):
I don't understand the command
Enter a command (or help): print
Current contents of deque:
o
1
1
e
h
2
3
1
Enter a command (or help): clear
Enter a command (or help): print
Current contents of deque:
Enter a command (or help): done
```

Hopefully, this gives you a good idea of how to work with collections and specifically the `deque` class, in Python. The other collections class that is new to Python with release 2.4 and above is the `default_dict` class. This class works almost exactly the same way as the `dict` class that we have looked at throughout the book. There is one major difference, however, in the way that keys which are not found in the dictionary are used. For a normal dictionary, if a key is not found in the dictionary, an exception is raised:

```
>>> d = {}
>>> print d['NotThere']

Traceback (most recent call last):
  File "<pyshell#9>", line 1, in <module>
    print d['NotThere']
KeyError: 'NotThere'
```

For the `defaultdict` class, you may specify an optional "generator function" that is used to create default entries when a key is not specified. You could, for example, generate a list of numbers in sequential order, or you could simply return a value that signals to the application that the value needs to be retrieved from the user. Let's take a quick look at how this works:

```
>>> from collections import defaultdict
>>> def gen_value() :
        return "<DEFAULT>"
```

```
>>> d = defaultdict(gen_value)
>>> print d["NotThere"]
<DEFAULT>
```

There are three steps to working with the `defaultdict` class. First, you need to import the class. The class, being part of the collections module, can be imported from that module using the `from` clause of the `import` statement. Next, you need a generator function. This function must take no arguments, and must be callable without an object associated with it, so it cannot be a method of a class. In this case, we have implemented a simple function that returns a string literal, indicating that the value is "defaulted." Finally, we create the `defaultdict` class using the standard object instantiation protocol. You will notice that when we now try to retrieve a key that does not exist, no error is generated. Instead of an error, the `defaultdict` class returns our defaulted string.

Math

Python provides a rich set of mathematical functions for working with various scientific and mathematical needs. Table 11-2 shows a list of the functions available in the math library for Python. The math module needs to be imported, as do all modules in Python with the exception of built-in functions like `range()`.

Table 11-2 The Python Math Functions

Function	Purpose
ceil	Returns the largest integer greater than or equal to the number passed in.
fabs	Returns the absolute value of the number passed in, as a floating point number.
floor	Returns the largest integer smaller than or equal to the number passed in.
fmod	Equivalent to the modulus operator, but using floating point math instead of integer math.
frexp	Returns the floating point representation of a floating point number as a mantissa and exponent.
ldexp	The inverse of `frexp`, this function returns the value passed in when multiplied by 2 raised to the power passed in.
modf	Returns the fractional and integer parts of a floating point number.
exp	Returns the constant "e" raised to the power passed in.
log	Returns the logarithm of the value passed in, using the base specified (or base "e" if no base is specified).
log10	Returns the logarithm of the value in base 10.
pow	Returns the number passed in raised to the power passed in.
sqrt	Returns the square root of the value passed in.

Working with the math library is not difficult—you simply use the function as specified, prefaced by the "math" prefix. For example, here are some basic usages of math functions in Python, as they would appear in the IDLE interpreter:

```
>>> import math
>>> x = 2.5
>>> print math.floor(x)
2.0
>>> print math.ceil(x)
3.0
>>> print math.sqrt(x)
1.58113883008
>>> print math.frexp(x)
(0.625, 2)
>>> print math.modf(x)
(0.5, 2.0)
```

As you can see, there is nothing dramatic about working with these functions. It should be noted that in addition to the functions listed in the table above, Python also supports the full range of trigonometric functions (sin, cos, tan, asin, acos, atan, and so forth).

Finally, there are two constants defined in the math library that might be of interest. First, we have the value "pi," which is so important that it has its own day on the U.S. calendar (March 14th). This value, which is used in many mathematical equations and scientific calculations, is used by entering:

```
>>> print math.pi
3.14159265359
```

The other constant in the math library is the value "e," which is also important in math and engineering calculations.

```
>>> print math.e
2.71828182846
```

Complex Math

If you work in engineering, or electronics, you probably know all about complex math. When we say "complex," we are referring here to the combination of real and imaginary numbers. Of course, if you are like me, you think of imaginary numbers as something you find in your checkbook. No, these numbers are really a different form of mathematics.

The idea behind complex math is that you have a real portion and an imaginary portion, and these two portions make up a complex number that can be used for a variety of important calculations. An imaginary number, represented in math by the value "i," is found by taking the square root of a negative number. Yes, I know, they told you in elementary school that you can't do that. You can, and the result is always an imaginary number. For example, this is what a complex number looks like in the math realm:

3i + 4

In this case, the 3i is the imaginary portion and the 4 is the "real" portion of the number. You can do all sorts of math with imaginary numbers, adding them, multiplying them, subtracting them, and so forth. For reasons unknown, Python chooses to write a complex number in a slightly different format than you might be used to. So the above complex variable, written in Python format, looks like this:

4 + 3j

Working with complex numbers is not difficult, but it has some odd behavior that you would not expect when working with regular numbers. For this reason, the Python libraries provide the cmath module that contains mathematical functions designed for the complex variable type, rather than the real variable type.

To work with complex numbers, you first need to know how to create one and extract its component parts. In Python, you just write out the number in complex format, and the interpreter recognizes it as a complex number. To work with the components, you use the real and imag properties of the variable:

```
>>> x = 4+3j
>>> print x.real
4.0
>>> print x.imag
3.0
>>> print x
(4+3j)
```

There is no need to load any special libraries to work directly with the complex type, because it is built into the language. If you want to apply functions to these values, however, you will need to import the cmath module:

```
>>> import cmath
>>> print cmath.sqrt(-1)
1j
```

Note that there is a big difference between the `sqrt()` functions in the `math` module and the `cmath` module. Taking the square root of a negative number in the math module is an error:

```
>>> import math
>>> print math.sqrt(-1)

Traceback (most recent call last):
  File "<pyshell#8>", line 1, in <module>
    print math.sqrt(-1)
ValueError: math domain error
```

The assumption is that if you want to work with complex numbers, you understand what it is you are doing and know that the result is likely to be imaginary. Thus, `cmath` allows the square root of negative numbers, while math does not.

The `cmath` module is mostly the same as the `math` module. It provides the trigonometric functions asin, acos, atan, asinh, and so forth, as well as the square root function. All of these functions will work with either real or imaginary values:

```
>>> print cmath.asin(100)
(1.57079632679-5.29829236561j)
>>> print cmath.asin(4+3j)
(0.917616853351+2.29991404088j)
```

Quite honestly, complex math is way beyond the scope of this book. If you know mathematics well enough to know how it works, you will understand what these functions are used for and what the returns should be. If you don't, it is unlikely that it could be explained to you in less than a full year's worth of math study. Suffice it to say that the functions are available to you, and if you need them, import the `cmath` module for your application.

Types

The types module contains information about the predefined types in the Python system. There are a number of built-in types, which are listed in Table 11-3. You can define variables of any of these types, check to see what type a given variable might be, and compare two types.

Table 11-3 The Python Type Module Types

Module Type	Contents
BuiltinFunctionType	Built-in functions in Python. This includes `print`, `dir`, `del`, and so forth.
BuiltinMethodType	Built-in methods for objects in Python, such as the `append()` method for lists, or the `__str__` method.
ClassType	User-defined classes.
ComplexType	Complex variable type.
DictType	Dictionaries defined within Python. Includes implicit dictionaries returned from functions and methods.
FileType	Any sort of file object returned by the `open()` function.
FloatType	A floating point number, in IEEE format. Does not include complex numbers with no imaginary portion.
FunctionType	User-defined function type. Does not include built-in functions, methods, lambda functions, or generator functions.
GeneratorType	A Python generator function.
InstanceType	An instance of a user-defined class. Does not include Python built-in objects such as dictionaries or lists.
ListType	A Python list object.
LongType	A long integer.
MethodType	Any method of a user-defined class.
NoneType	The unique no type, pretty much the same as the "C" NULL type.
StringType	Any Python string, including literal strings.
TupleType	Any Python tuple, including those returned by functions or methods.
TypeType	The type of an object returned by the `type()` function in Python.
UnicodeType	A Unicode string, which is different than a normal Python string or string literal.
XRangeType	The type returned by the `xrange()` function.

Using the `types` module isn't really difficult. You can find out the given type of an object, compare the types, and do something based on the type of an object. For example, you could write a function that only accepted floating point numbers. Since Python has no strong type-checking, you would have to do the checking yourself. A function like that might look something like this:

```
>>> def take_only_floats(obj) :
        if type(obj) != types.FloatType :
                print "Must be a float!"
                return
    print "ok"
```

You might then use such a function with various types of objects to test it, by doing something like this in the IDLE interpreter:

```
>>> take_only_floats("Hello")
Must be a float!
>>> take_only_floats(1)
Must be a float!
>>> take_only_floats(1.0)
ok
```

In general, working with the `types` module is pretty simple. It can be interesting to see what sorts of things you can deal with, however. For example, if you look at a class like this:

```
class Foo :
    def __init__(self) :
        self.x = 1
    def printme(self) :
        print "x = ", self.x
```

You can then look at a bunch of information about the class and its components. Let's look at some of them in the interpreter:

```
>>> f = Foo()
>>> print type(Foo)
<type 'classobj'>
>>> print type(f)
<type 'instance'>
>>> print type(f.x)
<type 'int'>
>>> print type(f.printme)
<type 'instancemethod'>
>>> print type(f.__init__)
<type 'instancemethod'>
>>> print type(f.printme())
x = 1
<type 'NoneType'>
>>> print type(dir(f))
<type 'list'>
```

If you ever want to know more about a given piece of data in the interpreter, the combination of the `dir` function and the `type` function will probably give you all you need to know. By far the nicest thing about working with an interpreted language is the wealth of information that is available to you within the environment without having to resort to looking at source code or documentation.

Strings

We've spent quite a bit of time looking at strings and functions for use with strings in the book so far. However, the `strings` module does contain a few functions that we haven't really talked about. The majority of the string manipulations in Python are built into the string class, but there are two functions worth discussing in this section.

The first function is called `capwords`. This function takes an input string and breaks it down into words, each of which is delimited by any of the valid delimiter characters defined by the `split()` function. The first letter of each "word" is then capitalized and extra spaces are removed before the words are recombined back into a single string. This sounds complicated, but it really isn't. Let's take a look at how you might use something like this:

```
>>> s = raw_input("Please enter your full name: ")
Please enter your full name: matt a telles
>>> import string
>>> print string.capwords(s)
Matt A Telles
```

Obviously, if you are working with legal or financial software, the ability to print out a name in this format is a very useful thing. The other rather nice thing about the function is that it automatically removes any extraneous spaces from the middle of words. For example, imagine that you had an input file that contained names that looked like "matt a telles," and you wanted to print them in a user-friendly way. You could write code that looked like this to accomplish this task:

```
>>> s = "matt          a              telles"
>>> print string.capwords(s)
Matt A Telles
```

The other function available in the string module is `maketrans`. This function is a bit strange, primarily because it does very little for you by itself. Instead, it is a utility function intended to help you with another task. To understand what you might want this function for, it is necessary to explain another function in Python: the `translate()` function for strings.

Imagine that you are creating some sort of a cipher, to pass codes to a secret agent in another country. You don't want the thing to be too difficult to read, since the agent is unlikely to have a huge amount of time to decipher and work with your messages. At the same time, you want your cipher to be as good as possible, so that others who found the message could not read it. The easiest way to accomplish both of these tasks is a simple substitution cipher. In such a cipher, one letter is replaced with another letter or number. Obviously, you can translate such a coded message easily, if you have the translation key. In Python, the translation key is a translation object. Let's look at a simple example:

```
>>> sIn = "abcdefghijklmnopqrstuvwxyz"
>>> sOut = "defghijklmnopqrstuvwzyzabc"
>>> sTrans = string.maketrans(sIn, sOut)
>>> print string.translate("This is a test of the emergency broadcast system",
sTrans)
Tklv lv d whvw ri wkh hphujhqfb eurdgfdvw vbvwhp
```

Looks like a foreign language, doesn't it? Worse, it is not very easy to translate, at least not if you don't have the right "key" to the translation process. Yet, using Python with the proper keys, doing the reverse translation is trivial:

```
>>> sRevTrans = string.maketrans(sOut, sIn)
>>> s = string.translate("This is a test of the emergency broadcast system",
sTrans)
>>> print string.translate(s, sRevTrans)
This is a test of the emergency broadcast system
>>> print s
Tklv lv d whvw ri wkh hphujhqfb eurdgfdvw vbvwhp
```

As you can see, the input and output can be reversed, giving you back what you want. If you are an old Internet person, you will recognize this type of transformation as the basis for the rot13() function, which relies on the letters from a-z being shifted around 13 positions in a string.

As a side note, if you were going to do something like this, one of the most important things you could do to make the resulting string harder to break is to replace the space character with something more innocuous. This makes it harder to figure out exactly what the words in the sentence look like.

```
>>> sIn = sIn + " "
>>> sOut = sOut + "~"
>>> print string.translate(s, string.maketrans(sIn, sOut) )
Tnoy~oy~g~zkyz~ul~znk~kskzmktie~hzugjigyz~yeyzks
```

Regular Expressions
You could easily write an entire book about regular expressions and pattern matching, and quite a few people have done just that. Regular expressions are patterns that permit you to

"match" various string values in a variety of ways. For example, you might want to pick out all strings that contain numbers. The purpose of this section is not to make you an expert on pattern matching or the regular expression powers of Python. The idea here is to introduce you to simple pattern matching and regular expressions, and show you how to use them in your application. Regular expressions are, without a doubt, one of the most powerful and confusing topics in computer science, but they really shouldn't be. The syntax and combination of various operators is what makes it hard, and we will do our best to wade through that complexity and explain how to use the `re` module to do what you want.

Patterns

The first thing you need to understand when working with regular expressions is the notion of a pattern. A pattern is simply one or more characters that represent a set of possible match characters. In regular expression matching, you use a character (or set of characters) to represent the strings you want to match in the text. For example, suppose that you wanted to match a string that looked like "xxx-xx-xxxx". This is obviously a Social Security Number. Now, suppose that you are looking for all such possible entries in a given string. Imagine that you are given some free form text that said:

My social security number is 000-00-0000 but it really should be 001-00-0001. Please change it immediately.

This is the sort of message that might be sent to the HR department of a major corporation. It would be kind of nice to be able to recognize the format of the message as referring to Social Security numbers and route it to the appropriate person in the department.

In order to use patterns to match expressions, you need to understand what the pattern matching characters are. Table 11-4 shows you the list of sets of characters for Python regular expressions and what they mean. First, review the table, and then we'll look at a couple of examples of how they would work.

Table 11-4 Regular Expression Characters In Python

Symbol	Meaning
. (period)	Matches any character except the newline character.
^ (caret sign)	Matches the start of any string.
$ (dollar sign)	Matches the end of any string.
* (asterisk)	Matches zero or more repetitions of a given regular expression. For example, .* matches zero or one of any characters except a newline.
+ (plus sign)	Matches one or more repetitions of a given regular expression. For example, .+ matches one or more characters.
?	Matches zero or one of the previous regular expressions. For example, ab? Matches a, b, or ab.

Symbol	Meaning
{}	Used as either {m} where m means to match exactly "m" instances of the previous regular expression or {m,n} where n > m, meaning to match between m and n instances of the previous regular expression.
\ (backslash)	Either a special character, such as one of the other regular expression characters (i.e., * matches an asterisk) or one of the special regular expression sequences (see later).
[]	Used to indicate a set of characters that a single character may match. May contain individual characters (0,1,2,3) or may use the – character to indicate a range (0-3).
| (pipe character)	Used to specify that two regular expressions, such as A | B can be found, where either of them may be the expression found.
()	Contains a set of regular expressions and defines a group that can be reused.

The characters listed above can be combined in various ways to define new character sets to match. For example, you could use *? combination to match as few characters as possible to accomplish whatever it is you want to match. Most of those combinations are simply too complicated to go into in a single chapter. Instead, let's focus on the simpler forms of regular expressions, to show how you might use them in your own applications.

The first thing to know about regular expressions is that the simplest form of a regular expression is a single character. That is, if I want to match something to "a," it has to be an "a" to match. The regular expression parser in Python recognizes this:

```
>>> import re
>>> print re.match("a", "a")
<_sre.SRE_Match object at 0x01195288>
```

Python then outputs a line indicating that a new object (sre.SRE type) has been created. The hex number following it is the address at which it was created.

The match() function tries to apply the first sequence as a set of regular expression characters to the second set of characters, called the *input string*, to see if it matches. Since there is exactly one character in the regular expression and it matches the only character in the input string, there is a match. If no match is found, the match() function returns None.

The next simplest form of matching is the single character match. Suppose that you are looking for anything that contains the letters "abc," followed by any given character. You can write that RE like this:

```
>>> print re.match("ab.", "abc")
<_sre.SRE_Match object at 0x01195288>
>>> print re.match("ab.", "abd")
```

```
<_sre.SRE_Match object at 0x01195288>
>>> print re.match("ab.", "dab")
None
```

As you can see, the sequence matches "abc," "abd," and anything else with "ab" and a single character. It does not, however, match the strings "dab" or anything else that does not start with "ab."

The beginning and end of string characters ('^' and '$') can be used to see if a string starts or ends with a given sequence of characters. For example:

```
>>> print re.match("^abc", "abcdef")
<_sre.SRE_Match object at 0x01195288>
>>> print re.match("^abc", "0123abc")
None
```

In this case, it doesn't matter what follows the string "abc" in the input string. As long as those three characters begin the string, the rest of it will match automatically. The start and end of string characters are said to be sequenced matches; they determine how the characters following them (up to another special character) should be interpreted. For example, to look for a string that starts with a "0," you write "0^," whereas to find a string that ends in "9," you write "9$."

Now suppose that you want to match certain words, but you don't know how the user is going to spell them. Suppose, for example, that you are in the United States, but your user base also extends into the United Kingdom (that's England for you non-geographic types). They spell things funny, like "colour" instead of "color." We could search for such a problem with the question mark. A warning to those who are used to database searching—the question mark does not do what you think it does. The question mark matches zero or one instance of the previous character (or set) in the search string. So you would have:

```
>>> print re.match('colou?r', 'colour')
<_sre.SRE_Match object at 0x011951E0>
>>> print re.match('colou?r', 'color')
<_sre.SRE_Match object at 0x011951E0>
```

Likewise, the asterisk "*" character matches zero or one instance of the previousexpression, but it will match as many as it can. So, if you have:

```
>>> s = re.match('[0-9]*-', '000-00-0000')
>>> print s.start()
0
>>> print s.end()
4
```

The start() and end() methods of the returned object from the match function indicate the positions of the start and end of the sequence that was matched. The match function is telling us that it matched characters zero through four (terminating at four). This makes sense, since you told it to search for a character in the set of characters "0-9" and to continue matching them until you hit a dash.

Special Sequence Characters

In addition to the standard set of characters shown in the previous table, there are also some special sequence characters associated with regular expression parsing in Python (and all other languages that support regular expression parsing). The six most important sequence characters are:

- ❋ \d: Matches any decimal digit. This is really the same as writing [0-9], but is done so often that it has its own shortcut sequence.

- ❋ \D: Matches any non-decimal digit. This is the set of all characters that are not in [0-9] and can be written as [^0-9]

- ❋ \s: Matches any white space character. White space is normally defined as a space, carriage return, tab, and non-printable character. Basically, white space is what separates words in a given sentence.

- ❋ \S: Matches any non-white space character. This is simply the inverse of the \s sequence above.

- ❋ \w: Matches any alphanumeric character. This is the set of all letters and numbers in both lower- and uppercase.

- ❋ \W: Matches any non-alphanumeric character. This is the inverse of the \w sequence above.

In addition to the sequences listed here, there are two others that are important. The \b sequence represents a word boundary, which is defined as anything that separates a character in \w and a character not in \w. The \p{L} syntax matches a single Unicode character, and can be useful when working in international settings.

Compiling Regular Expressions

One of the biggest problems with regular expressions is the time it takes to process them. The interpreter needs to scan through the tokens in your regular expression string each time that you want to match them to something. To avoid this problem, the re module supports "compiling" of expressions. Compiling a regular expression tokenizes it into a fast and compact form that can be scanned quickly and efficiently.

In order to compile things in Python, you use the compile() method of the re module. Somehow, this really shouldn't come as a huge surprise. The syntax of the compile method is:

```
>>> import re
>>> p = re.compile('[a-z]+')
```

In this case, you are telling the regular expression compiler that you want to match strings that consist of all letters. If an error occurs in the compile process, an exception will be raised by the re module:

```
>>> p = re.compile('[a-')
```

```
Traceback (most recent call last):
  File "<pyshell#4>", line 1, in <module>
    p = re.compile('[a-')
  File "C:\Python25\lib\re.py", line 180, in compile
    return _compile(pattern, flags)
  File "C:\Python25\lib\re.py", line 233, in _compile
    raise error, v # invalid expression
error: unexpected end of regular expression
```

If you get a valid object back from the compile() method, you can then move on to the next part of the process, matching the string to given input strings.

Matching Strings

The match() method of the regular expression system, in the Pattern object, will check to see if you have a match to a given string. For example, if you were using the check for all lowercase letters in a string, you might do something like this:

```
>>> p = re.compile('[a-z]+')
>>> m = p.match('123 matt')
>>> print m
None
```

The match() method will either return None, in which case there was no match found in the string, or a match object, which can be queried to see what sorts of matches were found and where in the string they began and ended. For example, let's use the same compiled string with an input that does match all lowercase letters:

```
>>> m = p.match('thisislowercase')
>>> print m
<_sre.SRE_Match object at 0x011531A8>
```

As you can see, we did get something back from the match this time, so now we can see what sort of match was involved in the process. To accomplish this, the match object provides a set of functions that will allow us to look at the information that was generated by the comparison. First, there is the group() method of the class, which returns the text that was found to match:

```
>>> print m.group()
thisislowercase
```

It might appear as if we simply got back the entire string, but that isn't always the case. For example, consider the following use of the match() function and returned matching string:

```
>>> m = p.match('this is lower case')
>>> print m.group()
this
```

Because the space character was not in the set of matching characters we asked for in the original compile statement, the matching process stops at that position. There are other methods of the match object that will give you positions of the start and end of the matching string. These methods are called, appropriately enough, start() and end().

```
>>> print m.start()
0
>>> print m.end()
4
```

If you prefer, there is also the span() method, which simply returns a tuple representing the start and end of the string.

One note about the match() method, it will always start at the beginning of the input string. If you want to search from arbitrary positions in the string, you need to use the search method instead. Here's a simple example of using search to break up the words in a sentence:

```
import re

p = re.compile('[a-z]+')

idx = 0
s = 'this is a test'
while idx < len(s) :
        m = p.search(s, idx )
        if m == None :
                break
        idx = m.end()
        print m.group()
```

Running this little test results in the following output:

```
>>>
this
is
a
test
```

As you can see, working with regular expressions really isn't that hard. It is really just a matter of building the strings properly. Now that you understand the basics, let's look at a bit more in-depth use of the `re` module.

Meta Characters

We've looked at the meta character sequences, but haven't really done anything with them. There are some slight subtleties working with meta character sequences, particularly those involving backslashes, in Python. Let's take a look at an example, so you can see the problem.

Imagine, for example, that you want to find the word "open" in a string. You might try writing something like this:

```
>>> m = re.search('\bopen\b', 'please open the door')
>>> print m
None
```

Your first thought, I'm sure, is that you made a mistake typing in the pattern string someplace, or that you failed to set some option flag. I know that's what I thought the first time I worked with regular expressions. Unfortunately, this isn't the case. What you typed is exactly what you thought, and it didn't find anything. Why is that? Well, in Python, if you are not using raw strings you will find that the string above has been "translated" by the interpreter into: `<backspace>open<backspace>` rather than the proper regular expression meta characters. This is because the '\b' escape sequence is treated as a special backspace character. To make it work, you need to trick the interpreter into reading what you meant, instead of what you said:

```
>>> m = re.search('\\bopen\\b', 'please open the door')
>>> print m
<_sre.SRE_Match object at 0x00A3F058>
>>> print m.span()
(7, 11)
```

It is important when using meta characters to be careful to escape the backslash sequences so that the interpreter properly reads them.

Grouping

It is often necessary to find groups of things in a string. For example, you might want to find a string, and find all of the duplicates of that string within your input text. Let's say that you have an input string that looked like ababababac. You want to match the string ab in the text. You might write something like this:

```
>>> m = re.match('ab', 'ababababc')
>>> print m.span()
(0, 2)
```

That certainly matches the first two characters, but what about the rest of them? Okay, you say, you will use something like this:

```
>>> m = re.match('ab*', 'ababababc')
>>> print m.span()
(0, 2)
```

Once again, it doesn't match any more, since the regular expression syntax does not look beyond what you ask it to. So how do you match all of the ab strings in the input string? The answer lies in grouping. By placing parentheses around an expression, you make it into a group. The regular expression matcher then looks for all of the occurrences of that group within the string:

```
>>> m = re.match("(ab)*", "ababababac" )
>>> print m.span()
(0, 8)
```

Now, as you can see, you have matched all of the entries of ab in the string, because they are considered to be groups. Groups can also be nested and extracted from the resulting match object using the groups() method:

```
>>> p = re.compile('(a(b)c)d')
>>> m = p.match('abcd')
>>> print m.span()
(0, 4)
>>> print m.group(0)
abcd
>>> print m.group(1)
abc
>>> print len(m.groups())
2
>>> print m.group(2)
b
```

This has been a very brief introduction to the world of regular expression parsing and matching in Python. Hopefully, you will have gotten enough out of it to begin really exploring the world on your own. However, before we go, let's look at one more complicated expression, one that finds an email address anywhere within a string. If you get nothing else useful out of this chapter, at least you can use this in your own applications.

```
>>> p = re.compile(r"\b[A-Z0-9._%-]+@[A-Z0-9.-]+\.[A-Z]{2,4}\b")
>>> s = 'The email address is: MATT@MATT.COM'
>>> m = p.search(s)
>>> print m
<_sre.SRE_Match object at 0x011961E0>
>>> print m.group()
MATT@MATT.COM
```

Note, for space saving, I did not include the a-z everywhere that A-Z was used, so you will have to either look for emails in uppercase, or use the upper method of the string library to find it:

```
m = p.search(s.upper())
```

Congratulations, and welcome to regular expression parsing!

System

The system module provides an interface to many of the Python specific routines that you need to provide a really nice user experience. In addition, it provides ways for you to get at information that you need when writing applications, and often the only way to get some of the information. For example, if you wanted to know what modules were compiled into the current interpreter, as opposed to those loaded at runtime, you would use the builtin_module_names attribute of the system module:

```
>>> import sys
>>> print sys.builtin_module_names
('__builtin__', '__main__', '_ast', '_bisect', '_codecs', '_codecs_cn',
'_codecs_hk', '_codecs_iso2022', '_codecs_jp', '_codecs_kr', '_codecs_tw',
'_csv', '_functools', '_heapq', '_hotshot', '_locale', '_lsprof', '_md5',
'_multibytecodec', '_random', '_sha', '_sha256', '_sha512', '_sre', '_struct',
'_subprocess', '_symtable', '_types', '_weakref', '_winreg', 'array', 'audioop',
'binascii', 'cPickle', 'cStringIO', 'cmath', 'collections', 'datetime', 'errno',
'exceptions', 'gc', 'imageop', 'imp', 'itertools', 'marshal', 'math', 'mmap',
'msvcrt', 'nt', 'operator', 'parser', 'rgbimg', 'signal', 'strop', 'sys',
'thread', 'time', 'xxsubtype', 'zipimport', 'zlib')
```

Exception handling information is all stored in the `system` module, as we have seen in the exception handling chapter and since. You use the `exc_info()` to retrieve the last exception, and `exc_clear()` to clear the current exception information, if you want to make sure that an error doesn't propagate past your application. In addition, there are three variables in the `system` module for exceptions: `exc_value`, `exc_type`, and `exc_traceback`. These three, although deprecated (that is, they won't be supported forever), provide information that you can get at directly, instead of having to rely on the `exc_info` method.

The `exit()` method is available in the `sys` module as well. The `exit()` method will exit the Python interpreter, and needs to be used with some care. Within the IDLE environment, using `exit()` will raise a `SystemExit` exception, which will prompt you to save your work and ask you if you want to exit IDLE. Outside of the IDE, of course, the `sys.exit()` method will simply terminate the program. In either case, the user may be surprised when your program simply stops.

There are also a number of attributes defined in the `sys` module that you should be aware of when you are programming. Some of these are listed below, so you can always look at the Python documentation for any others you might need.

Table 11-5 Attributes Of The `sys` Module

Attribute Name	Attribute Meaning
maxint	The maximum allowable integer value for the system.
path	Shows you the current path of directories used to locate modules for the import statement in the interpreter.
platform	A string representing the platform on which your Python script is running. For Windows this is usually win32. For LINUX, it might be LINUX1.
prefix	A string representing the directory for which all of the Python system code is relative to. For example, in Windows, this is likely to be `c:\Python25` or wherever you installed Python.
version	A string representing the current version of the interpreter.
winver	A string representing the prefix used by Python to create registry keys.
argv	The arguments passed into the script if the program was run from the command line or the currently loaded script.

Most of the attributes of the `system` module are pretty self-explanatory, as are the methods found within it. The `argv` attribute, however, is worth explaining a bit. If you run the program from the command line within whatever operating system you happen to be using, Python will pick up the arguments to the program that the user enters on the command line. For example:

```
python myscript.py filename matt telles
```

This run of the interpreter from the command line has four command line arguments. The first (argument 0) is the name of the script that is being run. In general, if a script is loaded, there will always be an argument in the zero position, and it will be the name of that script. Anything after that begins at position one, and it is stored in order. So, in the previous example:

```
argv[0] is 'myscript.py'
argv[1] is 'filename'
argv[2] is 'matt'
argv[3]  is 'telles'
```

If you want to pass in an argument with a space in it, simple enclose the arguments in double quotation marks: "matt telles" then becomes a single argument.

Random Number Generation

One of the most common problems you face when writing certain types of applications is the need to generate random numbers. Rolling dice is one of the most popular uses for random number generation as all players of Dungeons and Dragons™ will tell you, but there are quite a few uses for this functionality in the corporate world as well. Imagine, for example, that you want to show a user a security question each time he logs in to your corporate network, but you don't want him to know which question he will have to answer. There might be 10 questions, and you want the questions presented in a random order, so that the user can't get too complacent. This is an excellent place for random number generation.

The Python random module provides functionality for the production and control of random numbers. Besides the capability to generate simple random numbers, the module also provides methods for seeding the random number generator, selecting a random entry from any sequence, and quite a few other bits of functionality. Let's take a look at some of the uses now.

First, the random() function will generate a number in the range of 0 to 1, inclusive, as a floating point number. You can either use the generated number, or you can apply it to an integer number to produce the equivalent of a die roll:

```
>>> import random
>>> print random.random()
0.223679731938
>>> print int( random.random()*6 + 1)
5
>>> for i in range(0,6) :
        print int ( random.random() * 6 + 1 )
```

```
3
3
5
3
5
4
```

If you don't like having to do all of the multiplying and adding, you can use the `randint()` method instead:

```
>>> print random.randint(1,6)
1
```

Alternatively, if you happen to want to "weight" the rolls a bit, you can use the `choice()` method. This method allows you to randomly select a value out of a list of values. For example, in our "dice" example, we might want to only allow certain values to be rolled. In this case, we might use `choice()` this way:

```
>>> print random.choice( [1,3,5,6] )
5
```

The `choice` function has a similar "brother" method called `randrange()`. This method, which accepts three arguments, generates a range of values and selects one of them. The arguments are the start of the range, the end of the range, and the step value to use to get from the start to the end.

Oh, and finally, you can "seed" the random function with a given value, if you like. The `seed()` method accepts a single argument, which is the seed value. If you do not supply one, it will use the current system time. If you do not seed the random generator, it will tend to produce the same values each time it is used. A seed value represents a "starting point" for the random number generation, and will force the generator to create a new sequence each time it is used.

Dates and Times

The `datetime` module provides interfaces to the date and time methods within the Python library system. The module consists of the following classes:

✳ `timedelta`—Provides an interface to functionality that calculates differences between two times or dates.

✳ `date`—Provides functionality associated with dates only. Dates are represented by a month, day, and year value.

* `datetime`—Provides functionality associated with dates and times. A datetime value is represented by a month, day, and year, as well as an hour minute, second, and microsecond.
* `time`—Provides functionality associated with a time value. A time value is represented by an hour, minute, second, and microsecond value.
* `tzinfo`—Provides time zone information.

Creating a New Time

The `time` class provides functionality for creating new times, or for setting specific values for a given time object. For example, to create a new time object representing the current time of day, you would use:

```
import time
t = time.localtime()
```

You can print the time values using the `strftime()` method.

```
>>> print time.strftime("%I:%M")
```

Naturally, you can create your own time objects. For example, you could create a time object representing 11:59 a.m. However, this is done with the `datetime` class, rather than the `time` class. The reasons for this are myriad, but you get used to it.

```
>>> from datetime import datetime
>>> d = datetime(datetime.now().year, datetime.now().month, datetime.now().day,
11, 59, 0 )
>>> print d
2007-03-16 11:59:00
```

Time Operations

Once you have a time value, what do you do with it? If you just want to print it out, you can use the aforementioned `strftime` method. If you want to extract the individual pieces of the time value, you can do so as well:

```
>>> import time
>>> t = time.localtime()
>>> print t
(2007, 3, 16, 11, 53, 9, 4, 75, 1)
>>> print t[3]
11
>>> print t[4]
53
```

```
>>> print t[5]
9
```

As you can see, Python does not have the same notions of attributes for time values that you might find in other languages, such as C or Java. Instead, you get back a tuple of time values, which are the year, month, day of the month, hour, minute, second, and so forth. You can utilize these values, but please note that you cannot write to them. Attempting to change the time value via writing to the tuple element will result in an error from the interpreter, since tuples are immutable.

Creating a New Date

Similar to a time, you can create a date as well. The current date is stored in the today() method of the datetime class. To get to this class, you will need to import the datetime module and use the datetime class within it. This can be a bit confusing. For example, to use the today() function, you do this:

```
>>> import datetime
>>> print datetime.datetime.today()
2007-03-18 13:15:48.734000
```

You can create your own date objects, using the datetime class, by using the constructor for the datetime object. This constructor does permit you to specify a complete date and time, but you don't have to use all of it. Only the date portion is required, such as in this example, were you create a date of January 1, 2007. The time will automatically be set to midnight, as you can see here:

```
>>> d = datetime.datetime(2007,01,01)
>>> print d
2007-01-01 00:00:00
```

Date Operations

After you have a datetime object, what exactly can you do with it? As we've seen, you can use the today() method to get back a date representing the current date and time. There is also a method called utcnow(), which returns the current date and time in UTC (universal time coordinate) format. There are two methods for converting from a timestamp: fromtimestamp() and fromutctimestamp() that will work for taking the date and time of a file object modification time and converting it into a standard Python date object.

One of the more common methods in the datetime class is the fromordinal() method. This method accepts a single argument in the range of 1 to 366 and returns the date that represents that ordinal value for the year. For example, if you wanted the 32nd day of the year, which would be February 1, you could use:

```
>>> print datetime.datetime.fromordinal(32)
0001-02-01 00:00:00
```

Note that you would need to add 365 and account for leap years to move forward in time to get the current year. There is a corresponding `toordinal` function, which will convert the string value back into an ordinal one. In fact, since we are working with the calendar and date time functions, let's go ahead and do that now. These methods are in the `calendar` module, which we will need to import into our code. Here are the functions you will need to implement:

```
import calendar

def daysinmonth( month, year ) :
    if month == 2 :
        if calendar.isleap(year) :
            return 29
        else :
            return 28
    if month == 1:
        return 31
    elif month == 3:
        return 31
    elif month == 4:
        return 30
    elif month == 5:
        return 31
    elif month == 6:
        return 30
    elif month == 7:
        return 31
    elif month == 8:
        return 31
    elif month == 9:
        return 30
    elif month == 10:
        return 31
    elif month == 11:
        return 30
    elif month == 12:
```

```
        return 31

def toordinal( month, day, year ) :
    # Initialize ordinal value
    ord = 0
    # First, do the years from 1 to that year
    for y in range(1, year) :
        ord = ord + 365
        if calendar.isleap(y) :
            ord = ord + 1

    # Add in the days up to that month for the year
    for m in range(1,month) :
        ord = ord + daysinmonth(m, year)

    # And add the days for this month
    ord = ord + day
    return ord
```

You can test the function easily enough, since you have the `fromordinal()` method of the date time class to work with. Let's test it with a few possible entries:

```
>>> import datetime
>>> print datetime.datetime.fromordinal(toordinal(1,1,2007))
2007-01-01 00:00:00
>>> print datetime.datetime.fromordinal(toordinal(3,10,2007))
2007-03-10 00:00:00
>>> print datetime.datetime.fromordinal(toordinal(2,29,2004))
2004-02-29 00:00:00
```

You can see by the output that your function works just fine. There really isn't a lot more to say about dates and times. The calendar class is also available for things like the leap year calculation, and you can use the individual components of the date and time objects to print out dates in whatever format or use you want.

Time Zone Information

The last thing to mention in the date and time manipulation section is time zones. Python understands and works with time zone information in the date time objects. When you are creating a `datetime` object, you can supply an option `timezone` object as the final parameter to the class. If you do this, then the `datetime` object will have two methods that can be called `tzname()` and `tzinfo()`, which will return information about the time zone associated with this date. This allows you to enter dates in whatever time zone they are given, rather than relying on the current date. The time zone information will be used when converting the date representation into a string, if it is different than the current time zone.

Finally, if you do supply a time zone information object (`timezone`) to the `datetime` constructor, you can use the `dst()` function to determine whether or not this date is within daylight savings time. Note that with the recent change to DST, your version of Python may or may not be accurate. If you are relying on daylight savings information, please be sure to check this date before shipping your script.

Operating System Interface

It is inevitable, when working with programming languages, that you will have to eventually do something that is not generic to all operating systems. For example, you might need to get a list of files and directories, or create or "spawn," a new process, or simply retrieve information about the operating system for use in data reporting or debugging. Whatever the reason, sooner or later you will run into something that works differently on each and every operating system. Python provides the `os` module for working with operating system specific functionality in a more or less independent manner. The scope of the `os` module is such that it would be impossible to cover it for all operating systems in all cases, so we will simply look at a few of the more commonly used areas.

System Information

Quite often, you need to know a bit about how the operating system deals with things. Information like the separator for a file base name and its extension (i.e., in config.sys, the separator between config and sys), or for directory composition (i.e., c:/windows). You may want to know the current directory or the parent directory. All of this information, and more, is available in the `os` module. Let's take a quick look at how this works:

```
import os

def print_system_info() :
    print "Current directory: "+os.curdir
    print "Parent director: "+os.pardir
    print "File Separator: "+os.sep
    print "Extension Separator: "+os.extsep
    print "Environment strings:"
    for e in os.environ :
        print e
```

Obviously, the first thing you need to do is to import the `os` module in order to use the functionality exposed by that module. Once you have done this, there are a number of attributes that you can look at directly. If you run the above function in the IDLE environment, you will see the following output, which should give you a good idea of how it all works:

```
>>> print_system_info()
Current directory: .
Parent director: ..
File Separator: \
Extension Separator: .
Environment strings:
TMP
COMPUTERNAME
```

Should you ever want a complete listing of the functionality exposed by the `os` module, as well as any other module in the Python system, simply run the function: `dir(mod-name)` where `mod-name` is the name of the module you are interested in. The IDLE interpreter will then show you a list of all of the public attributes and methods available.

Process Management

Sometimes, you just need to run another program, or another script, or simply execute a command that the operating system provides. Why would you want to write yet another version of a function that copies files, for example, when you can simply run the `copy` command in the Windows shell? It makes no sense to constantly reinvent the wheel. Python was created primarily in the UNIX world, where calling other programs (a process called *spawning*) is the normal way of doing things. For this reason, and because the functionality is so useful, Python provides a fairly rich way of starting and controlling other applications from within a Python script.

There are a lot of methods listed under the process management section of the Help file in Python module Help. However, you will find that the majority of them are simply variants on a theme. For example, there are eight methods that begin with "spawn," and then take a variety of arguments to accomplish the same basic goal. They aren't especially different methods, and once you understand one, you will understand them all. We will only look at a few, one of each major subgroup.

Let's begin with the `spawn` functions. This group of functions will all you to launch an existing program with or without arguments. Let's imagine, for example, that you want to launch the Windows application, Notepad, in order to allow the user to view or modify some text. We could use the `spawnl` method of the `os` module like this:

```
>>> id = os.spawnl(os.P_NOWAIT, "c:/Windows/Notepad.exe")
```

Running this command will launch the Notepad executable as soon as the statement is executed. The return from all of the spawn functions is a process ID that can be used to check or end the process status. The `waitpid` method, for example, will wait until the process is complete and then return control to the program along with the exit status of the application. If you were to write some code like this:

```
>>> id = os.spawnl(os.P_NOWAIT, "c:/Windows/Notepad.exe")
>>> status = os.waitpid( id, 0 )
>>> print status
```

The Notepad program would launch, but the Python program would appear to "hang" until Notepad was closed. Once the Notepad application terminated, the program would then print out the exit status and ID of the program. The "status" return of the program is actually a tuple made up of the ID of the program (for comparison) and then the exit status shifted 8 bits to the left (don't ask, just accept it). If you run the above code in the IDLE interpreter, for example, you will see something like this when Notepad is closed:

```
>>> print status
(1824, 0)
```

The status returned is a tuple of two values, 1824, which is the ID and 0, which is the status of the application run.

Similar to the spawn methods, there are a group of methods that fall under the exec grouping. `Exec` is quite similar to `spawn` with one notable difference. When you run the `exec` function, the currently running process is replaced by the one you specify and the current process ends. For example, suppose you created a script that looks like this:

```
import os
os.execl( "c:/Windows/Notepad.exe", "c:/userlog.txt")
print "Running notepad"
```

You would assume that running this script would launch Notepad and then print out "running notepad" to the console. In fact, if you try this, you will see Notepad launch, but nothing will be displayed on the console window. The process has been completely replaced.

The next important method of the process category is the `kill` command. To kill a process means to shut it down, but *kill* seems to sound a lot more exciting to the programmer, so that is what it is called. The `kill` method accepts two arguments: the ID of the process to kill and a signal to send to it.

Under Microsoft Windows the `kill()` method is not defined, so you will need to write your own. To implement this, you will need the Python Windows Extensions, available on Source Forge. The function looks like this:

```
def kill(pid):
    """kill function for Win32"""
    import win32api
    handle = win32api.OpenProcess(1, 0, pid)
    return (0 != win32api.TerminateProcess(handle, 0))
```

Killing a process is a pretty extreme measure, and one you should only do for things you started or that you know should not be running. For your own process, you do not use the `kill` command, but rather the `exit` function. The `exit` function will terminate the current process, which may be your script or may be the interpreter. For example, consider the following script running in the interpreter:

```
s = raw_input("Enter a command (exit to exit): ")
if s == "exit" :
    exit()
```

If you run this script within the interpreter, you will see the dialog displayed in Figure 11.1, asking you if you want to terminate the program or not. If you say yes, it will exit the program and the interpreter. If you say no, you will see a display like this:

```
Traceback (most recent call last):
  File "E:/Python/ch11_7.py", line 3, in <module>
    exit()
  File "C:\Python25\lib\site.py", line 251, in __call__
    raise SystemExit(code)
SystemExit: None
```

The purpose of raising this exception is to give you one last chance to clean things up before you exit the process and the system. Use `exit()` with extreme care, as once you allow the system to exit, it is all over.

The final method we will look at in the process management category is the `system()` method. This method allows you to run a given system command within the Python interpreter. For example, suppose that you wanted to copy a file within your script to back it up before process the existing file. You might write something like this:

```
os.system("copy c:\\temp.dat c:\\temp1.dat")
```

This command will simply copy the file called "temp.dat" to one called "temp1.dat." If you run the command in the interpreter, and the file exists, you will see the following output:

```
>>> os.system("copy c:\\temp.dat c:\\temp1.dat")
0
```

Figure 11.1
Termination dialog in
Python.

Unlike many things in the programming world, a zero when running a program indicates a successful status, meaning the file was copied.

We talked about the files and directories portion of the os module back in Chapter 6, so there is no real reason to rehash it here. Instead, you should spend your time looking through the various components of the modules, to see what you will need when you are writing your own applications in Python.

By the way, the win32api modules are all available free of charge for download on the python.net site, and are really nicely done. If you are a Windows programmer, I highly recommend them. Python is all about reusing other people's work and giving your own work for them to reuse, so please do not hesitate to find the best modules and libraries out there and reuse them in your own applications.

In Conclusion

If you take one thing away from this chapter, it should be how very rich and varied the Python library system is, and how much functionality is provided for you in the existing code. Your first move, when you need a bit of functionality, should be to see what is already available in the Python libraries, rather than writing your own code. Writing code to learn how to do something is one thing, but writing code because you don't want to use anyone else's code is just silly. Python is there to provide you maximum functionality with minimum effort, so take advantage of that.

That concludes the first half of this book, which should wrap up all of the basic knowledge you need to work with Python. From this point on, we will be working with the other components of the WAMP/LAMP (Windows/Linux, Apache, MySQL, Python) development environment. In our next chapter, we start to explore using Python to create real GUI applications.

12} The GUI — TkInter

In today's programming world, the graphical user interface is king. Users no longer want command line programs that require them to type in commands or enter cryptic sequences of characters to accomplish their tasks. Instead, the computer world is all about point-and-click, drag-and-drop, Laurel and Hardy and, wait. No Laurel and Hardy, sorry, just got a bit carried away there. Hopefully, you get the idea. Today's world is about simplicity, and simplicity is about the easiest and most consistent way of doing things. In the software world, easy and consistent means a graphical user interface (GUI). In Python, using a GUI means working with TkInter. In this chapter, we will explore the TkInter functionality, learning how to use the module to produce GUI applications that make it simple to point and click, and, well, you get the idea.

What Is TkInter?

The TkInter library is an interface to the Tk (or Tcl) graphical user interface components, hence the name. The Tk graphical user interface is not a part of Python. It has been around for quite a few years on the UNIX platform and has been ported to most other operating systems as well. The Tcl system is a platform-independent way of creating high-quality graphical user interfaces with a minimum of effort and a maximum of functionality. As you will see, Tk allows you to build interfaces that scale well, can be used in differing environments, and take advantage of the native user interfaces wherever possible.

Terms and Conditions

Before you begin working with the Tk interface, there are a couple of terms that will become important as you start to write application code. Let's get them out of the way before we have to work with them.

Event Handling

In order to work with a modern graphical user interface library, you will need to understand the concept of events and event handling. Because users do not work in a linear fashion, you need to handle the things that a user does as they do them. The things users do are called *events,* and the way in which you deal with the events is called *handling.* For example, when the user clicks the mouse cursor in a given field in an input form, he generates a few events. First, he generates a mouse movement event, indicating that the mouse cursor has moved to its current location. Next, the mouse click event indicates that the user has clicked the mouse cursor within the event-handling window that we are interested in. Following the click come two higher-level events. First, the "old" input field loses its focus, and finally, the "new" input field gains focus. All of these events are sent to your application, if you are so inclined to be interested in them.

You handle events by "registering" your application for event handling messages. The Tk library, as well as most modern user interface libraries, allows you to register for virtually all events that occur within the system, or to ignore those events that you do not care about. If you do handle an event, you may either replace, or add to, the default handling for that event within the system. For example, when a key is pressed by the user, you may elect to process the key yourself and not pass it on to the underlying control in the user interface. Alternatively, you may elect not to process the keystroke at all, but to allow the underlying control to do all of the handling of the keystroke. Finally, you may select a combination of handling and default processing.

It is extremely important to think in terms of events and event handling when you are writing a graphical user interface application. You simply cannot afford to think in terms of linear programming, or you will drive the user completely insane. Users want to do the things they find most important at the time. If that means entering the first, third, and fifth fields of an input form before entering the second and fourth fields, then that is what they will want to do. If you prevent them from doing things in the order they feel most comfortable doing them, you will find that nobody will want to use your application.

Callbacks

A *callback* is the way in which the graphical user interface system notifies you that an event has occurred and allows you to process it. You "register" a callback function with the system for a given event, or a set of events for a given control. For example, you might register a callback with the system for the clicking of a button on an input form. When the user clicks the mouse button while the mouse cursor is over the button, a click event occurs. If you have registered to receive that click event, you will receive a message to the handler function that you have defined.

The important thing to realize about a callback function is that its behavior is asynchronous to the rest of the application. You do not know when your callback will be invoked, nor do you know at the time what the state of the system might be. You can elect to try to keep track of all of the changes in the states you are interested in, or you can query the system for the current state of anything you care about at the time of the event.

Consider the case of a button click on a form, as a simple example of a callback function. Imagine that you have a form with three input fields on it, containing the domain, user name, and password for logging into a given network system. The form will contain the three input fields and two buttons for either continuing or cancelling the operation. If the user clicks on the Cancel button, the input form is thrown away and the state returns to its previous settings. If the OK button is clicked, then the application needs to see if all of the input fields have been entered. You will not know whether the data is valid or not until the user clicks the button; this is the asynchronous part of the equation.

In the Tk library, you can register for callbacks for virtually all events, whether they are major ones, like the user clicking a button, or minor ones, like the user moving the mouse over a given form element. It is important to keep track of what it is you are doing with the given callback functions, since you can use the same function for multiple events, if you so choose. The important distinction is that a callback is used by the application, whereas an event is used by the control. Controls generate events, and applications listen for changes that are broadcast by those events via callbacks.

Widgets

In user interface parlance, a *widget* is anything that can have properties set and events generated for it. In general usage, however, a widget is really something that can be placed on a window and receive user input. Under certain circumstances, widgets can be invisible, yet receive events, such as when a widget is used for a database connection. For our purposes, however, you can consider the widget to be any user interface element, such as a button or input field. We will discuss widgets in more depth when we begin to look at all of the possible elements available to you for use in your applications out of the Tkinter library. For now, just think of a widget as a black box that does something for you in your code.

Layout Managers

A *layout manager* is a non-visual component that helps you place things where you want them on an input form. For example, if I had three input fields (places to type in values) on an input form and wanted them to align vertically so that one was directly below the next, I could do this in a few different ways. First, I could specify the positions of the input fields directly, placing each one at a given vertical position within the input form. This has the advantage of always looking the same, but has the problem that if the form is resized, the input fields look out of place.

The second approach is to move the input fields whenever the form is resized. In many environments, such as older C++ GUI libraries, this is the only way in which you can have the form look right when it is resized. This can involve a lot of coding, however, and often leads to problems when the form shrinks beyond a certain minimum size. If there are no other choices, however, this is really the only way to control your input form appearance, regardless of the scale of the surrounding window.

The third and final approach to resizing input forms is to use what is called a "layout manager" to handle the positioning of input fields and other fields on a given input form. A layout manager uses one of a variety of methods for defining the relationship between fields on an input form. For example, the layout manager might use a grid to define the rows and columns that input fields should appear in. Another possible approach is to define preferred positions, such as a button appearing always on the right-hand side of the input form. Whatever the method used, the layout manager then applies the rules of the method to determine where a given field should lie when the form is first displayed, and when it is subsequently resized or moved.

The Tk library relies heavily on layout managers for defining how a given input form should be displayed at runtime. Unlike many of the more modern programming languages, Tk/Tcl does not contain a WYSIWYG (what you see is what you get) layout tool for defining the format of input forms. Instead, you do all of your work in code. This is good for dynamic definition of input forms, but also requires that you do more work up front, thinking about how the form should look. This is neither a good thing, nor a bad thing, merely one trade-off that you must consider when writing applications.

Working with TkInter

There are two basic steps to creating a Tkinter application. First, you must import the Tkinter module. This is done using the standard import statement in Python. At the top of any application using Tkinter, you should add the following line:

```
from Tkinter import *
```

Normally, you would never do something like this in Python, since it means importing the entire module and all of its components into your application. This is usually overkill for a module, as it will often have a lot of things you really don't need. Tkinter, however, is an exception rather than the rule.

Once you have done this, you are now able to access all of the functionality provided by the GUI module. In order to work with a Tkinter application, you must have a "root" object. The root object is the basic window to which all other components are added. You can have multiple windows open at the same time in a Tkinter application, but only the first Tk object created is the root. Once the root object is destroyed, the windowing system is shut down, and the GUI portion of your application is complete.

Let's create the world's simplest Tkinter application, just to show you how it is all done in Python.

```
from Tkinter import *
root = Tk()
root.mainloop()
```

If you run the above code in the IDLE interpreter, you will see a single window appear on the desktop, as shown in Figure 12.1. The window contains no controls, nor does it have any sort of title, aside from the default "tk." It contains the usual close, minimize, and maximize that you would expect from a Windows application. To get rid of the window, simply click on the "x" (or Close) button on the top right of the window frame.

Figure 12.1
A basic Tkinter window application running on the desktop.

The components of a Tk program are really no more complicated than this; there are just more of them. Let's examine the three steps to creating such a GUI application in Python.

1. The Tkinter module is loaded into the application space by using the import statement.

2. A "root" is created to be used as the main application window.

3. The `mainloop()` method of the root object is invoked.

That is really all there is to a Tk program in Python. Once the `mainloop()` method is invoked, the underlying library will handle all of the events for the window until the window is either closed by the user or by some application code that is designed for the purpose.

Of course, you really don't care much about simply putting up a window. What you really want to do is to use the windowing functionality to create more complicated applications using the Python constructs that you have learned about so far. Let's take a step forward, and create a "hello tk" application that shows off how to create a window and place a control on it using the Tkinter module for Python.

Creating a Label

Everyone has to have a "hello world" sort of application for whatever graphical user interface system he is working with. It seems to be a requirement in the computer book world, so who am I to buck the tradition? Let's create a "hello tk" application that will put up a window and display some text upon it.

1. Create a new file in Python using the IDLE editor's File | New Window command.

2. Enter the following code into the new window and select File | Save. Save the file as ch12_2.py in the directory of your choice.

3. There's an inconsistency here where some programs get identified and others don't.

```
# Import the functionality we need
from Tkinter import *


# Create the root. This will be the
# "window" for all of our activity.
root = Tk()


# Add a new label to the root to display
# our message.
w = Label(root, text="Hello, Tk!")


# Force the system to put all of the controls
# on the window
w.pack()


# Start things running. Note that the only way
# to stop this program is to click the "close"
# button.
root.mainloop()
```

4. Press the F5 key or select Run Module from the Run menu of the Editor window. You should see a display similar to the one shown in Figure 12.2.

Figure 12.2
Hello Tk!

The only difference between the first example and the second, aside from all of the comments, is the addition of a label component. As you can see, there are two steps for putting a label on the screen. First, you need to actually create the label. The label object constructor accepts two arguments. The first argument is the root component on which you want to place the label. Normally, this is the window object you created via the Tk() function call; however, it may be a subcomponent of that window. The second argument is simply the text that you want to display within the label.

The second step to placing a component on a window is to call the `pack()` method of the component. This method tells the layout manager how to place the component onto its parent. In this case, we just want to layout the label in its default location, which is simply the next available space on the window.

Finally, we call the `mainloop` method of the root window to get the whole process started and display the window on the desktop. To close the window and exit the program, click the Close button in the corner of the window.

Frame Widgets and Centering

Now that you understand how to create a simple window and add a label to it, let's add a little bit of complexity to the process. In this case, you are going to create a new type of widget, called a *Frame*, to the window, and center it within the parent window vertically and horizontally. You will then add a label as a child of the frame, also centered within the parent. To make the whole thing even more useful, you are going to actually specify a size for the main window, so that you can see how Tk lets you define exactly what you want on the screen.

1. Create a new file in Python using the IDLE editor's File | New Window command.

2. Enter the following code into the new window and select File | Save. Save the file as `ch12_3.py` in the directory of your choice.

```python
# Import the module
from Tkinter import *

# Create the root
root = Tk()
root.geometry("600x500+10+10")

# Create a frame to hold the text, with a fixed height and width
myContainer = Frame(root)
myContainer.pack(side=TOP, expand=YES, fill=BOTH)

# Put a label in the frame
myLabel = Label(myContainer, text="This is a test")
myLabel.pack(side=TOP, expand=YES, fill=BOTH)


root.mainloop()
```

3. Press the F5 key or select Run Module from the Run menu of the Editor window. You should see a display similar to the one shown in Figure 12.3.

Figure 12.3
A centered window.

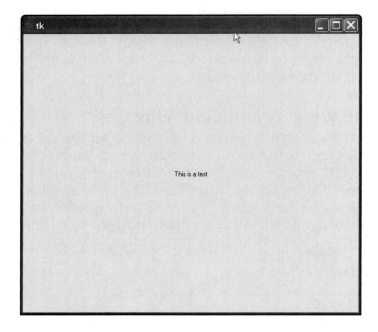

This is a test

Now, let's look at the changes to this program from the previous one and what those changes accomplished. You will notice that you have added a line below the creation of the root window object:

```
root.geometry("600x500+10+10")
```

The geometry method of the root object specifies the size and position of the window on the desktop. The basic format of the string that is passed to the function is "widthxheight+l+u," where width is the width of the window in pixels, height is the height of the window in pixels, and l and u are the inserts from the left and bottom of the screen respectively. For example, if I use a string of "600x400x50x20," it means I want a window that is 640 pixels wide by 400 pixels tall. I want the window to appear 50 pixels from the left-hand side of the screen and 20 pixels from the bottom of the screen. You do not have to specify all of the elements. If I only wanted the size specified, I could write the geometry string as "640x400."

The next component of the program is:

```
myContainer = Frame(root)
myContainer.pack(side=TOP, expand=YES, fill=BOTH)
```

The Frame object is a container object in Python. It simply defines a block of the root window to be set aside for an empty area. The Frame object can contain other objects, and it allows for the objects to be moved about within the frame. Once you have a frame object defined, you can define how it is to appear in the parent window, which in this case is the root window.

The `pack()` method takes a variety of options, some of which are shown here. The side parameter defines how the object is to be aligned to its parent. In this case, you have defined the frame to be anchored to the top of the parent window. The expand parameter tells Tk that you want the frame object to expand when the parent window of the frame is expanded. If you resize your main window, the frame will automatically resize with it, subject to the constraints of the rest of the geometry packing the frame. Finally, the fill option specifies whether the frame object should fill itself vertically, horizontally, or both. In this case, you have asked that the frame fill the entire window by expanding in both directions.

Now that the frame object is defined, you then build the Label object within that frame. The advantage to doing it this way is that you can change the behavior of the frame, such as making it take up half the window, and not have any impact to the children of the frame (our label, in this case). The frame is a "container," and the children within that container will be resized or moved, based on the container behavior.

```
myLabel = Label(myContainer, text="This is a test")
myLabel.pack(side=TOP, expand=YES, fill=BOTH)
```

The definition of the label object hasn't changed at all, but the packing logic certainly has. As you can see, you are defining the label to do exactly what the frame does, but within the frame, rather than within the root. If you changed the frame definition to, for example, fill only the vertical portion of the window, the label would be centered within that new space.

Now that you have a basic understanding of how to create elements within a window and how to position them, it is time to start working with elements that actually have some user interaction. Let's start with a button.

An Application with a Button

As I'm sure that you are aware, a button is a user interface element that allows the user to press a mouse button over and normally performs an action in response to that mouse click. A button has certain attributes, most important of which is the text that appears on its face. You can think of a button as a label with some user response to it, which is really what it is. To create a new button in a Tk application, you use the `Button()` class.

1. Create a new file in Python using the IDLE editor's File | New Window command.

2. Enter the following code into the new window and select File | Save. Save the file as `ch12_4.py` in the directory of your choice.

```
# Import the module
from Tkinter import *

# Create the root
root = Tk()

# Add a button to click
btn = Button(root, text="Push Me!")
btn.pack()



root.mainloop()
```

3. Press the F5 key or select Run Module from the Run menu of the Editor window. You should see a display similar to the one shown in Figure 12.4.

Figure 12.4
A button in Tkinter.

If you click the button, you will notice that it reacts to the event by displaying itself as "depressed," but does nothing else. The button object does not, by default, have any functionality associated with it. If you want to change the behavior of the application when you click on a button, you need to write your own function to handle the click event. For now, let's imagine that you want to write an indication that you received the event to the console in the IDLE interpreter.

To add button handling functionality to your application, you need to define a command handler for the button and a function that is to be called when that command handler is invoked. Let's do that here. Modify your program to include the lines shown in bold below:

```
# Import the module
from Tkinter import *


# Define a function to handle the button click
def button_click() :
    print "The button was clicked!"


# Create the root
```

```
root = Tk()


# Add a button to click
btn = Button(root, text="Push Me!", command=button_click)
btn.pack()



root.mainloop()
```

Now, when you click the button, you should see the string "The button was clicked!" shown in the console window. Try it out and see.

Working with Entry Fields and Grid Layouts

The most common use of user interface windows is to gather information from the user. Often, this information is in the form of free-form text, which cannot be collected by using a button or other selection mechanism, but must be typed in manually by the user. For this purpose, the Tkinter library provides the entry field widget. As a simple example, consider the input form shown in Figure 12.5.

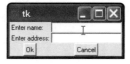

Figure 12.5
An input form in Tkinter.

There is nothing particularly special about this input form. You might see something like this in any standard application that needed to gather a few bits of information from the user. You would like to collect two bits of information here: the name and address of the user. Let's create a simple Python script that will put up the form (also called a *dialog* in many systems) and collect the information. You'll be using a different form of the layout manager here, which is a grid manager. The grid manager lays out controls on the form in a row and column grid-like structure. You'll see what it means as we go through the code.

1. Create a new file in Python using the IDLE editor's File | New Window command.

2. Enter the following code into the new window and select File | Save. Save the file as ch12_5.py in the directory of your choice.

   ```
   from Tkinter import *


   root = None
   ```

```
namentry = None
addressentry = None
name = None
address = None

def close_window() :
    global name
    global address
    global nameentry, addressentry
    name = nameentry.get()
    address = addressentry.get()
    root.destroy()

def DoInputForm(root):
    global nameentry, addressentry

    Label(root, text="Enter name:").grid(row=0, sticky=W)
    Label(root, text="Enter address:").grid(row=1, sticky=W)

    nameentry = Entry(root)
    addressentry = Entry(root)

    nameentry.grid(row=0, column=1)
    addressentry.grid(row=1, column=1)

    # Add an ok and cancel button
    Button(root, text="Ok", command=close_window).grid(row=2, column=0)
    Button(root, text="Cancel", command=close_window).grid(row=2, column=1)

root = Tk()
DoInputForm(root)
root.mainloop()


print "Name: "+name
```

3. Press the F5 key or select Run Module from the Run menu of the Editor window. You should see a display similar to the one shown in Figure 12.5.

Taking a look at what is going on in this application, you see a few new items. The Entry field is created in the `DoInputForm()` function. The entry field creates a text entry area that the user can type whatever they want into it. You might notice the use of the `grid()` layout manager to define where the text entry fields and prompts appear on the form. The concept of a grid is certainly not new in user interfaces; spreadsheets and such have been around for years. In Tkinter, the grid layout permits you to define things in terms of rows and columns. The row and column entries will be defined by the width and height of the fields that fall within them. For example, if you were to define a row that contained a field that was 100 pixels high, that row would then take on a minimum height of 100 pixels plus the spacing between the rows. Likewise, the width of the column is defined by the widest entry within the column. You can set absolute widths and heights in the entries, by using the width and height attributes, but it is generally best to allow the grid layout manager to do the work for you. Different items will appear in different resolutions for different users, so it is a good idea to allow the dynamic management of your layouts. Note that if you do not specify a column number, the column will default to zero, the leftmost column.

Another important thing to notice here is that if you do not need the object resulting from the creation of a widget, such as with the Label objects, there is no reason to assign them to a variable. This might be a bit confusing, since you would think that as soon as the object went out of scope it would be destroyed. Have no fear, the parent window maintains a list of widgets and will not allow them to be destroyed (and thus disappear from the window) before the parent is destroyed. If you have a need for the items, such as with the Entry fields that you want to retrieve user input text from, then you will need to keep a reference to the Entry object (or other object that you might be creating).

You assign a command handler to the buttons to close the window when the user clicks either of the buttons. This isn't the most elegant way to handle things, since you obviously would not want the OK and Cancel buttons to do the same thing, but it does illustrate that you can use a single event handler for multiple items in your own user interfaces.

When the user clicks the OK or Cancel button, the command handler, called `close_window()`, is invoked. Note that we have made the object references for the Entry objects on the window into global variables, and refer to them globally within both the command handler and the `DoInputForm()` functions. This allows us to get at the information in the Entry fields by using the `get()` method of the Entry object. The `get()` method returns the string that the user has entered for the field before he clicked the OK or Cancel buttons.

One note about tab order is probably important here. The order in which the tab key will move through the fields in a Tkinter dialog is normally defined by the order in which the fields themselves are added to the dialog. Fields that do not accept user input, such as labels, will not be in the tab order. So, for our data entry form, the order of the tabbing through the dialog will be:

* The name Entry field
* The address Entry field
* The OK button
* The Cancel button

Once the bottom of the list is reached, pressing the tab key will move back to the beginning of the list, so hitting tab while on the Cancel button will move you back to the name entry field. The Shift-tab (often called a *backtab*) will move you backwards through the list, in reverse order from above.

The above code will all work, and certainly does what we wanted it to do. However, it suffers from one particular problem—it is convoluted and ugly. What you really want is to make the code a bit more elegant and a lot less kludgy. To do this, you want to remove the references to global variables and the need for calling everything a global in all of the functions. The best way to implement this in Python is by using a class, so let's convert our existing set of functions and variables into a class with methods and members.

Creating a Class to Handle User Interfaces

There are two good reasons to wrap up the functionality for a given set of user interface code into a class. First, it makes it easier to read and edit the code for the user interface, and it makes the code a lot cleaner. Secondly, and more importantly, it makes it vastly easier to reuse and extend the code in other applications. It is extremely rare for a given piece of user interface functionality to be used only in one place at one time. Instead, it is much more common that you end up needing a form from one script in another script and so forth and so on. For these reasons, it makes a lot of sense to convert your procedural code that you developed in the previous example into a class that you can use again and again. It will also help us get rid of those ugly global variables and global statements within all of the code. So let's go ahead and do that.

1. Create a new file in Python using the IDLE editor's File | New Window command.

2. Enter the following code into the new window and select File | Save. Save the file as `ch12_6.py` in the directory of your choice.

```
from Tkinter import *


class AddressInputForm :
    def __init__(self) :
        self.root = None
        self.nameentry = None
```

```python
        self.name = ""
        self.address = ""

    def CloseWindow(self) :
        self.name = self.nameentry.get()
        self.address = self.addressentry.get()
        self.root.destroy()

    def CreateForm(self) :
        self.root = Tk()
        Label(self.root, text="Enter name:").grid(row=0, sticky=W)
        Label(self.root, text="Enter address:").grid(row=1, sticky=W)

        self.nameentry = Entry(self.root)
        self.addressentry = Entry(self.root)

        self.nameentry.grid(row=0, column=1)
        self.addressentry.grid(row=1, column=1)

        # Add an ok and cancel button
        Button(self.root, text="Ok", command=self.CloseWindow).grid
        (row=2,column=0)
        Button(self.root, text="Cancel", command=self.CloseWindow).
        grid(row=2, column=1)

    def Show(self) :
        self.root.mainloop()


af = AddressInputForm()
af.CreateForm()
af.Show()
print "Name: "+af.name
```

Running this bit of code will result in the same display as Figure 12.5 and will have the same output. Notice, however, how much cleaner the code looks and how much easier it would be to modify the entry fields or prompts with this style of coding. In the future, you should always use a class for your data entry forms, unless they are of the simplest possible variety.

Working with List Boxes

A common problem when dealing with user interface design is how to allow the user to select from a set of options, when that set of options may be variable in length. You might think to present a series of buttons, which we have already looked at, or a list of check boxes, which we will look at soon. A better alternative, however, is the list box. A list box displays a list of strings and allows the user to select one or more of the strings (at the programmer's discretion) to do something with. You might present a list of file names and allow the user to select which ones he wants to use to perform an operation. Perhaps you want to present a list of connection protocols for a communication system and allow the user to select only one of them. Whatever your need, if the data is in list or array form, the answer is probably a list box for your GUI element.

The Tk library provides the `Listbox()` class to provide access to the functionality of the list box in Python. You can create a list box, add items to it, delete items from it, and get back one or more items as a selection from the user. Let's take a look at an example of using the list box. For your example, you will pretend that the user has a list of items from which he needs to make selections. Once the item has been selected and processed, you will then delete it from the list box item list. In addition, you want to provide the user with the capability to select multiple items at one time and to process and delete them all at once. The work of processing the items certainly isn't exciting, but selecting and deleting items is interesting, to say the least. The list box you are going to create will look like the one shown in Figure 12.6.

Figure 12.6
Working with list boxes.

1. Create a new file in Python using the IDLE editor's File | New Window command.

2. Enter the following code into the new window and select File | Save. Save the file as `ch12_7.py` in the directory of your choice.

```
from Tkinter import *


class ListBoxTest :

    def __init__(self) :
```

```
        self.root = Tk()
        self.list_box_1 = Listbox(self.root, selectmode=EXTENDED)
        self.list_box_1.pack()
        self.delete_button = Button(self.root, text="Delete",
        command=self.DeleteSelection)
        self.delete_button.pack()


    def DeleteSelection(self) :
        items = self.list_box_1.curselection()
        pos = 0
        for i in items :
            idx = int(i) - pos
            self.list_box_1.delete( idx,idx )
            pos = pos + 1

    def Show(self) :
        for i in range(0, 10) :
            s = "Item " + str(i)
            self.list_box_1.insert( END,s )
        self.root.mainloop()


lbt=ListBoxTest()
lbt.Show()
```

If you run the application in IDLE, you will see the list box as it appears in Figure 12.6. Play around with the box a bit, selecting one or more items and clicking the Delete button. You will see that the item is removed from the list box properly.

One thing worth noting in this code is the use of the `Listbox()` constructor:

```
        self.list_box_1 = Listbox(self.root, selectmode=EXTENDED)
```

Notice that you pass a selectmode of "EXTENDED" into the constructor. This permits the user to select multiple items at once. If you omitted this argument, the list box would only allow single selection. Also, you might try selecting no items and clicking the delete button. You notice that nothing happens. The list box class handles the case of no selections in the `curselection()` method quite nicely. This is a nice change from some of the other GUI libraries out there. The `curselection()` method, by the way, returns a list of items that were selected. That means you can use all of the `list` methods that we have discussed to work with the list. Finally, note the slightly complex calculations to determine the index of the item to delete. This looks strange, but really isn't. Once you delete an entry, the ones following it in the list are then out of order. For example, if I select items 2, 3, and 4 in the list box, and try to delete them using those indices, I will actually delete items 2, 4, and 6. This is because the deletion is done based on the index of the entry in the list, not the original item number. So once item 2 is gone, item 3 is now in the position that item 2 used to be in, and so forth. For this reason, you need to calculate the offset you have already processed and use it for the real index of the item to delete.

One other thing before we move on to another part of the list box example. It has become common to use the "double-click" event to do default processing in a dialog. For example, if the dialog allows the user to select an item, then double-clicking that item in the list box should do the same as selecting the item with a single click and then pressing the OK button in the dialog. If you scan through the available methods of the list box, you will not find a command associated with the double-click. This is a hangover from the underlying Tcl/Tk system that underlies Tkinter for Python. Tcl uses something called "binding" to add functionality to widgets in the system. You can add a double-click handler by using the `bind()` method of the widget with the proper bind string, to call your method. Let's add that functionality now. Modify the existing `init` method with the method shown in bold:

```
def __init__(self) :
    self.root = Tk()
    self.list_box_1 = Listbox(self.root, selectmode=EXTENDED)
    self.list_box_1.pack()
    self.delete_button = Button(self.root, text="Delete",
    command=self.DeleteSelection)
    self.delete_button.pack()

    # Bind an event to the list box selection
    self.list_box_1.bind("<Double-Button-1>", self.DoubleClick)
```

Of course, you need to create the method that will be called when the double-click event is fired from within the Tkinter system. We've called this method "DoubleClick" (how original), so let's go ahead and define that method here. Add the following code anywhere in your class definition:

```
def DoubleClick(self, args) :
    item = self.list_box_1.curselection()
    self.list_box_1.delete( item[0], item[0] )
```

Now run the program again. It will look exactly the same as Figure 12.6, but if you double-click on an item, that item will be removed immediately from the list box. Try it and see! By the way, there is a "bug" in this code. If you double-click on an empty list, the program crashes because there is no current selection. See if you can fix it yourself.

Scrolling a List Box

One thing you might have noticed if you played with the above code at all is that if you added a lot of items, say, 50 or more, they can't be reached in the list box at runtime. That is, the Python list box does not have a built-in scrollbar. This seems rather strange, when you think about it, given that the list box is intended to allow you to select from potentially large numbers of items. If you can't scroll, does that mean you have to display a list box big enough to show all the items at once? That could be horrible, especially if you have a lot of items. Fortunately, it isn't true. While the list box itself contains no functionality for permitting the user to scroll, the Scrollbar class does. In typical Python and Tk fashion, you can combine the functionality of the two elements to produce a list box that appears to scroll for the user.

Figure 12.7 shows the new list box in our dialog, showing the scrollbar. In order to produce this dialog, however, you will need to make some modifications to your existing code for the list box display.

Figure 12.7
List box working with a scrollbar.

1. Create a new file in Python using the IDLE editor's File | New Window command.

2. Enter the following code into the new window and select File | Save. Save the file as ch12_8.py in the directory of your choice.

```
from Tkinter import *


class ListBoxTest :

    def DeleteSelection(self) :
        items = self.list_box_1.curselection()
        pos = 0
```

```
        for i in items :
            idx = int(i) - pos
            self.list_box_1.delete( idx,idx )
            pos = pos + 1

    def __init__(self) :
        self.root = Tk()
        self.frame = Frame(self.root)
        self.scrollbar = Scrollbar(self.frame, orient=VERTICAL)
        self.list_box_1 = Listbox(self.frame, selectmode=EXTENDED,
        yscrollcommand=self.scrollbar.set)
        self.scrollbar.config(command=self.list_box_1.yview)
        self.scrollbar.pack(side=RIGHT, fill=Y)
        self.list_box_1.pack(side=LEFT, fill=BOTH, expand=1)
        self.frame.pack()
        self.delete_button = Button(self.root, text="Delete",
        command=self.DeleteSelection)
        self.delete_button.pack()

    def Show(self) :
        for i in range(0, 50) :
            s = "Item " + str(i)
            self.list_box_1.insert( END,s )
        self.root.mainloop()


lbt=ListBoxTest()
lbt.Show()
```

The key to this code is the creation of the scrollbar object. You can use a scrollbar on its own, or in conjunction with other Tk elements, such as the list box, as you see here. If you look at the resulting display, you will notice that the scrollbar appears to be a part of the list box, rather than some separate element. This is due to the way in which we create the elements. Notice that we have added a new frame element to the display, which contains both the list box and the scrollbar. This is important, since if you do not use a frame, you will end up with a list box, scrollbar, and button all appearing at what seem to be random positions on a dialog background. Always place like elements in a frame so that you can align them properly for display.

The yscrollcommand is an attribute used to vertically scroll a list box. If you wanted to add a horizontal scrollbar as well, you would use the xscrollcommand attribute in the list box constructor. By associating one with the other, you are telling the list box to "listen" to the scrollbar scrolling method for hints as to when it should move its own positioning. Finally, the orientation of the scrollbar is set by the orient attribute in its constructor. Obviously, this can be either horizontal or vertical; in this case, we have chosen vertical.

You really don't need to understand a great deal more about the scrolling of list boxes than what you see here. Anytime you need a list box to scroll, you can simply drop in the code you see here, and it will simply work. That's the great thing about working with well-defined libraries such as Tkinter—you get a lot of predefined "recipes" that will do the things that you most commonly need accomplished in your own GUI systems. Just toss this one in your toolbox and pull it out when you need it.

Menus

Menus are a staple of modern graphical user interfaces. A simple, yet intuitive way for a user to invoke commands, menus were a natural outgrowth of the old command line interfaces for applications. Rather than having to remember a dozen cryptic and finger-wrenching commands such as Alt-Shift-Ctrl-Q for quitting the application, the user could simply click on the Exit menu command and terminate the program. Users flocked to menu-based applications, rather than the old clunky, hotkey-based systems. Every modern program that is not a simple utility tends to have a menu, so it is no surprise that you would want one for your Python applications.

Fortunately, working with menus in Tkinter is one of the easiest things there is to do. You can add main level menus, or submenus (also called *cascading menus*), quite simply using an object-oriented approach. To illustrate the use of menus in Python, let's take a look at a simple menu system, as shown in Figure 12.8. Notice that we have a main menu, with one submenu, under the Tools menu.

Figure 12.8
An application with
a main menu

1. Create a new file in Python using the IDLE editor's File | New Window command.

2. Enter the following code into the new window and select File | Save. Save the file as ch12_9.py in the directory of your choice.

```
from Tkinter import *


class MenuTest :

    def NewFile(self) :
```

```
        print "Creating a new file.."

    def OpenFile(self) :
        print "Opening an existing file..."

    def Close(self) :
        self.root.destroy()

    def notdone(self) :
        print "Not done yet!!"

    def __init__(self) :

        # Define the root window
        self.root = Tk()

        # Define a basic menu for the window
        self.main_menu = Menu(self.root)
        self.root.config( menu = self.main_menu )

        # Create the file menu
        fileMenu = Menu(self.main_menu)

        # Associate it with the window menu system
        self.main_menu.add_cascade( label="File", menu=fileMenu )

        # Now, add some commands to it
        fileMenu.add_command( label="New", command=self.NewFile )
        fileMenu.add_command( label="Open", command=self.OpenFile )
        fileMenu.add_separator()
        fileMenu.add_command( label="Exit", command=self.Close )

        # Try another kind of menu
        toolMenu = Menu(self.main_menu)
        self.main_menu.add_cascade( label="Tools", menu=toolMenu )
        toolMenu.add_command( label="Tool 1", command=self.notdone )
        submenu = Menu(toolMenu)
```

```
        toolMenu.add_cascade( label="Others", menu=submenu)
        submenu.add_command(label="Other 1", command=self.notdone)
        submenu.add_command(label="Other 2", command=self.notdone)


        self.root.mainloop()


    mt = MenuTest()
```

If you run the above script, you will see the display shown in Figure 12.8. There are a couple of things worth noting here. First, under the File menu, you will see a line dividing the functionality of the menu. Users expect this sort of thing to illustrate where some sorts of functionality end and others begin. This type of line is called a *separator* and can be added to any menu using the add_separator() method of the menu class. You can't select a separator, nor do anything with it. It is merely there to indicate a break in types of functionality.

The next interesting thing is how commands are associated with menu entries. When you add a new entry to a menu, you specify a block of executable code (by name) that will be called when the user selects that menu entry at runtime. As with all other callback functions in Python, you can specify either a stand-alone (often called a *static method* in other languages) function, or you can call a method of a class. To call a class method, you merely have to specify the self keyword in front of the method name (i.e., self.notdone). This indicates to the interpreter that this is a method, not a function, and that the self argument should be automatically passed to the method when it is invoked by the menu handler. This, by the way, is a vastly nicer way of doing things than most of the compiled languages, which cannot handle callbacks that are class methods.

How do we manage to create that submenu under the Tools menu? We associate a menu with the Tools menu, rather than the main menu. Every menu in Tkinter can have menus attached to it; they will be simple pop-up menus that are displayed when the user selects the main menu entry from the main window. This is rather nice, since you can easily move a menu from one place to another with relative ease.

One thing we haven't mentioned about menus is the tear-off capability of the menu. If you notice, all of our menus have a series of dashes ("---") at the top of the menu when it is displayed. If you click on this entry, the menu will tear itself off the menu and be displayed as a free-floating menu. If you don't like this behavior, simply specify tearoff=0 in the call to the constructor for the menu. For example, suppose that you modified the Tools menu:

```
toolMenu = Menu(self.main_menu, tearoff=0)
```

Modify the method call as shown and then re-run the application. You will notice that there is no longer a dashed line at the top of the tools menu, and that it cannot be torn off to free float around the application.

Context Menus

If you are accustomed to working on Windows or the Macintosh, you probably are accustomed to working with context menus. Context menus, or right-click menus as they are sometimes called, are menus that pop up when you press the right mouse button within a given context. For example, if you are working on an editing program, the context menu might contain editing commands like cut, copy, and paste. Adding these commands to your Python Tkinter program is really easy, and is something you should seriously consider when you are designing and writing your program. Making life easy for the user, when it is easy for you to do, is something that is just too good to pass up. To add a context menu, you only need to know one new method, the `tk_popup()` method of the menu class. Let's look at how it works.

1. Create a new file in Python using the IDLE editor's File | New Window command.

2. Enter the following code into the new window and select File | Save. Save the file as `ch12_10.py` in the directory of your choice.

```
from Tkinter import *

class ContextMenuTest :

    def Cut(self) :
        print "Cut"

    def Copy(self) :
        print "Copy"

    def Paste(self) :
        print "Paste"

    def OnContext(self, args) :
        # Define a context menu
        contextMenu = Menu(None, tearoff=0)
        contextMenu.add_command( label = "Cut", command = self.Cut )
        contextMenu.add_command( label = "Copy", command = self.Copy )
        contextMenu.add_command( label = "Paste", command = self.Paste )
        contextMenu.tk_popup(args.x_root, args.y_root, entry="")

    def __init__(self) :
        self.root = Tk()
```

```
        self.root.geometry("300x500")
        self.root.bind("<Button-3>", self.OnContext )
        self.root.mainloop()

    cmt = ContextMenuTest()
```

There are a couple of important things to note about context menus. For example, you will always want to specify the tear-off value to be zero when creating one. It makes no sense at all to have a context menu tear off anything, since it is free floating to begin with. Next, you will notice that the menu structure for a pop-up context menu is exactly the same as for any other menu. This is not an accident, because a context menu is a regular menu with no parent. Finally, notice the `tk_popup()` method call. This method accepts three arguments, the x and y position to display the pop-up menu on the window, and the entry to select to begin with. Normally, you will leave the third argument (the entry) blank.

In order to make the pop-up menu appear, you need to capture the right-click of the mouse. This is done with the `bind()` method of the Tk object. The right mouse button, for historical reasons, is button three. The left mouse button is button one, and for systems that support it, the middle button is button two. If there is no middle button, you will never get a callback for it, but it doesn't change the numbering system at all. You bind the "Button-3" event, which is a click from the rightmost button of the mouse, to your context handler method. This context handler will receive two arguments. First, it will get the object for which it is operating. This is simply your `self` argument that you've used in all of your functionality so far. The second argument is an event argument. This specifies where the mouse button was clicked on the screen. The `x_root` and `y_root` attributes of the event class specify the position relative to the window, which is what you want for our positioning.

When you select an item in a context menu, the menu will automatically disappear from the screen and the method you tied to that menu item will be invoked. That's really all there is to working with context menus. It is so simple that anyone can add this kind of functionality easily, and it makes you wonder why programmers so often leave it out. Don't be one of those evil programmers—give your users all the tools they need to do their jobs easily.

Scale Widgets

How often do you find yourself needing to enter a value within certain limits? The answer is quite often, especially if you work with numeric data. For example, imagine that you need to enter a percentage for use with transparency in an application. The valid values might be zero to 100 percent transparency for a given window, indicating whether the window is completely transparent or completely opaque. It is a pain in the neck to force the user to enter a value in that range, validate the range to make sure that it is proper, and then convert the input string into a number so that you can actually use it in your calculations. Wouldn't you think there would be an easier way? It turns out that, using the Tkinter libraries, there is a better way, and that way is called a *scale widget.*

The scale widget allows you to "slide" a value from one extreme to another, simply by pressing the mouse button down on the control and moving it from one side to another. The scale permits you to move in either scrolling increments, by using the mouse to slide a single block on the screen, or to move in single units by clicking on the end of the scale that you want to move toward. As a benefit, the scale widget also has a display that shows you the current value of the widget for the user to see exactly where he is in the process. You can use a scale widget for input, to allow the user to enter a value, or you can use it for display, to indicate how far along a user might be in a given process.

Figure 12.9 shows a simple dialog window that contains a scale widget. In this case, we have set the limits of the widget to be from zero to 100, and the user has moved the widget slider value to be 68.

Figure 12.9
A slider widget, showing a
user selected value.

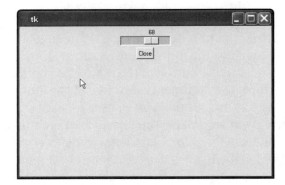

Let's go ahead and build the application that displays Figure 12.9, along with the button that closes the application and prints out the final selected value for the user.

1. Create a new file in Python using the IDLE editor's File | New Window command.

2. Enter the following code into the new window and select File | Save. Save the file as ch12_11.py in the directory of your choice.

```
from Tkinter import *

class ScaleTest :

    def CloseMe(self) :
```

```
        self.value = self.scale.get()
        self.root.destroy()

    def __init__(self) :
        self.value = 0
        self.root = Tk()
        self.root.geometry("500x300")

        # Create a scale widget
        self.scale = Scale( self.root, from_=0, to=100, orient=HORIZONTAL )
        self.scale.pack()

        # Create a button to close the app
        Button( self.root, text="Close", command=self.CloseMe ).pack()

        # And run the app
        self.root.mainloop()

st = ScaleTest()
print "Value = " + str(st.value)
```

If you run the script and move the widget around, then click the Close button, you will see the value displayed on the console. Note that if you are running the script from within IDLE, you will not see the final value displayed. This is just an oddity of the IDLE environment; don't let it concern you. By the way, if you don't like the slider showing the value above it, simply add the configuration option "showvalue=False" to the constructor for the class. This leads to an interesting question, however. Suppose that you wanted to display the value in your own label or another control. You could easily update a label text to display the value, but how do you know when the value changes? The answer is that the scale widget allows you to specify a command method to be called whenever the value changes. To illustrate how this works, modify the above code as follows (changes shown in bold):

```
from Tkinter import *


class ScaleTest :

    def CloseMe(self) :
        self.value = self.scale.get()
```

```
            self.root.destroy()


    def ShowTheValue(self, args) :
        self.value_label["text"] = str(self.scale.get())


    def __init__(self) :
        self.value = 0
        self.root = Tk()
        self.root.geometry("500x300")

        # Create a scale widget
        self.scale = Scale( self.root, from_=0, to=100, orient=HORIZONTAL,
showvalue=False, command=self.ShowTheValue )
        self.scale.pack()

        # Create a button to close the app
        Button( self.root, text="Close", command=self.CloseMe ).pack()

        # Create a label to show the value
        self.value_label = Label( self.root, text="0" )
        self.value_label.pack()

        # And run the app
        self.root.mainloop()


st = ScaleTest()
print "Value = " + str(st.value)
```

Now when you run the program, you will see the value updated in your own label in real-time.

RadioButtons and CheckButton

When it comes to allowing the user to make choices, there are really two ways programming languages go about it. First, you can allow the user to simply type in an answer to a question. This goes along the lines of "What color do you want the background to be?" followed by an input field that lets you type in things like "white" or "red." Obviously, aside from the problem of misspellings, this is a process that is fraught with error. You can get all sorts of answers you never expected, like "the color of my wife's eyes," for example. The usual alternative to this is to allow the user to select the color from some sort of a list. If you have a lot of possible entries, a list box is definitely the way to go. But what if you only have two or three possibilities to choose from? In this case, you don't want to use a list box, as they are rather daunting to the average user. What you want is to present a list of possible options and have the user select the one he wants, while not allowing him to select more than one. This is the purpose of the RadioButton class in Python's Tkinter library. On the other hand, what if you want to allow him to select from a short list of items and select more than one of the entries? In that case, you use the CheckButton class. These two classes, while similar, have slightly different behavior from the perspective of the user. Let's look at an example of using both types in a small application to see how it all works.

Figure 12.10 shows the application we are going to be building. It consists of two separate groups of radio buttons and one set of check buttons that the user can select from. The user will be able to select one option from the first group of radio buttons, one option from the second group of radio buttons, and as many options as they want from the group of check buttons.

Figure 12.10
Radio buttons and check buttons in Python

Let's go ahead and build the application that displays Figure 12.10.

1. Create a new file in Python using the IDLE editor's File | New Window command.

2. Enter the following code into the new window and select File | Save. Save the file as ch12_12.py in the directory of your choice.

```python
from Tkinter import *


class SelectionTest :
    def __init__(self) :

        # Create the main window
```

```
self.root = Tk()

# Create a few radio buttons in group 1
self.group_1 = IntVar()

Radiobutton(self.root, text="Option 1:", variable=self.group_1,
value=1).pack(anchor=W)
Radiobutton(self.root, text="Option 2:", variable=self.group_1,
value=2).pack(anchor=W)
Radiobutton(self.root, text="Option 3:", variable=self.group_1,
value=3).pack(anchor=W)

# Separate them with a label
Label(self.root, text="Group 2:").pack()

# Create a second group of radio buttons
self.group_2 = IntVar()
Radiobutton(self.root, text="Option 2-1:", variable=self.group_2,
value=1).pack(anchor=W)
Radiobutton(self.root, text="Option 2-2:", variable=self.group_2,
value=2).pack(anchor=W)
Radiobutton(self.root, text="Option 2-3:", variable=self.group_2,
value=3).pack(anchor=W)

# Now, create some checkboxes
self.check_1 = IntVar()
self.check_2 = IntVar()
self.check_3 = IntVar()
Checkbutton(self.root, text="Text", variable=self.check_1).pack
(anchor=W)
Checkbutton(self.root, text="RTF", variable=self.check_2).pack
(anchor=W)
Checkbutton(self.root, text="Word", variable=self.check_3).pack
(anchor=W)


self.root.mainloop()

st = SelectionTest()
```

```
print "Group 1 selection: "+str(st.group_1.get())
print "Group 2 selection: "+str(st.group_2.get())
print "Check Box 1: " + str(st.check_1.get())
print "Check Box 2: " + str(st.check_2.get())
print "Check Box 3: " + str(st.check_3.get())
```

If you run the program, you will see that you can select one item in group one, one item in group two, and as many of the check buttons in group three that you want. When you close the window, by clicking the Close button in the corner, you will see the values associated with the items you checked printed out to the IDLE console window. The general rule of thumb is simple—if you want a single choice out of multiple options, use radio buttons. If you want to allow the user to select mutually allowable, but related, items, use check buttons.

Note the use of the `IntVar` type. The `IntVar` class represents a reference to an integer within the Python system. We are using it here so that we can transfer data between the `CheckButton` objects and our scripting code.

Text Widgets

The final widget we are going to look at in this chapter is the text widget. The text widget can be used for either displaying large amounts of text for an application, or for allowing the user to edit text much like a word processor. The text widget provides a rich array of text editing functionality, allowing you to embed images or text in documents, select and operate on parts of the text, and do many other things with textual displays.

For this example, you are going to build a simple file viewer. You will be able to type in a file name to an entry (single line text input) field and then click a button to load the file into a larger text file. Fair warning—the Tkinter text widget is not the most efficient control. It can be slow to load very large amounts of text into the control, especially if you do it one line at a time. Loading an entire file at once isn't too bad, but this is not a replacement for a true text editor.

The text control does not contain scrolling functionality in its GUI elements. If you want to add scrolling to the display, you will need to do it in the same way that you did with the list box, by adding a scrollbar to the control. This is pretty much a standard in the Tkinter library, because the assumption is that you should not have to suffer through functionality you don't want, and that a function that exists in one place should not be duplicated in another.

Figure 12.11 shows the application you are going to be building. It consists of a field to enter a file name and a button that you can click to load the file into the text display field below.

Figure 12.11
Radio buttons and check
buttons in Python

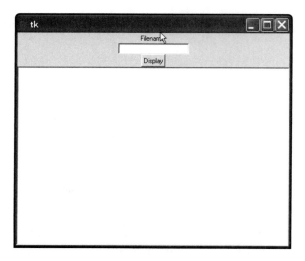

Let's go ahead and build the application that displays Figure 12.11.

1. Create a new file in Python using the IDLE editor's File | New Window command.

2. Enter the following code into the new window and select File | Save. Save the file as ch12_13.py in the directory of your choice.

```python
from Tkinter import *

class FileDisplay :

    def loadfile(self) :
        myFile=file(self.filename.get())
        myText= myFile.read()
        myFile.close()

        self.text_widget.insert(0.0,myText)

    def __init__(self) :
        # Create the elements
        self.root = Tk()
        Label(self.root, text="Filename: ").pack()
        self.filename = Entry(self.root)
        self.filename.pack()
        Button(self.root, text="Display", command=self.loadfile).pack()
```

```
        self.text_widget = Text(self.root)
        self.text_widget.pack(expand=1, fill=BOTH)


        self.root.mainloop()


    fd = FileDisplay()
```

If you enter a valid file name in the entry field and then click the Display button, you will see the file loaded into the text field properly. Again, note that we do not provide scrolling functionality for the text field. If you want to add scrolling functionality, simply modify the _init_ method as follows (changes shown in bold):

```
def __init__(self) :
        # Create the elements
        self.root = Tk()
        Label(self.root, text="Filename: ").pack()
        self.filename = Entry(self.root)
        self.filename.pack()
        Button(self.root, text="Display", command=self.loadfile).pack()
        self.frame = Frame(self.root)
        self.scrollbar = Scrollbar(self.frame, orient=VERTICAL)
        self.text_widget = Text(self.frame, yscrollcommand=self.scrollbar.set)
        self.text_widget.pack(side=LEFT, fill=BOTH, expand=1)
        self.scrollbar.config(command=self.text_widget.yview)
        self.scrollbar.pack(side=RIGHT, fill=Y)
        self.frame.pack()


        self.root.mainloop()
```

In Conclusion

In this chapter, you learned about the Tkinter library and how to use it to create GUI applications in Python. Tkinter, of course, is not a part of Python, but is an external system that happens to have an interface. In fact, the library is called Tk and the interface to it is called Tkinter. You can use this library to create many complicated and amazing things in Python; we merely scratched the surface of what is possible in this chapter.

Remember, this book is not intended to be a complete reference to the Tkinter system. There are many more widgets that were not covered, and many bits of functionality that were not discussed. You can find out a lot about the library on the Internet or through the documentation supplied with the Python system. Play around with the libraries, try to do different things, and you will learn more about it than you could possibly learn here. This was intended as an overview and an introduction to some of the things you probably wouldn't think about without trying them. When you install Tk in your Python system, you will also get a complete Help file that describes the methods and classes in the library. Please refer to that more complete documentation for anything we didn't cover here.

Tkinter is a well written and well debugged library. It has been around for a long time in the UNIX world, and has been ported to many operating systems. By using this interface for Python, you will find that your applications work transparently across systems, with no changes necessary.

In our next chapter, we will explore the second part of the WAMP system, the Apache Web server. We won't be using the Tk library there, but will later on in the book, so don't forget everything you've learned!

13} The Web Server—Apache

The most popular use of Python in the corporate world is for writing scripts to be called from Web pages. In order to use a Web page, of course, you must somehow serve up that page to the user, so that he can interact with your scripts. The serving up of pages is accomplished by a Web server. The most popular open source Web server is the Apache Web Server from the Apache Software Foundation. You can find the Apache Web server at `www.apache.org` or `httpd.apache.org`. The Web server itself is free, although there are various organizations that sell versions of it. For our purposes, the free basic server will be fine.

We often refer to the combination of Web server, scripting language, and database as either the LAMP or WAMP system. The "L" stands for Linux, while the "W" stands for Windows. In either case, the "A" is the Apache Web server, while the database is normally MySQL (thus, the "M") and the scripting language is either Python or Perl, completing the acronym. In the next few chapters, we will be looking at how to put together the WAMP system, although the process is essentially the same for LAMP once you get the software installed.

Setting Up Apache

In the Windows world, setting up the Apache Web server is one of the simplest jobs you will ever have. Download the installer (MSI file) from the Apache Software Foundation Web site and run it on the box on which you want to install the software. It is perfectly acceptable to run the software on your local machine, using the local address (127.0.0.1, or localhost). For our purposes, you can accept pretty much every default available, specifying only the directory that you want to install the program in. Note that you must be an administrator on the computer that you are trying to install Apache for in order for it to work properly. Please be sure to install the system as a Windows service, so that it will load and run properly at startup, and will be available at all times. If, for some reason, you do not want to install it as a service, you will need to run the command line version of the software (or launch it via the Start button) to bring it up. In any case, once you have the software installed, the next step is to verify that the Web server is running.

In this book, we are using the 2.2 version of the Apache Web server. If you are using a different version, you may get slightly different prompts or displays. The basics of what we are doing shouldn't change, however. Make sure that the version of Apache you are using is compatible with the version of Python you are using, however. This information is generally available on the Apache Web site.

Testing Apache

After you have installed the Apache software, the first step is to make sure that it is working properly. Apache ships with an index.html file that is located in the `$root\htdocs` directory, where `$root` is the root of the installation system. For example, if you used the default install options, the root of the system will be `\Program Files\Apache Foundation\Apache 2.2` (for the 2.2 version of the Web server, your directory could be slightly different).

Fortunately, the Web server really doesn't care where you place the files; it just cares about the URL (uniform resource locator) that you provide it to find files. To test the Web server, you enter the following line on the navigation line of your favorite Web browser: `http://localhost`.

The Web server will find the index.htm file in the `htdocs` directory of the installation tree and will display the contents on the screen. What you see varies, depending on the installation version you have, but you should see something that makes it obvious that the Apache Web server is running. If, for some reason, you do not see the Welcome screen, check to see if the Apache server is running. You can verify this, at least with version 2.2, by checking the tray in the bottom right corner of the screen (in a default Windows configuration, anyway) to see if you see the Apache server icon, as shown in Figure 13.1, is displayed.

Figure 13.1
The Apache icon as shown in the Windows tray.

If the icon is visible and you are still not seeing the Welcome page, refer to the Apache documentation to see what might be going wrong. Normally, this is not a problem, because the server installation process is pretty foolproof. Once you have verified that the server is running and that you can access files locally, the next step is to verify that the system works with Python. To do this, you will create a simple script to show that the program is working properly.

Your First Python CGI Script: Hello Apache

The CGI (Common Gateway Interface) protocol is a standard way for external programs and application environments to interact with Web servers. While a plain HTML file on the Web is static, a CGI program (or script) is executed at the time that the request is made from the user, and the content is created on the fly. To see how this works, let's create a simple script in Python and have it executed by the Apache Web server.

1. Create a new file using the IDLE editor or your favorite text editor.

2. Place the following code into the new file and save this file as ch13_1.py:

```
#!c:/Python25/python

from os import *
from cgi import *

print "Content-type: text/html\n\n"
print "<BR><B>Hello Python!</B>"
```

3. Save the file to the cgi-bin directory under the root of your Apache installation. For example, if the Apache system was installed to c:\Program Files\Apache Software Foundation\Apache 2.2, then save the file into:

```
C:\Program Files\Apache Software Foundation\Apache 2.2\cgi-bin
```

For this example, the file is called ch13_1.py, to indicate that it is the first program you created in this chapter, but you can call it whatever you like. Whatever you decide to name the file, remember that name for the next step.

4. Launch a Web browser and enter the following URL into the navigation box: http://localhost/cgi-bin/ch13_1.py

Obviously, if you have used a different name for the file, replace the ch13_1 in the above URL with your own name. In any case, the file must end with the .py extension and must be in the cgi-bin directory for this to work.

You should see a display similar to the one shown in Figure 13.2. Note that while this particular display is in the Firefox (Mozilla) Web browser, the resulting display would be the same in any Web browser. The output of your little program is simple HTML and will look the same no matter what you view it in:

Figure 13.2

Hello Python script output.

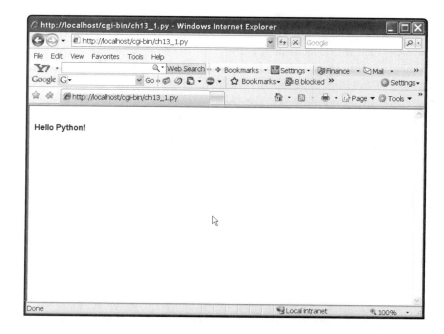

Examining the Hello Python Script

As you look at the rather simple code involved in the script, you should notice a few things. First, the code imports two new modules that you haven't really worked with before. The `os` module contains operating system specific functionality, while the `cgi` module imports functionality directly related to the CGI processing. We aren't actually using either of these in this script, but you should use them as a matter of course when you are working with Web-related coding.

The script uses the `print` statement to output data to the Web server. You will notice that the first line that is output is:

```
print "Content-type: text/html\n\n"
```

This line is required for the Web server to properly interpret the code. As a side note, this is not a valid HTML file, since it does not contain a starting `<HTML>` and closing `</HTML>` tag. Even with that problem, there are no Web servers on the market today that won't properly deal with this output so long as the header line is in place.

Once you have output the header line, the rest of the code generates simple HTML tags and text to display the line on the browser the way you want it to appear. The `<B>` tag outputs the data in bold, while the `<BR>` tag simply outputs a break (or blank line, in this case). This book is not intended to be a primer on HTML, as there are lots of books out there for that. The assumption, from this point on, is that you know enough about HTML to either write the kinds of statements you need to write, or that you can look them up elsewhere. We will focus mostly on the Python aspects of the scripts we are writing.

After the server loads the script, the `print` statement simply emits code that will be interpreted by the server as a file to send to the client. Thus, when the script has finished, your "file" that is shipped to the client looks like this:

```
Content-type: text/html


<BR><B>Hello Python!</B>
```

The two blank lines following the header line are required by HTML for the server to be able to know where the display code begins. There are other things that can go into the block between the header line and the beginning of the HTML code, so please refer to a solid HTML book for further information.

Note that while we are sending HTML data to the server, no file is ever created on your local machine.

The cgi-bin Directory

The next issue we need to discuss is why, suddenly, it matters where the script file "lives." Up to this point, we have created the file containing the Python code anywhere that we wanted to. For Web scripts, however, the files need to "live" in the cgi-bin directory. The reason for this isn't very complicated. The Web server needs to know that a given area is under its control and contains "safe" files. You can create subdirectories under the cgi-bin directory and use those, as well. Finally, you can actually place files in different directories and use them, but this requires configuration changes to the Apache configuration files. Please refer to your Apache documentation on how do accomplish this. For now, let's simply assume that all scripting files need to be placed in this directory and just move on.

When the Web server gets a request for a file, it looks at the extension on the file to determine what to do with it. If the extension is .htm (or, in some cases, .html) the file is considered to be static HTML text and processed directly. (There are exceptions to this rule, but for now just accept it.) If the extension is a known scripting language, such as `.py`, the file is passed to the Python interpreter to process. The difference between a normal script and a Web script is simply in the environment that is available to the script. For a Web script, not only does the output go to a specific place, but there are also certain values available to you in the script that are not there for non-Web scripts. Things like cookies, form values, and Web server information are all there if you know how to get to them. In the remaining scripts in this chapter, we will explore some of this information.

Oh, one final note on the script code. You will notice that at the very top of the Python code, there is a single line comment:

```
#!c:/Python25/python
```

This comment, which is ignored by the Python interpreter while in IDLE or on the command line, is used by the Web server code as a "hint" to tell it where to find the Python executable. Make sure that it points to the directory in which the Python application (`pythonw.exe` on Windows) is found.

A Script for Displaying the Environment

While it is all very well and good to display simple HTML text in a Python script, there is obviously nothing very exciting about static text. The purpose of using Python in a Web script is to generate dynamic data. In this example, you are going to output, for the user, the current environment variable settings on the system. Note that these settings will be for the machine running the scripts, not the user's machine containing the browser. For testing purposes, this is usually the same machine.

1. Create a new file using the IDLE editor or your favorite text editor.

2. Place the following code into the new file and save this file as `ch13_2.py`:

```
#!c:/Python25/python

from os import *
from cgi import *

print "Content-type: text/html\n\n"
print

print "These are the environment variables:<br>"
for key, value in environ.items():
    print key, " = ", value, "<br>"
```

3. Save the file into the cgi-bin directory under the Apache Web server root directory. In this example, the file is called `ch13_2.py`, but you can call it whatever you like.

4. Run the script by entering the following URL into a Web browser: `http://localhost/cgi-bin/<filename.py>`
   where file name is the name of the file that you used in step 3.

If you run the program in the Mozilla/Firefox browser, you should see a display similar to the one shown in Figure 13.3. Note that the environment variables that you see will probably differ radically from the ones shown here. Environment variables depend on what you have installed, what drives you have available, and what settings you have chosen in the Windows system. However, you should at the very least see a list of variables with their values.

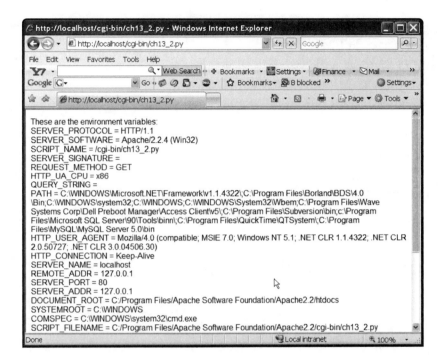

Figure 13.3
Python environment variables display.

Once again, we have imported the modules that are used for CGI and operating system interaction. The environ module is used to retrieve the environment variable settings, and they are displayed after the standard HTML header is displayed. Although there is nothing interactive about this script, it does at least generate dynamic data based on the current settings of the machine.

Now, the interesting part comes about. If you open a command prompt in the Windows environment, and then enter the command "set" followed by a carriage return, you will see a list of the environment variables set for your current user setting. Compare the entries that you see to the entries in the Web page displayed, and you will realize quickly that they are not in the least bit alike. In fact, if you run the script within the IDLE environment, you will see that the results are completely different as well.

When you run the script in the IDLE interpreter, or on the command line, you are running it under your own account. When a script runs in the Web server, however, it is running under a special account dedicated to the Web server. As a result, the environment that you are operating under is different. In addition, the environment within the Web server is different than that of the system environment. While things like this rarely make a huge difference, you do have to be aware of them when writing code that might be executed within the Web server environment and without.

Receiving Data from an HTML File

While one-sided conversations between a Web server and a Python script are often useful, it is considerably more interesting and useful to be able to supply a Python script with information from a Web page, and to generate output based on that input. In Python, the CGI module provides access to information sent by HTML pages containing input fields. These pages, called *forms* in the HTML world, can do the job of obtaining input from the user in a clean and user-friendly manner, and then pass them on to a simple script to do further processing.

As an example of this, let's collect some user information in an HTML form. In this case, you will use the form shown in Figure 13.4, which prompts the user for his first and last names. These bits of information will be passed on to a Python script, which will combine them and greet the user by his entire name.

Figure 13.4

An HTML input form for use with a Python script.

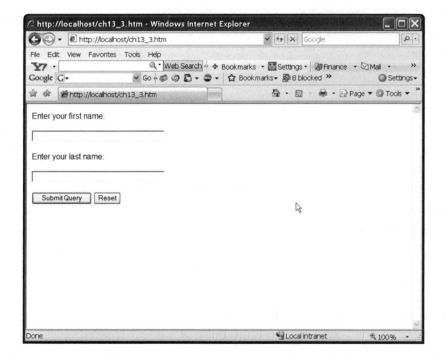

In order to accomplish this, you will first need an input form. This form, which is created in simple HTML, will then call your script.

1. Create a new file using your favorite text editor. In this case, I've chosen to use the Windows Notepad application, which is conveniently available in all versions of Windows.

2. Place the following code into the new file:

```
<HTML>

<! Define a form for inputting values for name and address>

<form action="cgi-bin/ch13_3.py">
 <p>Enter your first name:</p>
 <input type="text" name="firstname" size="40">
 <p>Enter your last name:</p>
<input type="text" name="lastname" size="40">
 <input type="submit">
 <input type="reset">
</form>
</HTML>
```

3. Save the file as `ch13_3.htm` and store it in the htdocs directory under the root of the Apache Web server installation directory.

4. Now create a new file using either your favorite text editor or the IDLE editor.

5. Place the following code in the new file.

```
#!c:/Python25/python
import cgi

reshtml = """Content-Type: text/html\n
<html>
 <head><title>Hello</title></head>

 <body>
  <h1>Welcome to a Python script!</h1>
  <p>You are identified as: %s</p>
 </body>
</html>"""

form = cgi.FieldStorage()
```

```
lastname = form['lastname'].value
firstname = form['firstname'].value
message = firstname + " " + lastname
print reshtml % message
```

6. Save the file as ch13_3.py and place it in the cgi-bin directory under the Apache root installation directory on your system.

7. Load the HTML file into your Web browser by entering the following string into the navigation control: http://localhost/ch13_3.htm.

8. Enter your first name and last name into the input fields and click the Submit Query button. The Python script file will be loaded and executed, and you should see something similar to the display shown in Figure 13.5.

Figure 13.5
The result of the Python script called from an HTML form.

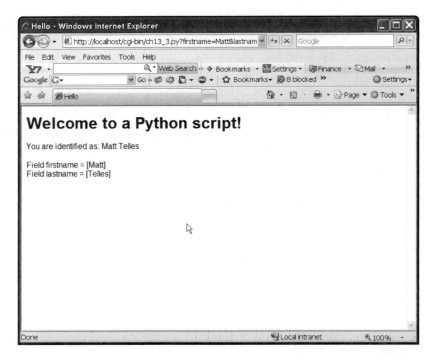

The FieldStorage() class of the cgi module will provide you with access to all sorts of information that is present in a multi-part form from HTML. Since the FieldStorage object is just a glorified Python dictionary, you can dump all of the data in the structure if you want to see what you are getting. For example, you could add the following code to the end of the script to print out the data that is received:

```
# Dump the dictionary of fields
for f in form :
    print "Field " + f + " = [" + form[f].value + "]<br>"
```

In this example, all you will see are the `firstname` and `lastname` fields, since that is all the data that is sent via the HTML form. However, if there were "hidden" fields in the HTML form, they would be present here as well.

Sending Data to an HTML File

Have you ever had to fill in a form with certain required fields? A lot of Web sites have a list of fields that you have to enter, along with a few that you don't necessarily have to fill in. For example, you might care a great deal about someone's name and city, but don't care particularly whether they fill in the apartment number of their address. After all, not everyone lives in an apartment, and those of us who live in normal houses with no apartment number tend to take it personally when you tell us that we need to fill in a number that does not apply. Do you ever wonder how the Web pages "know" that you haven't filled in certain bits of information and tell you exactly which ones you need to fill in?

In order to check the data entered in a form and send it back if it is incomplete, you need a scripting language. Python, fortunately, contains all of the information you need to do this task, and makes it easy to boot. To accomplish this task, you need a single Python script. This script will "know" whether or not data has been entered for a given input field by checking the `FieldStorage` object that comes in to see if a value is entered, and if not, it will change the color of the prompt for the entry field to red to indicate to the user that the field needs to be entered.

Ah, you say, but what about the first time the form is displayed? Won't the user immediately see all of the required fields in red? That would be disconcerting, to say the least. We need to take care of that problem. First, let's look at the form we will be displaying for the user, and then we will develop the Python script that resides behind the form in order to show you how it all works. Figure 13.6 shows you the basic form that you will be creating in this example.

1. Create a new file using your favorite text editor. In this case, I've chosen to use the Windows Notepad application, which is conveniently available in all versions of Windows.

2. Place the following code into the new file:

3. Save the file as `ch13_4.py` in the cgi-bin directory.

Figure 13.6

A generated input form.

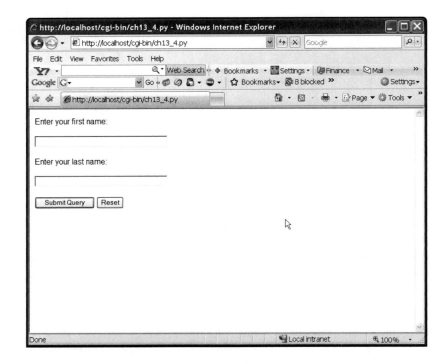

```
#!c:/Python25/python
import cgi

def send_form( dic ) :

    # Get the values we care about
    fName = dic.getvalue("firstname", "" )
    lName = dic.getvalue("lastname", "" )

    # See if we need to generate errors
    flag = int( dic.getvalue("flag", "0") )

    # Now, let's do the form
    print "<form action=\"ch13_4.py\">"

    if flag == 1 and fName == "" :
        print "<p><FONT COLOR='red'>Enter your first name:</FONT></p>"
    else :
```

```
          print "<p>Enter your first name:</p>"

     if fName != "" :
          print "<input type=\"text\" name=\"firstname\" value=\""+fName+"\"
size=\"40\">"
     else :
          print "<input type=\"text\" name=\"firstname\" size=\"40\">"

     if flag == 1 and lName == "" :
          print "<p><FONT COLOR='red'>Enter your last name:</FONT></p>"
     else :
          print "<p>Enter your last name:</p>"
     if lName != "" :
          print "<input type=\"text\" name=\"lastname\" value=\""+lName+"\"
size=\"40\">"
     else :
          print "<input type=\"text\" name=\"lastname\" size=\"40\">"
     print "<p>"
     print "<input type=\"submit\">"
     print "<input type=\"reset\">"

     # Add a hidden variable, so we know if we have been here or not
     print "<input type=\"hidden\" name=\"flag\" value=\"1\">"
     print "</p>"

def gen_output( dic ) :

     error = 0

     fName = dic.getvalue("firstname", "" )
     lName = dic.getvalue("lastname", "" )

     if fName == "" or lName == "" :
          error = 1

     if error == 0 :
          print "Hello there " + fName + " " + lName
```

```
    return error

# First, do the header.
print "Content-Type: text/html\n\n"
print "<HTML>"

form = cgi.FieldStorage()

res = gen_output(form)
if res == 1:
    send_form(form)

print "<form>"
print "</html>"
```

How It All Works

The first thing you need to understand before figuring out how it all works is to remember that the function definitions in the code will not be executed until they are called from the inline code. That means that the "script" actually begins executing at the comment that says, "First, do the header." Below this line, you generate the output HTML header that the Web server needs to read in order to know what to do with your generated file.

The next thing to do is to obtain the field storage information. This information will always be available in any Python script that is called from a Web server. However, the fact that it exists does not mean that it will necessarily have the information you need in it. You first call a function (getvalue) to verify that the data exists within the field storage. If a given field is not found, you know that you need to generate the form for the user to fill in and submit. If both values (last name and first name) are found and have valid values, however, the program will just display a hello message and quit.

Assuming that the user has not filled in the data, we move to the form generation. Note that we use a hidden variable (called flag in the code) to check to see if we have generated this form before. If the variable is not found in the field storage, this is the first time the user has selected this Python script file, and we don't want to tell him about any possible missing data, because he hasn't had an opportunity to actually fill it in yet. It would really be rude to tell him that we found errors when he didn't do anything.

The send_form() function uses the getvalue() method of the FieldStorage class to get back the values of the last name, first name, and flag. The second argument to the getvalue() method is the default value if the value was not found in the internal dictionary of the class.

We use that default value to see if there is anything there. After checking to see if the flag is set, you can either just output the input fields for the form, or you can set the prompt to be in red before doing the input field. The actual text does not change; you just set the font color (using the HTML font tag) to red.

This example illustrates how to use Python to generate a form dynamically for the user to enter data, and how to validate that data. You can see, hopefully, how easy it would be to check various pieces of data and require the user to re-enter them if they were wrong. Finally, this example illustrates the use of "hidden variables," which can be used to send data between HTML forms and back-end Python scripts to indicate state. You could easily use a hidden variable for something like a user session ID, to indicate a more semi-permanent set of data that is stored on the server for a given user at a given time. Naturally, you could easily use such a system to make sure that only a single user logs in using a given name at a given time, or to check for timeouts based on a long period of idleness.

Dynamic HTML Displays Based on User Input

Suppose that you were creating a Web site that allowed the user to trade stocks. This Web site might have various elements to it, such as looking at your current stock portfolio, trading stocks, or simply seeing an account overview of your account. It would really be nice if you could simply allow the user to log in once to the site and specify what he wanted to do at the same time. Once his login credentials had been verified, it would be nice to be able to take him directly to the page that he wanted to see, without forcing him to go through some sort of a menu system on the main page each and every time that he came into the system. This sort of personalization has become very popular on the Web lately, and it is something you should strongly consider for your own Web sites as you develop them. Naturally, Python provides methods for helping you out with things like this.

To begin with, use a form like the one displayed in Figure 13.7. This would be the login page of the Web site. It prompts the user for the user name and password that he wants to use (naturally, not displaying the password as you type it for security purposes) and then allows him to select where he wants to go from that point on.

To create this system, you will need the login form defined. Since this form will always look the same (at least for now), we will use a static HTML file to display it. Let's create that here. Create a new file and enter the following code into it. Save the file as ch13_5.htm. Of course, you will be saving this file into the htdocs directory, which is where all HTML files should be going from now on.

Figure 13.7
A specialized login form.

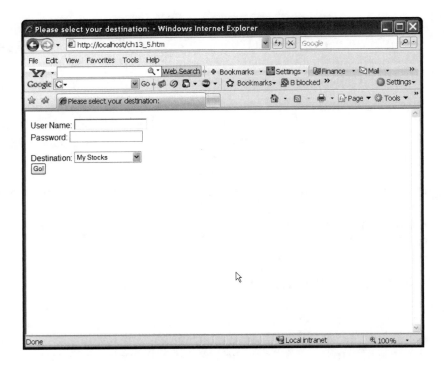

```
<html>
   <head>
      <title>Please select your destination:</title>
   </head>

   <body>
      <form name="SelectDestination" method="post" action="cgi-bin/ch13_5.py">
         User Name: <input type="text" name="name"><br>
         Password: <input type="password" name="pwd"><br><br>
         Destination: <select name=selbox single>
            <option value='1'>My Stocks</option>
            <option value='2'>Account Overview</option>
            <option value='3'>Trading</option>
         </select><br>
         <input type="submit" name="submit" value="Go!"><br>
      </form>
   </body>
</html>
```

After you have defined the form, you need to create the back end of the system. By the way, this is the normal way in which Web sites are developed in any language, not just Python. You first create the user interface, deciding what information you are going to need, and how to display it. Once you have the shell user interface in place, you then move on to implementing the back end of the system. In many cases, you will want to "dummy up" the back-end scripts so that they simply send you to the right place, adding the logic to do the hard work as you go along. In this example, we are going to follow that approach, dummying up the user login logic. In the next chapter, we'll look at how to do the work of actually storing the information for a user in a database, so that you can retrieve it and do real comparisons.

To begin with, let's just create a Python script that accepts the input from the form, so that you know what you are getting. Here's a potential start, which we will call `ch13_5.py` and store in the cgi-bin directory:

```
#!c:/Python25/python
import cgi
# See what they gave us
form = cgi.FieldStorage()

fUser = form.getvalue("name", "")
fPwd  = form.getvalue("pwd", "" )
fDest = form.getvalue("selbox", "")
# First, do the header.
print "Content-Type: text/html\n\n"
print "<HTML>"
print "UserName: "+ fUser + " <br>"
print "Password: " + fPwd + " <br>"
print "Destination: " + fDest + " <BR> "
print "<form>"
print "</html>"
```

As you can see, we aren't actually doing anything with the information yet. The first step is to check the user name and password. If he supplied us with valid information, we can move on to the next step. Once again, the idea here is to stub in the functionality and then fill it out as we learn what the true requirements are for the feature. Along the way, we will "re-factor" the code so that the pieces that we need to reuse are placed in separate functions. The new code looks like this:

```
#!c:/Python25/python
import cgi

def gen_html_header() :
    print "Content-Type: text/html\n\n"
    print "<HTML>"

def gen_html_trailer() :
    print "</HTML>"

def process_selection(sel) :
    gen_html_header()
    print "You selected: " + repr(sel)
    gen_html_trailer()

def check_credentials( user, pwd ) :
    if user == "admin" :
        if pwd == "admin" :
            return 1

    # Anything else is a failure.
    gen_html_header()
    print "Security Error: Either the user name or the password, or both, is
    invalid<br>"
    print "Click " + "<a href=http://localhost/ch13_5.htm>here</a> to return
    to the login page"
    gen_html_trailer()

    # Indicate to the caller that we failed
    return 0

# See what they gave us
form = cgi.FieldStorage()

fUser = form.getvalue("name", "")
fPwd  = form.getvalue("pwd", "" )
```

```
fDest = form.getvalue("selbox", "")

if check_credentials(fUser, fPwd ) == 1 :
    process_selection( fDest )
```

Now, if you enter a valid user name and password (currently, only "admin" is valid for both), you will see an output telling you what selection the user made from the drop-down list on the form. If, on the other hand, the user enters an invalid user name and password (anything but "admin"), he will see an error form that allows him to click on a hyperlink and return to the login page. Play with the forms for a bit, experimenting to see where everything happens and how it all works.

You might wonder, by the way, why we choose to send the user directly to a hard-linked location, rather than simply sending him "back" to the previous page. In a browser you would press "back" to go back to the input form, fill it out again, and then move on. Unfortunately, that isn't possible in this case, because we are on the server side of the equation, and don't know where the user came from.

However, once the user gives us a valid user name and password, and gives us the location of where he wants to go, it would make sense to actually send him there. There are a fair number of ways to do this, such as placing the code for the page generation in our Python script file, redirecting the user to another HTML page, and creating a new script for creating the new page. There is nothing special about adding a new function to the current script, so that wouldn't show you anything exciting. We will look at redirection in a little bit, as we explore how to send a user to a new address. That leaves only writing a new script to handle the page and using that from within our existing module. Since we really haven't explored that aspect of Python to this point in the book, it makes a lot of sense to do it that way.

Let's create a new script, in this case called ch13_5_1.py that will do the work of processing the "My Stocks" page for your Web site. To do so, just create a new file in the cgi-bin directory called ch13_5_1.py and place the following code into the new file.

```
#!c:/Python25/python
import cgi


def gen_html_header() :
    print "Content-Type: text/html\n\n"
    print "<HTML>"


def gen_html_trailer() :
```

```
    print "</HTML>"

def generate_mystocks_page() :
    gen_html_header()
    print "You have reached the My Stocks Page!"
    gen_html_trailer()
```

The code isn't complicated, nor does it do anything exciting, but it does illustrate how you would generate the new page. Note that even though we already have a `gen_html_header` and `gen_html_trailer` function declared in our existing module, this will not present a problem in the new module, because the names are scoped to the module level. So now we have our new module to handle the "My Stocks" page. The obvious question is, how do we "call" that module from the existing handler for the Web site. Remember, Python is an interpreted language. That means that it does not need to know at the time the files are created where something is—it just needs to be able to find the function you call when it is invoked. As a result, you can modify the existing `process_selection()` function in your original script to read as follows:

```
def process_selection(sel) :
    if ( sel == '1' ) :
        import ch13_5_1
        ch13_5_1.generate_mystocks_page()
```

Note that we are explicitly calling the `generate_mystocks_page()` function from the `ch13_5_1.py` file. If you make this change and then run the original form again, entering "admin" for the user name and password, and selecting the "My Stocks" option from the drop-down list, you will see that the page is properly displayed!

HTML Elements

Just to illustrate how all of the HTML elements map to their Python equivalents and how you can check to see what you are getting, let's write a very simple program that shows off the various types of HTML elements, such as radio buttons, check boxes, and so forth. Your input form is going to look like the one shown in Figure 13.8, which presents a very simple order form for pizzas.

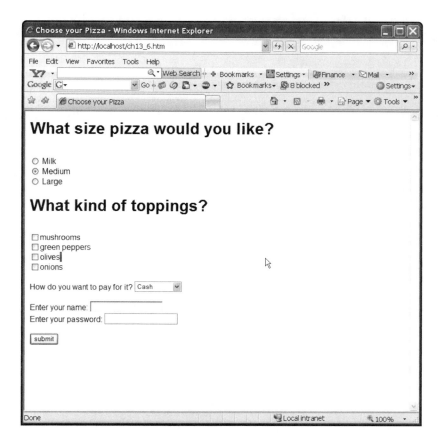

Figure 13.8
The pizza order form.

The HTML for this input form looks like this:

```
<HTML>
<TITLE>Choose your Pizza</TITLE>

<FORM ACTION="cgi-bin/ch13_6.py">

<! First, the pizza size >
<H1>What size pizza would you like?</H1><BR>

<input type="radio" name="size" value="Personal"> Personal<br>
<input type="radio" name="size" value="Medium" checked> Medium<br>
```

```
<input type="radio" name="size" value="Large"> Large<BR><BR>

<H1>What kind of toppings?</H1><BR>

<INPUT TYPE=CHECKBOX NAME="mushrooms"    >mushrooms<BR>
<INPUT TYPE=CHECKBOX NAME="greenpeppers">green peppers<BR>
<INPUT TYPE=CHECKBOX NAME="olives"       >olives<BR>
<INPUT TYPE=CHECKBOX NAME="onions"       >onions<P>

How do you want to pay for it?
<select NAME="payment">
<option>Cash</option>
<option>Check</option>
<option>Credit Card</option>
</select><BR><BR>

Enter your name: <INPUT TYPE=TEXT NAME="name"><BR>
Enter your password: <INPUT TYPE=PASSWORD NAME="password"><BR><BR>


<INPUT TYPE=SUBMIT VALUE="submit">
</FORM>
</HTML>
```

As this is not a book on HTML, we aren't going to take a lot of time to discuss the elements or how they work. Instead, let's focus on how these various element types are received by your Python script when the user enters the requested values and then presses the submit button. Here is the code for a very simple Python script that will simply print out the values you receive. We'll call this script ch13_6.py, since that is how it is referred to in the form action line in the above HTML.

```
#!c:/Python25/python
import cgi

def gen_html_header() :
    print "Content-Type: text/html\n\n"
    print "<HTML>"

def gen_html_trailer() :
```

```
    print "</HTML>"


form = cgi.FieldStorage()


gen_html_header()
for e in form :
    print "Received " + e + " = ["+form.getvalue(e)+"]<BR>"
```

This code doesn't do anything, obviously, since it is just there to print out the received values. If you enter some of the values requested in the HTML form and press the submit button, you should get the following output in a Web browser. Do not forget to place the ch13_6.py script file into your cgi-bin directory, however, or it won't work at all.

```
Received size = [Medium]
Received mushrooms = [on]
Received greenpeppers = [on]
Received olives = [on]
Received payment = [Check]
Received name = [matt]
Received password = [matt]
```

Radio buttons return the value associated with the group they belong to. Check boxes, however, will only return you a value if they are checked. If they are not, you get nothing back. Text entry fields, whether clear text or password fields, return the text you have selected, and the select (drop-down list) field returns the value assigned to the selected item. Knowing all this will help you when you are trying to figure out how to work with the input generated by an HTML form.

Cookies

At this point in time, you would have to be deaf, dumb, and blind not to know about the Internet and cookies. Cookies are simple bits of information that track information about the user so that you can make the user experience as nice as possible. Unfortunately, cookies have gotten a pretty bad reputation, due to the perception that they can somehow "inform" the Web sites of your behavior. To set the record straight, there is nothing wrong with cookies. You do not have to allow them in your client browser, but if you do, it will make your Web browsing experience much more rich and useful. As a server-side Python developer, you should be aware of the bad reputation of cookies and be prepared if the user will not allow you to store them. There are other alternatives, as we have seen, such as passing hidden variables that maintain state information. This isn't ideal, since you really don't know whether the user is the same user that used your system last, but it works.

The purpose of a cookie is to store a little bit of information that you need preserved on the client machine. This is accomplished by sending tagged information in the header space of the data that is passed back and forth between the server and the client. The details of how cookies work in HTML headers is a bit beyond this book, nor do you really need to know this in order to use them. Python provides a wonderful little module called the *Cookie module* (what else?) to provide the interface to the functionality you need to make cookies work in your application.

The typical example of a cookie is to show how many times a given user has visited a Web site. That particular example is stale and boring, and really doesn't show off the kind of functionality you are likely to need. So, instead, let's consider a different possibility, which is checking the membership status of a given user on a given machine. To accomplish this, you are going to have to first check to see if a given cookie exists on a user's machine, and then set it if it does not. You also want to make sure that the cookie expires, so that the membership is not permanent.

1. Create a new file using IDLE or your favorite text editor. Call this file ch13_7.py.

2. Place the following code into the ch13_7.py file:

```
#!c:/Python25/python
import os
import Cookie

def gen_html_header() :
    member = Cookie.SimpleCookie()
    member["membership"] = 1
    member["membership"]["expires"] = 30
    print member
    print "Content-Type: text/html\n\n"
    print "<HTML>"

def gen_html_trailer() :
    print "</HTML>"

def check_membership():
    if 'HTTP_COOKIE' in os.environ:
        cookies = os.environ['HTTP_COOKIE']
        cookies = cookies.split('; ')
        for cookie in cookies:
            cookie = cookie.split('=')
            name = cookie[0]
```

```
        value = cookie[1]
        if name == "membership" :
            return int(value)
    return 0

val = check_membership()
gen_html_header()
if val == 0 :
    print "You are not a member!"
else :
    print "You are a member!"
gen_html_trailer()
```

3. Save the file to the cgi-bin directory of your Apache install root.

4. In a Web browser, enter the URL of `http://localhost/cgi-bin/ch13_7.py` in your navigation area and press Return or Enter.

Notice that the first time you run the program, you are not a member. This is because the cookie does not yet exist. If you hit refresh within your browser, it will then tell you that you are a member. This indicates that the cookie has been set properly. This cookie is set for a "lifetime" of 30 seconds, mostly so that you can see it reset itself. In the real world, you would use a much longer time period. The expiration date is set by setting the "expires" attribute of the cookie value you want to set, and it is set in seconds from now. One last note about cookies: they are tied to the site that generates them. So you are unable to read cookies from another site, and if you were to change the URL of your own site, all of the existing cookies would become invalid. Otherwise, they really are about that simple to use. Import the Cookie module, create a SimpleCookie object, and then set the cookie strings and attributes that you want to set. All that and not even one bad pun about cooking up a new idea.

The process of creating a cookie is quite simple. You have the following code:

```
member = Cookie.SimpleCookie()
member["membership"] = 1
member["membership"]["expires"] = 30
```

The first line will create the actual cookie object. The second sets the value of the membership attribute within the cookie to 1. Finally, we set the expiration date (30 seconds from now) for the cookie.

Uploading Files

If you happen to be writing a Web server application that does things like customer support, source code control, or file sharing, you have likely run into the issue of allowing the user to upload a file to store on the server. Downloading a file is a simple process—just hand the link to the browser and off it goes. How do you manage to get a file from the user machine to the server, however? The answer, surprisingly, is quite easily. The majority of the work is done by the HTML on the client side. The processing of the file is handled by the browser and server, and all you need to do is acquire the file data and write it back to the place you want it stored on the server.

Here's how you upload a file from the client to the server. The first thing you need is the client side code that does the actual upload. To see how this works, create a simple HTML file and place the following code into it:

```
<HTML>


<FORM ACTION="cgi-bin/ch13_8.py" METHOD="POST" enctype="multipart/form-data">
    <input type="hidden" name="user" value="lola">
    <input type="hidden" name="action" value="upload">
    <BR><I>FILE:</I> <INPUT TYPE="FILE" NAME=upfile>
<br>
<input type="submit" value="Press"> to upload the file!
</form>


</HTML>
```

The work is all done by the input statement in the HTML file, which allows the user to select (or browse to) a file on the client side. When the submit button is pressed, the data will be appended to the form in multi-part format. This part is particularly important, as you will notice that in the form definition, you specify that the encoding type be multi- part form data. If you omit this part of the file, your file will not be transmitted properly and will not arrive at the destination in a usable format. Once you have everything set up on the client side, the only remaining problem is to process it on the server side.

1. Create a new file using IDLE or your favorite text editor. Call this file ch13_8.py.

2. Place the following code into the ch13_8.py file:

```
#!c:/Python25/python

import cgi
```

```
import sys

def gen_html_header() :
    print "Content-Type: text/html\n\n"
    print "<HTML>"

def gen_html_trailer() :
    print "</HTML>"

gen_html_header()
form = cgi.FieldStorage()
try :
    file_contents = form["upfile"].value
    print file_contents
except :
    print sys.exc_info()

gen_html_trailer()
```

3. Save the file to the cgi-bin directory of your Apache install root.

Note that in this example, we are simply printing out the contents of the file. If you wanted the file actually saved on your server, you would simply open a file using the file handling functions we discussed in Chapter 6, and write the contents to that file.

Redirection

One last topic with regards to working with Web pages and servers is the concept of "redirection." The idea of redirection is fairly simple. Suppose that you have a script on your server that was intended for, say, administrators only. If the user were not an administrator, you might want to send him to some other script. Alternatively, suppose that you were in the middle of updating a big chunk of your Web site and did not want people entering a given area. You might want to send them to another section of the system so that they did not get annoyed at functionality that didn't work. Finally, if you were working for a company that was bought by another company, you might want to redirect all of your traffic to a new Web site that handled both companies. In any of these cases, the idea is to send the user's browser directly to a new page without forcing him to see a half-implemented page, or non-working functionality.

Redirection in HTML is quite simple to implement. You just have to set a return value and set the redirection location. Here's how you would implement a redirection function in Python.

1. Create a new file using IDLE or your favorite text editor. Call this file `ch13_9.py`.
2. Place the following code into the `ch13_9.py` file:

```
#!c:/Python25/python

import cgi

def print_redirect(url):
        print 'Status: 302 Moved Temporarily'
        print 'Location:', url
        print 'Pragma: no-cache'
        print 'Content-Type: text/html'
        print


        print '<!DOCTYPE HTML PUBLIC "-//W3C//DTD HTML//EN">'
        print '<title>Redirect (302)</title>'
        print '<h1>302 Moved Temporarily</h1>'
        print '<p>The answer to your request is located at'
        hurl = cgi.escape(url, 1)
        print '<a href="%s">%s</a>.' % (hurl, hurl)


    print_redirect("http://www.yahoo.com")
```

3. Place the `ch13_9.py` file in the cgi-bin directory of your Apache install tree.

If you run the script, by entering `http://localhost/cgi-bin/ch13_9.py` in your Web browser, you will see the script start to run and then the Yahoo! Home page will come up. If you were using a program to "scrape" the Web page, rather than just browsing it via your Web browser application, you would see an error displayed briefly, indicating that the site had moved temporarily and then you would see the Web page for `www.yahoo.com` come up.

Note the use of the `cgi.escape()` method. This method takes ordinary characters in the URL that are invalid for the World Wide Web standards and "escapes" them by turning them into acceptable strings (such as hex values).

Redirection can be a very useful bit of functionality that you should keep in your Python toolbox for future uses.

Error Handling

Our final topic for Web browsing and the Internet is the problem of error handling in Python Web scripts. If you have been playing at all with the scripts we have been working on in this chapter, the odds are good that you have created a syntax error or two. There are really two ways to handle errors in creating scripts in Python. The first is to always run the script in the IDLE environment and see whether or not it generates any errors. Of course, because the IDLE environment does not have the same environment variables as a Web browser, this may not always work. However, checking a script this way for syntax errors is not a bad idea. When you run a Python script in a Web browser without checking it for errors, and run across a syntax error or other such problem, the Web browser will display something terribly useful like "Internal error," which tells you nothing about what went wrong. So how do you find out what really happened?

When you write a new script, consider adding these lines:

```
import cgitb
cgitb.enable()
```

Place them at the top of your script file. These lines will allow your script to display errors in the Web browser, rather than simply displaying an error message like "Internet Error" to the end user. For example, consider the following example:

1. Create a new file using IDLE or your favorite text editor. Call this file ch13_10.py.

2. Place the following code into the ch13_10.py file:

```
#!c:/Python25/python

import cgi

x = 1/0


print "More stuff here"
```

3. Put the ch13_10.py file in the cgi-bin directory of your Apache root directory.

If you now run the script via your Web browser, you will see an error reported, indicating that there was a problem running the page. Not very useful, so let's fix that. Add the following lines to the script, below the import cgi statement and above the problem line.

```
import cgitb
cgitb.enable()
```

This activates an exception handler that will show the error in your Web browser, if any error occurs. If you'd rather not show the details of the error in your script, you can instead write the problem descriptions to a file instead, with a line like this:

```
import cgitb
cgitb.enable(display=0, logdir="/tmp")
```

The arguments to the enable method are a value indicating whether or not you want the error message displayed, and a second argument indicating where you want the logs to be stored in the case of errors.

In Conclusion

That concludes our work with the Internet functionality of Python. We'll be using Web scripts more from this point on, as we develop applications using Python scripting and databases and such. However, you now have all of the tools you need to write a complete Web site using HTML and Python if you so desire. As you will see in coming chapters, the remainder of building a Web site tends to be either back-end work or graphical user interface design.

In the next chapter, we will begin to explore the world of databases and Python, using the MySQL relational database system. After that, we'll come back to the Internet and combine the worlds of HTML, Python, and MySQL to create a complete WAMP (or LAMP for your Linux folk) system.

14 } Working with Databases

Without a doubt, the biggest boon to the corporate world has been the database. Never before has so much information been available so easily to the average corporate user. On the flip side, never before has so much data been stolen, destroyed, or mangled either, but you have to take the bad with the good. The database is responsible for the massive growth of the computer industry, and particularly the Internet. Without databases, the data on most Web sites would be static, and things like shopping carts and "just-in-time" checking of quantities available of products would be impossible. Imagine, for example, ordering a book on some Internet Web site, only to be told a day or two later that they didn't have any in stock and that your order would be backfilled in "a period of time." Databases provide instant access to information, and allow users to find things in a way that they never could before.

In this chapter, we will explore the use of databases with Python. We will be using the MySQL database, which is freely available on the Internet for download. If you are not using the database for commercial purposes, there is no cost to using MySQL, which makes it particularly appealing for learning database technologies. We'll see how to create and open databases, how to read and write data for databases, and how to find information and display it for the user to view.

What Is a Database?

Put simply, a database is an organized collection of information. There are more technical definitions, but they really don't say much more than this. A text file is a database, as is a pile of magazines. There is nothing that says that a database must have a specific format, or be organized in particular ways, although we have come to understand that when a person says "database," what he really mean is a relational database. A relational database is an organized collection of information that is all related in some way. There are a lot of terms that database experts throw about, some of which we do not care about and some that you really do need to understand.

Let's look at some of the basic database terms, with explanations of what they mean. Note that these aren't clinical definitions; they are just intended to explain to you, the Python developer, what to expect when you hear the term in conversation or literature.

Simple Database Terminology

When you talk about databases, especially relational databases, you need to understand some of the verbiage that people are likely to throw your way. It really isn't necessary for a user of a relational database to be a database administrator, designer, or even programmer. What is necessary is that you understand the functionality provided with the database system. To do your job, you will often have to deal with people who do speak in "databasese," and the terminology will help you communicate with them.

Let's start with a ***column***. In database terms, a column is a single variable within a database object. For example, if you were storing an address as an object in the database, then one of the columns would be the street number. There is one column value for each variable stored for an object, although there will be as many of a given column as there are objects in the database

The next term is ***row***. A row is a single object in the database. A row is made up of columns, which represent the variables in the object. We could map a simple Python class instance to a row in a database by placing each of the attributes into a column. Multiple rows would represent multiple individual objects.

A ***table*** is a collection of rows and columns. You can think of a table as a spreadsheet if it makes it easier to visualize. Tables maintain all of the information about a single subject in a relational database. Unlike indexed sequential access method (ISAM) files, relational tables can be linked together through either indices or "keys" that point from one table to another.

A ***key*** is an index into a table. You can create a key from a single column in the table or multiple columns concatenated together. Keys are used for fast access to information within the table.

Referential Integrity refers to the ability of a relational database to maintain the integrity in relationships between bits of data. For example, if one table maintains a list of customer records and another table maintains a list of customer orders, there is a relationship between the two tables. If a customer order is deleted, that's fine, there is no problem created. However, if a customer record is deleted, it only makes sense that all of the customer order records need to be deleted as well. Referential integrity means that when an operation is complete, the integrity of all of the dependencies in the database is maintained. Thus, since the customer orders are dependent on the customer record, they have to be deleted when the original customer record is deleted.

An ***index*** is a fast way of getting back data in a database. Essentially, an index allows you to keep a specific ordering to a table, using a combination of the columns. Indices are always sorted in ascending or descending order, according to the way in which you will be accessing the data from your applications. For example, you might create an index on the Social Security Number in your customer record file, allowing you to quickly and easily report on things in SSN order.

What Is MySQL?

The relational database we will be using in this chapter (and for the remainder of the book) is the MySQL database. This database is open source, meaning that you can download and use it at no charge, which is one of the primary reasons for its popularity on the Internet. However, in addition to being free, MySQL is also important because it is fast, reliable, and well documented. Unlike some of the commercial database systems, MySQL has a ton of support and information available at no charge on various Internet Web sites, as well as many utilities that you can use for free. We'll explore the downloading and installing of the system, as well as the utilities that you might want to acquire at the same time.

Note that there are two versions of MySQL available. The first is an open source, free, edition that has no support available from the publishers. There is a second, commercial, version of the database system that you may want to buy if you are working on a commercial e-commerce site. There are no restrictions on the open source system, which is often referred to as the "community server" on the MySQL site. If you are comfortable with installing, administering, and tuning an e-commerce server, then the MySQL community edition is for you. If, on the other hand, you feel more comfortable letting someone else do all the hard work, you should probably invest some money and buy the enterprise edition.

Downloading and Installing

The first thing you will need to do to use the MySQL system in Python is to download it and install it. As of the writing of this book, the current version of MySQL is 5.0. You can obtain the binaries and installers for the system from `www.mysql.com`; just click the Downloads button and navigate to the Community Server edition. The remainder of the install is fairly automatic. Simply select all of the default values. You will be asked for a root password. Enter one and remember to write it down somewhere. Eventually, you will need to actually use the root password, and there is nothing quite so annoying as to not be able to remember what it was you used to set up the system and be forced to reinstall everything.

In addition to the actual core database system, you will need one other download. You will need the MySQL Python library. This set of modules, which is available on the popular Source Forge Web site (`www.sourceforge.net`) under the `mysql-python` project name, provides a complete set of modules for interfacing to the MySQL database from Python. You can write your own interface to the database system if you are feeling particularly masochistic. The interface is all socket-based, and the command set is a standard, but it isn't a good idea.

The Python module for MySQL is well defined, well documented, and handles errors you would never consider. You can find the complete download on the sourceforge site (`www.sourceforge.net`) within the `mysql-python` project. Be sure to download the right version for the version of Python you are using and the version of MySQL that you are using (the version of the Python interpreter we are using is 2.5 and the MySQL version is 5.0). The installer file is called `MySQL-python-1.2.2.win32-py2.5.exe`. If you install a version intended for a different version of the Python system, the installer will not find the registry keys (for Windows) or directory information it needs to install the modules properly.

Finally, back at the MySQL Web site, there is one more optional installation that you may want to seriously consider downloading. This is the GUI Tools download, which contains a bunch of useful utilities for working with the MySQL database. If you don't download this set of utilities, you will need to work directly with the command-line client for MySQL, which can be a bit complicated and terse. We will be using the GUI tools in this chapter, so it is essential that you download them as well to follow along. The tools are free, as well as the database, so there is no real reason not to use them.

Once you have the database and all of the utilities installed, make sure that the database is ready to run. You can easily check to see if the database interface modules are installed by simply trying to import the `MySQLDb` module in the IDLE interpreter:

```
IDLE 1.2
>>> import MySQLdb
>>>
```

If you get the above display in the interpreter, everything has been properly installed. If, on the other hand, you get an error saying that the `MySQLdb` module was not found, it is either not installed, or was not installed in the proper location. Go back and check to see where you told the thing to place its files and then try it again. Once you have everything working, you will need to create a new database in MySQL and define at least one table in that database. We'll look at doing that through the GUI tools now.

Creating a New Database

In order to create a new database, we will be using the "MySQL Administrator" GUI application. This application will be found in your MySQL group on the Start button of your Windows desktop. Launching the program will result in the display of the login screen, as shown in Figure 14.1. Your server host should be your local machine (`localhost`). You can leave all of the other bits of information alone, except for filling out the root password that you created during the install. You did remember to write down the root password, didn't you? Of course, the user name will be "root."

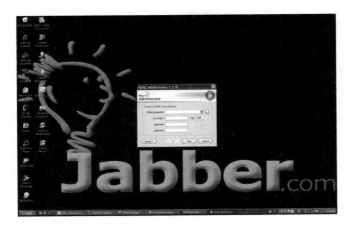

Figure 14.1
The MySQL administrator
login screen.

As soon as you log in properly to the administrator system, you will see the main screen of the administrator. This pane shows you the various possible options in the left-hand pane of the window, along with status information in the right-hand pane. The important things to notice are whether or not the server is running (it really has to be, or you wouldn't have been able to log in to the administrator) and some information about the server version and machine information.

The main screen is shown in Figure 14.2. Make sure that your display looks something like this, and then you can continue to your next task, ensuring that a database is created and that a table is available to the end user and your applications.

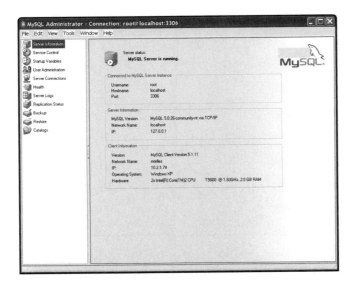

Figure 14.2
The MySQL administrator
main screen.

Clicking on the "catalogs" button in the top half of the left-hand side of the administrator display will show all of the available databases in the bottom half of that side. To add a new database, right-click in the area that displays the available databases and select "Create new schema." If you don't understand what a *schema* is, don't worry about it at this point—you can think of it as a new database.

We are going to call our new database "python-test," so that we can easily identify it within our applications. The addition of the "test" part of the name also allows you to find it easily when you want to deploy your database in the real world and remove any databases that do not belong. From a security standpoint, it is very important not to leave databases that are not part of the "real" system around, as they may lack security or have holes that allow dedicated hackers into the system. Clean up your database system, and it will run better too, which is something to consider later in the application lifespan.

Once you have created the new schema and selected the python-test database in the administrator, you should see the display shown in Figure 14.3 (or a reasonable facsimile thereof). We will be using this screen to create a new table for use in our application for testing Python with MySQL.

Figure 14.3
The MySQL administrator screen for new database.

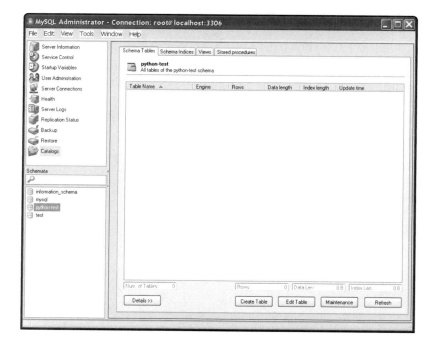

You are going to be adding a new table to your database, so the obvious choice is to click the "Create Table" button on the administrator screen. After you have clicked this button, you get what has to be the most confusing GUI screen ever created for a database manager application. The screen shown in Figure 14.4 shows the MySQL Administrator Table Editor dialog. The top half of the dialog seems straightforward enough; you enter the name of your new table. In our case, we are going to create a database for cataloguing books, so we are going to create a table called *Books*. This information goes into the main screen under the "Table Name" field. However, it does not seem obvious how we are going to add our variable definitions (columns) to the database. Ah, the joys of working with GUI applications, right?

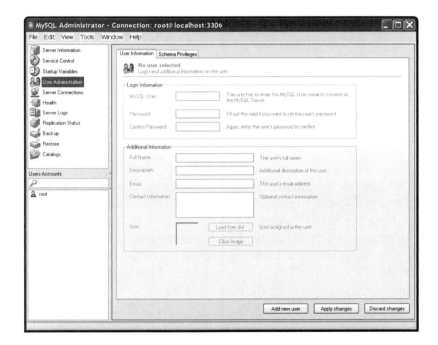

Figure 14.4
The MySQL administrator screen for user management.

Fortunately, all is not lost. A little experimentation (or simply reading ahead a bit in this book) will show that you can click in the Columns and Indices section of the screen. When you double-click in the Column Name area of the grid below the tab in that section, you will notice that it becomes an editable entry field. Enter the following information into the grid:

```
Column Name: BookID
Datatype: INTEGER
Not Null: Checked
Auto-increment: Checked
Flags: Unsigned checked
Comment: Put whatever you want here, I entered "The ID of the book
we are going to be creating."
```

You move between the fields by either pressing the Tab key or clicking in each field as you want to enter data into it. You can modify the field by either double-clicking it and changing the value, or by selecting the "Column Details" tab below and changing the specific values you want to change. Note that changes are applied to the schema (at least in memory) as soon as you leave a field, but that the actual database is unchanged until you click the Apply button on the bottom of this dialog box.

Fill in the remainder of the fields with the rest of the information you want to store for your books. The list is shown below.

Table 14-1 Book Table Columns

Column Name	Type	Flags	Description
BookName	VARCHAR(45)	None	The title of the book
BookAuthor	VARCHAR(80)	None	The author of the book
PublicationDate	INTEGER	None.	The publication year of the book.

After you have finished entering the data (remember, you will need to double-click on a blank row to add a new column), click the Apply Changes button at the bottom of the dialog box. A warning will appear asking if you really want to execute the given SQL statement shown on the database. This is simply converting the entries you gave it into a Structured Query Language (SQL) statement. SQL is the "language" that databases speak in order to add, delete, or modify data and contents. Say yes to the dialog box and close the create table dialog by clicking the Close button at the bottom right of the dialog. Congratulations! You have now created a new database within the system and created a new table for that database.

Creating a New User

The next optional step is to create a new user for the database. You do not actually have to create a user, because you already have one called *root*. It is a bad idea, however, to use the root user when working with the database from your Python script. For one thing, the root user has access to everything in the database and can cause all sorts of harm if you were to mess up a statement in your script. For another, and more important reason, you will likely be embedding the user name and password of your user in the script information. Even though that information never makes it to the Web page user, it can be found if there are holes in your Web server security. For this reason, and many more, it makes sense to create a new user.

Another really good reason to create a new user for every database that you create in your MySQL system is for tracking purposes. The MySQL system has a pretty good set of tools available for seeing what individual users do on the system. If you have a single user for all of the databases and tables in the system, it is difficult to see what a given user did that might have caused a problem. In general, you should create a new user for each system that you implement in the database.

The user modification system is found on the User Administration selection of the main window of the administrator application. Clicking on that tab will show you the screen to add a new user, as shown in Figure 14.4.

Obviously, you click the Add New User button to create a new user. When you do, you will be presented with a screen asking for a bunch of information about your new user. All you really care about here is the user name and the password. In this case, I have created a new user called "python-test" with a password of "python" within the environment. The purpose of using the "test" moniker is simply to indicate to us that this is not an account we want hanging around in the database should it ever be moved into a production environment. Having test accounts around is a security risk, because they tend to have very simple passwords (as shown in this example, certainly) and thus can be cracked by external users and used to gain access to the system. This is a bad idea, so you need to be able to find them and delete them before you put the system "live." When you are finished, click the Apply Changes and Add New User buttons to finish the process.

Now that you have the database defined, and a user defined for that database, it is time to get into the actual process of coding. The first thing is to connect to the database and log in using Python. Let's do that now.

Opening an Existing Database

In order to work with a database, you need to connect to it first. Let's write a very simple program that will do this:

1. Create a new file using the IDLE editor or your favorite text editor. Call the file ch14_1.py.

2. Enter the following code into your new file:

```
# Do the proper import
import MySQLdb
# Now, connect to the database
db = MySQLdb.connect(host="localhost", user="python-test",
passwd="python", db="python-test")
```

Note that although some lines may appear to be on multiple lines, they are really a single line in the editor. They may be too long to place on a single line in the final text. If you want, you can continue the line using the line continuation character ('\') at the end of the line instead.

3. Run the program by selecting Run | Run Module from the menu of the Editor window or by pressing F5 in that window.

You would think that, at this point, you would see the code run and that you would be connected to the database. Unfortunately, that doesn't happen. Instead, you get the following display in the IDLE window.

```
Traceback (most recent call last):
  File "E:/Python/ch14_1.py", line 4, in <module>
    db = MySQLdb.connect(host="localhost", user="python-test",
passwd="python", db="python-test")
  File "C:\Python25\lib\site-packages\MySQLdb\__init__.py", line 74, in
Connect
    return Connection(*args, **kwargs)
  File "C:\Python25\lib\site-packages\MySQLdb\connections.py", line 170,
in __init__
    super(Connection, self).__init__(*args, **kwargs2)
OperationalError: (1044, "Access denied for user 'python-test'@'%' to
database 'python-test'")
```

You might wonder why we got such an error. After all, we created the proper database, we added the user, and we verified that the password was correct. Why, then, did we *not* get a proper connection? The answer lies in the access privileges that apply to the database and the tables within that database. If you go back to the administrator application and select the user within the user administration screen, you will notice that there is another tab to the display called "Schema Privileges." By default, the new user was created with no privileges in any of the database. We need to change this in order to allow them to access our database. For now, we will simply give them all of the privileges available for the database we have created. Select the "python-test" database and add all of the privileges using the multiple selection and arrow buttons available on the screen. You should see a display similar to the one shown in Figure 14.5.

After you have made this change, go back to the IDLE interpreter and run the script again. You should now see that it runs properly, indicating that you connected to the database with no errors. This is a common mistake when creating new users, and it is important to remember to set privileges each time you add a new user to the system. Once you have made the mistake, you are unlikely to repeat it, so it was a worthwhile exercise to see the error occur.

Note that we are using the connect() method to actually create a session with the database. The connect() method takes several parameters, which are probably obvious from context, but are worth discussing. The host parameter, of course, is the name or IP address of the machine that is running MySQL. The user and password parameters specify the user we are going to

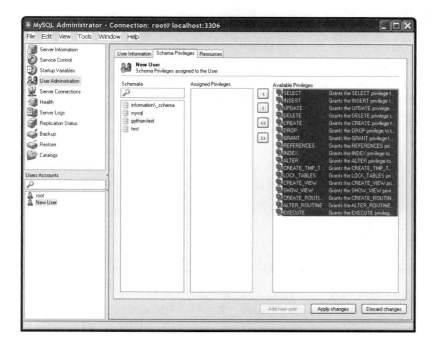

be using for security purposes to connect to the database. For our purposes, the account is the test account we created previously. Finally, the db parameter is the name of the database you want to use, since there can be several installed for a given MySQL server.

Writing to a Database

When you have a database defined, and a table added to it with some columns to fill, and a user to connect to that database, it only makes sense that you would want to put some data into the database so that it can be used later on. Let's look at the steps that are involved in writing data to a table of a database. We'll start out by simply presenting the code and working through the process of explaining how it works.

1. Create a new file using either the IDLE editor or your favorite text editor.

2. Place the following code in the new file:

```
# Do the proper import
import MySQLdb
# Now, connect to the database
db = MySQLdb.connect(host="localhost", user="python-test", passwd="python",
db="python-test")
# get user input for our book
```

```
try:
    title = raw_input("Please enter a book title: ")
    if title == "" :
        exit
    author = raw_input("Please enter the author's name: ")
    pubdate = int( raw_input("Enter the publication year: ") )
except:
    print "Invalid value"
    exit


# Echo back
print "Title: [" + title + "]"
print "Author: ["+ author + "]"
print "Publication Date: " + str(pubdate)


# create a cursor
cursor = db.cursor()
# execute SQL statement
stmt = "INSERT INTO Books (BookName, BookAuthor, PublicationDate) VALUES ('"
stmt = stmt + title
stmt = stmt + "', '"
stmt = stmt + author
stmt = stmt + "', "
stmt = stmt + str(pubdate)
stmt = stmt + ")"
cursor.execute(stmt)
print "Record added!"


cursor.close ()
db.commit ()
```

3. Save the file and call it "ch14_2.py". Run the script in the IDLE interpreter by either selecting Run | Run Module from the Editor window or by pressing F5.

4. Enter some data for the book information when prompted. You should see a display something like the following:

```
Please enter a book title: A Tale of Two Cities
Please enter the author's name: Charles Dickens
```

```
Enter the publication year: 1856
Title: [A Tale of Two Cities]
Author: [Charles Dickens]
Publication Date: 1856
Record added!
```

Okay, so you've seen the code run. How do you verify that the data was added? There are a variety of ways to do this, but for now, we will use the Command Line interface to the MySQL system. In your start group, under MySQL and mySQL Server 5.0 menus, you will see an entry for MySQL Command Client. It will be found under the MySQL Server menu. Run the Command Client command and enter your password for the root of the server.

Enter the following commands, and you should see the results displayed as a simple table in the command window:

```
mysql> use python-test;
Database changed
mysql> select * from books;
+--------+----------------------+----------------+-----------------+
| BookID | BookName             | BookAuthor     | PublicationDate |
+--------+----------------------+----------------+-----------------+
|      7 | A Tale of Two Cities | Dickens        |            1865 |
+--------+----------------------+----------------+-----------------+
2 rows in set (0.06 sec)
```

The "use database" command simply instructs the MySQL system to switch to the database you name. You can only work on a single database at a time, although you can work on multiple tables within the command window.

The second command, "select * from books," is a command to the SQL interpreter within MySQL to retrieve all of the records stored in the "books" table and to display all of the columns in the table on the console window. There are hundreds of variants of the select command, and you can read about them in any good SQL book. The purpose of this book is to teach Python, not SQL, so we will mostly assume that if you need more information about the syntax of a specific command, you will refer to a manual on the subject.

Hopefully, you can see that the record was properly added to the database. Now, the question is: How did it get there? Let's take a look at the individual components of your script and see what happened.

The first segment of the code simply imports the right modules and sets up your connection to the database:

```
# Do the proper import
import MySQLdb
# Now, connect to the database
db = MySQLdb.connect(host="localhost", user="python-test", passwd="python",
db="python-test")
```

As you can see, this is really nothing new—we've done this before. The next segment simply inputs the data from the user using the `raw_input` function to retrieve some strings to fill in the data fields you are going to store in the database. Following that section, however, is the real "meat" of the application:

```
# create a cursor
cursor = db.cursor()
# execute SQL statement
stmt = "INSERT INTO Books (BookName, BookAuthor, PublicationDate) VALUES ('"
stmt = stmt + title
stmt = stmt + "', '"
stmt = stmt + author
stmt = stmt + "', "
stmt = stmt + str(pubdate)
stmt = stmt + ")"
cursor.execute(stmt)
print "Record added!"


cursor.close ()
db.commit ()
```

A "cursor" is a pointer into the database. You use cursors to create "views" that you can work with in the database. The `cursor()` method returns us a reference to the database cursor for our execution. The `stmt` variable is a simple string that gets built into a valid SQL statement to insert the values into the database system. Once you have a valid SQL statement, you use the `execute()` method of the cursor object to run the statement within the database. Note that SQL statements will always be text strings, so you have to do conversions from numerics into strings and so forth.

Next, you invoke the `close` method on the cursor. This will tell the database that you are done with the object and free up the memory. The final step is to commit the changes with the `commit()` method of the database connection object. The `commit` is necessary because relational databases work in transactions. When you open a connection to a database, you begin a transaction. When you are finished with whatever work you are doing, you commit the transaction. If you fail to commit the transaction, the database will automatically "roll back" the transaction, which will result in no data being written to the disk. If you find that nothing is being saved after what seems to be a successful execution, check to be sure that you are calling `commit`.

One last note before we move on. If you remember from our database table definition, the book table actually has one more column than we listed in the insert function in our program. The reason is because that column was defined as an "auto-incrementing" field. This means that the database will keep track of the values in the field and will simply add one for the next value that is added. You might notice in the display that the value is not 1 for the book ID value. This is simply because I had played with the code before running it a final time, and the database remembered the current incremental value. The reason for using an auto-increment field is to create a value that is guaranteed to be unique so that it can be treated as a key into other tables.

Reading from a Database

Writing data to a database is easy enough, but the actual excitement for the user is seeing what is in that database. To find out what is in the database, you need to read the data from the database and then present it to the user. The reading function in SQL is called the `select` statement. The general form of the `select` statement is:

```
SELECT [column-names-or-asterisk] FROM [table-names] …
```

The reason for the ellipsis following the statement is that there are other, optional parts of the `select` statement. We will look at some of those later. For now, all you need to worry about is the list of columns and the table name(s) that you want to retrieve data from in the database. For our purposes, we want all of the values in the table, so the column name value we select is the asterisk ('*') value. To the SQL interpreter, the asterisk is interpreted as meaning "give me all of the columns defined for the tables." Since you have only one table in the database at this point, your "table list" argument is just the name of a single table, which is the books table.

Let's create a very simple script that will retrieve all of the values in the books table and print them out for the end user.

1. Create a new file using either the IDLE editor or your favorite text editor.

2. Place the following code in the new file:

```python
# Do the proper import
import MySQLdb
# Now, connect to the database
db = MySQLdb.connect(host="localhost", user="python-test", passwd="python",
db="python-test")
```

```
# create a cursor
cursor = db.cursor()
# execute SQL statement
stmt = "SELECT * from books"
cursor.execute(stmt)

# Now, get back the data values.
rows = cursor.fetchall ()
for row in rows:
    print "Row: "
    for col in row :
        print "Column: %s" % (col)
    print "End of Row"
print "Number of rows returned: %d" % cursor.rowcount

# Close the cursor
cursor.close()

# And then close the database connection
db.close()
```

3. Save the file and call it `ch14_3.py`. Run the script in the IDLE interpreter by either selecting Run | Run Module from the Editor window or pressing F5. You should see a display similar to the one shown here.

```
Row:
Column: 7
Column: A Tale of Two Cities
Column: Dickens
Column: 1865
End of Row
Number of rows returned: 1
```

The SQL statement is executed, followed by a loop to print out the data values. The `fetchall()` method simply returns all of the rows that were affected by the statement, in this case all of the rows in the table. There is also a `fetchone()` method, which will return a single row at a time, returning None when there are no more rows. So, we could have written the loop as:

```
rows = cursor.fetchone ()
while row is not None :
```

```
# Do the printing...
# Get the next row
row = cursor.fetchone()
```

This syntax is a little easier to read, and slightly more efficient with respect to memory, but it is also a little slower. Your implementation should depend on whether or not you have the ability to load all of the rows into memory. Note that some implementations will only return you the rows that you need, caching them as necessary. Check the documentation for your version to see which approach makes more sense.

As you can see, retrieving data from the database is not a complicated matter. You can elect to retrieve all of the columns, or just some of them. You can retrieve all of the rows, or just a few at a time. Finally, there is an "order" option available. You can sort based on the name of a column. For example, you could rewrite your SQL statement as:

```
stmt = "SELECT * from books ORDER BY BookName"
```

This statement will sort the returned values by the title of the book. You can sort on any column in the table, whether or not you print out that column. So, if you wanted to sort the returned table based on the book identifier, but didn't want to print out the numeric value, you could do that as well.

Before leaving the subject of reporting on database values, let's look at one final example. In this case, you want to be able to retrieve the values of the column names, as well as the column values, and display them for the user. You can see where this would be useful for spreadsheets and such, in cases where you want to be able to display data without knowing the order or name of the columns within the returned record set. Fortunately, for this purpose, MySQL provides a different form of the cursor object, called the `DictCursor`. This cursor type returns the name and values in a dictionary format.

1. Create a new file using either the IDLE editor or your favorite text editor.

2. Place the following code in the new file:

```
# Do the proper import
import MySQLdb
# Now, connect to the database
db = MySQLdb.connect(host="localhost", user="python-test", passwd="python",
db="python-test")
# create a cursor
cursor = db.cursor(cursorclass=MySQLdb.cursors.DictCursor)
# execute SQL statement
stmt = "SELECT * from books ORDER BY BookName"
```

```
cursor.execute(stmt)

# Now, get back the data values.
rows = cursor.fetchall()
for row in rows:
    for col in row :
        print "Column ["+col+"] = " + str(row[col])
    print ""

print "Number of rows returned: %d" % cursor.rowcount

# Close the cursor
cursor.close()

# And then close the database connection
db.close()
```

3. Save the file and call it ch14_3b.py. Run the script in the IDLE interpreter by either selecting Run | Run Module from the Editor window or by pressing F5. You should see a display similar to the one shown here:

```
Column [BookAuthor] = Dickens
Column [BookName] = A Tale of Two Cities
Column [PublicationDate] = 1865
Column [BookID] = 7

Column [BookAuthor] = Charles Dickens
Column [BookName] = A Tale of Two Cities
Column [PublicationDate] = 1856
Column [BookID] = 8

Number of rows returned: 2
```

Updating a Database

Data is rarely static. In the real world, things change, whether they are publication dates for new releases, or quantities for items for sale. Obviously, if you are using a database system to store information about your business, you need the ability to update the information when it changes. The SQL language was designed for such needs. The update statement is used to modify values in a database, allowing you to change data in a single record in the database or across all of the records at once.

In order to use the update functionality of the MySQL database, you will need to decide two things. First, you need to know exactly what records you want to change. Second, you need to know what values within the records you want to change. In general, you will not want to change values that are considered "unique" in a given record, since that could lead to conflicts with other records. MySQL enforces rules that you apply to a database, so when you tell it that a given value must be unique, it will not allow you to create two records with the same value in a unique column. This applies whether you are creating brand new records with the same column value, or whether you are changing an existing record's column value to be the same as another record within the database.

In order to create an application that changes data, you will need to prompt the user for which value he wants to change, and what he will be changing the existing value into. You can use the code you just wrote to get back the names of the fields that are available and ask the user which of them he wants to change, and from what value he wants to change them into. Then you can use the update function to modify the database. Now the basic syntax of the update function in SQL is as follows:

```
UPDATE <table-name> SET <column-name> = <value> [ WHERE <clause> ]
```

This looks confusing, but it really isn't. The table name argument is simply the table you are working with, which in this case is "books." The column name to set is the value you want to change, and the optional where clause specifies which records should be changed. Let's take a look at some code, and you will see just how the thing is supposed to be done.

1. Create a new file by using either the IDLE editor or your favorite text editor.

2. Place the following code in the new file:

```
import MySQLdb
import MySQLdb.cursors

def get_column_name( data, prompt, names ) :
    value=-1
    while value == -1:
        idx = 1
        for col in data :
            print str(idx) + ": " + col
            names.append( col )
```

```
            idx = idx + 1

        value = int( raw_input(prompt) )
        if value < 1 or value >= idx :
            value = -1
    return value


# Connect to the database and get back a cursor
conn = MySQLdb.Connect(
    host='localhost', user='python-test',
    passwd='python', db='python-test')
cursor = conn.cursor(cursorclass=MySQLdb.cursors.DictCursor)

# Get the column names and ask the user which one they want
# to use for changes.
cursor.execute("SELECT * FROM books")
data = cursor.fetchone()

names = []
old_value = get_column_name( data, "Which column do you want to change
records for? ", names )
names = []
new_value = get_column_name( data, "Which column do you want to change
records to? ", names )

old_val = raw_input("What value do you want to change for " +
names[old_value-1] + ": ")
new_val = raw_input("What value do you want to change to for " +
names[new_value-1] + ": ")

stmt = "UPDATE books SET " + names[new_value-1] + " = '"+ new_val +
"' WHERE " + names[old_value-1] + " = '" + old_val + "'"
print stmt
cursor.execute(stmt)
```

```
print "Rows affected: " + str(cursor.rowcount)



cursor.close()
conn.commit()
conn.close()
```

3. Save the file and call it `ch14_4.py`. Run the script in the IDLE interpreter by either selecting Run | Run Module from the Editor window or by pressing F5. You should see a display similar to the one shown here.

```
1: BookAuthor
2: BookName
3: PublicationDate
4: BookID
Which column do you want to change records for? 4
1: BookAuthor
2: BookName
3: PublicationDate
4: BookID
Which column do you want to change records to? 3
What value do you want to change for BookID: 7
What value do you want to change to for PublicationDate: 1999
UPDATE books SET PublicationDate = '1999' WHERE BookID = '7'
Rows affected: 1
```

The majority of this code is made up of functionality you have used already in the past or in this chapter. The only new part, really, is the update function call itself. You will note that the `update` function sets the `rowcount` variable of the cursor to indicate how many rows were affected by the change you wanted to apply. Basically, you ask the user what column they want to base the change on, printing out the column names by getting them out of the cursor information. Then you ask him what column he wants to change, and the values for both the column you are searching for and the column value you want to change for those records. Finally, you put together the `update` statement and ship it off to the database for execution. That's really all there is to it.

Deleting from a Database

Naturally, if you can add to a database, you need to be able to remove from it. The delete statement in SQL will delete a record or series of records, much the same as the update function will. The issue is figuring out what you want to delete and making sure that you are only deleting the records you expect to remove from the permanent storage system.

The basic syntax of the SQL delete statement is:

```
DELETE from <tableName>
WHERE <condition>
```

Where the `tableName` value is the table you want to delete values from, and the condition is the pattern to match for the records to be deleted. To illustrate what happens here, let's take a look at an example using Python. First, you will add a few records to your book database and then ask the user which ones to delete. You will delete books by the author's name, rather than the book identifier, just to illustrate how it all works.

1. Create a new file by using either the IDLE editor or your favorite text editor.

2. Place the following code in the new file:

```
# Do the proper import
import MySQLdb

def add_record( cursor, title, author, pubdate ) :
    try :
        # execute SQL statement
        stmt = "INSERT INTO Books (BookName, BookAuthor, PublicationDate)
        VALUES ('"
        stmt = stmt + title
        stmt = stmt + "', '"
        stmt = stmt + author
        stmt = stmt + "', "
        stmt = stmt + str(pubdate)
        stmt = stmt + ")"
        cursor.execute(stmt)
        print "Record added!"
    except :
        print "Error adding record!"

def delete_records( cursor, author ) :
    try :
        # execute SQL statement
        stmt = "DELETE FROM Books where BookAuthor = '" + author + "'"
```

```
            cursor.execute(stmt)
            print str(cursor.rowcount) + " Records deleted!"
        except :
            print "Error deleting record!"



# Connect to the database
db = MySQLdb.connect(host="localhost", user="python-test", passwd="python",
db="python-test")

# create a cursor
cursor = db.cursor()

# Add some records

add_record( cursor, "The Sun Also Rises", "Ernest Hemingway", 1850 )
add_record( cursor, "The Moon is a Harsh Mistress", "Robert Heinlein", 1960 )
add_record( cursor, "Friday", "Robert Heinlein", 1988 )
add_record( cursor, "Stranger in a Strange Land", "Robert Heinlein", 1970 )
add_record( cursor, "For Whom the Bell Tolls", "Ernest Hemingway", 1950 )

# Now, ask the user which author to delete

author = raw_input("Which author should we delete: ")
if author != "" :
    delete_records( cursor, author )

cursor.close ()
db.commit ()
```

3. Save the file and call it `ch14_5.py`. Run the script in the IDLE interpreter by either selecting Run | Run Module from the Editor window or by pressing F5. You should see a display similar to the one shown here.

```
Record added!
Record added!
Record added!
Record added!
```

```
Record added!
Which author should we delete: Ernest Hemingway
2 Records deleted!
```

You need to verify that the records you expected to be there are still there, and the records that were supposed to be deleted are really gone. To do this, log in to the Command Line client for MySQL and issue the following commands:

```
mysql> use python-test
Database changed
mysql> select * from books;
+--------+-----------------------------+-----------------+-----------------+
| BookID | BookName                    | BookAuthor      | PublicationDate |
+--------+-----------------------------+-----------------+-----------------+
|      7 | A Tale of Two Cities        | Dickens         |            1999 |
|      8 | A Tale of Two Cities        | Charles Dickens |            1856 |
|     10 | The Moon is a Harsh Mistress | Robert Heinlein |            1960 |
|     11 | Friday                      | Robert Heinlein |            1988 |
|     12 | Stranger in a Strange Land  | Robert Heinlein |            1970 |
+--------+-----------------------------+-----------------+-----------------+
5 rows in set (0.02 sec)
```

As you can see, your Ernest Hemingway books are gone, and the Robert Heinlein books that you added are properly there. That's all there is to deleting records. Naturally, you can delete anything you can find in the database, using the Where clause. The Where clause is really a type of searching in the database.

Searching a Database

As you've seen, the various SQL statements that operate on databases work by locating a group of records on which you want to perform an action. The process of locating the records is called *searching* or *selecting*. The selection process in SQL is quite capable of very complex operations. You can select a group of records based on the contents of one or more fields, as well as by using various built-in functions on those fields. In addition, you can link multiple tables together (called *joining tables*) through a common field. Imagine, for example, that you have a table with employee information and another table with the employee pay information. Both tables might have a single column called "Social Security Number" (or SSN for short) that serves as a unique "key" into both tables. By joining the two tables on the SSN, you can retrieve all of the information about an employee and all of his or her pay stubs with a single request. That is the real power of SQL.

For now, however, let's look at an example of doing simple searching in a relational database using the SELECT statement. The basic format of the SELECT statement is as follows:

```
SELECT <fields> FROM table [,table] [WHERE <condition>]
```

Where:

The <fields> argument is either a list of the columns in the table(s) that you want back, or the asterisk ('*') symbol. The asterisk indicates that you want all of the various fields from all of the tables listed in the select statement.

The table(s) argument lists one or more tables that contain the information you want to retrieve from the database. If this is a single table, you may only list fields that are in that table in the <fields> argument. If there are multiple tables listed, you can select any fields from any of those tables.

The <condition> argument is one or more clauses that identify the record(s) you are interested in finding. You do not have to specify a Where clause in a SELECT statement. Thus, a statement like this is perfectly valid.

```
SELECT * from books;
```

This statement will return all of the columns in the Books table, and will return all of the rows in the Books table with no regard for what those records contain.

To begin with, you are going to clear out our Books table, so you know that there is nothing surprising there to find. Issuing the following command will delete all of the records from a table:

```
mysql> delete from books;
Query OK, 5 rows affected (0.21 sec)

mysql> select * from books;
Empty set (0.00 sec)
```

Now you can start working with the database knowing that it is "clean" and contains no extraneous records. You'll write a simple script to add a bunch of records to the table and then search it in various ways.

1. Create a new file using either the IDLE editor or your favorite text editor.

2. Place the following code in the new file:

```
# Do the proper import
import MySQLdb
```

```
def add_record( cursor, title, author, pubdate ) :
    try :
        # execute SQL statement
        stmt = "INSERT INTO Books (BookName, BookAuthor, PublicationDate)
        VALUES ('"
        stmt = stmt + title
        stmt = stmt + "', '"
        stmt = stmt + author
        stmt = stmt + "', "
        stmt = stmt + str(pubdate)
        stmt = stmt + ")"
        cursor.execute(stmt)
    except :
        print "Error adding record!"

def print_result_set( cursor ) :
    rows = cursor.fetchall()
    for row in rows:
        for col in row :
            print "Column ["+col+"] = " + str(row[col])
        print ""

# Connect to the database
db = MySQLdb.connect(host="localhost", user="python-test", passwd="python",
db="python-test")

# create a cursor
cursor = db.cursor(cursorclass=MySQLdb.cursors.DictCursor)

# Add some records

add_record( cursor, "The Sun Also Rises", "Ernest Hemingway", 1850 )
add_record( cursor, "The Moon is a Harsh Mistress", "Robert Heinlein", 1960 )
add_record( cursor, "Friday", "Robert Heinlein", 1988 )
add_record( cursor, "Stranger in a Strange Land", "Robert Heinlein", 1970 )
add_record( cursor, "For Whom the Bell Tolls", "Ernest Hemingway", 1950 )
add_record( cursor, "Fellowship of the Ring", "JRR Tolkien", 1950 )
```

```
add_record( cursor, "The Two Towers", "JRR Tolkien", 1952 )
add_record( cursor, "Return of the King", "JRR Tolkien", 1954 )
add_record( cursor, "The Hobbit", "JRR Tolkien", 1948 )

# Search for all titles by Robert Heinlein
cursor.execute("select * from books where BookAuthor = 'Robert Heinlein'")

# Print out the results.
print "Books by Robert Heinlein: "
print_result_set( cursor )

# Now, search for all records made after 1960
print "Books printed after 1960: "
cursor.execute("select * from books where PublicationDate > 1960")

# Print out the results.
print_result_set( cursor )

# Finally, all records that contain the word "the" in the title
print "Books with a title containing 'the': "
cursor.execute("select * from books where BookName like '%the%'")

# Print out the results.
print_result_set( cursor )


cursor.close ()
db.commit ()
```

3. Save the file and call it `ch14_6.py`. Run the script in the IDLE interpreter by either selecting Run | Run Module from the Editor window or by pressing F5. You should see a display similar to the one shown here. Note that the BookID values will likely be different in your case. This is perfectly okay, since the BookID field is filled in by the database and is based on how many times you have added data to the table.

```
Books by Robert Heinlein:
Column [BookAuthor] = Robert Heinlein
Column [BookName] = The Moon is a Harsh Mistress
```

```
Column [PublicationDate] = 1960
Column [BookID] = 69


Column [BookAuthor] = Robert Heinlein
Column [BookName] = Friday
Column [PublicationDate] = 1988
Column [BookID] = 70


Column [BookAuthor] = Robert Heinlein
Column [BookName] = Stranger in a Strange Land
Column [PublicationDate] = 1970
Column [BookID] = 71


Books printed after 1960:
Column [BookAuthor] = Robert Heinlein
Column [BookName] = Friday
Column [PublicationDate] = 1988
Column [BookID] = 70


Column [BookAuthor] = Robert Heinlein
Column [BookName] = Stranger in a Strange Land
Column [PublicationDate] = 1970
Column [BookID] = 71


Books with a title containing 'the':
Column [BookAuthor] = Ernest Hemingway
Column [BookName] = The Sun Also Rises
Column [PublicationDate] = 1850
Column [BookID] = 68


Column [BookAuthor] = Robert Heinlein
Column [BookName] = The Moon is a Harsh Mistress
Column [PublicationDate] = 1960
Column [BookID] = 69


Column [BookAuthor] = Ernest Hemingway
Column [BookName] = For Whom the Bell Tolls
```

```
Column [PublicationDate] = 1950
Column [BookID] = 72


Column [BookAuthor] = JRR Tolkien
Column [BookName] = Fellowship of the Ring
Column [PublicationDate] = 1950
Column [BookID] = 73


Column [BookAuthor] = JRR Tolkien
Column [BookName] = The Two Towers
Column [PublicationDate] = 1952
Column [BookID] = 74


Column [BookAuthor] = JRR Tolkien
Column [BookName] = Return of the King
Column [PublicationDate] = 1954
Column [BookID] = 75


Column [BookAuthor] = JRR Tolkien
Column [BookName] = The Hobbit
Column [PublicationDate] = 1948
Column [BookID] = 76
```

As you can see, there are three separate examples of searching the database using the `select` statement. In the first case, you do a simple comparison for all authors based on a single name. This returns a set of records that you can then print. In the second example, you are looking for all records where the publication date is after 1960. As you can see, SQL is perfectly capable of doing math and math comparisons to return a set of records. Both of these examples are pretty straightforward.

The final example uses the "like" operator along with pattern matching syntax to search for all records that contain the word "the" in the title. There are really two things to notice about this one. First, you use the percent ('%') character to match zero or more characters, much as you do in regular expressions matching in Python. By placing the percent character on either side of the phrase you are looking for, you find all strings that have "the" anywhere in them. Also, note that the returned values are not case sensitive. Thus, you get back both "the" and "The" from titles. If you just wanted to search for titles that began with the word "the," you could have used "The%" instead and found them all. Play around a bit with the searching functionality if you like, using the Command Line client in MySQL. The syntax is the same; just remember to enter a semi-colon (';') at the end of the line to tell the interpreter you are finished entering a command.

In Conclusion

As we've seen in this chapter, Python can be combined with the immense power of relational databases, using MySQL, to create really amazing applications. Now that you have a good handle on using the basic commands of SQL, you can do almost anything you want with it. In our next chapter, we'll combine the things we've been learning to this point, using the Internet, relational databases, and the power of Python, to create a full-blown Web site.

15 } Putting It All Together

At this point in the book, you have learned all about the basic syntax of Python. You've learned how to write scripts that can be called from Web servers, and how to write scripts that work with databases. It's time to put all of this together into a nice package that uses all of the pieces in one place. We will be creating a reference application that is run from a Web server, uses a database, and shows you the steps involved in putting together a complete Python application for the Web.

The purpose of our Web application will be to create a Web site for maintaining personal book information. We are going to store what books you own, who wrote them, when they were written, and allow people to post reviews about the books for others to read. This will mean being able to present forms to the user to fill out, being able to store data in a database for later retrieval, and being able to report on the information stored in that database. That should really about cover all of the aspects of Python that might be used in a typical Web application.

Designing the Application

The first stage of any system creation is the design of the application. We aren't going to go into amazing detail here, because that really isn't the focus of this book. However, with Python, as with most programming languages, you need to have a good understanding of what you are going to be implementing before you start. In this case, there are three areas that you need to understand before you start coding.

Program Flow

Before you can begin to write an application, it is important to understand how the user flows through the system. Essentially, a user flow is a "path" from starting point to ending point. In our case, there are several user flows to consider.

* Logging into the system
* Logging out of the system
* Adding a new book record to the system
* Modifying an existing book record in the system
* Deleting an existing book record from the system
* Adding a user review of a book in the system
* Viewing book records in the system
* Viewing book reviews in the system

Certainly, there are considerably more flows that you might want in a production environment, but this will easily do for now. Note that not all of these flows require their own individual screens or scripts; some can be combined into a single script with a single user interface to them.

Your system will consist of a single main menu that supports the flows, as well as the logging in and logging out. We aren't going to do a lot of high-level security here. We'll just set a cookie on the user machine so that you know who your users are. In a real system, you would want a complete user database with strong passwords and error checking. This isn't necessary in a simple prototype application like the one we will be developing.

User Interface Design

Once you understand what it is you will be implementing and how the user will move through the system, the next step is to design the actual user interface (UI). At this stage, there is no real reason to come up with hard and fast designs for the UI, but you should be able to mock up simple pages that are at least placeholders for the steps in the user flow process. For our purposes, simply listing the forms we are going to be creating and what information we will need on those forms will suffice for now. This isn't going to be a beauty contest for user interface design, because these forms will be purely functional. So let's look at the forms you are going to need.

* Main menu form
* Add book record form
* Select book record form
* Add review form
* Book report form
* Review report form

You might wonder where the forms are for logging in and out, and for modifying and deleting records. As it happens, the login and logout can be done on the main form, simply listing the information stored in the cookie for the system. The modification form is really exactly the same as the add book record form, except that it comes pre-populated. You may or may not use the same script behind the scenes to work on the forms, but the design is the same.

The purpose of the user interface design segment of the project plan is to discover what elements you need and what elements can be combined together. In addition, by figuring out what you are going to need to do, you can design flexible forms more easily that are consistently provided to the end user.

Database Design

As we've mentioned before, the database is the fundamental driver of most applications these days. Although we are developing a fairly simple application, we need to figure out what information we are going to be storing before moving on and implementing the real database tables and writing the code that will store the information in the databases. Database tables are notoriously hard to change once they have data in them, so it behooves us to make sure that the design of our tables is correct before we start working with them. In general, a relational database should be set in stone long before you start writing the first line of code to access it. This does not mean that the data you store has to be set in stone, because you can always add subsidiary tables to your database to store information as you come across it. However, any tables that exist on the first day that your application goes "live" should keep the same layout for the life of your application. This can be a difficult thing to accomplish, but if you strive to accomplish this goal, your application stands a much better case of being bug-free and surviving in the long-term.

In your case, you are going to need two database tables. The first will maintain the book records, which are descriptions of the books you are storing. The second table will maintain the book review records, which are the descriptions of how people feel about the books.

One note here: In a typical system, you would actually have more tables to remove the redundancy in the book records. For example, rather than storing the author name over and over, and wasting a lot of space for the text of the name, you would create a single record for the author name and use an identifier to "link" the author name to the book record. A good book on database design and relational database will give you all the information you need to make your database as solid as possible.

Our two database tables will consist of the following information:

- ❋ **Book Table**
  - ❋ **Book identifier**—The unique identifier that represents this book in the system.
  - ❋ **Book name**—The title of the book. This need not be unique.
  - ❋ **Book author**—The name of the author of the book. This will not be unique.
  - ❋ **Publication date**—The date this book was published. Not unique.

- ❋ **Book Review Table**
  - ❋ **Review ID**—The unique identifier that represents the review in the system.
  - ❋ **Book ID**—A link to the book table. There can be multiple reviews for a single book in the system, so this ID is not unique in this table.
  - ❋ **Reviewer**—The name of the person doing this review. This will be the same as the "login" name of the user, and need not be unique. We will store this name as text in the database.
  - ❋ **Review text**—The text of the review. No checking will be done for this. It will simply be free form characters.

Now that you have the basic skeleton of the application design done, it is time to move on to actually creating things. Let's start with database tables, since they form the core of our implementation.

Implementing the Database Tables

In order to implement your new application, you are going to need a new database in which to store the data. Let's call this database "books," since that is the kind of information you are going to be storing in the database. To create a new database, you will use the MySQL Administration GUI application, as shown in Figure 15.1. This screen assumes that you have launched the administrator program and logged in as a root-level user with the correct password, as we covered in the previous chapter. You will also need to click the Catalog button and press Ctrl-N to bring up a new window for creating schema.

The next step is to create the table within the database in which to store the information about all of the books. To do this, just add a new table to your new database and fill in the form with the columns for the table, as shown in Figure 15.2. Clicking Apply Changes will create the new table, with no data in it, in the database so that you can begin to populate it with your application. You may notice that this is the same structure that we used in the previous chapter, and might wonder why we are recreating the table. The answer is that tables must be created anew in each database in which they are used. You can export the schema and reimport it to create the same table, but a new version of the table must exist in every database in which it is used.

❋ Checking the Settings

Depending on your initial configuration settings, as well as the version of MySQL you are using, your settings may be slightly different than those shown. In addition, of course, your comments will likely be different. Neither of these things matters in the running of the application.

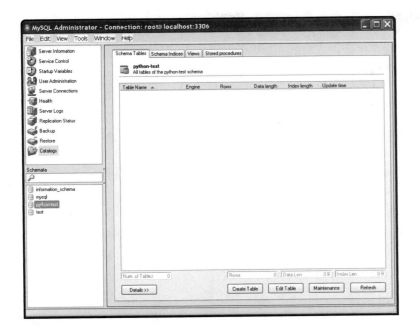

Figure 15.1
Creating a new database
in MySQL Administrator.

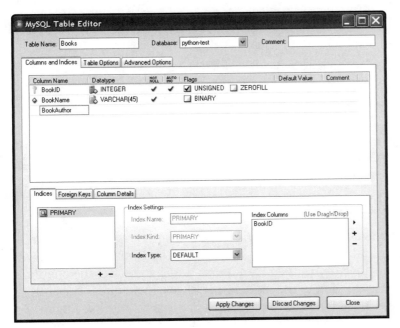

Figure 15.2
Creating the Books table in
the database

You will need a table for the book reviews as well. This table should contain the book identifier
to use for cross-referencing to the book title table. Let's refer to this information as a "foreign

key" within the book review table. It is a key into another table, not your current one. You will also need a unique identifier for this table, which we will refer to as the review id.

Figure 15.3 shows the table you will be creating using the MySQL Administrator GUI application in order to implement the BookReview table. Enter the values as you see them and click the Apply Changes button to create the new table.

Figure 15.3
Creating the Book Review table in the database.

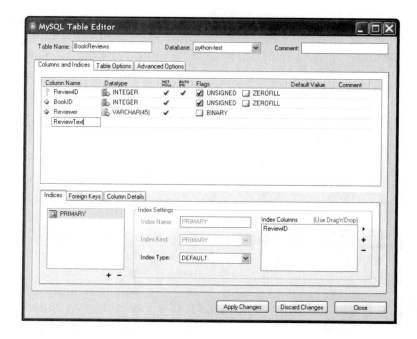

At this point, you have all of the tables you will need to implement the system created. The next step is to start building the actual application. To do this, you are going to need to create the forms and scripts that make up the main application. Let's do that now.

Implementing the Forms

The forms for your application will be created in scripting code, because you need to have various parts of the forms generated dynamically, based on the state of the system and what the user has selected. We'll begin with the main menu form, which looks like the one shown in Figure 15.4. Note that this is the view of the main form only when no one is currently logged in. When someone has logged into the system, it will appear to look like Figure 15.5. However, through the magic of Python scripting, we are going to create a single script that generates both of these form views, without any need for separate HTML or Python files.

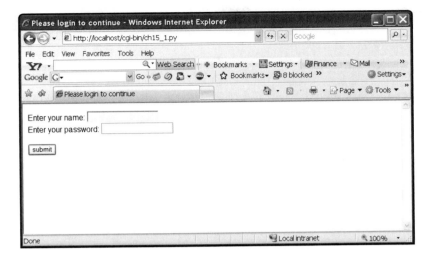

Figure 15.4
The login form.

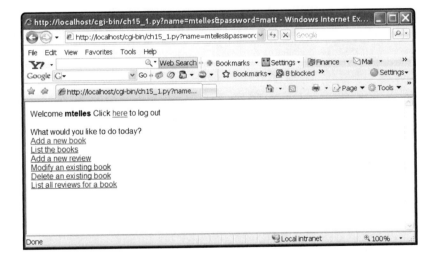

Figure 15.5
The main menu form.

These are not the prettiest forms in the world, but that isn't the point of this exercise. You are more than welcome to use your creative talents to create whatever you want to make them look nicer. The point here is to show off the underlying functionality of Python, Apache, and the MySQL database.

In order to implement the functionality shown here, you need to create a new script. In this case, I have placed the script in a subdirectory of the Apache cgi-bin directory. You can put it wherever you want, but your links and screen displays will be correspondingly different. To implement the functionality, follow this procedure:

1. Create a new file using the IDLE editor or your favorite text editor.

2. Enter the following code into your new file:

```
#!c:/Python25/python

import cgi
import sys
import cgitb
import os
import Cookie

def gen_html_header(username) :
    if username != None and username != "":
        member = Cookie.SimpleCookie()
        member["username"] = username
        member["username"]["expires"] = 60*60*60
        print member
    print "Content-Type: text/html\n\n"
    print "<HTML>"

def gen_html_trailer() :
    print "</HTML>"

def get_user_cookie():
    if 'HTTP_COOKIE' in os.environ:
        cookies = os.environ['HTTP_COOKIE']
        cookie = cookies.split('=')
        name = cookie[0]
        value = cookie[1]
        if name == "username" :
            return value
    return ""

def print_menu() :
    print "<BR><BR>"
    print "What would you like to do today?<BR>"
    print "<a href=../../ch15_2.htm>Add a new book</a><BR>"
```

```
    print "<a href=ch15_3.py>List the books</a><BR>"
    print "<a href=ch15_4.py>Add a new review</a><BR>"
    print "<a href=ch15_6.py>Modify an existing book</a><BR>"
    print "<a href=ch15_3.py?mode=3>Delete an existing book</a><BR>"
    print "<a href=ch15_3.py?mode=2>List all reviews for a book</a><BR>"
cgitb.enable()

# See if we have the cookie we need
form = cgi.FieldStorage()
username = get_user_cookie()

# See if we got some user arguments
try :
    uname = form.getvalue("name")
    username = uname
except:
    uname = ""

# Output the header
gen_html_header(username)

# If we have the user name, output it
if username != None and username != "" :
    print "Welcome <B>" + username + "</B> Click <a href=ch15_1.py>here</a>
    to log out"
    print_menu()
else :
    # Output the login information
    print "<TITLE>Please login to continue</TITLE>"
    print "<FORM ACTION=\"ch15_1.py\">"
    print "Enter your name: <INPUT TYPE=TEXT NAME=\"name\"><BR>"
    print "Enter your password: <INPUT TYPE=PASSWORD NAME=\"password\">
    <BR><BR>"
    print "<INPUT TYPE=SUBMIT VALUE=\"submit\">"
    print "</FORM>"
# Output the trailer
gen_html_trailer()
```

3. Save the file to the directory you have chosen, whether it is the cgi-bin directory of Apache or a newly created directory under the cgi-bin directory. Use the name `ch15_1.py`.

4. Run the program by entering the following location into your local Web browser. `http://localhost/cgi-bin/<your path>` where `<your path>` is the location of the file you just created. You should see the output shown in Figure 15.4.

How does it all work? First, check to see if your cookie has been set. If it hasn't been set, then you should look to see if the form variables have been passed in. If either of these things is true, the user has set the cookie, and you will use their username for all further processing. If he has not been here before, you should put up a login screen and make him enter his user name and password. In a normal Web application, you would verify his password in some sort of user table before proceeding. For now, we will just assume that he is who he says he is.

Assuming that the user logged in properly, he will then be shown the main menu for the system. This menu will contain all of the options that we have discussed previously. The menu display code is shown in the `print_menu` function. Notice also that you greet the user by name, which is a nice touch.

For the menu items, we will now implement the functionality for each one. Start with the Add Book command. This command will be implemented as a combination of an HTML form and a Python script. Here's the HTML form you will be using (which we will call `ch15_2.htm`):

```
<HTML>

<! Define a form for entering a book>

<form action="cgi-bin/ch15_2.py">
 <p>Book Title:</p>
 <input type="text" name="title" size="45">
 <p>Author:</p>
 <input type="text" name="author" size="45">
 <p>Publication Date:</p>
 <input type="text" name="pubdate" size="45">
 <p>
 <input type="submit" value="Add Book"><BR><BR>
 <a href="cgi-bin/ ch15_1.py">Return to Main Menu</a>
</p>
</form>
</html>
```

You are simply defining a form for inputting the three bits of data you need to create a new book. When the user clicks the button to add the book, it calls your Python script. You need to write that script. Let's do that now:

1. Create a new file using the IDLE editor or your favorite text editor.

2. Enter the following code into your new file

```
#!c:/Python25/python

# Do the proper imports
import MySQLdb
import cgi

def gen_html_header() :
    print "Content-Type: text/html\n\n"
    print "<HTML>"

def gen_html_trailer() :
    print "</HTML>"



def add_record( cursor, title, author, pubdate ) :
    try :
        # execute SQL statement
        stmt = "INSERT INTO Booktitles (BookName, BookAuthor,
        PublicationDate) VALUES ('"
        stmt = stmt + title
        stmt = stmt + "', '"
        stmt = stmt + author
        stmt = stmt + "', "
        stmt = stmt + str(pubdate)
        stmt = stmt + ")"
        cursor.execute(stmt)
    except :
        print "Error adding record!"

# See what they gave us
```

```
form = cgi.FieldStorage()

fTitle = ""
fAuthor = ""
fPubDate= -1
try :
    fTitle = form.getvalue("title", "")
    fAuthor  = form.getvalue("author", "" )
    fPubDate = int(form.getvalue("pubdate", ""))
except:
    # Something isn't right.
    print "Error: Bad data"


# Connect to the database
try :
    db = MySQLdb.connect(host="localhost", user="python-test",
    passwd="python", db="books")

    # create a cursor
    cursor = db.cursor(cursorclass=MySQLdb.cursors.DictCursor)

    add_record( cursor, fTitle, fAuthor, fPubDate )

    cursor.close ()
    db.commit ()
except:
    print "Exception in database!<BR>"


gen_html_header()
print "The record was added: <BR>"
print "Title: " + fTitle + " <BR>"
print "Author: " + fAuthor + "<BR>"
print "Publication Date: " + str(fPubDate) + "<BR>"
print "<BR>"
print "<a href=\"../../cgi-bin/ ch15_1.py\">Return to Main Menu</a><BR>"
gen_html_trailer()
```

3. Save the file to the directory you have chosen, whether it is the cgi-bin directory of Apache or a newly created directory under the cgi-bin directory. Call the file ch15_2.py.

4. You should now be able to go from the main menu to the Add a Book Page and back again.

Adding Reviews

Our next bit of functionality involves the next two menu items, which are surprisingly closely related. The first menu item is listing the available books, and the second menu item is adding a review to a given book title. In fact, most of the remaining menu items are built around the idea of getting a list of books and applying some sort of action to them. In order to do this, you need the ability to list out the available book titles. In the last chapter, we saw that the select statement in SQL was the method available for getting back a list of items from a database, and that is exactly what you are going to do here in order to get back a list of the book titles and display information about them. The output from the list of books will just be the information available to them. What differs from case to case is that you want the ability to do different things to the titles. Let's create the code that will generate the book title report to see what is going on here.

1. Create a new file using the IDLE editor or your favorite text editor.

2. Enter the following code into your new file:

```python
#!c:/Python25/python

# Do the proper imports
import MySQLdb
import cgi
import sys
import cgitb
import os
import Cookie

def gen_html_header(username) :
    if username != None and username != "":
        member = Cookie.SimpleCookie()
        member["username"] = username
        member["username"]["expires"] = 60*60*60
        print member
    print "Content-Type: text/html\n\n"
```

```python
    print "<HTML>"

def gen_html_trailer() :
    print "</HTML>"

def get_user_cookie():
    if 'HTTP_COOKIE' in os.environ:
        cookies = os.environ['HTTP_COOKIE']
        cookie = cookies.split('=')
        name = cookie[0]
        value = cookie[1]
        if name == "username" :
            return value
    return ""

def list_records( cursor, username, mode ) :
    try :
        # execute SQL statement
        stmt = "SELECT * from BookTitles"
        cursor.execute(stmt)
        recs = cursor.fetchall()
        for rec in recs :
            print "Title: " + rec["BookTitle"] + "<BR>"
            print "Author: " + rec["BookAuthor"] + "<BR>"
            print "Publication Date: " + str(rec["PublicationDate"]) + "<BR>"
            # Mode 1: Allow review.
            if mode == "1" :
                print "<a href=\"../../cgi-bin/ ch15_4.py?name=" +
username + "&id=" + str(rec["BookID"]) + "\">Add a Review</a><BR>"
            # Mode 2: Allow viewing reviews.
            if mode == "2" :
                print "<a href=\"../../cgi-bin/ ch15_5.py?name=" +
username + "&id=" + str(rec["BookID"]) + "\">Show Reviews</a><BR>"
            if mode == "3" :
                print "<a href=\"../../cgi-bin/ ch15_6.py?name=" +
username + "&id=" + str(rec["BookID"]) + "\">Delete books</a><BR>"
```

```
            print "<BR>"

    except :
        print "Error listing record!"

cgitb.enable()

# See what they gave us
form = cgi.FieldStorage()
try :
    mode = form.getvalue("mode")
except:
    mode = "0"

username = get_user_cookie()

# Connect to the database
try :
    db = MySQLdb.connect(host="localhost", user="python-test",
    passwd="python", db="books")

    # create a cursor
    cursor = db.cursor(cursorclass=MySQLdb.cursors.DictCursor)

    gen_html_header(username)
    list_records( cursor, username, mode )
    print "<a href=\"../../cgi-bin/ ch15_1.py?name=" + username + "\">
    Return to Main Menu</a><BR>"
    gen_html_trailer()

    cursor.close ()
except:
    print "Exception in database!<BR>"
```

3. Save the file to the directory you have chosen, whether it is the cgi-bin directory of Apache or a newly created directory under the cgi-bin directory. Call the file ch15_3.py.

4. You should now be able to go from the main menu to list the books and back again.

There is really very little new in this script. You'll get back the list of book titles from the database and display them, one at a time, on the Web page. Note the addition of the "mode" command line variable to the incoming URL. This will be used to determine what to do with the list. If the mode is absent, or zero, you will just display the books. If the mode is set to the value "1," then you are going to allow the user to add a review to that book title. You do this by calling a new script with the identifier for the book. We need this identifier, you may recall, because the book identifier is a foreign key into the book review database.

Adding the Review to the Database

Now that you have a list of the books displayed for the user to select from, you need to actually process the request, get the information back from them, and place it into the database. To do this, there are really two parts. First, you need to display the proper data entry form for the user to enter his review information in. Then you need to process that information when he submits it to the server and adds the record. You can use a single script to accomplish this same task by simply passing the appropriate variables and commands to it. Let's look at what the form will look like, since it is displayed in Figure 15.6.

Figure 15.6
The book review form displayed.

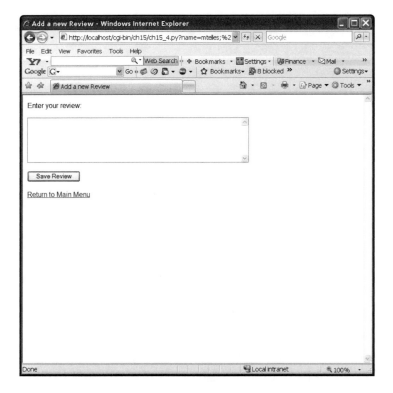

We will generate this form on the fly, primarily to show you how easy it is to do things like this, along with the information you will need to save the record. In order to do this, you need to create a new script in Python. This script will display the form, and then be called again for processing the form. When the user clicks the button, it will be run again, but this time to process the request to store the information in the database.

1. Create a new file using the IDLE editor or your favorite text editor.

2. Enter the following code into your new file:

```python
#!c:/Python25/python

# Do the proper imports
import MySQLdb
import cgi
import sys
import cgitb
import os
import Cookie

def gen_html_header(username) :
    if username != None and username != "":
        member = Cookie.SimpleCookie()
        member["username"] = username
        member["username"]["expires"] = 60*60*60
        print member
    print "Content-Type: text/html\n\n"
    print "<HTML>"

def gen_html_trailer() :
    print "</HTML>"

def get_user_cookie():
    if 'HTTP_COOKIE' in os.environ:
        cookies = os.environ['HTTP_COOKIE']
        cookie = cookies.split('=')
        name = cookie[0]
        value = cookie[1]
        if name == "username" :
```

```
            return value
    return ""


def generate_form( username, id ) :
    print "<TITLE>Add a new Review</TITLE>"
    print "<FORM ACTION=\"ch15_4.py\">"
    print "Enter your review:<BR><BR> <TEXTAREA NAME=\"review\" COLS=60
    ROWS=6></TEXTAREA><BR>"
    print "<BR><INPUT TYPE=SUBMIT VALUE=\"Save Review\">"
    print "<INPUT TYPE=HIDDEN NAME=name VALUE=" + str(username) + ">"
    print "<INPUT TYPE=HIDDEN NAME=action VALUE=\"add\">"
    print "<INPUT TYPE=HIDDEN NAME=id VALUE=\""+ str(id) + "\">"
    print "</FORM>"


def save_review( username, id, form ) :
    try :
        # execute SQL statement
        stmt = "INSERT INTO BookReviews (BookID, ReviewedBy, Review) VALUES ('"
        stmt = stmt + id
        stmt = stmt + "', '"
        stmt = stmt + username
        stmt = stmt + "', '"
        stmt = stmt + str(form.getvalue("review"))
        stmt = stmt + "')"
        cursor.execute(stmt)
        print "The review was successfully saved!<BR><BR>"
    except :
        print "Error adding record! Stmt: [" + str(stmt) + "]<BR>"
        print sys.exc_info()


cgitb.enable()


# See what they gave us
form = cgi.FieldStorage()


# Get the information we need from the field storage
```

```
    username = ""
    id = ""
    action = ""

    #try :
    username = form.getvalue("name")
    id       = form.getvalue("id")
    action   = form.getvalue("action")
    #except:
    #    username = ""

    if username == "" :
        username = get_user_cookie()

gen_html_header(username)

# Connect to the database
try :
    db = MySQLdb.connect(host="localhost", user="python-test",
    passwd="python", db="books")

    # create a cursor
    cursor = db.cursor(cursorclass=MySQLdb.cursors.DictCursor)

    if action == "" or action == None :
        generate_form(username, id)
    else :
        save_review( username, id, form )

    print "<a href=\"../../cgi-bin/ ch15_1.py?name=" + str(username) +
    "\">Return to Main Menu</a><BR>"

    cursor.close ()
    db.commit()
except:
    print "Exception in database!<BR>"
```

```
        print sys.exc_info()
    gen_html_trailer()
```

3. Save the file to the directory you have chosen, whether it is the cgi-bin directory of Apache or a newly created directory under the cgi-bin directory. Call the file `ch15_4.py`.

4. You should now be able to go from the main menu to the Add a Review page and back again.

As you can see, the code is fairly straightforward. The data is retrieved from the form storage area and placed into the database via an SQL statement. One note about this script: The assumption made here is that the review data is valid for inserting into an SQL statement. That is, that it does not contain characters that are invalid for the database field in which it is to be stored. If that isn't true in your case, you will need to "massage" the data so that it consists of valid characters.

Note the use of "hidden" form values to pass information from the form to the Python script. This is an excellent method for sending data from one place to another without having the user have to enter it or see it.

Listing the Reviews

Obviously, if you are going to have people review books, you will want the ability to see what other people have said about the book. Listing the reviews is the step we will approach next. The process is pretty much the same as listing the books themselves, but with one important twist. Rather than simply selecting all of the books and displaying them, you need to use the information about the book to display all the connected records in the database. This is done by the `select` statement in SQL, just as it was before, but in this case, you will be attaching a condition to the statement. Let's look at how this is going to be done.

Remember, back when we were writing the list function for the books, we placed several "mode" statements into the list, which generated various kinds of links, depending on the mode. One of the things that we passed along with those links was the identifier for the book. We are now going to take advantage of that information. In addition, you might recall that the main menu link for displaying reviews looked like this:

```
print "<a href=ch15_3.py?mode=2>List all reviews for a book</a><BR>"
```

As you can see, we are just calling the list routine, but this time with a mode of two. This will indicate that the link to print out the reviews for the book will be displayed after the book title information.

1. Create a new file using the IDLE editor or your favorite text editor.

2. Enter the following code into your new file:

```
#!c:/Python25/python

# Do the proper imports
import MySQLdb
import cgi
import sys
import cgitb
import os
import Cookie

def gen_html_header(username) :
    if username != None and username != "":
        member = Cookie.SimpleCookie()
        member["username"] = username
        member["username"]["expires"] = 60*60*60
        print member
    print "Content-Type: text/html\n\n"
    print "<HTML>"

def gen_html_trailer() :
    print "</HTML>"

def get_user_cookie():
    if 'HTTP_COOKIE' in os.environ:
        cookies = os.environ['HTTP_COOKIE']
        cookie = cookies.split('=')
        name = cookie[0]
        value = cookie[1]
        if name == "username" :
            return value
    return ""

def list_records( cursor, id ) :
    try :
        # execute SQL statement
        stmt = "SELECT * from BookReviews where BookID = " + str(id)
        cursor.execute(stmt)
```

```
            recs = cursor.fetchall()
            for rec in recs :
                print "Reviewed by: " + rec["ReviewedBy"] + "<BR>"
                print "Review: " + rec["Review"]+ "<BR>"
                print "<BR>"


        except :
            print "Error listing record!"


cgitb.enable()


# See what they gave us
form = cgi.FieldStorage()
try :
    id = form.getvalue("id")
    username = form.getvalue("username")
except:
    id = "0"


if username == "" or username == None:
    username = get_user_cookie()


# Connect to the database
try :
    db = MySQLdb.connect(host="localhost", user="python-test",
    passwd="python", db="books")


    # create a cursor
    cursor = db.cursor(cursorclass=MySQLdb.cursors.DictCursor)


    gen_html_header(username)
    list_records( cursor, id )
    print "<a href=\"../../cgi-bin/ ch15_1.py?name=" + username + "\">
    Return to Main Menu</a><BR>"
    gen_html_trailer()


    cursor.close ()
```

```
except:
    print "Exception in database!<BR>"
```

3. Save the file to the directory you have chosen, whether it is the cgi-bin directory of Apache or a newly created directory under the cgi-bin directory. Name the file ch15_5.py.

4. You should now be able to go from the main menu to view all of the reviews for a given book.

Deleting Books

The final piece of the system that we will look at in this chapter is the deletion of books. There is one other component that will need to be written, modifying a book, but that code has really already been done here several times, and there is no good reason to go over it again. Simply placing the current value into the form fields and using an update statement rather than an insert statement will accomplish this task. Deletion, however, requires something new. You need not only to remove the record for the book that the user selects, but you must also delete the associated book review records. Let's look at how that works.

When you select a book to delete, the database must delete the book record. This is straightforward, and is done via the delete statement in SQL. After this has been done successfully, you then need to find and delete all of the associated review records. Remember that you store the book identifier in the book review record, so you can use that information to tell SQL which records to delete.

1. Create a new file using the IDLE editor or your favorite text editor.

2. Enter the following code into your new file:

```
#!c:/Python25/python

# Do the proper imports
import MySQLdb
import cgi
import sys
import cgitb
import os
import Cookie

def gen_html_header(username) :
    if username != None and username != "":
        member = Cookie.SimpleCookie()
```

```
            member["username"] = username
            member["username"]["expires"] = 60*60*60
            print member
        print "Content-Type: text/html\n\n"
        print "<HTML>"


def gen_html_trailer() :
    print "</HTML>"


def get_user_cookie():
    if 'HTTP_COOKIE' in os.environ:
        cookies = os.environ['HTTP_COOKIE']
        cookie = cookies.split('=')
        name = cookie[0]
        value = cookie[1]
        if name == "username" :
            return value
    return ""


def delete_records( cursor, id ) :
    try :
        # First, delete the book id records.
        stmt = "DELETE FROM BookTitles WHERE BookID = " + str(id)
        cursor.execute(stmt)
        print "Book record deleted<BR>"
        # Now, delete the book reviews for this book
        stmt = "DELETE FROM BookReviews WHERE BookID = " + str(id)
        cursor.execute(stmt)
        print str(cursor.rowcount) + " reviews deleted<BR>"
    except :
        print "Error deleting record!"
        print sys.exc_info()


cgitb.enable()

# See what they gave us
form = cgi.FieldStorage()
```

```
form = cgi.FieldStorage()
try :
    id = form.getvalue("id")
    username = form.getvalue("username")
except:
    id = "0"

if username == "" or username == None:
    username = get_user_cookie()

# Connect to the database
try :
    db = MySQLdb.connect(host="localhost", user="python-test",
    passwd="python", db="books")

    # create a cursor
    cursor = db.cursor(cursorclass=MySQLdb.cursors.DictCursor)

    gen_html_header(username)
    delete_records( cursor, id )
    print "<a href=\"../../cgi-bin/ ch15_1.py?name=" + username + "\">
    Return to Main Menu</a><BR>"
    gen_html_trailer()

    cursor.close ()
    db.commit()
except:
    print "Exception in database!<BR>"
    print sys.exc_info()
```

3. Save the file to the directory you have chosen, whether it is the cgi-bin directory of Apache or a newly created directory under the cgi-bin directory. Call the file `ch15_6.py`.

4. You should now be able to go from the main menu to view all of the reviews for a given book.

That's really all there is to it. You have implemented a more or less complete system for managing books and book reviews in a few hundred lines of Python! That's pretty impressive.

In Conclusion

In this chapter, we have learned quite a bit about working with Web servers, dynamically generating HTML and HTML forms, working with databases and linking tables, and passing data around between Python scripts. This chapter is not a replacement for a more complete book on SQL or HTML. Instead, it is intended to show you how to work with these concepts within the Python environment. If you plan to work extensively in the Web or database world, I strongly suggest that you find reference works on both these subjects.

16 } Python and Graphics

In the beginning, there was text. In the computer world, the beginning has always meant a text-based interface with text-based displays. This was true in the mainframe days, in the early personal computer days of MS-DOS, and originally on the Internet. The early Internet Web pages were plain text, with nary an image or graphic to be seen. As things progressed, however, text was complemented by graphics. It makes sense, therefore, to be able to create and use graphics in Python, just as you do on the World Wide Web. This chapter will be a short introduction to the graphical world of Python.

The PIL Library

Python, by itself, contains no graphic capabilities. The language core is all about looping and decision-making and assignments and string handling, as we have seen in the chapters leading up to this one in this book. To implement any sort of graphic capability in your Python applications, you need an external library. This isn't unusual, as we have seen in the use of CGI functionality and relational database functionality in previous chapters. As with the MySQL library that we downloaded in order to use the relational capabilities of that database, we need to download a library in order to work with graphics in Python. In our case, the library that we will be downloading is called *PIL*, for the Python Image Library. Much like the MySQL system, the PIL modules are distributed in a two-fold manner. You can use the system as a free library, available for use to anyone, or you can pay for support and such. Since we are experimenting with the library, we will just download the free version and use it. However, as you will see, a lot of effort went into creating a high-quality system such as PIL, and it is well worth supporting such endeavors by paying for the commercial version of the library. This is something you might consider doing in the future, as you use Python in your commercial systems.

Downloading

In order to begin using the PIL modules, you must first download the installation package. The basic system for PIL is available on the www.pythonware.com Web site. You will find the entire download system here: http://www.pythonware.com/products/pil/index.htm. As of the writing of this book, the current version of the library is 1.1.6 and supports Python versions 1.5.2 and higher, which includes the 2.5 version that we are using in this book. If you are using other versions, refer to the Web page for instructions on which module to use. In any case, the basics of what we are doing here should be the same no matter what version you are using. The interface has become quite standard over the years.

Installing

For the Windows operating system, the installer for PIL is a standard Microsoft executable (.exe) file. You run the installer from Windows Explorer or from the command line. When you run the installer, you should see the dialog box displayed on the screen as shown in Figure 16.1.

Figure 16.1
The PIL installation main screen.

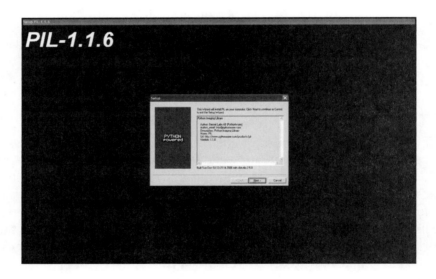

Clicking on the next button will take you to the screen that determines which version of Python you are running. It is important to select the correct version so that the modules for PIL are installed in the proper location. If you only have the single version 2.5 of Python installed on your system, as I do, you will see the screen displayed in Figure 16.2 on your computer monitor.

If, for some reason, your Python version is not displayed, the Python interpreter is probably not registered with your system. The easiest way to fix this is to reinstall Python from the Python Web site. There are certain registry entries that need to be created and set properly in order for Python to work and for other modules to find it, and the installation process will do this for

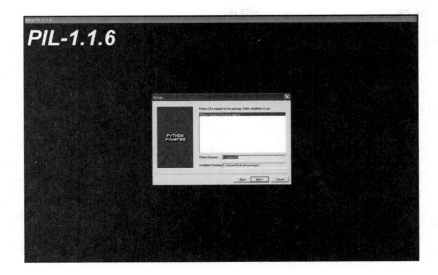

Figure 16.2
Determining the Python
version installed.

you. Alternatively, you may go to the PythonWare site and find the registration script that they have so nicely provided, which will create all of the registry entries that are necessary for the system to run properly.

In any case, once you have finished with the installation program, the PIL modules will be installed on your system under the proper Python directory, and it will be possible to start writing graphical applications using the modules. Let's take a look at the basic steps necessary to create a new graphical image using PIL.

Verifying Your Installation

Before you actually begin to write some code using the PIL modules, the first thing to do is to verify that the installation is properly in place. To do this, the easiest way is to try to import the right module within the IDLE environment. Type the following line in the IDLE editor:

```
import Image
```

and press the Return or Enter key. If the system comes back with a normal prompt, the PIL modules are properly installed. If an error is displayed saying that the system could not find the module image, please go back and check to see that the installation process ran properly and that you installed the PIL modules in the right place on your system.

Creating a New Image

First, create an image. In the PIL world, an "image" is just a blank drawing surface of a given height and width. You create a new image by using the Image module within the PIL library. For example, to create a new one, you would use the following piece of code. You can actually just type the code into the IDLE editor, since all of the work is done "behind the scenes." The image will not be displayed until you actually tell it to show up.

```
>>> import Image
>>> im = Image.new("RGB", (50,80), (255,255,255))
```

The code above does two things. First, you import the Image module from the PIL library. This gives you access to the Image functionality, which includes creating a new image. Next, you create a new image by using the function of the Image module called "new." This function takes three arguments, of which only the first two are required. The arguments are as follows:

Function Parameters

The first parameter to the function is the mode of the drawing. In this case, we are only going to use RGB values, but there are other modes. Officially, you may use any of the modes listed in Table 16-1. The strings are the values passed into the function, while the meaning is simply the type of image that is produced. The mode value represents how the pixels are stored in memory and what values can be assigned to individual pixels.

Table 16-1 Pil Image Modes And Their Meanings

String	Meaning
"I"	Single-bit (monochrome) image
"L"	8-bit pixels black-and-white images
"I"	32-bit signed pixel values color images
"F"	32-bit floating point pixel values color images
"P"	8-bit pixels using color palettes
"RGB"	3×8 pixel Red/Green/Blue encoding
"RGBX"	True color images with padding
"RGBA"	4×8 pixel Red/Green/Blue/Alpha encoding
"CMYK"	4×8 pixel color separation encoding
"YCbCr"	3×8 pixels color video format

In the above table, the size of the pixels (for example, 1 or 3×8) defines the number of values you need to pass in for a given pixel entry. For example, in single-bit pixels, there is only a single value, zero or one for monochrome images, or an eight-bit value for color pixels.

The second parameter to the method is the size of the image. The size is represented by a two-value tuple containing the height and width of the desired image. Drawing outside of this area will result in cropping being done and parts of the image not being rendered properly.

The final parameter, which is optional, is the background color to use to fill the image when it is first created. These are RGB values, because our image is in RGB mode, so the values will be 255 for each of the red, green, and blue "guns" of the display monitor. That particular combination results in a white background. You can create a black image by selecting zero (0) for each of the red, green and blue values. There are numerous RGB tables on the Internet that can show you the various other options for displaying color.

Drawing on the Image

It really isn't a great deal of excitement to create a blank image. What people want to see is some sort of information displayed on the image surface. That's what we live for, as programmers, after all. The PIL modules provide a pretty rich set of functionality for drawing on an image surface, as well as ways in which to load existing images and modifying them. For now, however, let's just consider the various ways in which you might want to draw things on an image canvas.

To do this, follow these steps:

1. Create a new file using the IDLE editor or your favorite text editor.

2. Enter the following code into your new file:

```
import Image
import ImageDraw

# Create the new image
im = Image.new( "RGB", (100,100), (255,255,255) )

# Create a drawing surface.
draw = ImageDraw.Draw(im)

# Now, draw an 'X' across the surface
draw.line((0,0)+im.size, 128)
draw.line((0, im.size[1], im.size[0], 0), 128)

# And display the image using the built-in image viewer.
im.show()
```

3. Save the file, giving it the name ch16_1.py.

4. Run the file by either selecting Run Module from the Run menu or by pressing the F5 key within the IDLE edit window.

5. You should see an image displayed in the program you have configured to view bitmap files (the default is the Windows Picture and Fax Viewer application) that should look something like the one shown in Figure 16.3.

Figure 16.3
Generated image within Python using PIL.

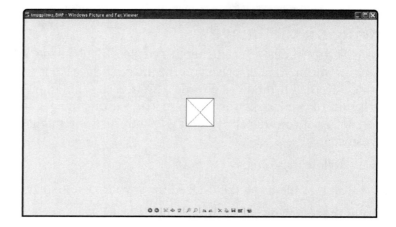

As you can see from the displayed image, we got exactly what we expected to get, a box with an "x" displayed through it. Let's look at the code to see just what we did here. First, you need to import the modules that are needed for this script. In this case, we are using both the draw and image modules, so they are imported with the first block of code:

```
import Image
import ImageDraw
```

Drawing the Image

Next, you need to create the image file itself and the drawing surface that you will be using for that surface. The image file can already contain information, as you will see, but the drawing surface that you get back will be a blank canvas that you can do whatever you like with. The Draw() function will return you the canvas you need to work with. This functionality is accomplished by these lines:

```
# Create the new image
im = Image.new( "RGB", (100,100), (255,255,255) )
# Create a drawing surface.
draw = ImageDraw.Draw(im)
```

The interesting part of the application is the actual line drawing. The draw class contains functionality to draw a line. The code to do the drawing looks like this:

```
# Now, draw an 'X' across the surface
draw.line((0,0)+im.size, 128)
draw.line((0, im.size[1], im.size[0], 0), 128)
```

The line method of the `Draw` object takes three arguments, of which only the first one is required. The arguments are the following: xy, options, list.

The x and y points are used to draw the line from and to. You can do this in several ways, as shown in the previous example. In the first example, we use the starting point of the image (0,0) and the ending point as the size of the image. Because these are both tuples, you can add them together to get a resulting tuple that can be passed to the line method. In the second example, we specify the two points that we want to connect as separate x and y values.

The options list contains the fill value, which is the color to use for drawing the line, and the width value, which can be ignored, which is the width of the line to use. If you do not otherwise specify a width, a default width will be used for the system. The fill value can either be an RGB value or an index as defined in the documentation.

In addition to lines, you can draw several other types of image components on the drawing canvas. Table 16-2 lists the various drawing primitives supported by the PIL module `ImageDraw`.

Table 16-2   Drawing Primitives In Pil

Function	Purpose
arc	Draws an arc given a starting point and a starting and ending angle.
bitmap	Draws a bitmap at a given position on the drawing canvas.
chord	Draws a chord between two points, given a starting point and a starting and ending angle. This is the same as the arc method, but with one important difference: the ends of the points are connected by a line.
ellipse	Draws an ellipse inside a set of bounding rectangle coordinates. The ellipse may be optionally filled with a user-specified color.
line	Draws a line between two or more coordinates defined in the list of points passed to it.
pieslice	Draws an arc given the starting point and starting and ending angles of the slice. Also connects the center of the circle with the ending points.
point	Draws a single point on the screen given the x and y coordinates for that point. The color of the point can be specified.
polygon	Draws a polygon, given a set of coordinates in the passed-in parameters. Note that the starting and ending point will be connected by a line to close the polygon. You can specify the color of the polygon using the outline option and optionally fill it using the fill option.
rectangle	Draws a rectangle on the screen, given a starting and ending coordinate pair.

Displaying the Image

You may have noticed the last call to the `show()` method of the image. Python has no built-in functionality to display images. Obviously, in a desktop environment, you would want a way to show the images you create, whereas on the Web you can simply send the images out to the user in the form of a Web page. The `show()` method uses the built-in functionality of the operating system to display a given image type. For the Windows operating system, the `show()` method simply brings up whatever application has registered itself for the image type. In our example, the Windows Image and Fax Viewer application will be the default program to use if nothing else is specified. When you call the `show()` method, this program will be used to display a temporary version of the image stored on disk. It is important to note that once the application is spawned to display the image, you will no longer have any control over it.

In the UNIX world, the xvt application is used by default (although others can be configured to work with images as well). This primitive application is definitely not the optimal choice to work with images, much as the Image Viewer is not in Windows. Note that if no applications are configured for image viewing, calling the `show()` method will simply do nothing. Without a configured image viewer, no error message is displayed, nor is any status information passed to the application.

Saving the Image

One of the nicest features of the PIL modules is its capability to save images in a variety of formats. Since the module also supports the loading of existing images in various formats, this means that you can easily use the modules to convert from one format to another. As an example, you can create a simple Python script that accepts an input file in one of the supported formats and saves it to a different format.

1. Create a new file using the IDLE editor or your favorite text editor.

2. Enter the following code into your new file:

```
# Do the proper imports for this script
import os, sys
import Image

# Process input files.
inFile = raw_input("Enter name of the input image file: ")
try:
    im = Image.open(inFile)
except:
    print "Unable to open input file!"
```

```
        exit(1)


    # Now, see what format they want
    formats = ("JPG", "GIF", "BMP")


    print "What format do you want the output file in?"
    print "(1) JPEG"
    print "(2) GIF"
    print "(3) BMP"
    try :
        fmt = int( raw_input("Enter choice [1-3]: ") )
    except:
        print "Invalid selection!"
        exit(1)
    if fmt < 1 or fmt > 3 :
        print "Invalid entry!"
        exit(1)


    # See if we can do this conversion.
    fileName, extension = os.path.splitext(inFile)
    if extension.upper() == formats[fmt-1] :
        print "Cannot convert to same format!"
        exit(1)


    outFile = fileName + "." + formats[fmt-1]


    try :
        im.save(outFile)
        print "File Converted Successfully"
    except IOError:
        print "cannot convert ", inFile
```

3. Save the file, giving it the name ch16_2.py.

4. Run the file by either selecting Run Module from the Run menu or by pressing the F5 key within the IDLE edit window.

You should see something like this in your script run.

```
Enter name of the input image file: c:\test.jpg
What format do you want the output file in?
(1) JPEG
(2) GIF
(3) BMP
Enter choice [1-3]: 2
File Converted Successfully
```

If you go to the directory where you stored the original file, you will then find a new file there with the proper extension and type for the file conversion you asked for. In our example above, I should see the file c:\test.gif in the root directory of the c:\ drive. In fact, checking the directory list, I find that to be the case. See how easy it is to do a conversion using PIL? Imagine, for example, writing a simple script to do batch conversions of files from whatever format they are in into a standard format for a Web site. That would certainly be a useful project, and one that would likely be only a few lines of Python and PIL code. All of this is accomplished via the save() method of the PIL module.

Loading an Existing Image

As you have seen, the open() method can be used to load an existing image into the Image drawing surface. Once you have an existing image loaded, you can do a number of things with it. For example, you can draw on the surface of the image. Imagine that you have an image and want to place the infamous circle with a line through it on top of the image. Let's take a simple look at doing so, with an image. Here is some simple code that will load an image called *cockroach.gif* (you may prefer your own image that isn't so insect-like) and draw the circle and line. The following code, which we will call, ch16_3.py, accomplishes this.

```
# Do the proper imports for this script
import os, sys
import Image
import ImageDraw


# Load the image
try:
    im = Image.open("c:\\cockroach.gif")
except:
    print "Unable to load image"
```

```
    exit(1)

# Get a drawing surface for the image
draw = ImageDraw.Draw(im)

# Draw the circle
draw.ellipse((0,0)+im.size)

# Draw the line
draw.line((0,0)+im.size)

# and show off the result
im.show()
```

The result of this script running is the image shown in Figure 16.4. As you can see, your image is displayed properly with the circle around it and a line across the entire thing. If you wanted to do the coordinate calculations, you could even draw the line entirely within the circle.

Figure 16.4
A loaded image with drawing on it.

Now, it would hardly be useful to just be able to draw on top of images. You often want to be able to modify given parts of an image in order to draw just the portions you want. For this, the PIL library provides the crop() method. The crop() method operates on a given image and selects a given bounding box. For example, using the cockroach picture from the previous code, you could select a box in the center of the image. If you wanted, say, 50 pixels on each side of the center of the image, you could write the following code (which we will call ch16_4.py) to accomplish this task:

```
# Do the proper imports for this script
import os, sys
import Image
import ImageDraw

# Load the image
try:
    im = Image.open("c:\\cockroach.gif")
except:
    print "Unable to load image"
    exit(1)

# Now, just grab the center of the image.
width, height = im.size
center_x = width / 2
center_y = height / 2
center = im.crop( (center_x-50, center_y-50, center_x+50, center_y+50) )

# And display that section
center.show()
```

If you try this script, you will see only the middle of the bug displayed on the screen. Once you have the image, you can easily modify it. Simply obtain a drawing surface for the image, do what you want to it, and either display or save it in whatever format you want. This is the real power of the PIL modules—the ability to modify images quickly and easily and save them to disk.

Displaying Text

Graphics are not all about lines and colors and images. They are also about displaying text on a graphical image. For example, you might want to place a copyright notice on an image that you use in your own system so that other people can't just claim it and use it on their own Web sites. If you have an existing image, placing a copyright message at the bottom of it really isn't difficult using the PIL modules. The `ImageDraw` module contains a text function that allows you to output a text string at a given position on the output image, in a specified font. The actual syntax of the `text()` method is as follows:

```
text( position, string, options)
```

where:

`position` is the x and y position where you want the string to appear on the output image.

`string` is the text string that you want to output.

`options` is a list of potential options to use for display. The main two options are font and fill. The font option should specify an `ImageFont` instance, while the fill option specifies the color in which to display the text.

If you need to know what the size of a text string will be, so that you can center it or place it at a given location on the screen, you can use the `textsize()` method of the `ImageDraw` module. The `textsize()` method takes two arguments: the text to size and any options (font, color, etc) that you want to use to display the text.

Let's look at a simple example of using the `textsize()` and `text()` methods of the `ImageDraw` module to place a copyright notice at the bottom of a given image. In this case, you will create your own image with a box and lines through it and then place the copyright information over it.

To do this, follow these steps:

1. Create a new file using the IDLE editor or your favorite text editor.

2. Enter the following code into your new file:

```python
import Image
import ImageDraw

# Create the new image
im = Image.new( "RGB", (200,200), (255,255,255) )

# Create a drawing surface.
draw = ImageDraw.Draw(im)

# Draw a rectangle on the surface
draw.rectangle((10,10,im.size[1]-10, im.size[0]-10), fill=(255,255,255),
outline=(0,0,0))

# Now, draw an 'X' across the surface
draw.line( (10,10, im.size[1]-10, im.size[0]-10), 128)
draw.line((im.size[1]-10, 10, 10, im.size[0]-10), 128)

# Now, our text string
```

```
ts = draw.textsize("(C) Copyright 2007")

# And draw the text
draw.text( (10, im.size[0]-ts[1]), "(C) Copyright 2007", fill=(0,0,0))

# And display the image using the built-in image viewer.
im.show()
```

3. Save the file, giving it the name ch16_5.py.

4. Run the file by either selecting Run Module from the Run menu or by pressing the F5 key within the IDLE edit window.

5. You should see an image displayed in the program you have configured to view bitmap files (the default is the Windows Picture and Fax Viewer application) that should look something like the one shown in Figure 16.5.

Figure 16.5
An image with text.

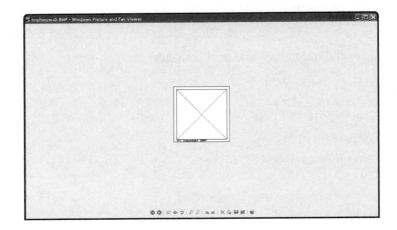

As you can see, working with images and text is not at all difficult using PIL. One of the best uses for the PIL library is to create image representations of text for the infamous "Enter the text as you see it in the box below" for Web pages that want to avoid spiders and such (a process called CAPTCHA).

Identifying an Image

We have seen how you can load an existing image and look at certain information about it, such as the size of the image. There are, however, other bits of information about an image that can be useful when you are working with it. Let's take a look at the information you have available to you when you load an existing image. There are really two types of information available about an image. First, you can get some of the basic information, such as the type of image (format), the size, and the mode (color type) of the image. This information is available directly from the Image objects. Then you can get some statistical information available about the internals of the image, such as the number of pixels, the mean and standard deviation for color bands, and the extremes of the colors displayed. This information is available in an object defined in a class in the ImageStat module. Let's create a simple script to display information about an image.

1. Create a new file using the IDLE editor or your favorite text editor.

2. Enter the following code into your new file:

```
# Do the proper imports for this script
import os, sys
import Image
import ImageDraw
import ImageStat

name = raw_input("Enter the image for statistics: ")

# Load the image
try:
    im = Image.open(name)
except:
    print "Unable to load image"
    exit(1)

# Print out statistics about the image
print "The image is in " + im.format + " format."
print "The size of the image is " + str(im.size)
print "The image is in " + str(im.mode) + " mode."

# And get the internal statistics as well
stat = ImageStat.Stat(im)
print "There are " + str(stat.count) + " pixels in the image"
print "The average pixel level is " + str(stat.mean)
print "The extrema for all bands is " + str(stat.extrema)
```

3. Save the file, giving it the name `ch16_6.py`.

4. Run the file by either selecting Run Module from the Run menu or by pressing the F5 key within the IDLE edit window.

For this example, we will run the script on the aforementioned "cockroach.gif" file that was used in a previous example, but you can choose any image you like. When I run the script and give it the file name of the image, I get the following output:

```
Enter the image for statistics: c:\cockroach.gif
The image is in GIF format.
The size of the image is (614, 619)
The image is in P mode.
There are [380066] pixels in the image
The average pixel level is [22.342585235195994]
The extrema for all bands is [(0, 31)]
```

While this information is not always the most useful thing to know, it can sometimes mean the difference between writing a lot of special case code and knowing exactly what sort of processing to do for an image. Keep the statistical functions in mind, particularly when worrying about printing images on color printers and saving them to disk in particular formats.

Rotating an Image

A common problem when working in various image applications is the need to rotate an image about its center. This is particularly noticeable when working with photos, for example, where the photographer chose to rotate his camera so that he could get a better angle for a shot. Displaying an image rotated on the screen forces the user to turn his head to see it correctly, which leads to neck strain and annoyance with the programmer. Rather than have your users be angry with you, it is usually nicer and easier to simply allow them to rotate the image the way that they want it to display for ease of viewing and printing.

The PIL module provides a number of transformation methods, including the ability to rotate an image. To see how this works, let's create a simple script that produces an image with some text on it, and then rotate that image so that the text is running up and down, instead of side to side.

1. Create a new file using the IDLE editor or your favorite text editor.

2. Enter the following code into your new file:

```
import Image
import ImageDraw
```

```
# Create the new image
im = Image.new( "RGB", (200,200), (255,255,255) )

# Create a drawing surface.
draw = ImageDraw.Draw(im)

# Draw our text string
draw.text( (10, im.size[1]-20), "This text will be rotated", fill=(0,0,0))

# And rotate the image 90 degrees
out = im.rotate(90)

# And display the image using the built-in image viewer.
out.show()
```

3. Save the file, giving it the name ch16_7.py.

4. Run the file by either selecting Run Module from the Run menu or by pressing the F5 key within the IDLE edit window.

You should see a display that looks a lot like Figure 16.6. As you can see, the text is rotated 90 degrees and displays vertically. An important thing to note here is that the rotate() method of PIL does not actually modify the existing image. Instead, it creates a new image that represents the original image rotated. The original image is still intact, so there are actually two copies of the image in memory.

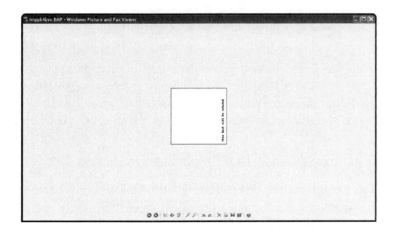

Figure 16.6
Rotated text display.

Postscript Printing

The PSDraw module provides the ability to create Postscript drawing capabilities to your applications. Postscript is an excellent way to define exactly how your output will look on a printer. You begin your documents with a begin_document() method call and end them with an end_document() call. Otherwise, the majority of the functionality is exactly the same as with drawing on the screen. After all, that is really the whole point of Postscript—it is supposed to look the same on the printed page as it does on the display screen. For example, if you wanted to display an image with a box around it on a Postscript printer, you would do something like this:

```python
# Import the proper modules
import Image
import PSDraw
# Load our image
imageName = raw_input('Enter the filename: ')
# Try to load the image
try :
im = Image.open(imageName)
except:
        print 'unable to load image'
        exit(1)
# Define the box to display, in printer points
box = (1*72, 2*72, 7*72, 10*72)
ps = PSDraw.PSDraw()
# Create the document
ps.begin_document(title)
# draw the image using 75 dots per inch
ps.image(box, im, 75)
ps.rectangle(box)
# draw centered title
ps.setfont("HelveticaNarrow-Bold", 36)
w, h, b = ps.textsize(title)
ps.text((4*72-w/2, 1*72-h), title)
# And close the document
ps.end_document()
```

Note that the default output for the Postscript file will be sys.stdout. You can change that via the PSDraw method. Simply pass in a name of a file:

```
ps = PSDraw.PSDraw("myfile.ps")
```

and the resulting document will be created ("myfile.ps") and all output sent to it for later printing.

Creating Thumbnails

Our final topic for this chapter will be one of the single most useful things you will ever run into in any library, creating thumbnails for images. By far and away, the most common complaint from users is the slow load time of Web pages. A Web page that contains many large images will load extremely slowly, simply because of the time necessary to download each of the images from the server to the Web browser and then to render the images on the user screen. The larger the image, the more bytes that the image takes up in space, and therefore, the longer it takes to transmit over the wires.

If you want to shrink the size of your images, the best way to do this is to create a "thumbnail" version of the image. A thumbnail contains all of the most important aspects of an image, but is considerably smaller. The alternative to thumbnails is to cut off the image at certain boundaries. While this does make the image smaller, it also has the unfortunate side effect of losing bits of information that might be stored in the image. If the image is a picture of a rally, for example, and contains a picture of your child in the corner, this is not exactly what you wanted to see when you bring it onto your machine. Using a thumbnail approach, you instead shrink the image by cutting down the total number of pixels for the image, while still maintaining all of the components of the original image.

Creating a thumbnail of a given image in PIL is really easy. The ImageDraw module contains a specific method called *thumbnail*, which will take an existing image and create a thumbnail out of it. The resulting thumbnail image is also an image, so it can be displayed, or saved, as you wish in your application. Let's take a look at how you would go about doing this.

1. Create a new file using the IDLE editor or your favorite text editor.

2. Enter the following code into your new file:

```
import os, sys
import Image

name = raw_input("Enter the image file name: ")
ht = int ( raw_input("Enter the height to use for the thumbnail: ") )
wd = int ( raw_input("Enter the width to use for the thumbnail: ") )

outfile = os.path.splitext(name)[0] + ".thumbnail"
if name != outfile:
```

```
try:
    im = Image.open(name)
    im.thumbnail((wd,ht))
    im.show()
except IOError:
    print "cannot create thumbnail for", name
```

3. Save the file, giving it the name ch16_8.py.

4. Run the file by either selecting Run Module from the Run menu or by pressing the F5 key within the IDLE edit window. Use whatever image file you like, and give it the size of 50 pixels wide and high.

You should see a display that looks a lot like Figure 16.7 (assuming, of course, you used the same cockroach image I did). Compare your original image to the final thumbnail, and you will see just how much it has shrunk.

Figure 16.7
A thumbnail in PIL.

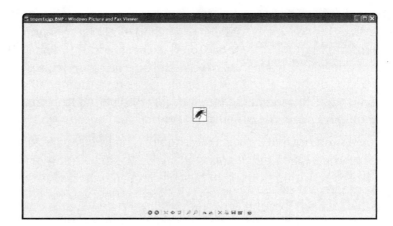

If you give your users one thing you have learned in this book, please supply them with thumbnail images and cut down the amount of time it takes to view your Web pages. By doing this, you will have happier users and lower bandwidth requirements for your applications.

In Conclusion

Hopefully, this chapter has given you a good introduction to working with images using the PIL modules. This free library provides an excellent way to integrate high-quality images and image processing into your own Python scripts. One of the main goals of working with Python is to stop reinventing the wheel and use what is already available to create the best possible scripts and Web pages. Using libraries like PIL will help attain that goal for your own applications.

This also concludes this book. I hope that you have enjoyed reading about Python as much as I have enjoyed writing about it. This is not an ending, so much as a beginning. Go out there and play with the language, write new scripts, and create new things that people want to use. When all is said and done, that is really what it is all about.

Index

except statement, 30, 226—228
Exception class, 227, 298
exception classes, 297—299
exception handler, 406
exception handling, 4, 73, 170, 228
    else clauses, 232—234
    finally clause, 234—235
    keywords, 29—30
    system module, 329
exceptions, 29—30, 119, 170, 221—222
    arguments, 222, 237—238
    automatically opening Stack Viewer, 73—74
    blank except clauses, 231—232
    catching, 30, 222, 226—228
    categories, 230
    cleaning up, 243—244
    clearing, 329
    code that might throw, 30
    comparing type values, 239—240
    delegating, 244—246
    division by zero, 225—226
    error message, 222
    errors, 222
    information about, 222
    logging, 239
    multiple except clauses, 229—231
    parts of state, 240—241
    position where error occurred, 222
    printing information about, 242
    raising, 30, 222, 235—237
    re-throwing, 244—246
    retrieving last, 329
    syntax error, 222
    throwing, 27, 73
    traceback example, 223—224
    tracebacks, 224—225
    type, 239
    user-defined, 238, 297—299
    working with, 239—243
exc_info() function, 241—242
exc_info() method, 329
exc_traceback variable, 239, 241, 329
exc_type variable, 239, 329
exc_value variable, 240, 329
exec statement, 34
exec() function, 338
execute() method, 420
exit command, 150
exit() function, 339
exit_functional() function, 150
exit() method, 329
Expand Word command, 70

exp() function, 312
exponential operator (**), 46
exponentiation, 46
exponentiation operator (shorthand) (**=), 46
expressions
    conditional, 38
    evaluating, 27
    highlighting parentheses, 69—70
    immediate mode and side effect, 36—37
extendleft() method, 306
extend() method, 306
extensible language, 1
extensible scripts, 2
external scripts, 79

F
fabs() function, 312
fact() function, 236
factorial functions, 210—212
factorials, 210—211, 235—237
    negative number, 236
    undefined for negative values, 212
fchdir() method, 183
fdel() function, 277
fetchall() method, 422
fetchone() method, 422—423
fget() function, 277
fields, 413
    storage information, 390
    tab order, 355—356
FieldStorage class, 386, 387, 390
File | Class Browser command, 58—61
File | New Window command, 57, 93, 152
File | Open command, 57, 94, 113
File | Open Module command, 58
File | Path Browser command, 61—62, 88—89
File | Recent Files command, 57
File | Save command, 152, 176
file input, 175—177
File menu, 57—62
file methods, 177
file names, 67
file object, 175, 243—244
file output, 177—179
file viewer, 373—375
fileno() method, 177
files, 183—186
    append access, 176
    binary, 176
    bytecode version, 11
    with clause, 243—244
    closing, 179—180